WRECKERS OR BUILDERS?

A History of Labour Members of the European Parliament 1979-1999

Other books on the European Parliament:

The European Parliament, 7th edition
By *Richard Corbett, Francis Jacobs* and *Michael Shackleton*

Since 1990 this has been the standard textbook on the Parliament covering every aspect of how it is elected, organised and does its work. *"An indispensable guide... both an excellent primer for students and a reliable reference tool for practitioners"*, Hans-Gert Pöttering, President of the European Parliament in 2007-09. (2007, ISBN 978-0-9551144-7-2)

Six Battles that Shaped Europe's Parliament
By *Julian Priestley*

The former Secretary-General of the European Parliament describes six turning points in Parliament's struggle for power and recognition. *"One could hardly imagine a better commentator on the evolution of the European Parliament than Julian Priestley "*, Jean-Claude Juncker, Prime Minister of Luxembourg. (2008, ISBN 978-0-9556202-3-2)

For full details of these and other books, please visit

www.johnharperpublishing.co.uk

Wreckers or Builders?

A History of Labour Members of the European Parliament 1979-1999

Anita Pollack

JOHN HARPER
PUBLISHING

Wreckers or Builders? A History of Labour Members of the European Parliament 1979-1999

Published by John Harper Publishing
27 Palace Gates Road
London N22 7BW, United Kingdom.

www.johnharperpublishing.co.uk

ISBN 978-0-9556202-9-4

Printed and Bound in Great Britain by Cromwell Press Group.

To Phil and Katy and the Labour Party

TABLE OF CONTENTS

PART III: 1989-1994 – BUILDING A BETTER EUROPE

PART IV: 1994-1999 – AN ADVENTURE PLAYGROUND

FOREWORD

by Neil Kinnock

At last we have a history of Labour MEPs in the first twenty years of the directly elected Parliament. This piece of Labour history has not been written before and there's reason to be grateful, therefore, to Anita Pollack who has produced a well-researched record – warts and all – of the period when Labour in the European Parliament grew from 17 to 62 Members and Labour's policy on the EU changed from withdrawal to committed support for membership and reforms.

Using a combination of her own experience, interviews with MEPs and others with substantial engagement in European affairs, and thorough examination of the official European Parliament records, Anita has tracked the turbulent years from the first direct elections of 1979 to the change of electoral system in 1999. From the leadership of Barbara Castle to the Labour Government of Tony Blair, fascinating stories emerge of a Labour group which mixed members who were hell-bent on fundamentalist anti-Europeanism with mainstream European social democrats; of a long Labour march from the devastating defeat of 1979, through the advances of the 80s and early 90s, to the landslide victory of 1997; and of a growing Labour contribution to the joint efforts of the Socialist group to promote progressive policies on workers' rights, gender and race equality, European enlargement, international development, social justice, environmental and consumer protection and the endless list of other issues which rightly engage the world's only elected international parliament.

The events, conflicts and progress of these decades will be of interest to political activists, students and those working in the European institutions – particularly as the law-making power of MEPs has grown to become an equal partnership with the Council of Ministers. The work of MEPs rarely gets much publicity, the value which they give to European democracy is too often ignored, and the importance of the victories and defeats which they experience is largely unknown. This book helps to make the Parliament, its people and its workings more visible and understandable. It is, therefore, an account which adds to accountability. Every democrat must welcome that.

Neil Kinnock

Westminster
April 2009

ABBREVIATIONS

ACP	Africa Caribbean Pacific group of developing countries
AECA	American European Community Association
AEU	Amalgamated Engineering Workers (union)
AGM	Annual General Meeting
ANC	African National Congress
ASEAN	Association of South East Asian Nations
ASTMS	Association of Scientific, Technical and Managerial Staffs (union)
BBC	British Broadcasting Corporation
BLG	British Labour Group
BP	British Petroleum
BSE	Bovine Spongiform Encephalopathy, "mad cow" disease
CAP	Common Agricultural Policy
CBI	Confederation of British Industry
CCC	Coalfields Communities Campaign
CDU	Christian Democratic Union, principal German conservative party
CFSP	Common Foreign and Security Policy
CJD	Creutzfeldt-Jakob's Disease
CLES	Campaign for Local Economic Strategies
Cllr	Councillor (in local government)
CLP	Constituency Labour Party
CND	Campaign for Nuclear Disarmament
Confed	Confederation of European Socialist Parties
Co-op	Co-operative Party/Society
COREPER	Committee of Permanent Representatives (in Council of Ministers)
CRS	Co-operative Retail Society
CSC	Campaign Strategy Committee (in the Labour Party)
CSU	Christian Social Union (Bavarian sister party of CDU)
CWS	Co-operative Wholesale Society
DAEA	Draft Act of European Union
DUP	Democratic Unionist Party (Northern Ireland)
EAPN	European Anti Poverty Network
EBRD	European Bank for Reconstruction and Development
EC	European Community/Communities
ECB	European Central Bank
ECJ	European Court of Justice
ECLP	European Constituency Labour Party
ECOFIN	European Council of Finance Ministers
ECOSOC	Economic and Social Committee
ECOSY	Youth section of European Socialists
ECU	European Current Unit (a monetary calculation mostly used for agriculture prices)
EDF	European Development Fund
EDG	European Democratic Group
EEA	European Economic Area
EEC	European Economic Community
EFTA	European Free Trade Area
EMAC	Economic and Monetary Committee (in European Parliament)
EMS	European Monetary System

EMU	European Monetary Union
END	European Nuclear Disarmament
EP	European Parliament
EPLP	European Parliamentary Labour Party
EPP/PPE	European People' Party, the Christian Democratic (centre-right) Group in the European Parliament
ERDF	European Regional Development Fund (Structural Funds)
ERM	Exchange Rate Mechanism
ESF	European Social Fund
ESPRIT	An EU research programme
ETUC	European Trade Union Confereration
EU	European Union
EUROPIA	non profit organization representing oil industry
FIELD	Foundation for International Environmental Law and Development
FPTP	First past the post electoral system
GATT	General Agreement on Tariffs and Trade
GC	General Committee (local Labour Party organization)
GCHQ	Government Communications Headquarters
GDP	Gross Domestic Product
GDR	German Democratic Republic (East Germany)
GLC	Greater London Council
GLOBE	Global Legislators Organised for a Balanced Environment
GMB	General Municipal and Boilermakers' Union
GMC	General Management Committee (local Labour party organization)
GMO	Genetically Modified Organism
GUE	European United Left, group in European Parliament
HACAN	Clear Skies organization against expansion of Heathrow airport
ICL	International Computers Limited
IEEP	Institute for European Environmental Policy
IGC	Inter-governmental conference
IIED	International Institute for Environment and Development
IMO	International Maritime Organisation
IPPR	Institute for Public Policy Research
ITN	Independent Television Network
ITV	Independent Television
JPC	Joint Parliamentary Committee (European Parliament delegations for countries negotiating accession to the EU)
KGB	Soviet Union state security organisation
LCC	Labour co-Ordinating Committee
LCE	Labour Committee for Europe
LDDC	London Docklands Development Corporation
LEONARDO	A European adult education fund
LME	Labour Movement for Europe
LSE	London School of Economics
MBE	Member of the British Empire
MECU	Million ECU
MEDA	EU fund for Mediterranean countries
MEP	Member of the European Parliament
MFA	Multifibre Agreement
MP	Member of Parliament

MSF	Manufacturing, Science and Finance Union (formerly ASTMS)
NALGO	National Association of Local Government Officers (union)
NATO	North Atlantic Treaty Organization
NEC	National Executive Committee (of the Labour Party)
NGO	Non-governmental Organization
NUM	National Union of Mineworkers
NUPE	National Union of Public Employees (union)
OMOV	One Member One Vote
PASOK	Greek Socialist Party
PES	Party of European Socialists
PHARE	EU fund for Central and Eastern Euope
PLO	Palestine Liberation Organization
PLP	Parliamentary Labour Party
PPC	Prospective Parliamentary Candidate
PPS	Parliamentary Private Secretary
PQ	Parliamentary Question
PR	Proportional Representation
PSB	Public Sector Broadcasting
PSOE	Spanish Socialist Workers' Party
QMV	Qualified Majority Voting
RACS	Royal Arsenal Co-operative Society
RCV	Roll Call Vote
RECHAR	European fund for coal areas
REX	External Economic Affairs Committee (dealing with trade)
RSPCA	Royal Society for the Prevention of Cruelty to Animals
SAARC	South Asian Association for Regional Co-operation
SAVE	EU fund for energy efficiency
SDLP	Social Democratic and Labour Party (Northern Ireland)
SDP	Social Democratic Party (UK)
SEA	Single European Act
SEEDA	South East Economic Development Association
SEPA	Scottish Environment Protection Agency
SLD	Liberal Democratic party in UK
SME	Small and Medium Enterprises
SNP	Scottish National Party
SPD	Social Democratic Party (Germany)
STASI	East German state security organization
TACIS	Technical Fund for Independent States (former Soviet)
TENS	Trans European Networks
T&GWU	Transport and General Workers' Union
TUC	Trades Union Congress
TVWF	Television without frontiers
UDF	French Democratic Union, political party on the right
UDM	Union of Democratic Mineworkers
UEFA	European Football Association
UKIP	United Kingdom Independence Party
UKRep	United Kingdom Representation to European Community
UNED	United Nations Education section
UNISON	Public sector union in UK
UUP	Ulster Unionist Party

USDAW	Union of Shop, Distributive and Allied Workers
VAT	Value Added Tax
WAC	Women's Action Committee
WEA	Workers' Educational Association
WEU	Western European Union
WHO	World Health Organization
WI	Women's Institute
WTO	World Trade Organization

A note on terminology

The EEC, EC, EU and "Common Market"

Three European Communities were established in the 1950s, with some shared institutions – the European Coal and Steel Community, the European Atomic Energy Community and, by far the most important for the longer term, the European Economic Community (EEC). Although these were collectively formally known as the "European Communities" (EC), in Britain the term "Common Market", strictly-speaking referring to the programme of progressive economic integration provided for in the Treaty of Rome establishing the EEC, became shorthand for the whole European project and its institutions. This usage remained widespread into the 1970s even after Britain joined the Communities itself in 1973.

By the 1980s the term "Common Market" was primarily used as short-hand by those opposed to the EEC – including the "anti-marketeers" in the Labour Party. The term "European Community" ("European Communities" never entering general usage) was by this time especially favoured by those supportive of the European project. Under the Treaty of Maastricht (signed in 1992), the European Union was created, comprising the European Communities, the two intergovernmental pillars of the Common Foreign and Security Policy and Justice and Home Affairs, as well as the European Monetary System and Economic and Monetary Union. While the term European Union (EU) has since become the normal catch-all term, EEC and EC were also widely used in the 1990s and some older diehards continued to refer to the "Common Market".

The European Parliament

The three communities founded in the 1950s shared a Common Assembly. It referred to itself (though not consistently) as a "parliament" from the early 1960s although it remained primarily a forum for national parliamentary delegations without significant powers at that stage. It began to acquire meaningful powers, notably in respect of the Community budget, during the 1970s. The first direct elections were held in 1979 and this new legitimacy hastened the expansion of the Parliament's powers. By 1979 the term "European Parliament" was that normally used to describe the institution, but as will be seen below, those in the Labour Party opposed to the "Common Market" were reluctant to call it a Parliament, preferring the name "Assembly". The term "European Parliament" was not actually formally recognised in the treaties until the Single European Act of 1986.

INTRODUCTION

This book tells the story of the Labour Members of the European Parliament over four electoral terms during an historic period for the Labour Party. Having been first (from 1980) an assistant to Barbara Castle, the first Leader of the British Labour Group in the directly elected Parliament, and then an elected MEP for the two terms from 1989-99, I felt both compelled and qualified to take on this task, which has not been tackled before. The study has been undertaken within the prism of Labour's attitude to "Europe" but the subject matter is much wider.

While ensuring accuracy has been a consistent challenge, as great a problem has been what to leave out. With eighty-three Labour MEPs during this twenty year period there is an immense range of topics to cover and any such history, if it is to be of a length tolerable to the reader, can therefore only provide a partial record. To do full justice to everything and everyone would have taken several volumes. I have attempted to cover most of the major events and controversies and to be as objective as possible rather than make this my story.

I have been able to interview, either in person or by phone, e-mail and questionnaire, all but one of the Labour Members who are still living and thank those who generously assisted with time and recollections. Sadly some of the most notable characters are no longer with us and they are sorely missed. Versions of events over these twenty years are sometimes as numerous as the Members, and cannot always be reconciled – and one or two former Members were reluctant to have old coals raked over. I have also spoken to senior officials, journalists, party workers, assistants, academics and some politicians from other parties, both in Brussels and the UK to tease out their impressions and memories. The Debates and Minutes of the European Parliament during this period have been pored over. It has not been possible to uncover all the records of EPLP and NEC meetings and assorted strategy groups, nor the Socialist Group, but reference has been made to those where information has been found. A warehouse fire destroyed many of the pre-1994 EPLP archive documents and photographs.

For a number of Members, and certainly in the early years, being an MEP was seen as a route to becoming an MP, or something to fill in time between losing one House of Commons seat and gaining another. Party members and MPs tended to think that any MEP wanted to become an MP so there was always some rivalry. The reality is that MEPs have more power than an average back-bencher in the House of Commons and by the 1990s many realized that the European Parliament was a more satisfying place to be in terms of changing the world – which is what most politicians want to do. The biggest problem was and remains the relentless travel. During the 1980s MEPs were not often seen to be much of an asset to the party, but this changed during the 1990s, particularly with their help in securing the Labour victory of 1997. Visibility with the electorate, however, shrank after the 1999 election with the introduction of the new regional list system.

Many have said there is little interest in MEPs and their work, and undoubtedly a patronizing attitude prevails in the Westminster village. Widespread misinformation, lack of interest and ignorance is the rule in the press and elsewhere. The strength of lobbying when MEPs are dealing with important legislation contradicts that. This history may help to extend knowledge and understanding about the range and importance of the work of these semi-detached politicians.

There are many to thank. All the Labour Members were contacted and all are mentioned in the book. Some were exceptionally helpful with time, reminiscences, documents, photographs, endless questions and corrections. Amongst these were Sir Ken Collins, Glyn Ford, Carole Tongue, Richard Corbett, Wayne David and Ken Coates. Many other actors were kind enough to give their time in interviews and supply information and particular thanks are due to Lord (Neil) Kinnock, Sir Julian Priestley, Rt Hon John Prescott, Manfred Michel, David Earnshaw, David Wilkinson, Baroness (Jan) Royall, Peter Coleman, Lord (Chris) Smith, Lord (Alan) Haworth, John Palmer, Jane Enright, Geoff Harris, Dick Gupwell, Maggie Coulthard, Tessa Ryan, Tony Robinson, Dagmar Roth-Behrendt, Marijke van Hemeldonck, Terry Ashton, Reinhold Hack, Michael Wood, David Lowe, Charles Clarke MP, Gerhard Stahl, Janet Anderson MP, Mike Gapes MP, Nick Sigler, John Carr, Baroness (Glenys) Thornton, Greg Cook, Frazer Clarke, Derek Reed, Jan Kurlemann, Jesper Schunk, Patrick Costello, Michael Contes, Emma Whelan, Dr Dianne Hayter, Jim Murphy, Belinda Pyke, Lord (Tom) Sawyer, Lord (Larry) Whitty, Lord (David) Triesman, Jane Stowell, Liz Mills, Pat Healey, Jo Oxenbould, Nick Crook, Adrian Cunningham, Lord (Henry) Plumb, Bryan Cassidy, Anthony Simpson, Peter Beazley MEP, Joan Woodman, Baroness (Joyce) Gould and Brendan Donnelly. Thanks are due to the staff of the European Parliament libraries both in London (particularly Avis Furness before she retired and her successor Michelle Kneeshaw) and in Brussels, including Catherine Juckler in the photo library, who have been exceptionally helpful, as were the staff of the People's History Museum in Manchester and Mark Foster at the Foreign and Commonwealth Office.

Special thanks should also be extended to all who worked for me during my years as a MEP without whom I could never have managed to survive to write this book, many of whom are not named here. Gareth Harding, Aaron McLoughlin and Christian Farrar-Hockley were repeatedly called upon to assist with facts, but everyone made valuable contributions at the time, particularly Kim Dewdney, Catherine Eden and David Keen. Making people redundant when a politician loses is an unhappy experience. Staff of the European Parliament and Socialist Group, past and present were outstanding in their hard work, intelligence and loyalty. Solidarity from Labour Party members, far too many to mention, in the various permutations of London South West European constituency from 1984 to 1999 was more valued than they can realize, and in particular those from Battersea, in whose premises my office lodged. Thanks, too, for co-operation from the constituency's Labour MPs and those on the shadow front bench and government. Staff in Labour Party headquarters, London and South East England regional offices who are often taken for granted, also deserve thanks. Warm thanks, too, to John Harper for his wise counsel and patience in producing the book.

My husband and daughter have been uncomplaining and supportive during more than two years of having documents strewn throughout the house and their solidarity has been most welcome.

It goes without saying that those errors that remain in the text – and there will inevitably be some – are my responsibility and I will welcome any corrections that are notified to me for any future printings. Should the reception of this volume merit it, a subsequent volume is planned to cover the period from 1999 onwards.

Anita Pollack

London
May 2009

Prologue

Britain joined the "Common Market" – as the European (Economic) Community was at that time generally referred to at home – in 1973 and Labour was entitled to sixteen of the 198 seats in the European Parliamentary Assembly. The UK delegation was made up of MPs and peers, but Labour did not take up its seats until after the "Yes" vote in the June 1975 referendum confirming British membership and even then rather reluctantly. So at the beginning the delegation consisted of seventeen Conservatives, two Liberals and an independent peer, with sixteen seats vacant. Manfred Michel, the respected General Secretary of the Socialist Group at the time, says he pleaded with Harold Wilson to fill the empty seats, but the latter's hands were tied by party policy. For a period one of these was temporarily taken up by Dick Taverne MP. He had supported entry and was deselected by his local party, resigned, fought and won a by-election in Lincoln under the label Democratic Labour in March 1973, but lost it in the first 1974 general election which was won by Labour.

After the referendum the TUC and PLP reversed their boycotts. Eighteen seats went to Labour (by then in government), sixteen to the Conservatives and one each to the Liberals and SNP. Labour sent seven pro-market and five anti-market MPs and four pro- and two anti-market peers. The delegation's address was St Stephen's House, Westminster (Victoria Embankment) and it was originally serviced in London by Harry Mitchell from the PLP staff until his retirement with Phyllis Birt acting as the group's secretary.

Labour's first Leader and Vice-President of the Socialist Group was pro-marketeer and former Foreign Secretary, Michael Stewart, with Tam Dalyell as Deputy, also on the Group Bureau. Barbara Castle described Stewart as "the most intransigent Europeanist of them all" back in November 1966. Others included Sir Geoffrey de Freitas (pro), Willie Hamilton (pro), Gwyneth Dunwoody (anti), Bob Mitchell (pro), John Evans (anti), John Prescott (anti) and Betty Boothroyd (pro). The rest of the team consisted of Guy Barnett, John Evans, Bob Mitchell, Tom Ellis, Mark Hughes and Lords Ardwick, Bruce (formerly a director of *Tribune*), Castle (Barbara's husband), Watson and Gordon-Walker, and Baroness Fisher of Rednal. Barnett resigned to become a Minister in April 1976 and William Molloy was appointed. Lord Gordon-Walker resigned in October the same year, to be succeeded by Lord Murray of Gravesend. When Stewart resigned in November to become chair of a House of Commons Committee, Frank Tomney was appointed. Betty Boothroyd and Tom Watson resigned early in 1977. The Labour Members joined the Socialist Group, against the wishes of prominent and vociferous domestic anti-marketeer Peter Shore, and were its largest component right up to the 1979 elections, the German SPD being the next largest.

After Stewart retired the young and pugnacious John Prescott, an anti-marketeer who had already served on the Council of Europe, was elected to lead the Labour delegation in a close vote. Prescott says it was thought that Dunwoody would stand, but she was not entirely popular – "she left people savaged", he said, so he became the candidate of the anti-marketeers. The pro-market candidate was de Freitas and Prescott won. The group was very split between the two camps, but as a whole they earned respect, says Prescott, because "we were grafters and took on reports."

According to Roger Broad (Broad, 2001) Prescott soon became aware that he "could get a debate on, for example, the international activities of British Petroleum that would have been impossible at Westminster", and concluded that there were "new kinds of accountability that aren't available to national parliaments". The British Members found the committee system a good way of working and that it was easier to get answers out of Commissioners and Ministers from the Council than from Ministers at home. This would be borne out in the democratically elected Parliament that followed. The Assembly at this stage was a lower-key organization than the later Parliament. Sir James Scott-Hopkins, a Conservative Member who later became a Parliament Vice-President, said it rather resembled a gentlemen's club.

Jan Kurlemann, who was a press officer with the Socialist Group during this period, recalls that the British Members were poorly paid in contrast to the others, but they were always gentlemanly with the bar bills. He remembers a collection in the Socialist Group for the family of a Member who died.

Despite Labour's negative policy on the European Community, the Labour Members were active and influential in the Parliament and the Socialist Group which then had Members from all nine Member States. They produced three written annual reports in the form of little red pamphlets to the Parliamentary Labour Party at home, outlining their work in a fair amount of detail, with the assistance of Geoff Harris, a British member of the Socialist Group, a pro-marketeer who had written a Young Fabian pamphlet in December 1976 entitled "A Wider Europe".

In the delegation's first report, dated April 1977, Stewart in his foreword said: "The European Parliament is a forum in which policies can be advanced which can and do influence governments, an instrument for making the EEC more publicly accountable."

Lord Bruce took the influential role of budget rapporteur during his term of office. Dunwoody and Prescott were both internationalists but anti-Community. They didn't like the way the parliamentary chamber was arranged as a hemicycle (with MEPs ranged approximately from political left to right in a half-circle, rather than with opposing benches facing each other as in the House of Commons), or the different political culture, both of them being combative politicians.

In the second report to the PLP, dated July 1978, Prescott's foreword included the assessment that:

> "It is probably fair to say that our influence in the policy sphere has grown as our European colleagues have got used to our style and approach,

which at first came as something of a surprise, if not a shock to them. Our members are the most active members in the Assembly (time there, speeches made and questions asked)... The Parliament as a whole and the Socialist Group has gradually got used to the British Members' habit of challenging what sometimes appears to be a prevailing consensus amongst members from other nationalities and political groups".

The delegation for 1978-79 consisted of Rob Brown and George Cunningham, Tam Dalyell and Willie Hamilton, Gwyneth Dunwoody and Alan Fitch, Bob Edwards, Sir Geoffrey de Freitas, John Prescott, Mark Hughes, Tom Ellis, and Bob Mitchell from the PLP. The peers were Lords Ardwick, Brimelow, Bruce, Castle, Kennett and Lady Fisher. Chris Price, who had been a Member for a short period did not stand for re-election.

Manfred Michel spoke impeccable English and was often referred to as "the Englishman". He made strenuous efforts to persuade the Labour Party to change its policy, and extended warm solidarity and hospitality to the British delegation, saying that they worked constructively. The President of the Confederation of European Socialist Parties (Wilhelm Droscher) as a gesture of solidarity invited the Labour Group to his wine growing area in Germany, a visit that included Jenny Little from Labour HQ and Ian Mikardo MP from the NEC. Prescott was seen as energetic and worked on some important staff representation rules that were appreciated. He also generously invited Socialists to his home in Hull when there was a meeting on fish in Grimsby.

Prescott recalls an occasion when there was a parliamentary debate on a Monday on agriculture and regional funding and the Council meeting was on the Wednesday. He went to see Prime Minister James Callaghan wanting to line up the Labour Group's vote with the government position but Callaghan would not give him information about what the British position was to be. Prescott noticed that the Prime Minister's briefing contained incorrect facts and says he told him so in front of his civil servants. It was not the warmest of meetings.

The final report from the group was presented to the PLP in May 1979, just before the first elections. Prescott's foreword recorded: "The growth of our impact on the thinking of Parliament and the Socialist Group has enabled us to defend British interests quite openly at the same time as trying to convince other parliamentarians of our views on fundamental aspects of Community policies, and how they should be reviewed." In response to a survey conducted by Kevin Featherstone from the Department of Government at Manchester University, one of the Members said: "At home it is very difficult to get information out of Ministers whereas here on the committees you can really sit down and cross examine members of the Commission and the Council". From October 1978 the delegation appointed Michael Wood as a General Secretary and Jan Royall as an assistant from January 1979.

Roy Jenkins, a leading Labour revisionist figure before he formed the SDP, was President of the European Commission from 1977-81, having left Callaghan's government. He campaigned constantly but at the time unsuccessfully for a change in Labour's European policy. Callaghan asked Prescott whether he would like to be the UK's Commissioner when Roy

Jenkins' term came to an end, but Prescott said he didn't believe in a united states of Europe and did not want to take it on, wishing to remain in domestic politics. In the end the job went to Ivor Richard.

Altiero Spinelli led the European Federalist Movement as its Secretary-General between 1948 and 1962. Together with Paul-Henri Spaak and others, he saw to it that the early ad hoc Assembly had adopted a draft treaty on a statute of the European Community, back in March 1954. In 1970 he became a European Commissioner and continued his federalist mission.

The European Monetary System (EMS), precursor of the euro and coming into operation in March 1979, was negotiated by Chancellor Schmidt of Germany who was also a Member. The Labour delegation showed some independence from the party's policy at home in that Lord Ardwick, who was rapporteur for the Parliament on EMS, felt it was a welcome development if it created a zone of monetary stability and that it could provide a major contribution towards wider international monetary reform. The European Currency Unit (ECU) became the common denominator for currency parities. Whilst the UK joined the EMS under the Conservative government in 1979, it remained at that time outside the Exchange Rate Mechanism (ERM).

The European Act introducing direct elections was signed by Council in Brussels on 20 September 1976, leading to the EEC-wide elections to a new European Parliament in June 1979. At this stage the electoral systems were widely different in the various Member States. Remuneration for Members would be at the rates of national parliamentarians.

Socialist Group staff remembered the Labour delegation as good participants in Europe. However, none of the Labour Members stood in the first direct elections. In contrast eight of the Conservative Members were elected in 1979 to the new Parliament.

There was no sense of a handover from the old delegation to the newly elected Members, and there is no recollection of the reports recording the work that had gone before being distributed to the new MEPs. They were on their own. Most of the newly-elected Members did not even know their predecessors.

PART I

1979-84
Elected to withdraw

The Scene

The first five years of the democratically elected European Parliament had a reluctant Labour Group split down the middle on membership of the European Community. Budgetary problems, the British rebate and agricultural over-production dominated the debates. Thatcherism, unemployment and recession took hold in the UK. The Parliament, without much power apart from the ability to block the budget, was seen in the UK as a mere talking shop. The Labour Party was committed to withdrawal. Cruise missiles caused dismay. Debates began on the draft Treaty on European Union. The Isoglucose judgement of the Court of Justice in 1980 gave Parliament a de facto delaying power on legislation. Some Labour Members changed their mind on EEC membership. Four of them were to migrate to the House of Commons by the end of the five year period. The Labour Party at home was facing internal battles against the Trotskyist Militant Tendency. The 1983 general election was decisively won by the Conservatives. By the end of the Parliament three Labour Members had been dese-lected, one of whom defected to the pro-European SDP- Liberal Alliance.

Hard times

It was the worst of times for Labour. The world's first direct elections to a multinational parliament in June 1979 came just five weeks after the Callaghan Labour government's shattering landslide defeat to Margaret Thatcher's Conservatives. The successful Conservative slogan was epitomized in a broad-sheet poster advertisement entitled "Labour Isn't Working". The Labour government had lost a confidence vote following the "winter of discontent", a failed incomes policy, the demise of the Lib-Lab pact and on 1 March the fail-ure of the Scottish and Welsh devolution referenda. Even Cabinet Minister Shirley Williams had lost her House of Commons seat. (Williams came back for the SDP in the Crosby by-election in November 1981 but lost it to the Conservatives in 1983.) Morale was at rock bottom. Worse still, a substantial proportion of Labour Party members and MPs were not convinced of the merits of contesting the European elections at all. The timing could not have been worse. The electorate and the parties were weary, with disunity and half-heartedness the order of the day.

The Labour Party had not yet recovered from its splits during the 1975 ref-erendum on membership of the EEC. Many members had campaigned for a "No" vote and the two-to-one national majority in favour of membership still rested uneasily upon the left body politic. Whilst most Labour Party members considered themselves internationalists, they were generally of the view that the EEC was a "capitalist club". Castle thought it perpetuated Cold War div-isions. The party had only reluctantly filled its empty seats in the UK del-egation to the European Parliamentary Assembly after the referendum, having boycotted any participation from Britain's accession in 1973 until late 1975. Labour in government had declined to join the European Monetary System that came into operation in March 1979, leaving that to the new Conservative administration. There was an internal argument as to whether Labour should fight the elections at all but John Prescott, Leader of the Labour Group in the Assembly, wrote in *Labour Weekly* that it was the "least worst sol-ution". He maintains that even at that early stage it was evident to some that the pro-Europeans were working up to a breakaway party.

The party was engaged in an internal right versus left battle over the right to reselect MPs, greater grass roots involvement in policy making and the rise of women's committees on councils and black sections within the party. Internal struggles in constituency party organizations between moderates, Militants and the traditional left had reached a peak and elections for the European Parliament did not rise to the top of many activists' agenda. As a result, the election campaign was notable for its lack of enthusiasm, and this gave Labour a woeful result. The Conservatives returned sixty of the eighty-one UK MEPs, Labour seventeen and the SNP one. Voting by proportional representation, Northern Ireland returned one SDLP (John Hume), one Democratic Unionist (Reverend Ian Paisley), both of whom held dual mandates with the House of Commons and one Ulster Unionist (John Taylor). The Liberal Party, despite 12.6% of the vote, won no seats at all under the UK's first-past-the-post system, to discontent on their part. Overall turnout, reflecting the electorate's lack of interest in voting in two consecutive months, was 31.6%, the lowest in Europe. Some parts of the country had turnouts substantially lower than that and many Constituency Labour Parties boycotted the campaign.

The vagaries of the electoral system assisted the Conservatives. Given 45% of the vote they won three-quarters of the seats, with Labour's 31% only giving it one-fifth of the Members, in part due to poor turnout in traditional Labour-voting urban areas. Only two Labour MEPs were returned for Scotland. Another factor was that the hastily drawn up constituency boundaries were felt to be less than favourable to Labour. In particular, big cities such as London were divided as slices on a cake, with the thinnest part at the Labour-voting centre, and the widest part of the wedge on the Conservative peripheries.

The election had been delayed across Europe from the planned date of 1978 because of arguments in the House of Commons over whether it should be run on a system of proportional representation as elsewhere, or first-past-the-post as in UK domestic elections. The lengthy debate caused delays in the passage of the European Assembly Elections Bill. The 1977 White Paper on European elections faced six votes against it in Cabinet alone and eventually ran out of parliamentary time. The Act, when finally passed in 1978, supported the UK's electoral status quo and specifically opposed any increase in the powers of the European Parliament. Immediately after this Act was signed Labour conference voted for withdrawal from the EEC.

Labour's band of seventeen in Strasbourg consisted of local Councillors, public sector workers and polytechnic lecturers, led by their only star, Barbara Castle. She had substantial Cabinet experience in Harold Wilson's Labour governments, and was a committed anti-marketeer. There were four women, four academics, one journalist, one local government worker, a teacher, one from the private sector, two Labour movement administrators, one former MP and no previous Assembly Members. Most had trade union or Co-operative movement backing. Twelve were Councillors, some of whom kept their seats until the next local government election. Well over half were firmly against the Common Market. Many of them would have preferred to have been in the House of Commons rather than this new so-called Parliament with few powers, and a good number of them had unsuccessfully tried to win seats at general elections and were to try for a seat again in the future. Indeed, by the end of the first parliamentary term, four of this intake had become MPs, with a further three taking the Westminster road three years later.

In contrast, the large Conservative team included businessmen, bankers, four peers and three former MPs, six knights, a former ambassador, journalists, lawyers, landowners and eight former Members from the Assembly. Amongst them were six former Commission officials. Sir Peter Vanneck was a former Lord Mayor of the City of London; Sir Fred Warner was former Ambassador to Tokyo and the UN. Sir Fred Catherwood was one time Chief Economic adviser to the Department of Economic Affairs and director general of the National Economic Development Council. Sir Tom Normanton had ministerial experience and had been a MEP since 1973. Basil de Ferranti was deputy chair of Ferranti Ltd and past president of ECOSOC. David Harris was chief political correspondent of the *Daily Telegraph* and a former Member of the GLC. Madron Seligman was marketing director of a firm with sixty world-wide companies and the oldest Oxford friend of former Prime Minister Ted Heath. Sir David Nicholson was Chairman of Rothmans International. Stanley Johnson, father of Boris and not as right-wing, had been head of the environmental pollution division of the European Commission. Only five of the Conservatives were women. In contrast to today's Conservatives, they were in favour of the EEC and had a strategic idea of the way they wanted to shape events and protect their business interests. Members have since said they felt this was the best intake they ever had. They were on a surge of optimism at the start of the Thatcher era.

Labour candidates

None of the Members of the earlier European Assembly were candidates for Labour. The selection process had been lacklustre to say the least. It was only in October 1978 that conference approved the procedure for selection of candidates and proposals for MEPs' accountability to the party. Each local constituency party was entitled to send ten delegates to a European Co-ordinating Committee covering European constituencies to constitute the selection body and not all parties sent their full quota of delegates. There was unsurprisingly far greater enthusiasm from the right-wing pro-European minority in the party to take part and show up to selection meetings than from the left, who in the main were against the whole process.

The pro-Europeans' chief coordinator was Jim Cattermole, Chair of the first Labour Committee for Europe (LCE) and a former Labour regional organizer. Cattermole, who died in 2007, was a strong figure in the Labour Movement for Europe for many years and at that time was busily organizing for as many pro-marketeers as possible to be selected in winnable seats. Traditionally from the 1960s to that time Labour's pro-Europeans tended to be enthusiastic federalists and substantially on the right of the party, so his efforts did not bear a great deal of fruit.

The Labour Party had required any sitting MP to announce they would stand down at the next general election before they could be eligible to stand as candidates for the European Parliament. A number did so, including Michael Barnes and Dick Leonard – rebels on EEC votes in the past. However they were not selected. Barbara Castle was the only former Labour

MP who was both selected and elected. Other well-known Labour pro-Europeans (such as Dr Ernest Wistrich in Cleveland, Director of the European Movement) did not win their seats.

Prominent former MPs, too, were absent. In part at least this was because Labour MPs knew that in contrast to their continental colleagues, they could not progress to ministerial office if they were in the European Parliament rather than the House of Commons. Once they left, their route into government closed down. Sir Geoffrey de Freitas, a pro-marketeer, had been a Labour MP from 1945 on and off. He had a stint as a British High Commissioner in Africa and considerable European experience, as President of the Council of Europe from 1966-69 (a Member of that body from 1950-70) and one of the Labour delegates to the European Parliament from 1975-79. He might have lent some weight to the British Labour Group but did not move (and died in 1983). Similarly, Dr Colin Phipps who had been Labour MP for Dudley West from 1974-79 and before that for Walthamstow East (and was regarded as a right-wing federalist) stood down from Westminster but also did not get his name on a ballot paper. He later became a founding member of the SDP. Labour's policy of abolition of the House of Lords doubtless swung the balance against selecting a peer, ensuring that even Lord (Donald) Bruce of Donnington, an active member of the Labour delegation to the European Assembly from 1975-79 and a former editor of the left-wing paper *Tribune*, was not in the running. John Prescott MP, Leader of the former Labour Group, did not put himself forward, preferring to stay in Westminster.

Julian Priestley, a pro-market European Parliament official later to be General Secretary of the Socialist Group and then of the Parliament itself, was an unsuccessful Labour candidate in his home town of Plymouth in the general elections in 1974, 1979 and 1983, but did not put himself forward as a European candidate. "The time was never quite right", he said, "and then my European Parliament career was taking off."

Having been dropped from Callaghan's Cabinet in April 1976, Castle was not finding the back benches to her taste and had already told her Blackburn constituency party in 1978 that she would not stand for re-election to the House of Commons. As such, at nearly seventy, she was available to serve. Her political adviser and protégé Jack Straw had been selected to stand for her House of Commons seat. Barbara's husband, Labour life peer Ted Castle, was one of Labour's nominated Members of the Assembly, and she had accompanied him a few times on trips to Strasbourg and even more exotic locations. Her autobiography *Fighting All the Way* (Castle, 1993), reveals that Jo Richardson MP wanted to put her forward as Chair of the Equal Opportunities Commission but Barbara was not taken by that proposal. She was a political animal through and through. When she was approached by party workers in the North West asking if she would stand, she records that the idea interested her. "We anti-marketeers had to face the realities," she wrote.

> "We had been defeated on both the issues to which we were opposed. If there was to be a directly elected European Parliament, ought we not to be inside it, fighting the creeping federalism we could sense on every hand? I had never believed in vacating any political platform for the Tories to occupy."

To this day, some party workers from the North West recall the passion behind her speeches to this effect. Of the selection process itself, Castle says it was long, and "the delegates [in Greater Manchester North] were as indifferent to, and ignorant of, Europe as most of the electors were, so they jumped at the idea of having a candidate who was nationally known." She was opposed by a young local Councillor Glyn Ford, who went on to be elected himself in 1984.

Joyce Quin (now Baroness Quin) was selected for and won South Tyne and Wear as Labour's second youngest Member. One of a small band who were members of the European Movement, she had some European experience, having been a researcher in the Labour Party International Department early in the 1970s and as a linguist had travelled to the Council of Europe with parliamentary delegations and there met many European politicians. She faced some formidable opposition at her selection and had started with only a Fabian Society nomination. Later when she contested selection for her parliamentary seat, she faced opposition from a Militant candidate. On election she was the only female politician in the North East and as a result always enjoyed good media coverage.

Win Griffiths in Wales, a moderate pro-marketeer, former history teacher, Councillor and member of CND, had attempted to stand for Westminster but had not won the selection. "This was lucky", he said in retrospect, "since I won selection for Europe on the fourth ballot and stayed for two terms". He was lucky a second time in declining to stand for Westminster in 1983, saying that he felt he should undertake two terms in Europe, as Labour lost the seat. He was then persuaded to run in 1987, when Labour won, sending him to Westminster as MP for Bridgend, the only MP who won a non-Labour seat.

Ken Collins, another moderate pro-market Councillor and European Movement member, former apprentice metallurgist and town planner, went on to become the longest serving Chair of the Environment Committee, a powerful figure in the Parliament, and Deputy Leader of the Labour Group. He only narrowly squeaked his selection, however, by one vote on the third ballot. He could not have been more different from his neighbour in Glasgow, Janey Buchan, who was left-wing and anti-market. They were not the best of friends throughout their term.

It has been estimated (Butler and Marquand, 1981) that despite the anti-market climate, just over thirty of the seventy-eight Labour candidates were pro-market, although not many of them were elected. One example was the East London pro-market candidate, Peter O'Neill, a freelance journalist. He was selected at least partly because some of the left-wing inner city parties (still absorbed with their internal battles against Militant) did not send all their delegates to the selection meeting, leaving the field at the mercy of the traditionally more right-wing parties from the Essex end of the constituency. Election canvassing in Labour areas of London East was almost non-existent and very little literature was distributed. The Conservatives won and he later defected to the SDP. In later years piles of undelivered leaflets could be found languishing in party members' garages and dusty corners of Labour halls.

Alf Lomas (Leader of the British Labour Group 1985-87) was selected as an anti-marketeer in London North East against another anti-marketeer,

Ron Leighton, a founder of the Labour Common Market Safeguards Committee and fond of spouting facts and figures about the iniquities of the CAP. By the time of the European election Leighton had become MP for Newham North East. Lomas, a former railway signalman then political secretary for the London Co-op, had a congenial and persuasive manner of speaking. He was selected on the first ballot with around seventy votes and says that Ron only won fifteen. Lomas and Richard Balfe (a Greater London Councillor until 1977), although unlikely friends, had a common bond in that they had both been opposite numbers in the London and Southern Region Co-operative movements. Lomas later said Balfe did not fit any particular ideological slot.

One outstanding victor of the elections was Roland Boyes, a local government researcher from Durham and strong defender of social policies for the working class who later became an MP (1983-97) for Houghton and Washington. He was also a talented photographer. Fraser Kemp, his successor as MP, said that Boyes' selection speech in 1978 was "inspirational, speaking about the need for working people to have representation at every level". A strong anti-marketeer at the outset, Boyes was later to soften his position, partly under the influence of colleague Ann Clwyd. (She had fought Westminster seats unsuccessfully in 1970 and 1974.) Tam Dalyell, who was an MEP from 1976-79, maintained contact with various European Parliament officials during the 1980s, and asked which of the Labour Members was making an impact. It seems that Boyes was always mentioned.

The other members of that first Labour team were: Gordon Adam, a Northumbrian mining engineer who had fought in general elections in 1966 and 1974 and a by-election in November 1973; Richard Balfe, Political Secretary of Royal Arsenal Co-op; Janey Buchan, a Strathclyde Regional Councillor, Richard Caborn, a Sheffield trade unionist; Ann Clwyd, a Welsh journalist; Derek Enright, a Leeds schoolmaster and Yorkshire Councillor; Michael Gallagher a former miner and Leader of Nottingham Council; Brian Key, the youngest, a Barnsley Councillor and Yorkshire local government officer who had been active in the European Socialist Youth Movement; Tom Megahy MBE, a lecturer and first Leader of Kirklees Council; Dr Barry Seal, a Yorkshire polytechnic lecturer and Councillor; and Allan Rogers, a Welsh geologist. Adam, Boyes, Buchan, Collins, Enright, Gallagher, Griffiths, Key, Megahy, Seal and Rogers, were all local or County Councillors, quite a number of them having been Council Leaders or chairs of committees. Balfe, formerly from the Foreign Office, had been a GLC Chair of Housing and had fought Paddington South in the election of 1970. Lomas was Co-op and Castle had been an MP.

Some of the candidates who were not elected at that time came to prominence in later years in other ways but only Michael Elliott made the eventual journey to the European Parliament. He won London West in 1984 and served as an MEP until 1999, but stood unsuccessfully in Bedfordshire against Conservative Peter Beazley in this first election. He was pro-market and very keen to fight in the first European election, but was not on that occasion selected in his home seat of Ealing in West London, where he was a Councillor. Ian White, a pro-marketeer from Bristol attempted to get selected but was not to succeed until 1989. Albert Bore (now Sir Albert, who later became Leader of Birmingham City Council and then President of the Committee of the Regions in Brussels), came close to winning in Birmingham South, standing unsuccessfully against Conservative Norvella Forster. Mildred Gordon, later a Campaign Group MP, fought unsuccessfully in London North West as an anti-marketeer against Conservative Lord Bethell. Tony Hart, later a GLC Member and the husband of Dame Judith Hart (the Labour government Minister who played a major role in securing the Lome Convention of 1975), fought Shelagh Roberts, herself a Conservative GLC member (1970-81), in London South West. John Ennals, an academic and son of David Ennals (former head of Labour's International Department and then an MP and Secretary of State for Social Services), stood in Thames Valley against Conservative Baroness Elles who later became a European Parliament Vice-President. Steve Bundred, later Chief Executive of the Audit Commission, stood in London South East against Sir Brandon Rhys Williams MP. In Liverpool a Militant candidate, Terry Harrison, was put up and the Conservatives enjoyed a swing of 11% to them from their high vote in the general election a month before, with one of the lowest turnouts in the UK at 23.7%. There was only one minority ethnic candidate, P.S. Jariwala in Hampshire West.

Labour's left of centre activist grouping Labour Co-ordinating Committee (LCC), with a majority of anti-marketeers on its executive at the time, was wedded to the Alternative Economic Strategy based on controls on trade and capital movements which many felt was incompatible with the Treaty of Rome. Frances Morrell, a founder member who had worked for Tony Benn when he was Secretary of State for Energy was a member of its Executive and a GLC Member from 1981-86 (and subsequently leader of ILEA until its abolition), was in favour of a more positive approach to Europe but sceptical of its institutions, believing in international socialist co-operation. The Committee was formed in 1979 and its first Executive included people with an extraordinary mixture of views on the EEC, including Bob Cryer MP, Stuart Holland MP, Chris Mullin (later an MP and government Minister), Jeff Rooker MP, Michael Meacher MP, Brian Sedgemore MP and Audrey Wise MP. Nevertheless, after much discussion, the Committee drew up eleven probing questions for prospective candidates that were circulated to Constituency Labour Parties. There was no doubt from the way the questions were framed that the "correct" answers would be anti-market.

Manifesto machinations

European policy at the Labour Party (then at Transport House in Smith Square) was handled jointly by the Research Department, headed by Geoff Bish and by the International Department, headed by Jenny Little. Both of these individuals were anti-market. It was the latter who sent representatives to meetings of the Confederation of European Socialist Parties (Confed), together with National Executive Committee (NEC) members where the European manifesto was drawn up. The composition of staff in both departments was mainly anti-EEC and the same went for the NEC itself. Inside headquarters Nick Sigler was working on the Common Agriculture Policy (CAP) and Europe in the Research Department and argued that Europe was a domestic issue. Always a Eurosceptic, Sigler wrote substantial policy documents over two decades for the party. On the other side, David Blackman, a pro-marketeer working for the Socialist

Group in the European Parliament, was co-opted on to a European sub-committee as a specialist. A pro-EEC academic from Lancaster University, David Lowe, was also co-opted and by 1982 he too was working for the Parliament in Brussels. At the time of this first election he was writing briefing notes for Eric Heffer, frontbench spokesman on European affairs and recalls Heffer telling him: "don't come to me with the facts – I just want to get England out of the Common Market". According to Lowe, despite this, Heffer was not by any means an isolationist or nationalist, and was not against "Europe", but against the "capitalist EEC" and always remained baffled as to why no other Socialist party in Europe agreed with him on something which he felt was so obvious.

The EEC Liaison Committee was set up in March 1979 and became the de facto campaign committee, being chaired by Tony Benn who had become strongly anti-market. Disputes about whether the Parliamentary Labour Party should be involved in drawing up the manifesto left the PLP thwarted.

Labour's ideological divide on Europe was largely a left versus right split in the 1970s and 1980s, although there were some exceptions. In general the pro-marketeers were seen as the intellectuals from the Croslandite/Gaits-kellite wing of the party. There was a massive battle going on for the heart and soul of the Labour Party between the right, who had formed the Manifesto Group, on one hand and Militant supporters who were seeking to take control of the left on the other, squeezing the Tribune Group who were the more traditional left. Michael Foot and Tony Benn had, amongst others on the left, been strongly against direct elections to the European Parliament, as was Clive Jenkins, leader of the influential white collar trade union ASTMS. Most of the Labour Party saw themselves as international-ists, but were more interested in solidarity with the Commonwealth and developing countries than in Europe.

During the time of the Labour delegation to the unelected European Assembly (1975-79), Peter Shore MP, a prominent anti-marketeer, opposed the Members joining the Socialist Group on the grounds that the latter was comprised of "dangerously federalist social democrats, irredeemably com-promised by sitting in national coalition governments with centre and right-wing parties" (Broad, 2001). The Secretary of the Common Market Safeguards Committee, John Mills, insisted that direct elections were neither sanctioned by the referendum nor written into the Treaty of Accession. Anti-marketeers harboured fears for Britain's sovereignty and British democracy, Castle call-ing it a "rich man's club" and fearing it would prop up Cold War divisions. Anti-EEC feelings were still strong, as seen by the 1978 Labour Party confer-ence passing composite resolution 42 calling for Labour's next election man-ifesto to include the:

> "amendment of the European Communities Act to restore to the Commons the power to decide whether any EEC Regulation, Directive or Decision should apply in Britain, to reform fundamentally the CAP to permit freer food imports and deficiency payments, to curtail the powers of the Commission, to give express right to the Member states to pursue their own economic, industrial and regional policies, to reject EMU, and to ensure that Britain could keep the benefits of its indigenous fuels".

This was despite John Prescott MP, former Leader of the Labour Group in the Assembly and himself a Eurosceptic, saying he felt it would not be possible for Britain to leave the EEC.

With this bi-polar mindset, the manifesto was being negotiated on two fronts – in Europe and at home. The Confed had prepared a draft manifesto as early as June 1977 but it was proving difficult to reconcile the positions of socialist parties across Europe. The British sent observers only to the working parties, refusing to take part in their deliberations. The UK party's negative attitude had ensured that by June 1978 the text had been modified, particularly in terms of curtailing any transfer of powers from national governments to Community institutions. The Brits were not the only ones who were proving difficult, since the French were also finding disagreements, this time on enlargement policies. There was a stumbling block between British and Germans over the use of the term "European Parliament", with the British maintaining that it was an Assembly. Dick Gupwell, a pro-European Briton from the Socialist Group staff finally brokered a compromise by suggesting the terminology in the Treaty: "the Assembly of the European Community (European Parliament)". There was also widespread resistance to the word "manifesto". Manfred Michel, Secretary General at the beginning of the process, recalls that party Leaders came up with the idea of calling it a "platform". Ron Hayward, General Secretary of the Labour Party, had said on a visit to one of the meetings in 1978 that it was inevitable that an elected parliament would demand more power and that was one reason he was against direct elections.

The European manifesto failed to win support from the various parties, and was reduced to a 31-point "Political Declaration" by party Leaders of the Confed, with the names of Ian Mikardo MP and Hayward attached. These two had been sent to the Leaders' Summit in Brussels in June 1978 to sign the document. Labour was the only European Party not to send its Leader. To combat the press feeling that this was simply the lowest common denominator, a further document, the "Appeal to the European Electorate" was prepared for the Brussels Congress of the Confed immediately following the Leaders' meeting. This contained seven main aims, also fairly general in tone.

Labour's lack of enthusiasm for the European joint text came to a crunch when the NEC refused to endorse the final version of the "Appeal", necessitating a covering note by Hayward giving the official more negative slant. It was the only country not to use it as a platform. It was another decade before the Labour Party was fully to endorse an election manifesto of the European socialist parties. The Appeal was graced with a foreword from Hayward as party General Secretary, saying:

> "This Declaration… is not a statement of party policy but is issued for information as an indication of our general approach. The Labour Party Manifesto for the Direct Elections, published in January 1979, sets out the policy upon which the British Labour Party will be fighting the campaign this summer."

It had been necessary to publish these documents in order to take advantage of the much-needed financial assistance from Brussels channelled via the Socialist Group.

Labour's own manifesto published simultaneously was also controversial, with Callaghan abstaining on the vote on its text at the NEC, after a lengthy debate on whether it should be called "Labour in Europe", "Labour for Europe" or "Labour and Europe". It said: "The EEC Assembly is not a real Parliament... Labour would vigorously resist any further extension of the powers of the Assembly" and aimed "to restore to the Commons the power to amend or repeal legislation applicable to Europe". The penultimate paragraph carried the sting:

> "We declare that if the fundamental reforms contained in this manifesto
> are not achieved within a reasonable period of time, then the LP would
> have to consider very seriously whether continued EEC membership was
> in the best interests of the British people".

This was following a call for a major revision of the Treaty of Rome. Callaghan refused to launch the campaign and Hayward, the anti-marketeer, had to preside. Even the venue was subject to a last minute change due to double booking and many journalists arrived as it was ending. Nevertheless, the pro-marketeers argued that they could still sign up to this piece of party policy as the wording was sufficiently oblique.

In May Callaghan was due in Paris for a "Springtime for Socialists" rally attended by twenty thousand Europeans. It can't have been a happy meeting of minds. He warned the Leaders that each party must be free to pursue its own economic and political strategy. The Europeans had organized a series of eleven conferences and events between December and May in different countries and on topics covered by their campaign document. Two weeks before the election there was a final European socialist event at the foot of the Eiffel Tower in Paris, again without official participation of the British.

To campaign or not to campaign?

This was the election about which Tory Deputy Prime Minister Willie Whitelaw famously spoke of people going about the country stirring up apathy. There was little media publicity. Labour Party workers were dispirited and tired after the catastrophic general election a mere few weeks before and the devolution referenda in Scotland and Wales in the spring. All three manifestos of the main British parties called for reform of the CAP, leaving Labour candidates no unique selling point on which to campaign except the withdrawal policy. Complaints of lack of funding and poor organisation abounded. Conservatives did not campaign too hard for fear of awakening a dormant Labour vote. Their main advantage was that campaigning was held back until after the Whitsun break, effectively giving only two and a half weeks to win voters' hearts and minds.

Labour candidates had a meeting in Birmingham on 11-12 May financed by the European parties. There had also been a large candidates' meeting in Luxembourg in April with the socialist parties at which Willy Brandt had spoken to the Labour candidates trying to persuade them to take a more pro-European line. Castle made a barnstorming anti-market speech and Brandt as the next speaker tore up his prepared speech and refuted what she had said with a passionate off-the-cuff return. He spoke about international comradeship and the need for European socialists to be together to combat the international capitalist movement. Brandt was a strong supporter of the social dimension of the EEC – the idea that the Community should concern itself not only with economic growth, but also with the living and working conditions of its citizens. This meeting revealed the unpreparedness of Labour's candidates. Most did not even know what their salaries would be. Barry Seal recalls that Tom Megahy took the wrong train to the airport and wanted the plane held, phoning the airport saying he was Leader of Kirklees Council. The plane left without him. A Labour official in the Commission who was also travelling that way helped him get to Brussels and he finally arrived in Luxembourg the next day just as the meeting was finishing. Seal says:

> "None of us were used to getting planes then and I had trouble finding the money for the fare and had to do a deal with Co-op Travel [the travel agency used by many of the Labour MEPs] to be billed in arrears. Many of us were in the same boat as no-one was highly paid at the time."

Many of the Labour Members attest to tales of local parties within their constituencies completely boycotting the elections and this undoubtedly affected turnout and the Labour result. Caborn, who had led the Yorkshire "Get Britain Out" campaign, said the North East Derbyshire party in his Euro-constituency refused to participate at all. Joyce Quin attributes a similar position to Jarrow (where Alan Donnelly, later a pro- European MEP and Leader of the EPLP, was constituency secretary and where Quin had defeated their local candidate, Michael Campbell, favourite to win the selection) although by election day they had started to participate. There were many more examples of this kind. The Militant effect precluded winning seats in Liverpool and Birmingham. Collins was told by Rotherglen, one of his constituencies, that they would boycott the election, although he says the MP much later became supportive. Speaking at conference in the autumn of 1979, a Lancashire candidate said "we couldn't make up our minds and so half-fought". At the same conference Lomas spoke of a combination of indifference and hostility to the Common Market. (A more detailed account of these events can be found in *Britain's Emerging Euro-Elite?* (Westlake, 1994).)

Perhaps it was the demoralization and lack of coherence after the defeat of the Labour government, but it seemed the Labour Party could do nothing right. Millions of election leaflets were recalled, pulped and reprinted at vast expense because it was brought to the attention of the National Executive Committee by Dennis Skinner MP that the slogan on the leaflets read "Labour for Europe". He took umbrage at this and the NEC agreed it had to be changed. The reprinted versions said "Labour and Europe" but some of the original versions were apparently distributed by several pro-market candidates. Terry Ashton, former London Regional Director, recalls that was the case in West London with pro-marketeer Jim Daly, a former GLC Councillor and its Chair of Transport. Daly did not win the seat and later defected to the SDP, unsuccessfully fighting a parliamentary seat under that banner. He had set up an organization (the Radical Centre for Democratic Studies) to keep the Brussels-based Roy Jenkins briefed on the UK political scene, possibly with a view to later defection.

In Putney, part of London South West constituency, the Labour candidate Tony Hart was an anti-marketeer, as were most of the constituency party members at the time. There was not much of a campaign and to their annoyance the London South West election had to be re-run in the autumn because Shelagh Roberts (later Dame Shelagh), the Conservative winner and Greater London Councillor, had been disqualified on a technicality, not having resigned in a timely fashion from an office of the Crown (the Occupational Pensions Board). Mike Gapes, later a Labour MP, living in Putney at the time, recalls a lonely time touring the roads around tower blocks of the Alton Estate with a loud hailer in an attempt to drum up some voters. (Roberts was finally confirmed as Conservative Member for London South West in a by election in September 1979, though Labour increased its vote on a sharply reduced turnout, and the Conservative vote was halved.)

Because Britain votes on a Thursday and much of Europe at the weekend, the European election counts do not take place until Sunday. The suspense is awful for candidates, but the gap means that there is less excited interest by the press and party members, who do not bother to turn out in large numbers for the count. Enright, who had been a County Councillor, won the first seat to be declared and became the UK's first MEP. He was to be deselected by the next election by his local parties who objected to his pro-market stance.

Jan Royall worked in the European campaign office from January 1979, as did Michael Wood, a Labour Party member from the European Parliament who was General Secretary of the British Labour Group in the Assembly under John Prescott. (Royall later worked with Neil Kinnock and the European Commission and became Baroness Royall and Leader of the House of Lords). They remember that leaflets sent over to London during the campaign by the European Socialist Group were so out of touch with Labour's political position that they were quickly binned.

The lowest turnout in the country was in London North East, notorious for low turnouts, where Lomas, despite a strong majority of 24,804, had only 20.4% voting. Labour's safest seats were South East Wales (Rogers, majority 41,615), Yorkshire South (Key, majority 36,834), Glasgow (Buchan, majority 32,702) and Durham (Boyes, majority 28,804). Castle's Manchester seat had the seventh highest majority. Conservative victories were narrow in Strathclyde West and Midlands West, and Seal's Labour seat in Bradford was won on a far from comfortable majority, though he hung on to it until 1999.

An unrepentant Labour conference in autumn of 1979 carried Composite 40, saying (in part):

> "The only way to remedy this situation is by carrying out the policy of radical reform set out in the Party's Manifesto for the Euro elections. Should changes not be made by the early 1980s the question of Britain's continued membership of the EEC should be reconsidered."

Castle, speaking in the debate, said "we have found things worse than we anticipated… dairy production is costing £250,000 per hour…We must use the European Assembly as a platform for our socialist policies… the Community must go socialist or we will come out." Lomas also managed to speak, reminding delegates of the withdrawal policy and that Labour should be in the EEC for only one term. He was finally to retire in 1999 after twenty years.

This, then, was the policy under which Labour's small band of MEPs were mandated to work.

Getting started

The British Labour Group (BLG) held its first meeting shortly after the election in Labour's Westminster headquarters, then at Transport House, with Tony Benn chairing and Prescott speaking as former Leader of the Labour delegation to the Assembly. Most members did not know each other, except for the pro-marketeers who had previously met in St Helens at a meeting chaired by Bill Rodgers MP and more informally earlier with Jim Cattermole. The pro-marketeers' plan was to put forward a slate for election of officers, comprising Collins as Deputy Leader, Gallagher as secretary and Enright as Leader. Originally the plan was for Leader and Chair to be one and the same. Allan Rogers saw that, given Castle's penchant for simply moving on if people did not agree with her, this would not work and he proposed separation, moving anti-market Caborn as Chair. This strategy threw the European Movement group off balance, as it was an unexpected proposal. When Castle was nominated as Leader she seemed an obvious choice as the only one with government experience, so Enright withdrew, leaving the right in some disarray. Seal was then nominated versus Collins as Deputy Leader and the voting was eight votes each with one abstention, the result remaining stubbornly the same through two re-runs. After a lunch adjournment where Quin appeared to have persuaded Adam that he would get on politically with Collins because he was in the European Movement, the vote shifted to 9 – 7 for Collins. The abstention throughout was Lomas who took the principled attitude of refusing to vote for people he did not know. Following her election as Leader Castle lost no time in persuading the General Secretary of the Labour Party that she should remain on Labour's NEC in an ex-officio capacity as Leader of the European Group.

The pre-1979 Labour group had use of a parliamentary office courtesy of its Leader, Prescott, in St Stephen's House, on the Embankment where Wood and Royall worked. This was the venue for a second BLG meeting after the election to decide on committees which they did by ballot. In the autumn of 1979 the European Parliament Information Office in London was in the throes of moving from its old base in Kensington Palace Road to an elegant building in Queen Anne's Gate, SW1, rather handier to the political hub. Since the parliament option was no longer available as MEPs were not now MPs, Caborn, together with Barbara Castle's assistant Janet Anderson negotiated space there for the political groups. Castle took office in a fine room on the first floor looking out over St James's Park and installed Anderson and Royall. She tenaciously managed to hold on to an office space in that building until July 1986, a full year after she had been deposed as BLG Leader. Anderson later followed another Castle assistant Jack Straw and became an MP, for Rossendale and Darwen, from 1992 and Minister for Tourism 1998-2001. When Anderson left in the Spring of 1980 to work for Jack Straw, Anita Pollack, who had been working for an MP, was recruited.

The Brits hit town

The BLG formed one sixth of the 112-strong Socialist Group, the largest political grouping in the European Parliament of nine nations. Roy Jenkins, then President of the Commission, referred to "an unbalanced result" in the

UK. Claude Cheysson, the French Socialist Commissioner, was more scathingly outspoken, being quoted in the *Times Guide to 1979 European Election* as saying: "the Labour Party has made a ridiculously low effort that is going to reduce the Socialist Group in the European Parliament." Whilst some of the Socialist Group's Members were critical of the EEC, no other member party had a withdrawal policy except that of Finn Lynge, representing Greenland, from 1979 an internally self-governing part of the Kingdom of Denmark. (Greenland ultimately left the Community as the result of a local referendum in February 1982.) At the first meeting of the Socialist Group the position of Leader was contested between Ernest Glinne from Belgium's Socialist Party and Ludwig Fellermaier from Germany's SPD. Both of these had been MEPs in the Assembly. Barbara Castle persuaded her BLG colleagues to vote for Glinne because she told them he was the more left-wing of the two, probably relying on her experience of European Assembly visits with her husband Ted.

Members of the Socialist Group were disappointed that Labour had not won more seats, and a little suspicious of these vociferous anti-Europeans, who appeared to be less conciliatory than their predecessors in the Assembly. For the most part, however, they accepted their new British comrades as part of the family. Labour Members were somewhat uneasy. They did not know how long they would be working in the EEC. Many felt that the next general election would be won by Labour and they would not serve a second term because a Labour government would withdraw. It was not to be. The Conservatives were in government for the long haul.

There was also some bad blood between the Labour Party officialdom in the UK and the Socialist Group. The NEC unrealistically wanted funding for researchers that was part of the Socialist Group's institutional funding to be remitted to Labour headquarters to help pay for its staff, since it was always strapped for cash. Grumbling about this rumbled on for some time. Eric Heffer when Chair of the NEC proposed that the British staff of the Socialist Group should actually work for the Labour Party, blithely indifferent to the fact that this would never be permitted under the Parliament's rules. NEC endorsement of candidates had depended on a written undertaking "to adhere to support for the party manifesto and to vote for the payment of any sums of money made available for research or administrative purposes to the British Labour Assemblymen or women collectively to the Labour Party which would employ staff for this purpose".

Northern Ireland's SDLP member, John Hume, was deemed by the Socialist Group to be nominally a member of the BLG making it large enough to qualify for delegation status. Although he did not attend their meetings, he was counted as part of their quota for posts under the Parliament's complicated D'Hondt system – a proportional system of allocation based on the numerical strengths of political groups, named after the Belgian lawyer who devised it. In later years he was to say that all the parliamentary positions gained by BLG members were attributable to his joining the delegation. He was also part of their social group. Hume and the Reverend Ian Paisley were also Westminster MPs and maintained dual mandates during their terms in the European Parliament

The Conservatives remained fairly aloof, forming the European Democratic Group with two Danes and a UUP Member. This was because some of their Members, although pro-European, were put off by the more federalist rhetoric of some of the Christian Democrats. Dropping the name "Conservative" was the subject of some debate, particularly after their spectacular victory, but felt to be necessary in the European context where the word was not included in the names of political parties or well understood. They were led by Sir James Scott-Hopkins, a former MP and Assembly Member, and were the largest single national group in the Parliament. It was not until the Spanish joined in 1986 that their group was to become more multinational, since they failed to attract any of the Greeks who arrived in 1982. One of their number, Baroness Elles, coming from a long career in local government, became a Vice-President of the Parliament in 1982 and used the post to great effect to put down Labour Members in plenary sessions. Sir Henry Plumb (often called "Sir Plumb"), later Lord Plumb, having been President of the National Farmers' Union in the UK, gained the post of Chairman of the Agriculture Committee. This was not without some angst from the French who were against reform of the CAP and did not like to see such an experienced opponent in a strong position. The Agriculture Committee included five former national presidents of farmers' unions. Some of the Conservatives were instrumental later in forming the Kangaroo Group, dedicated to removing barriers to trade and developing the Single Market. Plumb was to take over the leadership of their group before the next election.

Winnie Ewing, SNP Member for the Highlands and Islands, having lost her House of Commons seat in May, was quick to point out that she had a high turnout at 55%, with a constituency larger in area than Belgium. As an MP she had already served on the UK delegation to the Assembly and was to remain active in the Parliament for a good number of years, becoming known as a good speechmaker.

The Socialist Group operated fairly chaotically, as did the Parliament itself, both finding the transition from the previous smaller institution less than smooth. Glinne, the new Chairman, likened the job to chairing a kindergarten. Most of the Members did not know each other and it took a while to settle down. The Group in the former Assembly had been fairly cohesive, despite some policy differences, but it was smaller and more amicable. Manfred Michel, Secretary General of the Group until the end of 1980, said that in the pre-1979 Assembly Labour played a constructive role and the comradeship was excellent, despite their divided views on the Common Market. On one occasion he had taken them to his home in Luxembourg for a social evening, but such efforts had no effect on softening the anti-market policy of the party and things were different in the new, larger system.

Immediately upon arrival the Labour Leader was thrown into complex negotiations as to who would be endowed with what post in the Parliament, with the help of Michel who was experienced in working the machinery to best advantage. The BLG won entitlement to one Parliament Vice-Chair, which went to Allan Rogers as one of the Group's senior anti-marketeers. He said Enright's name had first been mooted but this did not find favour with the Group and it took him by surprise when his own name came up. It soon became apparent that one chair of committee post was also available. The Labour Members had, after a certain amount of jostling including a toss of a coin, agreed which committee they desired. Collins was startled to be called up on his holiday by David Blackman, a senior British member of the Socialist Group staff, to say he had been given Chair of the Committee on Environment, Public Health and Consumer Protection as a result of Castle's negotiating. He was never to look back from this beginning, holding the post for the majority of his twenty years in the Parliament – save for 1984-89 during which he was the Socialist Group's Coordinator (spokesperson), when the German Socialist Beate Weber held the post. Under Collins' leadership the Environment Committee became a powerful and forward-looking force, constantly pushing the powers of the Parliament, holding the Commission accountable and negotiating policies with the Council of Ministers. But at the beginning such positions were rare for the reluctant BLG Members. The only other trophy was for Seal as Vice-Chair of the REX Committee, covering external trade.

Castle railed against the "backstairs negotiations" that were the result of the proportional representation system. She hated the d'Hondt system and argued that the Socialist Group, as the largest, should put forward its own candidate as President of the Parliament. As she later put it in her autobiography: "To Ernest Glinne, wheeler dealing was a way of life because of the way Belgian politics worked" (Castle, 1993). She accompanied him in the negotiations, as senior Vice-Chair of the Socialist Group and he was somewhat discomfited by her disapproval of the system. She impulsively called a press conference with Glinne on the lawn outside the Parliament (not being able to obtain a room), to lodge a protest against the election of Simone Veil (French Liberal) as President on party lines. Castle argued that the President should be more like the Speaker of the House of Commons. This was rather obscure to a lot of the foreign journalists who were not familiar with the concept and it offered a slightly sour note, since Veil was accorded cross-party respect as an Auschwitz survivor. The complaints boiled down to a protest against the thirty-month term of office that had been agreed by the political groups. There was some suspicion that President Giscard d'Estaing's influence had been at work in the high level of support for Veil. However the deal finally struck was for Veil to be President for two-and-a-half years, then for it to be the turn of a Socialist. This so-called gentlemen's agreement was to come unstuck when the half way point came round at the end of 1981 and, partly as a result of Conservative machinations, it took several rounds of balloting for the Socialist candidate to be elected.

Castle's modest effort was not the only political demonstration at the first session. The Liberals staged their own protest with prominent British Liberals, including Russell Johnston and Christopher Mayhew, neither of whom had been elected. They occupied ten seats in the hemicycle at a point when it was empty and called a press conference to highlight the size of their vote in Britain with no members resulting, and to argue for a uniform election procedure. The European Liberals invited Russell Johnston, who had been a MEP from 1973-79, to attend their group meetings and have some access to the parliamentary buildings.

UK Members were the third lowest paid in the Parliament, earning less than many officials, whilst their German colleagues were the highest paid. This was the result of a prior agreement that had taken quite some negotiating, that MEPs would be paid the same as national MPs. When the MEPs arrived they did not know how much they could claim on expenses for their travel, and this was not settled until the first plenary. Rogers, who worked well with President Veil, says they set in train the first of the expenses reforms. Originally mileage was paid from national capitals and this rather generous system led to gravy train accusations. In the early days the mileage system of expenses also operated if a Member had to return to their own country for a mid-week engagement, which meant it was possible to make a substantial profit; it was also permitted to have allowances paid into a range of different currencies, thus benefiting from currency speculation. Many other nationalities also enjoyed good pension provisions and this, too, was not the case for the UK. In due course a voluntary pension scheme was set up for all those who wished to join, enthusiastically supported by the British but less so by the Dutch and Germans.

The Labour Group quickly polarised into two main camps, with some Members caught in the middle. The early pro-marketeers comprised Collins, Enright, Griffiths, Key and Quin, soon joined by Adam after a certain amount of teasing about his membership of the Labour Common Market Safeguards Campaign (which he maintained was for information purposes). Adam says that he always felt Europe should be taken seriously.

Gallagher, also a pro-European, remained throughout his term rather semi-detached from the Labour Group, though he had attended a pre-election meeting of the pro-marketeers as a member of the Labour Committee for Europe. When he later left the party he said the BLG was "really two groups of people who don't see eye to eye on anything". He had earlier worked in the same mine as Ken Coates (Bilsthorpe colliery). Later Coates was his lecturer at university, and then his agent when he fought against Ken Clarke at Rushcliffe in the election of 1974. Gallagher was sponsored by the NUM although he was a self-confessed moderate and against the miners' strike when it occurred, believing that Scargill should have agreed to attempts to deal with overstaffing in above-ground jobs. He says that when he was leader of Nottingham Council he had been passed a document, "Topic 12", outlining which pits were to be closed in the next twenty years and he ensured it was passed to Scargill, possibly adding to the momentum for the miners' strike. He later supported the breakaway Union of Democratic Mineworkers (UDM), based in the Nottinghamshire coalfield, which drew criticism from some other members of the BLG. The refusal of the Nottinghamshire miners to join the strike in March 1984, claiming it was unconstitutional, was to lead to the violent picketing and allegations of strike breaking that took place during that year. Gallagher spent most of his social time with what he felt were more convivial Irish Members, supporting their pro-European and good social welfare stance (and said they referred to the Tories as cave men). He was eventually to defect to the SDP when he was under threat of deselection by his constituency party in the run-up to the 1984 election.

Gallagher became a first Vice-Chairman of the Energy and Research Committee and was challenged by Adam when he defected, but maintained that he still kept his place in the Socialist Group and was in post under their quota and as such not beholden to the BLG. Gallagher many years later said that after he was elected he regretted giving up Nottingham Council for Europe, where he found everything was very slow, whereas "in local government you could see a result every day." His defection to the SDP was not entirely happy as he was not at all in favour of the European Liberals nor a supporter of Shirley Williams. In 1987 he set up a moderate Labour Party in Mansfield and by that time was associated with the UDM. He says "now the whole Labour Party is moderate" and rejoined the party in the early 1990s.

The anti-marketeers, largely Tribunites, formed a group of six: Balfe, Buchan, Caborn, Lomas, Megahy and Seal. Barbara Castle as Leader, whilst also firmly anti-market, saw it as her duty to keep aloof from internal fractions. In the middle were Clwyd, Boyes and Rogers, still largely on the left, and fairly anti-market, but over time some shifted their position, as did Balfe and even Castle. Rogers remained a Eurosceptic and in favour of pulling out on the grounds that Britain was a net importer from Europe and that it would not harm the economy. He preferred to deal with the Commonwealth, but in the BLG saw himself as trying to bridge the gap between the Members and so did not join the anti-market faction. By the end of this parliamentary session there was a two-to-one majority in the BLG to stay in the EEC.

Working partners

The Socialist Group included quite a few Members who had been in the Parliamentary Assembly prior to June 1979, and many had national parliamentary experience. There were some interesting and eminent characters amongst Labour's new group of comrades.

In the European Parliament and the Socialist Group, Members sit alphabetically rather than in national delegations. This meant that firm anti-marketeers Buchan and Caborn found themselves seated near Willy Brandt, the charismatic former German Chancellor. Whilst there was obvious disagreement on the merits of membership of the EEC, the comrades found other points of mutual interest. Buchan, a formidable Glaswegian with a life-long and vibrant interest in working class culture, poetry and folk music, recalls that Brandt had an excellent singing voice. Caborn, a doughty shop steward from the steel industry in Sheffield and later a long-serving Minister in the Blair government, and whose father had been District Secretary of the AEU and a Communist Party member, found a common interest in the economic situation and trades unions. It was not long after there had been a debate on the Brandt report at Cancun and development issues were high on the British agenda. Economic confrontation was on the rise in the UK and the debate on access to information for workers in multinational companies was in full swing. Francois Mitterrand was a member of the Socialist Group after the election, but immediately resigned, devoting himself to his presidential campaign in France. British Members always found it a strange practice that some continental parties would put well-known figures at the top of their party lists for campaigning purposes and then they would resign and be replaced by those lower on the list, but this was a common occurrence.

Leading the Socialist Group was Ernest Glinne, a Belgian Socialist former MP and Minister for Employment and Labour, who had also been a member of the Parliamentary Assembly and Chair of its Economic and Monetary Committee. Jacques Delors, a French Socialist of whom much more was to be seen later, became Chair of the Economic and Monetary Committee from

1979-81. Carlo Ripa di Meana, an Italian who was later to become Commissioner for Environment was there, as was Heidemarie Wieczorek-Zeul, later a long serving Minister in German governments. Others included Rudi Arndt, a writer and former SPD Minister who was also in the earlier Assembly; Katherina Focke, a former German Federal Minister; Edith Cresson, in 1981 to become French Minister for Agriculture, then Prime Minister and later a Commissioner; and Erwin Lange, Chair of Budgets since 1975 in the former Assembly, a long time SPD Bundestag member who had suffered imprisonment under the Nazis. There was also Karel van Miert, Vice-President of the Confederation of Socialist Parties from 1978-80 and later a Belgian Commissioner; Bettino Craxi, national Italian Socialist Party secretary and former MP; Jiri Pelikan, a former Czech member of the "Prague Spring" movement standing as an Italian Socialist; and many others. The Group also included a member from Greenland, Finn Lynge, who said it took him three days to travel to meetings and ostentatiously wore seal-skin waistcoats to the annoyance of the animal lovers.

There were numerous high-flyers from other parties too, including Altiero Spinelli, subsequently to found the federalist Crocodile Club within the Parliament, who had been elected on the Italian Communist list, having been a European Commissioner until 1976. Other notables and nobles included Otto Habsburg; Philipp von Bismarck; Martin Bangemann, a German Liberal later to be a Commissioner; Enrico Berlinguer, the Italian Communist leader; Emma Bonino, an Italian Radical later to be a Commissioner; Polish Prince Michel Poniatowski, as a Member for France who became the influential Chair of the Energy and Research Committee; and Prince Casimir Zu Sayn Wittgenstein Berleburg from Germany. Jacques Santer, later to become the ill-fated President of the Commission, was also elected as a MEP, but quickly resigned to join a new Luxembourg government. There were ten former heads of state and government: Willy de Clerq and Leo Tindemans from Belgium, Willy Brandt from Germany, Gaston Thorn from Luxembourg, Pierre Pflimlin, Jacques Chirac, Edgar Faure, Pierre Messmer and Michel Debre from France, Emilio Colombo, Giulio Andreotti and Mariano Rumor of Italy.

Despite their differences, Labour Members found much common cause with their Socialist colleagues. This was the heyday of the peace movement and campaigns for nuclear disarmament. American Cruise missiles were being deployed in Europe and the Greenham Common Women's Peace Camp was soon to be set up. There was agreement on a policy against nuclear weapons and many joint campaigns on these issues. A large number of Labour Members were at that time members of the Campaign for Nuclear Disarmament. Unemployment, workers' rights, social welfare and human rights were also largely uncontroversial matters across the Group where many Members had trade union roots. In contrast to Castle's combative style, many of those Labour Members who had been involved in local and county authorities had a clearer idea as to how the politics of compromise worked and were sometimes more willing to negotiate with others. All was not entirely peaceful, however, since Castle managed to tread on the toes of the German delegation led by Arndt and relations between the two delegations were often in conflict.

Getting down to work

This world's first multinational Parliament elected by direct suffrage representing 260 million voters in nine Member States elected former French Minister of Health and concentration camp inmate Simone Veil as its President with "founding father" Robert Schuman present in the gallery. (Jean Monnet had died earlier that year.) Setting the standard for years to come, this momentous event was largely ignored in the British press. As remains the case today, there was simultaneous interpretation into all the languages. Because the term of office of President was not laid down in the rules, the centre and right parties got together and proposed a two-and-a-half year term. Glinne for the Socialists proposed that it should be based on the Speaker of the House of Commons system, and that it should go to the largest group, obviously put up to it by Castle. The proposal was greeted with laughter.

Parliament's first five years were dominated by inter-institutional struggles over on-going budget crises. Once the elections to parliamentary posts had taken place, business took over from the posturing. Immediately Members were thrust into dealing with real issues in committees rather than simply pro and anti arguments. The work was a continuation from the old Parliament, with most of the procedures remaining intact, inefficient though they sometimes proved to be. During this Parliament the Christian Democrat and Liberal groups succeeded in dominating the votes because they found much common cause, often thwarting the Socialists despite the fact that the latter were the largest group.

The opening scenes of what was to be a lengthy budget battle took place with Balfe, as a Budget Committee member, putting the BLG position and unsurprisingly wanting the budget reduced. He spoke of "people in Bermondsey and Deptford [his constituency] having to go without a Sunday joint whilst in their midst is an EEC intervention store packed with red meat". He also paid tribute to his predecessor on budgets, Labour's Lord Bruce, in the tradition of House of Commons maiden speeches. Robert Jackson, the Conservative budget spokesman, who as early as September was seeking more powers for the Parliament, launched an attack on Labour by saying that Balfe had "brought out very clearly the radical flaw in the whole approach of his party to the question of Europe: full of criticisms of the Community but determined that we in this House should not have any power to do anything about them".

Brandt's speech on the next Helsinki follow-up conference on security and co-operation was an inspirational beginning. He spoke about hunger in the world, energy policy and trades unions and of constructing a treaty with Yugoslavia and on a European Community Charter of Human Rights. He also said: "Strasbourg is where the heart of Europe is beating. This city is living testimony to the reconciliation and subsequent friendship that has been forged between the German and French peoples, and which has brought progress to the whole of Europe and not just to our two peoples."

There was plenty of procedural tussling and adjournments as well as substantial business in that very first session in Strasbourg. The Irish President of the Council, Jack Lynch, drew a protest from Reverend Ian Paisley by beginning his speech in Irish. This was the first of many colourful interjections over the years from Paisley, who also complained that the Union flag was being flown upside down. Paisley, according to journalist John Palmer, shouting amongst other things: "Jack Lynch you are a murderer – you have blood on your hands" was removed by the ushers after "prolonged and vigorous protests". Lynch responded by saying "Madame President, I had hoped that the Member for Northern Ireland would not mar the historic opening of this newly-elected European Parliament by introducing a note of acrimony, particularly so early in the session". Roy Jenkins as President of the Commission (having left the House of Commons in 1977 after Callaghan refused him the Foreign Office) spoke about the energy crisis. The Thursday debates lasted until 4.05 am after endless adjournments, none long enough for dinner, to much grumbling from Castle. There was a break from 1.50 am to 3.30 am for some amendments to be printed where she managed a catnap in her office. The Friday sitting, still with the budget debate in full swing, did not close until 6.30 pm. Many of the Members must have missed their planes and crawled home utterly exhausted and not a little frustrated.

Derek Enright wrote the following in his "Our Man in Europe" bulletin to his party members:

> "In June it all sounded very romantic going to Luxembourg for the Socialist Group meeting, then Strasbourg for the first directly elected European Parliamentary Assembly. By the end of July I wondered why I had left security and the imminent prospect of an exciting headship, sharing each day with my family in a settled existence, for a nomadic life amid people who did not know how to conduct business in a proper fashion.
>
> It was well illustrated late one evening by the interpreters. My translation headphones were switched on to them when one of our British politicians came in heatedly, after an Italian whose excited gestures did not match the cool translation on the earphones.
>
> From our translation box, in addition to this MEP's impassioned speech, we heard from the interpreter, 'Oh... he's going over the same...ground again! I'm fed up of this...job, I want something to eat and get home to sleep.' The moment was further enlivened by another MEP asking: 'Is the British translation I heard on the headphones correct?'
>
> But September came, the committee work started and I remembered my aims and beliefs – a strong feeling for the Third World... The full Parliament had a seven-hour debate on how to tackle this problem."

Castle found the European Parliament a strange institution, not at all like the House of Commons where she had been for over thirty years. She and other British Members enjoyed and fully exploited Question Time which became widely popular as a form of participatory sport. It was, however, a pale imitation of what she felt was the real thing (i.e. the House of Commons) and she never understood why the Commission treated questions in a cavalier fashion, preferring not to give straight answers to anything at all. Her personal assistant at the beginning, Janet Anderson, said they were surprised at first at the reduced amount of constituency casework that arrived and that most of it came from businesses.

As a former government Minister for many years, Castle was not used to having to look after herself, deal with different currencies and work in disorganized conditions. Her autobiography (Castle, 1993) records:

"Used as I was to the austere and regulated life of the House of Commons, my arrival in Europe in 1979 was a culture shock. Brussels is a fine city and we British Members... soon discovered the delights of its many restaurants... But as far as I was concerned these delicacies [lobster, mussels etc] were not enough to offset the frustrations I felt as someone who had come to do a serious parliamentary job. In those early days the facilities provided for us MEPs was laughably inadequate. We were the Cinderellas all right. While the Commission dominated Brussels with its great sprawling mass of glass and concrete at the Berlaymont, we MEPs were corralled in some makeshift cramped quarters in the Boulevard de l'Empereur a couple of miles away, where we had not even a locker for whatever Parliamentary papers we were able to lay out hands on, let alone a desk. This was all the more annoying when I was elected Leader of the British Labour Group and I wanted to keep on top of things. I spent my first year in impotent fury trying to find out what was going on....."

However it was not too many months before MEPs were in much closer offices, albeit rather cramped together, at 97 Rue Belliard, in what is now the office of the European Economic and Social Committee and the Committee of the Regions in a substantial European *quartier*. It was not until the second term that they had individual offices in Brussels. In Strasbourg they occupied offices in the building used by the Council of Europe, and this, with new additions added from time to time as the Parliament expanded, served the MEPs right up until a new Parliament building was built and opened in 1999.

Because Strasbourg has never been well served by international flights, the French government for some years laid on "special" Air France flights for Members from some of the major European capitals, to facilitate the monthly journey to Strasbourg. These only functioned on the Monday, Thursday and Friday of plenary session weeks. The travel was always fraught with difficulty. Timings of flights were rarely convenient, connections were missed due to delays and parliamentary sessions frequently heard laments from Members about their travel problems. Lord Plumb recalls that for his very first Strasbourg session, his connecting flight from Birmingham was late, he missed the "special" and had to wait hours for another plane, which touched down en route in Lille, adding to the delay. This was not at all unusual. Hours were often spent in airport lounges waiting out delays, sometimes from strikes or fog. Many had to make several connections to get to Strasbourg, or fly into Frankfurt or Basle, each necessitating a two hour car journey from the airport. This difficult journey is still the situation today, since the Council of Ministers has refused to agree a single place of work.

By September, the first session after the short summer recess, Labour Members were already energetically tabling questions on coal policy, agricultural expenditure and budgetary contributions, misuse of Community funds and fraud, butter export subsidies, sugar surpluses, qualifications of veterinary personnel, energy, and fisheries. They were beginning to make their mark on what would become their long-term campaigning issues. Of the nine Oral Questions without debate tabled on Monday 24 September, for instance, Castle was involved in four and Brian Key in one. The Tories were in the ascendant on Oral Questions with debate (their experience showing here as these were more important), being involved in sponsoring five of the sixteen questions tabled, Labour only two. All of this was their initiative, instructions from "home" being non-existent.

Leading the attack for Labour, Castle pulled no punches against the British Conservatives. With a Conservative question on Community arma-ments procurement on the agenda, Castle accused Scott-Hopkins of trying to silence them because:

> "the Tories are deeply implicated in an attempt to turn this Community into a defence organization... We in the British Labour Group do not believe that the problem of unemployment in Europe can be solved by set-ting up an industrial-military complex and then telling the workers of Europe that their jobs depend on an arms race".

This was not her only attack on the Conservatives that session. She weighed in on butter prices, particularly the 50p a pound export subsidies and accused the Conservative Minister of Agriculture of selling out the interest of the British consumer in agreeing to the last price increase in the Council of Agriculture Ministers. At the same time she attacked Conservative MEP Neil Balfour on butter surpluses going to the Soviet Union, saying "what he was trying to do was bring a serious agriculture problem into the heart of the Cold-War philosophy of the British Conservatives!"

Michael Gallagher made his first of very few public interventions in five years, speaking on coal stockpiles and energy policy and cheap coal imports from South Africa, and opposing a nuclear programme. The next time he would speak in the chamber it was to be as a member of the SDP in the run-up to the 1984 election.

Socialist Group colleagues were astonished at the British Members' com-bative parliamentary style, which was very different from the more restrained approach they were used to. "They did not like our adversarial politics and thought it was insulting to other Members" says Caborn. One of the senior German SPD members said "you are not in your own Parliament now", in response to Labour's rough and tumble attacks. It was a slow cultural learning curve for the comrades.

An early attempt to set up a women's rights committee was opposed by British Conservatives, particularly Lady Elles, and withdrawn at the first session. A successful bid was made in October to set up a special Committee of Inquiry into the Situation of Women in Europe, which evolved into a per-manent Committee on Women's Rights after the 1984 election.

As Barbara Castle was starting to get into her stride in her mission to reform the CAP and budget, she was dealt a blow. Her beloved husband Ted died on Boxing Day 1979 during family celebrations at home. She was touched by the warm support of colleagues. Griffiths and Rogers drove all the way from Wales to the funeral. Plumb sent a supporting note, as did people from many quarters. She had lost a strong supporter and friend. When Barbara next met Sir Henry back in the Parliament, she told him "the old bugger promised not to die before me". BLG Members rallied round for months on her return, accompanying her to dinner in her favourite restaurants.

By March, she was back on form again making speeches demanding agri-culture reforms. She was starting to work out the line that she was to pursue for some years, that is to stop "open ended commitment to buy up all the milk the farmers can produce... we believe prices should be reduced and support

the smallest non-viable farms for social reasons through direct aids."
Unfortunately most of her continental colleagues felt this would be a re-
nationalisation of the CAP. Castle was furious that the Agriculture Committee
(scandalously packed with farmers) sometimes voted increases in farm prices
that were even higher than those proposed by the Commission. She established a good working relationship with Finn Gundelach, the Danish
Agriculture Commissioner, who supported moves for reform, but sadly, it
was not too long before he died and his successor Poul Dalsager was not quite
as zealous in his attitude to reforms as she hoped. The reform battle continued
for long years, running from crisis to crisis. In 1982 an increase of 3% was
agreed despite the Community budget being bankrupt and this led to yet
another budget crisis.

Priestley led a staff strike at the commencement of the March plenary
session, brought about by a decision to hold all sessions henceforth in
Strasbourg. There was strong support for Luxembourg from that quarter, as
many of the staff were based there and some sessions continued to be held
there for a time.

Despite Labour's anti-market approach its MEPs were good attenders and
became fully engaged in the work. They were always active in the hemicycle
during plenary sessions, most even staying on for the Fridays, generally without Castle who soon preferred to go home on Thursday nights as she was constantly in demand for speaking engagements. They also were assiduous in
their committee work. Lord Plumb, who was then Chair of the Agriculture
Committee, tells of the formidable line-up of Barbara Castle, Joyce Quin and
Edith Cresson (soon to be Agriculture Minister in Mitterrand's government)
in the front row of his committee, where the first part of the meeting was
always a fuss about whether or not Castle had her papers. She did not normally take an assistant to Brussels for meetings and after years of having
everything done for her as a government Minister, often struggled with
organizational matters. He says "she was a fighter, but she was a sweetie".
Castle's combative nature was often goaded to fury by Plumb's emollient
approach. This was the time of rising production leading to huge food mountains and escalating CAP costs culminating in the ridiculous situation for
some years of butter and beef being distributed free at Christmas to charities
simply to help reduce the storage and export restitution costs. Every
Agriculture Committee meeting was concerned with debates on how to deal
with the surpluses for sugar, butter and milk.

Roland Boyes developed a reputation for dry wit and rumbustious interventions that followed him into the House of Commons. He relished attacking the Tories, and made his mark early on. In January 1980 he said "it
grieves me a little to hear the hypocrites across the floor talking about unemployment, when their government in Westminster is cynically and deliberately creating it."

Budget battles and the UK rebate

Arguments about the size of Britain's contributions had been around since
Harold Wilson's attempts to renegotiate terms of entry for Britain. It had
been clear then that Britain would have a substantial budget deficit in its contribution to the EEC. This was also the case for Germany, but there was a tacit

understanding that their economy was strong and did well on export trade which made up for their heavy contribution. Back in 1973 it was felt that Britain would also gain in this way as a form of compensation, but Britain was being overtaken in productivity and competitiveness and its industrial strength was falling. By 1980 big industry in the UK, particularly steel, was being hit by the world recession and unemployment was rapidly rising. This brought the matter of the British contribution to the fore once more.

The Labour government of 1974 had negotiated a "Corrective Mechanism" on British contributions to the EC budget, but it had not solved the problems that were coming to a head as the transitional arrangements for EC membership came to their end. Britain was the second largest con- tributor after Germany, but one of the poorest Member States. The status quo could not continue and Margaret Thatcher was hell-bent on getting a better deal, seeking a broad balance between Britain's receipts and contri- butions. Her efforts were to put Labour Members in something of a quan- dary. They hated supporting her, but could not oppose attempts to improve the unhappy budgetary situation for Britain. Labour's NEC set up a study of the alternatives to EC membership.

In October 1979 Castle was complaining that the projected £1,000 million British contribution for 1980 was the equivalent of a 3p in the pound tax rate. In a November debate she said: "We heard a lot... about... *juste retour* ... is this an unjust *retour*? Poorer nations subsidising the rich ones. I offer this solidarity to Margaret Thatcher: for heaven's sake stand firm, and I will back you up". It is not recorded what Thatcher thought of this piece of unin- vited solidarity.

By the time of the Dublin Summit at the end of 1979 a major row over the 1980 budget was gathering momentum, the main problem being that agri- culture spending was getting out of control. CAP reform was something on which Labour MEPs had a clear mandate to get involved. Agriculture was taking around 78% of the total budget. Increases in milk prices alone were in danger of pushing spending through the permitted resources ceiling. Every 1% increase in milk prices added 100 million European Units of Account to the budget and clearly this was untenable. The first parliamen- tary reading on the budget achieved some limited modifications to reduce spending on milk, but Castle and others tried without success to put a check on open-ended commitments to agricultural spending. At home the *Daily Express* said that the CAP added 12% to the cost of food. Although the Conservatives would table amendments to reduce agricultural spending Castle accused them of supporting only token reductions.

A more comprehensive account of this first budget battle can be found in Sir Julian Priestley's *Six Battles that Shaped Europe's Parliament* (Priestley, 2008), where he describes the European players (particularly Erwin Lange, chair of the Budget Committee and Piet Dankert the rapporteur – both Socialists), the process by which the rejection was developed and its impact on the reputation of the Parliament. Parliament had gained substantial powers over the non-compulsory part of the budget in 1977 and a Qualified Majority in the Council of Ministers was needed to reject Parliament's pos- ition at that time. That meant that if two large and one small country had not opposed the amendments the whole budgetary reform process might have started, but at the lengthy Council meeting the UK government went with the majority and threw away the chance of more CAP reform at that moment. At the Dublin Summit Thatcher unsuccessfully sought a permanent solution to Britain's inequitable contribution and this was where the British negotiators focused their main attention.

Finally in December, after lengthy and unsatisfactory negotiations with a Council that did not appear to realize how serious the situation was, Parliament, including the Labour Members, rejected the budget by a substantial majority (288 – 64). This threw the Community into an unprecedented situation which resulted in a financial mechanism coming into place known as "provisional twelfths"- a monthly limit on spending at the level of the previous year's budget. The crisis thus precipitated could be seen as something of an own goal, however, since the Council was under no pressure to rectify the situation speedily. Provisional twelfths meant that Parliament was operating on an inadequate budget designed for the old Assembly of 198 members rather than the new one of 410, lower travel expenses and fewer staff. It was to be September 1980 before this particular problem was resolved, with a cobbled-together solution. The delay meant, amongst the more obvious constrictions, that allowances and salaries were frozen and there was a block on new staff being recruited, including interpreters.

In March 1980 Castle argued against the Socialist Group but with the support of the Conservatives in favour of a super tax as an instrument to close the open-ended commitment to buy surplus milk products. Her amendments argued for a 1% decrease in price overall, but did not win majority support.

When Parliament voted in favour of the budget in June 1980, after the Council had agreed slightly more moderate farm price increases, the BLG remained opposed to it. Indeed they put forward a Motion to reject the budget again, which was comprehensively voted down on 9 July by 171 – 22 with 9 abstentions. This time they were against the more pragmatic position of the Socialist Group who thought it was the best deal possible at the time, particularly as some increases had been made in the regional fund and there was an agreement to carry out a review of the budget as a whole in time for 1982. The BLG was still critical, on the grounds of the budget's many flaws and in particular the failure realistically to tackle agriculture spending. On the one hand the Group shared the view that the overspending had to stop. On the other, it was clear that many of the Socialist Group and the active Conservatives on the Budget Committee were keen to build up the reputation and power of the Parliament. Labour did not support that at all, particularly outspoken being Megahy. Not for the last time there was a moral dilemma. It was the start of eight consecutive years in which the Labour Members voted to reject budgets.

Whilst the general line of Labour and the Socialist Group was for spending reductions, some of the BLG were also working to restore cuts in social and regional spends. In December 1980 Win Griffiths supported a proposal to set up a European Regional Development Fund (ERDF), the Assembly in 1977 having allocated funding to an embryonic regional fund. Parliament's demand for the EDF (European Development Fund – spending on development aid – not the same as ERDF) to be "budgetised", i.e. placed under the powers of the Parliament, was ignored and to this day remains an unresolved battle.

The Dublin Summit in December that year debated an adjustment to the financial mechanism but it was not settled until the Fontainebleau Summit in May 1980 by means of "special measures". Stephen Wall, later the UK Permanent Representative (Wall, 2008), says that a three-year deal for Britain had been negotiated by Foreign Secretary Lord Carrington and Ian Gilmour, his deputy. Thatcher was less than thrilled with their negotiation and it did not hold, taking another three years of battles before a long-term solution was agreed. To some extent the Council was spooked by Parliament's earlier rejection of the budget and there was concern that the same fate might befall the rebate. Council came up with a way of paying the temporary refund under a different mechanism (using unanimous decision) so as to avoid the possibility of rejection. The Parliament in future would have to confine its intervention to complaining about the substantive content of the relevant Regulation. It was not greeted with great enthusiasm by the European colleagues. Dankert, the Socialist Group budget spokesman, said "the British agreement has shown that the policy of blackmailing the Community works" and that "the British deal means that the Community will hit the own resources ceiling a year earlier than we expected."

Nevertheless Castle was quick to condemn the delay at Dublin: "seldom have I read a more superficial document... inability of the Community to reform itself". She taunted Thatcher for backing down on a deal worth £350 million as "willing to nag, but afraid to fight." Derek Prag counter-attacked for the Conservatives accusing her of "the usual dose of repetitious clap trap". In the debate on a the BLG motion to reject the budget in July 1980 Labour was becoming aware that the rebate would be put to use to reduce the UK's public sector borrowing requirement and not for regional development and were furious about this state of affairs. The rebate settled at Fontainebleau was £550 million, so by holding out in December Thatcher had managed to increase its value by £200 million.

Castle was mistrustful of the BLG's budget spokesman, Balfe, and preferred wherever possible to make budget speeches herself because of the high profile of the subject, despite not being a full member of the Budget Committee. She was not concerned about this, being more intent on ensuring that the right message was conveyed to the British press via her speeches. It meant that she was simultaneously trying to master the vagaries of the agricultural prices and budgetary mechanisms, with very little help. She took her assistant to Strasbourg, mainly to act as a runner, but did not have anyone in Brussels to help her with committee work.

In a major debate in September 1980 on the Regulation for the financial mechanism, Castle said the whole thing was an elaborate farce. She later revealed that Thatcher had told the House of Commons the money would not go on much-needed industrial development and local authorities but simply flow back to the Treasury. She accused Thatcher of planning further cuts in public expenditure. This was a difficult moment. Castle felt between a rock and a hard place. Smoking and fuming in her office over a gin and tonic, she realized the rebate that she had supported was worthless, but felt she could not be seen by the British press to be against it. By November she and Balfe failed to agree on whether to oppose the rebate. Acrimonious debate over the British rebate was to continue for years both in Parliament and in Council.

Late in 1980 in the debates on the 1981 budget Parliament sought to limit agricultural spending and to increase funding for energy policy, development and social and regional efforts. By the time of the second reading later in the year there was also a supplementary 1980 budget in progress to make up for the deficiencies of the period when the earlier version had not been agreed and Parliament voted an increase in this. Some tricky manoeuvres were undertaken to achieve a satisfactory deal enabling the necessary spending. Labour remained generally critical.

A further stand-off occurred in 1981 when veteran European Spinelli was budget rapporteur and Parliament once again attempted to cut agricultural spending. This time Council agreed some of the reductions, but only a part of the proposed increases for social and regional spending. There were some arcane arguments as to whether or not Parliament's proposals went over the limit for "non-compulsory" expenditure (non-CAP). Matters came to a head with Council appealing to the Court of Justice against the Parliament. This struggle carried on for some time, finally culminating in a new inter-institutional agreement being signed in June 1982 between Parliament and Council.

The anti-marketeers were vigilant on other sections of the budget, notably Lomas, Buchan and Caborn attempting to cut subsidies to European Movements, always a bone of contention and described as propaganda vehicles by the comrades. Buchan too, kept a vigilant eye on attempts to increase subsidies for European schools which were one of her many bugbears. At that time the general budget was voted line by line, taking hours to vote and it was relatively easy to put forward amendments to increase or decrease specific "lines".

Spring 1982 saw the UK government attempt to block the annual package of farm prices so that some concessions could be found on "the bloody British question", as it had come to be known, and this found enthusiastic support from Castle and the BLG. Negotiations on the British rebate were complicated by taking place at the same time as there was general opposition in Council to Britain's uncompromising approach to the Argentine invasion of the Falkland Islands (Wall, 2008). There was a meeting of leaders in March to celebrate the 25th anniversary of the Treaty of Rome and Thatcher proved intransigent in her demand for a five year deal on Britain's funding. This was vetoed by Mitterrand who was clearly piqued by Britain's coupling of the issues of farm prices and the rebate. Britain thought it could invoke the "Luxembourg Compromise" as a veto. This had come into being as a political understanding in January 1966, following French boycotts of the Council. It was understood by Britain as a veto, but in fact was little more than an agreement to disagree. The idea was that in the case of majority vote decisions in Council, if an important national interest was at stake the Council would endeavour to reach a solution acceptable to all. Wall's account is that several other countries put a different interpretation on the so-called veto. Priestley points out that majority voting on agriculture prices was already in the Treaty. At the Agriculture Council on 11 May, Britain threatened "to bring the business of the EEC to a halt if the other members persisted in trying to force through a farm price increase against the wishes of the British government" (Wall, 2008). Plumb in Parliament voted to support the principle of majority voting on price fixing, "publicly distancing themselves [the EDG] from the policy of their own government". At the Council on 18 May, Peter Walker representing the government fell on his face when votes in Council were taken and Britain was defeated. This was a crisis for Britain and relations with France were at a low point for the next year. The Labour Party called on the government to withhold its contributions to the EC, and although this would have been against EC law it was considered for some time as a possible strategy.

The unsolved problem of the UK rebate continued to cause grief, and Parliament rejected the next supplementary budget containing the UK refund by 259 – 78, saying it was not going to have any more ad hoc solutions. Castle made a fine four minute attempt in December 1982 to win over the majority before the vote. She said:

> "I am not speaking for the Socialist group. I am speaking for my country's rights… So when you are talking about this rebate today, you are not talking about charity. You are talking about something that was built into the terms on which Britain joined the European Community… What is at stake here today is one simple issue. That is that some of you want to punish Britain for the fact that the Community has failed to reform itself…It is absolutely true that Mrs Thatcher will not spend a penny of this on any item of regional policy or public works on which she had not intended to spend it in the first place. But whatever rules you may apply at this moment you will not force her to do that... So what I say is, let us all be honest with ourselves, realize that the fundamental solution is not being fought for by anybody and that it is intolerable that one Member State should be penalized for the collective cowardice of you all."

Her passionate patriotism did not sway the majority.

The Commission President, Gaston Thorn, published a Green Paper on EC financing in the first part of the year. Its main proposal was an increase in Community "own resources" and suggested money for research, regional and social initiatives. This only led to fears of an even greater demands for funds from the UK. Thatcher was in any case opposed to research funding. There began complicated negotiations lasting the rest of the year right through the general election, the German Presidency and into that of Greece. The Stuttgart Summit of 1983 came and went (having been delayed to cope with the UK general election) with only a partial and temporary ad hoc solution for a rebate of £457 million despite the very real prospect of the EC running out of money. The proposed increase in "own resources", comprising a one per cent levy of VAT across the Community, required the unanimous agreement of the Member States. There was no solution at the Athens Summit, where the French (Delors being by then Finance Minister) were not prepared to see the Greeks find a way forward.

In October Castle was castigating the Parliament again on the huge cost of disposal of agricultural surpluses on a proposal for an astonishing 10.5% increase in milk price. She said: "we have milk coming out of our ears…" She pointed out the absurdity of pouring milk into calves at one end, milking cows at the other and then having to pay to dispose of the product.

In November there was yet another round of debates about Christmas butter (the scheme to donate free butter to charities for distribution so as to reduce the cost of storing surpluses), with the BLG again voting against the budget. There was a huge row at that time since, with the financial cupboard bare, one of the ruses being contemplated to save money was a proposal to put the UK rebate in Chapter 100. This was a reserve section which meant the money would be effectively frozen and would require a further vote in Parliament to release it. Encouraged by Labour MEPs, Parliament wanted the UK's 850 million ECU refund to be used on specific infrastructure programmes rather than as a direct reimbursement to the UK Treasury. Thatcher ensured there was no chance that this would be the case.

The 1983 budget was being considered at the same time as a supplementary and amending budget for 1982 that was to pay the UK's compensation. Parliament demanded that this should be the last ad hoc solution to the British refund, but never gained satisfactory assurances from the Council, which also rejected CAP reductions in the main budget. During the debate in December 1982, making a speech critical of the budget, Balfe said: "I challenge any Tory to come back to Britain and defend the Common Market against me publicly this weekend". The Conservatives abstained and the budget passed its second reading with Labour and the Socialist Group against.

The Budget Commissioner, Christopher Tugendhat (who had been a Conservative MP during the Heath government), was forced to admit that the 1983 budget was in ruins. In the projections for 1984, agriculture's share of the expenditure was still going up and there was not sufficient money to go round. The Council came up with a solution that was for a budget to cover only ten months' spending, technically illegal. Yet again Council proposed that the 1983 British rebate should be put in reserve. In October Castle again attempted to ride to the rescue. "Now really, to put in the budget the statement that the British rebate should go into reserve until the rest of us have managed to reform something, is to penalize the British people with a vengeance for the failure of the Community to reform itself." She suggested putting half of the agricultural spending in reserve instead. "We in the British Labour Group will oppose the proposal...It is absurd even to be contemplating an increase in the Community's own resources at the present time. You know you do not give more money to an unreconstructed delinquent. That is what this Community is." This unfortunately meant the BLG would vote against the report of the Socialist Group leader, Arndt, despite Castle praising his speech as being brilliant. It did not endear them to the Group members. Conservatives supported the Socialist text.

Labour again opposed the budget in December 1983. There were several different resolutions, including one from the Conservatives for rejection. Castle accused Conservative Neil Balfour of cowardice because many of his group were abstaining. Andrew Pearce accused Castle of representing a group of wreckers. There was a certain amount of confusion during the vote and some Conservatives did vote for rejection. Enright in an explanation of vote said:

> "I dissociate myself from the craven cowardice of the British Tories who had the hypocrisy to vote for all the measures for their farmer friends and then vote for the rejection instead of joining with Mrs Castle's motion, which was asking, not for a battle of Britain, but for a battle of equity and transparency in this budget."

Griffiths pointed out that the Tories had voted against money coming to Britain from the Regional Fund.

The 1984 budget was in real crisis in that the ceiling of "own resources" had been reached. Parliament froze both the UK rebate and five per cent of CAP spending, leaving the mess to be resolved in yet another Fontainebleau Council in June 1984 (France holding the Presidency of the Council once again). This had been preceded by intense negotiations between Geoffrey Howe for the UK and Roland Dumas for the French. A system was agreed in Parliament to compensate the UK on the revenue side of the budget and a new inter-institutional agreement was reached to increase the Community's own resources from one per cent to 1.4%. Thatcher in March had indicated she was prepared to accept the rise in the VAT contribution in time. This relieved pressure for the following year and the budget was passed. Yet again the BLG voted against on the grounds that the reforms were insufficient, but Parliament agreed to unfreeze the frozen funds and thus avoided a stalemate.

The Brussels Summit in March of 1984 collapsed in the face of British intransigence, with France and Italy blocking payment of the rebate. Britain threatened to withhold payments into the Community coffers and had even prepared some draft legislation to this effect, although this proposal was not popular with some Conservative MEPs. This threat, coupled with the leverage Thatcher had concerning the extra resources that would be needed in future as a consequence of Spain and Portugal's forthcoming accession, appeared to do the trick. The French opened negotiations, settling on a deal to cut milk output and a package of financial reforms including a modest increase in own resources. They had been reluctant to do this, not wanting to be seen to be giving way to the UK in the run-up to the European elections in June that year.

The inter-institutional agreement was to be a turning point in budgetary reform, giving Parliament a greater say in the structure of the budget. Somehow, via intense negotiations, Thatcher held out and won a two-thirds figure for the rebate that was to last two decades. It did not, however, win any friends in Europe.

More years were to pass before the various crises were able to be dealt with in a more coherent fashion and farm prices ceased to be the deciding factor. Clwyd battled furiously throughout for a doubling of the funding for social policy, supported by other Socialist colleagues from her committee, despite the general shortage of funds. Griffiths and others spoke out for strengthening the regional development fund and schemes to alleviate unemployment, and Adam plugged away for a reasonable research investment programme.

In those days the budget votes were a marathon line taking up to six hours, because each line was dealt with individually. In later years the negotiations mostly took place at the committee stage, with a "package" being put before plenary, thus considerably lessening the pain of hour upon hour of voting on matters of minute detail.

Fighting Thatcherism

By the beginning of 1980 unemployment was hitting hard in the constituencies of Labour Members and the Parliament became a battle ground of Labour against the Conservatives, who were forced into defending their government at home. The years 1980-81 saw recession blight the UK, particularly in the North, and 5,000 factories closed. The government failed to protect British interests on steel where the industry was being decimated in the face of international competition.

By the end of 1982 unemployment in the UK had hit three million. This situation persisted up to the 1983 general election and beyond as monetarist practices in the UK began to bite and it continued to be raised by Labour Members despite complaints from continentals that they should stick to European matters. Boyes, Seal, Griffiths, Caborn, Clwyd, Adam and others from hard-hit industrial areas joined in the fray, leaving Castle to continue her agriculture reform attempts and Quin valiantly struggling to try to save fishing communities. Fishing was frequently debated on a Friday morning before a thinly-attended House when many other Members had returned home. Boyes raised the problems of Consett in his constituency where the steelworks had closed – "a town destroyed" – but was attacked on one occasion by Tory Tom Spencer who said he could have taken some action in the Social Affairs Committee but had instead been at the Labour Party conference discussing withdrawal. Boyes also worked on nuclear disarmament issues (in June 1980 it was announced that 160 Cruise missiles would be sited in the UK) and constantly harangued the Tories and UK government over unemployment, with typical overstatement. In March 1982 he said "the butchering swine governing Britain are probably making decisions today – Budget day – that will ensure that tens of thousands more people go to an early grave."

Margaret Thatcher wound up for the British Presidency in Strasbourg in December 1981 as the first head of government of a Member State occupying the Presidency to attend a session of the European Parliament for the purpose of giving an account of the European Council (London Summit). Despite three chapters of the Mandate of 30 May 1980 still not having reached agreement, she gave quite a conciliatory speech: "Our future lies in working together". No Labour Member had the floor in her presence, though Castle had a good rant the following day: "Hope deferred makes the heart sick...stubborn adherence to a bankrupt monetarist policy has pushed up unemployment in GB to nearly 3 million... we are sick and tired of gesture politics, what we want are action politics" – and plenty more on the failings of the budget.

Labour MEPs were always actively campaigning at home alongside their local parties, MPs and Councils in opposing Conservative policies and presenting the Labour argument and used as much of their time and resources as they could to support local candidates in elections. One small blessing was the willingness of Commission officials to receive delegations from local authorities and businesses and to spend hours advising Councils how to get their hands on some of the structural funds. Most of the BLG Members, including Castle, were to take advantage of this and bring such groups across for meetings. Various Members also brought out to Brussels or Strasbourg delegations of workers either made redundant or about to become so, to demonstrate the problem and lobby the Commission for help. Boyes brought an NUM delegation in February 1982, and Clwyd brought redundant steelworkers, whilst Quin brought a delegation of shipyard workers.

The Social Affairs and Employment Committee wished to hold a meeting in the UK in 1980 but the Conservatives managed to have the idea quashed, clearly realizing that it would be used as an opposition platform in the home media. This idea had been supported by Labour Members for precisely that reason.

Events leading to the British miners' strike held sway for a substantial period in the latter part of this Parliament and the strike itself dominated the early part of the next. It became increasingly bitter as the situation of the miners and their families became more and more desperate. In March 1984 Caborn, in one of his last interventions (having been elected to Westminster) hit out at the curtailment of civil liberties in the restrictions on people's movement in the UK. This had been put in place by the government in a vain attempt to stop flying pickets supporting the miners who were attempting to block the way of "scab" labour.

Labour at home and the birth of the SDP

The Labour Party grudgingly offered only a marginal role to its MEPs in party structures. Whilst MPs could not stand as MEPs without first resigning, the NEC in its wisdom agreed in June 1981 that: "A European Member of Parliament will be allowed to seek nomination for a UK Parliamentary constituency provided that he/she gives an undertaking in writing that if elected he/she will resign as a Euro MP at a time agreed with the NEC."

The BLG Leader was able to attend but not vote at NEC meetings (some suggested that Castle virtually invited herself to the NEC having been a member of it for so many years) and MEPs were exiled to the gallery at Labour conference at first unless, as in the case of some, they managed to be sent as delegates from some other organisation. In a few years they were at least included in the "ex-officio" MPs section where they could attempt to speak without a vote. At a meeting with Callaghan soon after the election Castle had proposed that MEPs should have full access to the House of Commons but after negotiations Rogers on the BLG's behalf settled for limited access. It was not until 31 January 1989 that MEPs were permitted passes to the Westminster palace complex. There was no formal European Leader's speech to conference.

MEPs often had to ask to be invited to speak at General Management Committee meetings in their constituencies and sometimes were pointedly not invited. Rogers recalls an attempt by one of his local MPs, Roy Hughes, to veto his attendance and when the party went ahead with inviting him to speak the MP ensured that he was not present at the same time. Even when they were present and eager to report, MEPs were often relegated to a few minutes of "any other business" after ten o'clock when the comrades were anxious to repair to the pub. This has not substantially changed.

Following a winter of civil war, the Labour Party on 31 May 1980 held a special conference at Wembley at which the principle of a rolling manifesto was agreed. This conference was the setting for a debate on voting mechanisms for a new system of an electoral college for election of Party Leader to include trade unions and constituency parties as well as MPs. The other main purpose of the conference was to approve the "Peace, Jobs and Freedom" policy statement. It was not entirely harmonious, with Militant delegate Terry Fields telling the right-wingers to get out of the party. Immediately following that, the Labour Common Market Safeguards Committee produced a document saying that the next Labour government should be elected on a clear mandate to withdraw from the European Community. Shortly afterwards, in an early development that would later lead to the formation of the SDP, David Owen, William Rodgers and Shirley Williams wrote to *The Guardian* opposing this notion. There had, of course, been earlier indications of this split when Roy Jenkins floated the idea of a breakaway party on 22 November in the Dimbleby lecture. Dianne Hayter, later General Secretary of the European Parliamentary Labour Party, records in her book *Fightback* (Hayter, 2005) that it was a failure of the right-wing Manifesto group to hold the social democrats within the Party, saying that some in that group thought at the time that the Labour Party was finished.

Nevertheless, by the time of Labour's conference in September 1980, a resolution (Composite 15) in favour of withdrawal was able to be carried by five million votes to two million on a card vote. With a two-thirds majority, the effect of this was that it was official policy and should be included in the next election manifesto. This was greeted as a "fantastic victory" by Tony Benn, and was to lead to substantial strife during the next few years in the BLG. Benn failed to be re-elected to the Shadow Cabinet. It was this conference that also approved a resolution in favour of unilateral nuclear disarmament. In December 1980 Benn attended a meeting of the Socialist Group in Brussels, speaking on full employment, and defending the conference decision on withdrawal. He was comprehensively attacked by a line-up of continental heavyweights from a range of countries – Mario Dido, Gerhard Schmid, Katherina Focke, Eva Gredel, Hans-Joachim Seeler, Hellmut Sieglerschmidt, Giorgio Ruffolo and Antonio Cariglia.

In 1981 conference supported a Common Market resolution sponsored by Clive Jenkins' white collar union ASTMS reaffirming the contents of Composite 42 of 1978 and Composite 40 of 1979.

> "It further recognizes that not only has no progress been made on these reforms but the position of the UK vis-à-vis the EEC has worsened in every respect… accordingly, Conference does not believe the demands to which we are committed are capable of being fulfilled and urges the Labour Party to include the withdrawal of the UK from the EEC as a priority in the next general election manifesto".

Buchan, speaking in support of this resolution, said: "Let us be clear. We are for Europe – the real Europe… the only way we can be for these things is out of the Common Market."

The manifesto, largely the work of Callaghan for the general election in 1979, had taken only a marginally more considered position, saying that Labour would be the only major party offering the prospect of bringing about fundamental and much needed reform of the EEC. However it did include a pledge to restore to the Commons the power to amend or repeal legislation applicable to Europe. Bill Rodgers, not long afterwards to become a founding father of the SDP, called the conference "a disaster".

Not long after, Callaghan resigned as Labour Leader. Candidates for Leader were Michael Foot, Denis Healey, Peter Shore and John Silkin. On the second ballot, Foot won and Healey became Deputy Leader, contrasting left and right in the top team. This combination of events seems to have been the last straw for the Jenkinsites. The SDP was formed in March 1981, after Jenkins had completed his term as European Commission President at the end of 1980 and returned home to give substance to the Gang of Three. Twenty-eight Labour MPs joined and a number of peers, seriously splitting the Labour Party. They had mostly been active in Labour Committee for Europe. After this, Enright and Collins joined the Red Rose Group chaired by George Foulkes MP, wanting disaffiliation from LCE. It was not as starry-eyed pro-market as LCE but its members wished to see Britain's EEC membership continue and wanted to change the conference policy. Over a hundred other MPs on the right formed Labour Solidarity under the chairmanship of Roy Hattersley. Jenkins fought the Warrington by-election for the SDP in July 1981, but the seat was held for Labour by Doug Hoyle.

Some MEPs remember David Owen MP and other SDP heavyweights visiting Strasbourg to try to recruit the pro-marketeers. Collins, Key, Enright, Adam and Quin attended a dinner at one of Strasbourg's better restaurants, *Jean de Carolis*, but surprised their British hosts when their suggestions of joining the SDP were turned down by the MEPs, who maintained they were not interested in leaving the Labour Party. They remained loyal to the people who elected them. Quin later said "I am tribal Labour". None of this group ever left the Labour Party.

Considerable division existed in the party ranks at home, where support for mandatory reselection of MPs had gathered momentum. The next issue was on what basis. Solidarity put forward a proposal for "one person, one vote" in order to circumvent what was sometimes seen as "unrepresentative" local General Management Committees (GMCs). Trades unions, backed by the left, had put forward a 40 – 30 – 30 formula which scraped through early in 1981. One person, one vote was universally opposed by the left, including the so-called Campaign for Labour Party Democracy. The latter's argument was that it was the GMC delegates to which the MP reported and was accountable rather than the membership as a whole whom they maintained might not know the full story. With the left in the ascendancy the next few years saw eight Labour MPs deselected by their constituency parties.

In May of 1981 Labour gained control of the Greater London Council and left-winger Ken Livingstone ousted "moderate" Andrew McIntosh from the leadership of the Labour Group, and consequently the GLC. Shortly after this there was a challenge from left-winger Benn to Healey as Deputy Leader unleashing a massive battle between left and right in the party with six months of bitter campaigning. The right-wing Manifesto Group was calling on Foot to take action against Militant infiltration of more Constituency Labour Parties. In Parliament, a Group of Ten young MPs who felt they might never see a Labour government (thus losing their chance of ministerial posts) was formed, linking some right-wingers and some Tribunites. This group included Phillip Whitehead, later to become an MEP after losing his Westminster seat. Slowly the beginnings of a more pragmatic line from what started to become known as the "soft left" began to emerge. Healey hung on by a whisker as Deputy Leader, with some notable abstentions in the voting from Neil Kinnock and Joan Lestor. A report on an inquiry into Militant was published in December 1981, proposing a register of organizations operating within the Labour Party. The report said that: "It is our opinion that the Militant Tendency as presently constituted would not be eligible to be included in the proposed register..."

Over the next two years the party's internal battles reached crisis point. A hot debate was raging about expulsion of Militant supporters, numbering 3,500 by late 1982 at the time the organization was proscribed. In February 1983 the NEC bit the bullet and by 19 – 9 expelled five members of the *Militant* (newspaper) editorial board, a decision later upheld by conference. Immediately after that, a divided Labour Party lost the Bermondsey by-election. Life became more complicated, however, when Militant-controlled Labour in Liverpool recorded a better-than-average swing to Labour and returned a Militant MP. They had stood on the 1982 City Council elections on a policy destined for confrontation with the Tory government over Council tax.

By 1981 a written European Parliamentary report was permitted to be incorporated into the NEC Report to Conference, and Castle was able to chronicle some of the achievements of the MEPs in that and subsequent years.

Regular meetings took place between senior members of the PLP and officers of the BLG, in this and the next Parliament, and these were sometimes less than harmonious. There was disquiet in Westminster, to say the least, about there being no restrictions on MEPs putting in for House of Commons seats under party rules, but that MPs could not stand for the European Parliament (not that they generally wished to). However MPs slowly became aware that MEPs had budgets and offices in their constituencies producing literature, about which some MPs were far from happy. Caborn had told Fred Mulley MP he would stand against him and did so, successfully. Seal recalls accompanying Castle to one of these meetings and being faced with Healey shouting about MEPs setting up offices and circulating leaflets, using these superior resources to oppose MPs, few of whom at that time had staffed offices in their constituencies. Seal tried for selection in Bradford South in 1982 against a sitting MP but was not successful. Lomas applied for Newham North West where there was an acrimonious reselection battle against incumbent Arthur Lewis, but the NEC barred him from the list. Given attacks from Militant at one level, MPs were hyper-anxious about additional threats from across the Channel. By January 1981 the NEC had to modify its permission for MEPs to stand for Westminster seats, saying "that while no rule is being broken by any MEP standing against a sitting Westminster Labour MP, the NEC nevertheless urges that at the present time it would be in the interests of Party unity if they did not do so". Fear and jealousy reigned at a time of huge insecurity in the run up to the 1983 election.

Seal was on the Campaign Committee for the 1983 general election representing the BLG and was frustrated at the amateur nature of the way the party was shaping up. He suggested employing a firm to do public relations work and finally at a later stage a compromise was reached. Although Peter Mandelson, a pro-European with extensive Young Socialist International experience, was not brought in until 1985, Seal believes he was in part a mover in improving the professionalism of the Labour Party.

Labour in Europe

The BLG annual meeting in April 1980 re-elected Castle as Leader and Caborn as Chair. Future differences began to be seen, however. There was a straight right/left contest between Collins and Megahy for Deputy Leader, won by Collins, and a contest between Buchan, Rogers and Balfe for Secretary/Whip. Rogers won that and Buchan was given the prize of press officer. Clwyd was elected for the Socialist Group Bureau in addition to the Leader.

Castle was so well-known that she did not stoop to putting out press releases during her time in the European Parliament. Her technique, when she had made a controversial speech or a *Daily Mirror*-type sound bite, was to go down to the Press Bar and chat to the British journalists there. They would often come knocking on her door "to ask Mrs Castle if there were any good stories". Barbara did not use her courtesy title of "Lady" based on being the spouse of Lord Castle, but Parliament officials, tending to be sticklers for protocol would often use it which always infuriated her. It was another decade before she graciously accepted a life peerage in her own right.

Gaston Thorn, leading the Luxembourg Presidency from July 1980 beat off an offensive from Seal, who asked in a PQ: "what amendments would have to be made to the Treaty of Rome in order for a national Parliament to enact legislation to restore powers to decide whether Community legislation should be applicable to itself?" This zealous pursuit of official Labour policy was enthusiastically followed up by Megahy. Thorn suggested the idea seemed inconceivable and poured cold water on it, as one who had been involved in negotiating and signing the UK Treaty of Accession, pointing out there was no mention of such a right. Castle in her office later, scathingly used Margaret Thatcher's terminology and referred to him as "poor little Gaston".

The general policy of the BLG was to share out speaking time, but it was not always amicable. Clwyd recalls that Castle was furious that she was to speak against Norman Tebbit when he visited as Employment Secretary in September 1981 during the British Presidency. Clwyd was the logical speaker, the subject being the social situation and unemployment, as she was on the relevant committee, but it caused Castle to stalk out in a huff from Parliament's chamber as Clwyd started speaking. The two never saw eye to eye and much later Clwyd wrote an article about Castle, mentioning an incident about a "fur" coat. This enraged Castle even more, since she was a strong supporter of animal welfare and her coat was *faux* fur. In a bar where this argument surfaced Castle threw her coat on the floor and shouted at Clwyd: "you be bloody Leader then" and stormed out, leaving colleagues to deliver the coat to her hotel room later on.

Quin also recalls Castle being angry when she took on a report on New Zealand butter – a hot issue in a time of butter surpluses. Supporting the old Commonwealth was a point of honour for Labour and Castle felt it would end up being a sell-out because of committee pressure. Quin, however, was a natural conciliator and, using her diplomatic strengths, managed to steer through a pro-New Zealand report which went to the vote on a Friday morning when British Members were in attendance and many of those opposed to New Zealand imports had gone home. Labour and Tories were in agreement on this subject. A settlement on the import agreement was reached in October 1982.

The Bureau of the Socialist Group sent Castle, Rogers and Hume as a delegation to Athens in 1980 to talk PASOK into joining the Group. The Greeks had been inclined towards the Communist Group, but the team managed to win over the leftist party. Greece had not long emerged from the control of the Colonels and clearly must have felt that the Socialists offered a more powerful haven than the smaller group. Greek accession to the Community therefore brought a few more left-wingers from PASOK into the Socialist Group, and some of the BLG made new friends. At that time PASOK policy was also anti-market but it was not long before it changed, perhaps in acknowledgement of all the funding being poured into Greece. When January 1982 saw the halfway point of the Parliament, Labour gave up its Vice-Presidency so that the Greeks could have it (PASOK having won the Greek elections in October 1981). Dutch Socialist Dankert was elected President, but only after four ballots, following machinations by the Conservatives. Collins managed to retain his position as Chair of the Environment and Consumer Protection Committee.

Labour's anti-EEC policy at home often hit the press. In an article in *The Scotsman* in January 1981 Collins wrote: "while ultimate withdrawal must remain a possibility… it is certainly not a simple option nor is it a solution to all our problems." As yet Labour policy did not extend to the wide range of subjects that were being debated in Europe. The MEPs had no guidance on the vast bulk of policy that was being put before them for consideration, and soon learned to make it up as they went along, based on what they felt was the right thing to do. This approach was to last well into the second term before the party in the UK started taking some more notice and occasionally suggesting a line to their European wing.

The AGM in April 1981 re-elected Castle as Leader and Caborn as Chair. There was a re-run of the Deputy leadership contest between Collins and Megahy with Collins the victor again, and a new contest for Secretary/Whip between Balfe, Boyes and Rogers, with the latter re-elected. This time there was a contest for press officer and in Buchan's absence, Clwyd won. There had been some arguments about press releases, and a change to the Group's standing orders was agreed that insisted that all Group and individual press statements should be distributed to all. (It rarely happened.) Other standing orders included a provision that meetings should not last more than three hours (!) and also that elections should be by recorded vote. Socialist Group colleagues were astounded that Labour Members were expected to show their secret ballot papers to a BLG Member when voting in the Group. It was seen as Stalinist. This was the start of what was to become a bitter period lasting until the end of the decade. At home there had been a study group working to make a statement from the NEC to the 1981 conference but it was postponed when the chairman died.

Feelings became more heated during the year and in October 1981 several of the Group staged a press conference in Strasbourg and issued a statement to the effect that they would do everything possible to support Labour's policy of withdrawal from the Community. It was signed by Balfe, Buchan, Caborn, Lomas, Megahy and Seal. Balfe was not present. Caborn in the Chair insisted that there was no split in the BLG, to a barrage of questions from the journalists, asking why Castle was not there and why they did not leave the Socialist Group. Geoff Meade of the Press Association asked that if Labour Party policy was so crystal clear, why was there so much confusion? Buchan's final word to the journalists was "please don't call us anti-Europe. We are for Europe, against the Common Market". The journalists didn't really get the distinction but enjoyed the spectacle of the BLG split. There was a fulsome bit of pre-publicity in *The Guardian* saying: "A week of tensions and bitterness among the seventeen British Labour members of the European Parliament will spill into the open in Strasbourg today...", and reporting that Seal and Lomas were understood to be seeking selection for UK parliamentary seats.

All the angst about potential restrictions on a Labour government's economic policies was beginning to look a little thin once the French Socialists under President Mitterrand, coming to power in 1981, began to operate the beginnings of a socialist economic policy that left Brussels able to do little more than wring its hands. Mitterrand let it be known that he thought the Labour Party was "not left enough".

Argentina invaded the Falklands on 2 April 1982. Labour Members in a debate on the crisis in May argued for a diplomatic and economic rather than a military solution. Arndt of the Socialist Group, and a former conscientious objector, was angry with the UK over the war. On 14 June Healey, the Shadow Foreign Secretary, was in Strasbourg and there was a dinner at one of the better restaurants, *L'Arsenal* with the BLG officers present, and also Thomas von der Vring, a Socialist MEP who was a professor of economic philosophy. Collins recollects that the company started an argument about Descartes and Popper, the conversation started in English and finished in German and when the topic of discussion moved on to jazz piano Castle fell asleep and had to be woken up for the dessert course. (This was after a long day starting at 5am.) The next morning, Healey was heard to remark very pointedly: "Good morning Barbara, did you have a good sleep?" She was not amused. It was the date of the Argentine surrender and it is said that Healey heard about it from his taxi driver (BBC radio and TV not being piped into hotel rooms in that town).

One of the Socialist Group's "study days" meetings was held in Bradford in 1982, acting on Seal's persuasion. He wanted to highlight the problems in the textile industry and get some publicity for that. It had mixed results in terms of media coverage. Seal had persuaded the Group not to bring the parliamentary chauffeured cars over because of fear of a bad press about luxury (there were already "gravy train" accusations in the press from time to time) and he had to do a deal with local car dealers for transport. However this was a mixed blessing because of the Parliament's Sicilian drivers who were imported. There was a picket line on one route about a hospital closing and a driver forgot which side of the road he was on and managed to demolish some road works. Embarrassment also came from Willy Brandt's bodyguards who were stopped at the airport because they had guns. On a slightly more amusing note, one of the parsimonious Dutch Members camped out in a tent rather than use a hotel. This caused quite a fuss, according to Jan Kurlemann, then a Socialist Group press officer. The Dutchman had been on to the local press complaining that his family could not rent bicycles and it turned out that the reason was that they had no address, because of the camping. *The*

Yorkshire Post was most interested in this story. There followed a row in the Bureau about potential misappropriation of expenses and the upshot was that this particular Member did not make it onto his country's list at the next election. The whole event was a disappointment for Seal, with the bad press overshadowing his hopes of being seen as a champion of the textile industry. He was furious about the way things had turned out and turned his fire on Dick Gupwell, the staffer in charge of its organization, wanting him sacked. That did not help Labour's relations with the Group Secretariat.

Rogers produced a report on a natural gas policy for Europe, with the help of British members of the committee staff and both British and Germans staffers for the Socialist Group and today he maintains that the content of the report still holds true. It is an example of an anti-European seeing that in some areas the European dimension did offer advantages.

Castle, when not working to reform the CAP, was busy on the Bureau of the Socialist Group trying to make changes to its organization. Her work there was largely unsung, but considered important and her combative nature did not extend to her relationship with the staff, where she was seen as a conciliator. She wanted a research department to be set up, something that she never achieved. Pensions for the staff of Members were also to receive her attention and her own assistant convened a working group amongst British Labour assistants to share experiences. Assistants generally had a poor deal, lacking benefits such as maternity leave and pensions and Castle began a campaign to change this, a process lasting for decades and culminating many years later in a draft Statute for Members' Assistants. This was eventually agreed in 2008.

Parliament's positions were renegotiated in January 1982. For the BLG, Rogers was no longer a Vice-President of Parliament, but Collins retained his Chair of Environment and Gallagher held on to his Vice-Chair of Energy and Research. Clwyd became Chair of the Portugal Joint Parliamentary Committee (JPC) helping to negotiate accession; Adam took Vice-Chair of the EFTA Committee from April 1983. Key won Vice-Chair of the JPC for Spanish accession. Megahy became a Vice-Chair of the Credentials Committee, Quin was Chair of the Australia and New Zealand delegation from April 1983 and Rogers Vice-Chair of the Canada delegation. Seal hung on to his REX Vice-Chair.

Change afoot

Michael Foot and Eric Heffer visited the Socialist Group in Brussels on 10 February 1982, with Foot stating that he expected a firm withdrawal policy to be included in the next general election manifesto, "as not a policy in isolation, but part of Labour's Socialist alternative". Despite genuine warmth for him as a person, he met with a barrage of strong criticism from Group members. A senior German, Erwin Lange, spoke of the dangers of the national socialism that had led to World War II, saying we needed each other. Seeler, also SPD, said: "we are being hard in our comments to stop our UK comrades making a monumental error". Arndt said that Benn's comments on his earlier visit had been patronizing. Italian and French colleagues spoke of the need for the solution to be European and said that Labour was not helping in the fight against conservative forces. Even

PASOK members from Greece spoke of real prospects for change in the CAP and budget. It was an uncomfortable reception for the British visitors.

A few days later on 19 February 1982, Clwyd wrote in the *New Statesman* on "Why I have changed my mind on the Common Market". This was a courageous piece given the climate at home, and she says that explaining to constituents how she had changed her mind was quite tough. "They were hostile and it took a lot of time", she said many years later. The secretary of Cardiganshire constituency was John Marek (later an MP) who would not let her speak since she had become pro-market. In her article, she spoke of international solidarity in practice, when a Dutch Socialist colleague helped organize a meeting between workers' representatives in a multinational in her constituency and the Netherlands. She said that:

> "The Parliament does lack power to back its sometimes radical pro-posals… but Labour policy is set firmly against increasing the power of the 'Assembly'. You can't hobble a horse and then criticize its lack of speed. The French government at the moment is about to challenge EEC rules on import controls and if it succeeds then one of Labour's many reasons for withdrawal will be challenged."

She asked the Labour Party to think again with the example of Mitterrand's new socialist government in France pursuing its own economic strategy.

This piece was seized upon with joy in the Socialist Group. Its Secretary General, Paolo Falcone, circulated it to all Members with a cover note that read: "Dear Comrades, At the request of several Group members, the Secretariat has pleasure in enclosing the text of the above-mentioned article which we hope will make pleasant reading". Clwyd recalls that the staff were markedly more friendly to her after that.

The article caused a stir and it was not without a certain amount of poison. Clwyd says Janey Buchan did not speak to her for years afterwards, and accused her of losing the Hillhead by-election by writing the article. (This by-election on 25 March 1982, caused by the death of the incumbent Conservative MP, was contested by Roy Jenkins for the newly-formed SDP following the victory of Shirley Williams in Crosby and Jenkins' own failure to win Warrington earlier. He won, with Labour coming third after the Conservatives. It was not likely to have been won by Labour and indeed was not to be a Labour seat until George Galloway's victory in 1987.)

At the AGM of 1982 again Castle was re-elected Leader, Caborn was Chair, and Collins was Deputy (still opposed by Megahy). Rogers once more beat off an attempt by Boyes to oust him as Secretary/Whip. An understated Leader's report from Castle mentions "some disagreements over policy". It also said that the work of individuals on their committees had impressed the Socialist Group, which had shown remarkably little resentment towards the BLG despite the fact that during his visit to the Group earlier in the year Michael Foot had re-affirmed the Labour Party policy of withdrawal from the EEC. Clwyd and Castle were elected to the Socialist Group Bureau and Clwyd was subsequently sent on a three week tour of the USA to explain the Group's policy to control multi-nationals and what the European Parliament was all about.

A Walworth Road (by then Labour Headquarters) Research Paper in

April 1982 was a last-ditch attempt to dissuade the party from fighting the next Euro-elections. It countered all arguments in favour, by saying:

> "If we fight the election the public would be confused and would not understand our reasons, and thus our case for withdrawal would be severely undermined. They would not understand how a party committed to leave an institution was nevertheless seeking to be represented in that institution. One could draw the analogy here with the House of Lords – the public are confused by the creation of Labour peers when we are committed to abolishing the second chamber."

Nevertheless, in May the NEC narrowly decided that the party should contest the 1984 elections.

In response to the intemperate earlier NEC paper, the members of the Brussels Labour Group took the unusual step of publishing their own pamphlet in May with a suitably red cover, entitled "British withdrawal from the EC?" Not to be confused with the British Labour Group (of MEPs) – the BLG, the Brussels Labour Group consisted of Labour Party members working in the Community institutions, who unsurprisingly were entirely pro-EEC. Their pamphlet was a 34-page closely argued commentary on the NEC's 1981 report to conference on withdrawal. It was full of facts and figures about trade and the like and cited the socialist economic policy being pursued by Mitterrand in France. This did not endear these officials to the BLG, but they were unrepentant.

Collins had also written a paper as a commentary on the NEC paper, saying that it was a pessimistic and confused document and that "its main argument is a piece of punk Marxism". He also produced a substantial paper on environment, public health and consumer protection policy, pointing out their importance to people at home and explaining the reasons that the best place for their development was in Europe. The Labour Movement for Europe also put out a pamphlet entitled "The Economic Consequences of Withdrawal", arguing that it would be damaging for the economy.

By September Castle was making an attempt to influence Labour's conference policy on the EEC. It was now her turn to write a piece in the *New Statesman* (17 September 1982) entitled "Let Them Throw Us Out". She saw it as a pragmatic article, still holding on to her anti-market stance. But others such as Lomas and Balfe saw it as a U-turn. They attacked her in a letter published in that magazine, calling her dishonest and naïve in wanting to stay in the Community but break the rules and saying that she was not fit to be Leader. Megahy called the article "a formula for fudge", preferring his out-and-out opposition to the EEC. Although Castle remained defiant, insisting that she had not become pro-market, jibes such as this did hurt. In the article she argued that Labour was always being negative and as such was failing to get its policies across. Thatcher was being radical, positive and populist. A Labour government should simply proceed with its policies and wait for the European authorities to react to us; it was not, she argued, too late for the Labour Party to adapt its approach. Again, this piece was received well in the Socialist Group. She records in her diary that Carlo Ripa di Meana said: "your article is very, very important". Castle also maintained that her change of mind influenced both Michael Foot and Neil Kinnock's views of the EEC.

Although Labour's conference did not change its policy in 1982 the mood was arguably beginning to soften in some quarters. Quin and Boyes wrote an article in *Labour Weekly* prior to the 1983 general election asking why not, if Labour were elected, to proceed with its economic policies and see how Europe would react.

Whilst Castle was keen to attend NEC meetings in London, she was less interested in attending some of the Socialist Group "study days" meetings that were normally held at the same time as Socialist Confederation party meetings. She referred to them as "junkets" and did not bother to attend the Confed's congress in Paris in November 1982, leaving her representation to her assistant and Jan Royall. She would have received a warm reception had she attended, but was preoccupied with her traditional family Guy Fawkes celebrations at her home in Buckinghamshire.

Castle was also not present at the BLG's annual meeting in April 1983, being at home actively campaigning for the hoped-for Labour government. As a former Cabinet Minister she was still one of the most well-known and popular Labour figures. She was re-elected as Leader, along with Caborn as Chair, though the latter was opposed by Griffiths on the grounds of trying to improve the left/right balance amongst officers. Caborn had, by this time, been selected for a safe Westminster seat. A battle this time between Collins and Lomas for Deputy ran to a second ballot, with Collins maintaining his position. There were, however, grumbles that one person should not hold a position in the Parliament in addition to one in the BLG (Collins being chair of a major committee). Rogers was re-elected Secretary/Whip and Enright was elected press officer. For the second Socialist Group Bureau member, there was a contest between Clwyd and Seal. After a tie on the first ballot Clwyd withdrew. Boyes successfully moved an amendment to standing orders that henceforth all BLG votes should be recorded. Members had to call out on a roll call whether they were for or against every proposal. This was to cause bad feelings for many years until it was finally rescinded in 1991.

MEPs at work

Bit by bit Griffiths, Boyes and Clwyd, supported by some of their other colleagues, fought for regional and social funds to be put to use to help combat unemployment, poverty and disability. This was given more impetus after the accession of Greece in 1981. Their arguments began to fall on fertile ground in Brussels, and the seeds of the urban part of the European Regional Development Fund were sown during those years. There were to be arguments about additionality (the policy that EEC funds should be additional to national funding). Boyes would oppose Griffiths on the latter's attempts to develop an urban fund outside the geographic distinctions of assisted areas, fearing dilution of financial assistance, but the impetus for change was growing.

Derek Enright, a former classics master, was always prominent in the Chamber with his distinctive deep voice, witticisms and ability to demolish opponents. He managed to confuse the interpreters from time to time by breaking into Latin, classical quotations and literary puns. They loved him for the challenge of it, whilst not always managing to do more than simply tell the audience that the speaker had made a joke. In addition to pursuing

development issues he busied himself by taking up the cudgels to stop plenary sessions being held in Luxembourg and arguing for Brussels. Once,
when attempting to circumvent the smokescreen being put up by the
Parliament Bureau on decisions for meeting places, he observed: "the
Bureau is showing about as much sensitivity as a herd of elephants attempting a ballet dance on ice". Luxembourg, holder of the Presidency for the
latter half of that year, hosted a plenary meeting of the Parliament in June
1980 to substantial protest from British Members about extravagance and
inconvenience. Tom Spencer for the Conservatives attacked the (lack of)
aesthetic qualities of the new hemicycle. Castle and others grumbled about
the shortage of facilities for Members, the "narrow seats like battery hens
and not even allocated tables at which we could write our speeches."
Enright's campaign eventually met with some success. Another
Luxembourg plenary was held in December 1980 and the last one in that
electoral period was held in February 1981, despite the government having
built a new plenary especially to house the Parliament. After much more
pressure from Luxembourg, a final plenary was held there in July 1985, but
thereafter meetings in that city were generally for the Council of Ministers
or committees. The first Brussels plenary meeting, described as an open
meeting of the enlarged Bureau, was held in April 1983, followed by another
in June. Eventually "mini" plenary sessions in Brussels were to become part
of the accepted timetable of the Parliament.

Acting on a Socialist Group suggestion, Parliament had set up an ad hoc
committee on the position of women in the Community, after an unsuccessful
early attempt to set up a women's rights committee. Chaired by a formidable
French socialist feminist, Yvette Roudy, the committee produced a massive
multi-subject report debated in February 1981. London Conservative Dame
Shelagh Roberts was active in tabling amendments (mostly defeated) in an
attempt to reduce some of its ambitious proposals and the Conservatives had
a free vote. Roberts felt that including issues about women from the developing world was outside its mandate. She objected to attempts to redefine conditions in which support was given by the regional and social funds, and said
Members should "look very carefully at proposals for providing the same benefits for part-time workers as are provided for full-time workers... and at proposals for job sharing..." Derek Enright, Labour's "honorary woman" on the
committee attacked her position and made points about the need for improvements in benefits and pensions for women. In defence of taking up a post on
the Women's Committee, he had much earlier said "unless we fight for the
status of women, we degrade the dignity of men".

The Socialist Group put forward a successful resolution in April 1982 to
set up inter-parliamentary delegations to various parts of the world and
over the years many Labour Members were to become active on these delegations, using them as a vehicle to pursue human rights and economic
development in a way that far outreached their formal role. There were
always some, however, who simply enjoyed the interesting opportunities to
travel to foreign countries. At first this was in first class, and Members were
also able to use the price of such a ticket to buy tickets in economy and take
their spouses. Barbara Castle was given special dispensation to take her
niece after Ted died. But by the nineties purse tightening reduced this to
business class. On one occasion there was a parliamentary delegation to

Sierra Leone, and as a substitute member of the Development Committee Castle went along, with Enright. However she could not resist drawing attention to the trip as a "gravy train" in the press, earning the wrath of her fellows on the delegation. Enright and his wife Jane stuck by her and they forged a friendship despite their political and European policy differences.

Parliament's first public hearing was held on a consumer action plan during 1980 and the committee, chaired by Collins and assisted by staffer Michael Wood, went to Dublin Castle for the event, with an Irish rapporteur. It was a high profile event including Charles Haughey, the Irish Prime Minister, and was so well attended that there had to be an overspill room. It was one of the first indications of real interest in the work of the Parliament other than on budgetary matters.

Meanwhile, Collins and his committee were working on proposals to protect workers from lead and also pressing for a ban on the toxic herbicide 245-T. Jack Cunningham, Shadow Environment Minister at home, had given Collins the green light to develop policy, as it was ahead of any Labour position taken to date. Ken pursued this vigorously and was instrumental in Parliament's resolution criticizing the delay in introduction of lead free petrol in May 1984. Policy development of this kind was to take place on numerous occasions over the years, not only on environment policy. Matters were being dealt with at the European level in advance of home policy being developed. MEPs began to get used to using their own judgement as to the best position to take. Following the Seveso disaster the Environment Committee pushed for a Committee of Inquiry which was set up in July 1983 on the Treatment of Toxic and Dangerous Substances and reported in May 1984. A heavy industrial lobby on packaging of liquids earned Collins' wrath in July 1983 where he attacked the unsatisfactory level of democracy and lack of transparency on the part of the Commission in a vitriolic speech in the Chamber.

The Environment Committee became active in work on the prevention of acid rain and many other topics. Indeed an environment issue was to be a pivotal tool in giving Parliament a de facto delaying power which it could use to bargain for amendments, this being used to great effect by Collins and others. This was the famous Isoglucose judgement of the European Court of Justice in 1980 that struck down legislation because the Council of Ministers had adopted it before Parliament had given its opinion. Collins was to make good use of that judgement in delaying tactics over the years in order to force policy concessions from the Commission and Council. His first use was threatening to refer back to committee a proposal about meat inspection in the face of the Commissioner's refusal to negotiate. Within a very short time he had representatives of both Commission and Council in his office concerned about disruption of the meat industry and prepared to make concessions. He delighted in saying the Parliament at that time had no teeth but made effective use of its gums.

Castle worked furiously hard at reform of the CAP but was sometimes her own worst enemy. She eschewed the assistance of the Socialist Group staffer on the Agriculture Committee, at that time a genial and bright Dutchman Rob Van de Water, and would table her own amendments, since they were often unlikely to receive the blessing of the Socialist Group. On voting mornings she could be found at her desk at 7am, furiously cursing and smoking, trying to read dozens of amendments and produce an unofficial BLG voting whip, since on CAP reform Labour differed from the Socialist Group much of the time. On one occasion she was so exasperated with the text of a report by Plumb that she submitted a "delete all and insert...." lengthy amendment, which was ruled out of order.

As a distraction from the ongoing drama of the budget, the British rebate and the regional and social funds, Parliament was also deliberating the Vredeling Directive, the right for workers to have information about the intentions of their multinational companies. It was yet another area where Labour had some doubts, despite supporting the principle. On the one hand, as Boyes put it as rapporteur, powerful companies were lobbying against it. "With 12 million unemployed, if we reject this directive, how can we expect trade unionists to take us seriously?" On the other hand, there were some differences of nuance. Labour Members were firmly of the view that representatives on the boards should come from trades union members. But the prevailing continental view was that they should simply be worker representatives, and not necessarily from the unions. Caborn later voiced the concern that in the UK experience at the British Steel Corporation, workers who were not unionists went on the board and were isolated. Ivor Richard, the British Commissioner for Social Affairs and Employment from 1982, who was attempting to steer this directive through the system, was not greatly loved either in the Socialist Group or the BLG, due to his aloofness and his campaigning to change Labour policy on Europe.

In the end, the BLG and Socialist Group voted against the emasculated proposal. Caborn in 1983 said it had been watered down to an unacceptable extent. Even right-winger Enright attacked Commissioner Richard as "a wee sleekit timorous cowering beastie". (No idea what the interpreters made of this quote from Robbie Burns but it was the sort of challenge they enjoyed.) This was despite a special meeting of the BLG in December 1982 where Labour Members voiced their concerns and heard a threat from Richard to withdraw the proposal altogether. It was to take years before it finally succeeded. Nevertheless the BLG supported the final vote on the directive in this parliament which was defeated by only six votes (Conservatives against). Those rights would have been relevant to workers' struggles in numerous companies making redundancies in this period, such as Times, Hyster and Caterpillar. There was more ideological arguing in October 1983 on a report on the control of concentrations between undertakings. Once again the Vredeling proposals were relevant and Caborn, gratuitously insulting two at once, said: "Mr von Bismark does for transparency of multinationals and workers' rights in this report what Mr Bangemann does for hang-gliding" (Bangemann being of substantial physique). The Irish Presidency established an ad hoc working party in 1984 to seek a compromise but it proved to be a knotty issue. The directive setting up works councils was not finally agreed until 1994.

Most of the BLG waded in from time to time with numerous human rights concerns and defence of left-wing movements in countries such as Nicaragua, Chile and El Salvador. South African apartheid, the need for sanctions and the plight of Nelson Mandela were also constant topics for protest. Generally these actions were across the board and not a left or right prerogative, but there were also frequent political differences.

Anti-market views did not stop them speaking in favour of EU institutions being located in the UK in the hope of creating jobs. For instance Castle in March 1982 was arguing for the European Trade Mark Office to be given to Manchester.

Adam concentrated through his parliamentary career on energy and research subjects and became particularly engrossed in this once a research fund had been set up in the budget. He was for many years budget rapporteur for that committee and rarely strayed from that subject unless he was putting forward something directly concerning his constituency in North East England such as fishing. He said that his budget work often kept him working through the July and August holiday periods, and clearly was deeply committed to the work. His main point of controversy with some of his fellows was a quiet but diligent support for nuclear energy.

Covering up public disunity had not yet become a high priority for the BLG, who were divided North/South on whether or not to support proposals for a Channel Tunnel. Those from the North were fearful that it would cause further unemployment in their regions. In general the tunnel was seen as a violation of British virginity. In later years when the proposal became more concrete concerns were voiced on a number of levels, including fears that rabies-ridden animals would run through it and bring the disease to Britain.

Boyes and Balfe were on opposite sides on whether to support NATO in November 1983, when Boyes opposed Cruise missiles (deployed in the UK on 14 October and rolled out within months to Germany and Italy) and Balfe offered an explanation of vote in favour on a matter concerning the defence of Western Europe. Liberals supported the Conservatives in a joint resolution opposed by the BLG.

One subject on which there was universal agreement, however, was on proposals for the extension of VAT to food and children's clothes. This battle ran on for years, with the BLG vociferously opposed. They tabled frequent questions to the Commission and lost no opportunity to put their point of view for the retention of zero-rating. It remains as an unresolved matter today.

Seal was working on the renewal of the Multifibre Agreement (on textile trade with other countries) in a vain attempt to offer some protection to the textile industry at home, which was being badly hit by closures and redundancies. He spoke in favour of socialist planning and said he was constantly trying to persuade his local factories to modernize in the face of aggressive competition, but to no avail. He would sometimes meet with Larry Whitty, then with the GMB union, at Heathrow airport on textile workers' matters. In the UK, Freddie Laker planned to extend his transatlantic "Skytrain" budget airline concept to intra-European flights, to protests from Seal who complained that if Thatcher's ideas were to continue we would see regional airports disappearing. He had a personal interest in this, having taken his pilot's licence and a part share in a small plane. Key took issue about proposals for deregulation of air transport.

By mid-term Castle and some others, including Conservatives, were raising animal welfare issues, including cruel battery farming methods. Five million signatories were tabled on a petition in March 1982 against imports of baby seal products. There was something of a cross-party alliance here in that an "own initiative" report was produced pressing for an import ban, finally resulting in a Commission proposal (but remaining controversial six-teen years later). Tory Spencer was complaining about the cruel production of foie gras (which BLG members boycotted in restaurants). Collins joined him in a debate where it was revealed that exports to the UK of foie gras had increased saying: "I can only point out that this is yet more evidence that life under the Conservatives is bad for geese." In February 1984 Castle was call-ing for harmonization of legislation on the import of pets. There was much more on animal welfare to come in the second term.

Enright, right-wing credentials notwithstanding, was still able to make a vicious verbal attack on Conservative Adam Fergusson. In October 1983 making an explanation of vote about arms sales, Enright said he was speak-ing as a member of Parliamentarians for World Order and that it was a "dis-grace that Mr Fergusson, otherwise known as 'stop me and buy bombs' has not been present... he is trying to peddle arms throughout the world to create war elsewhere..." There was some bitterness at this time, as the American-led invasion of Grenada had just taken place. The attack clearly did not deter Fergusson, who a month later was speaking in support of Cruise missiles.

Ann Clwyd spent time travelling round during International Year of the Disabled, comparing how other countries treated their elderly and disabled people. She used the unfavourable comparisons to campaign against the Conservatives at home and also argued for a directive on disability based on the West German system.

In Spain the Spanish Socialist Workers' Party (PSOE) won the election in October 1982, becoming the first left-wing government since 1936. Relations with the Socialist Group were being strengthened in preparation for acces-sion. Despite being against the EEC, British Members supported enlarge-ment, particularly to include Greece. The accession of Spain and Portugal had been put back and in November 1983 the BLG spoke out against delay. They and the Socialist Group were keen to bring the countries that had so recently suffered under the fascist regimes of Franco, Salazar and the Greek Colonels into the democratic European influence.

Draft Treaty on European Union

Hans-Dietrich Genscher and Emilio Colombo, the German and Italian Foreign Ministers, in November 1981 launched an ad hoc working party to look at treaty reform and consider a European act at the same time as there were similar stirrings in the European Parliament. The Council initiative was to complicate Britain's fraught negotiations on the UK budget rebate and was used by Thatcher as a negotiating tool in rebate discussions.

Altiero Spinelli, the veteran Italian former General Secretary of the European Federalist Movement and European Commissioner, who been imprisoned for seventeen years under Mussolini, took the initiative in June 1980, circulating a letter to all MEPs setting out his ideas for a parliamentary initiative to reform the Treaty. The first dinner of eight cross-party Members took place in the restaurant *Le Crocodile*, hence the name. Those present included Altiero Spinelli (Independent), Richard Balfe (Labour), Brian Key (Labour), Stanley Johnson (Conservative), Paolo Gaiotti de Biase (EPP), Karl von Wogau (EPP), Hans August Lucker (EPP), Silvio Leonardi (Italian

Communist) and Bruno Visentini (Italian Liberal). Balfe points out that "the founding of the Crocodile Club, like many things in the EP was a confusing affair with a number of dinners... before it was officially founded". After the first dinner Key dropped out and Collins joined the group. This group began to meet monthly and issued the first Crocodile Newsletter in October. By December there were eighty MEPs interested and the group became instrumental in developing a draft "Crocodile resolution" which by the summer of the next year had attracted 179 signatories, proposing a Parliament working party. In July 1981, just after Thatcher had asked for "our money back", the cross-party group, now constituted as the Crocodile Club, supporting European federalism and treaty reform succeeded in getting a resolution passed by the Parliament by 164 – 24, to set up a Committee on Institutional Affairs. Public statements critical of the EEC notwithstanding, Balfe was a founder member. The new committee was constituted in January 1982. Richard Corbett (who became a Labour MEP in December 1996) was on the Parliament staff for this and Geoff Harris followed it in the Socialist Group secretariat.

The majority of the BLG had nothing to do with this initiative, and it did not appear to register on the radar of the Labour Party at home at that stage. However the Genscher/Colombo initiative was seen by the government as something on which it was important to remain constructively engaged, with the proviso that it would not require major treaty amendments. Officials tended to think that its proposals were neither new nor particularly pivotal. At the very moment when use of the Luxembourg Compromise was being floated in the Council over farm prices in 1982, the other issue on the table in the Council was negotiations on the draft declaration on European Union.

Meanwhile in Parliament the debate and proposals had begun laying the foundations for a draft Treaty Establishing European Union in February 1984. There were to be three Spinelli reports and votes over the next year whilst the treaty was being developed. In one such debate we saw Rogers beginning to manifest a more positive attitude to the Community; on the Spinelli report in July 1982 he said "... if it is to be a Europe for the deprived... that is clean and fit for people to live in ... freedom from fear of poverty, sickness and old age... that is a Europe we could support." Another debate in October saw numerous Conservatives taking part in the debate but no BLG Member speaking. Treaty reform of the federalist kind was definitely not part of Labour's European policy. Some felt it was simply Euro-Thatcherism. Megahy for Labour spoke in Parliament's April debate to say that here we have the "same old platitudes about the drive towards European integration... stop all this European flag waving and so-called advance to a European federalism that nobody in Europe in their right senses wants". He had another stab during the debate in September, calling it "a dangerous illusion". Needless to say the BLG remained against on all three votes. Collins, Enright and Adam abstained, although five had signed the Crocodile resolution. There appeared to be no particular input from the Labour HQ to its MEPs on this subject.

In April 1983 the draft Act (rather less ambitious than the original Genscher/Colombo proposals) was adopted in Council and this became the "Solemn Declaration on European Union" at the Stuttgart Council in June

1983. The British government took part in the European "re-launch" by putting forward a paper pushing for a Single Market.

One of the spinoffs from the Declaration was that the Heads of Government agreed to report to the European Parliament after each European Council meeting and that there would be an annual report on progress towards European union, which would be presented by the President of the Council. Additionally, each Presidency was to put forward its work programme to the Parliament at the beginning of its work. Parliament could also vote on the programme of a new Commission and give an opinion on international agreements and accession. This was a quiet increase in Parliament's powers that would be put to good use in the years to come.

It was always a surprise that Margaret Thatcher was prepared to put her signature to the Solemn Declaration. Whilst she was in favour of a Single Market for economic purposes, she did not support more power being given to the European Parliament, which the Solemn Declaration embodied. Thatcher, uncharacteristically pragmatic said: "I took the view that I could not quarrel with everything and the document had no legal force. So I went along with it." (Thatcher, 1993). She had, however, prevented the document being called an Act and anything that might require a treaty change and the government had done its best to water down the final text. One of the shreds that she clung on to was that the Declaration spoke about the EU as being a process and not a goal. Harris, Socialist Group staffer and a strong federalist, was jubilant, saying it was a very important step forward, but many Labour MEPs saw it simply as another piece of European wishful thinking. Harris proved to be right in the long run.

Federalist enthusiasts in the Parliament, however, were not content to let developments rest with the Stuttgart Declaration. Spinelli pushed forward and produced Parliament's own draft Treaty on European Union, voted through in February 1984. This proposed that Parliament and Council would become a bicameral legislative body. In the debate, Rogers maintained that the majority of European people did not want to be led down this federalist road. Megahy gave an explanation of vote saying that it would take us to a European super state and remove the national veto. Balfe said that "it means nothing in Catford, Peckham or Deptford" (his constituency) and voted with the BLG against it. Gallagher said that as the only representative of the UK Social Democrat/Liberal Alliance he would vote in favour and cited an opinion poll in the UK saying that the majority of voters would like the Parliament to have more control over Community affairs. The Tories had a free vote, and Labour remained against. There were numerous amendments and a range of different votes. In the final roll call vote the draft Treaty was supported 237 – 31 with 43 abstentions. Castle in her autobiography (Castle, 1993) records: "I sat helplessly as the Parliament passed Spinelli's draft Treaty of Union." Most of the Socialists and Conservatives voted in favour, but for the Tories Brian Hord and Christopher Prout were against, as was Revd. Ian Paisley. The Labour Members voting against were Balfe, Buchan, Caborn, Castle, Clwyd, Griffiths, Megahy, and Quin loyally following the Group decision. Labour abstentions were Adam, Collins, Enright (saying that it was an attempt to substitute slogans for action) and for the Tories, Peter Price and Michael

Welsh. Boyes, Seal, Lomas, Key and Rogers were not recorded as having voted. None of the Labour Members voted in favour.

The upshot of this was that the Heads of Government at Fontainebleau set up a special committee, chaired by Senator Dooge of Ireland to study the Community's future development. The British representative was Malcolm Rifkind, then Europe Minister at the Foreign Office, whose main aim was to pursue the government's "Europe – the Future" document outlining a vision for a Single Market. There was to be more during the next parliamentary period.

General election disaster

The atmosphere in the Parliament became highly charged in the run up to the UK general election of 1983 with Labour and Conservative MEPs frequently trading insults on farm prices, on South Africa, on unemployment, on equal treatment for women and any number of other matters.

Lomas accused the Commission of bias for holding a press conference in London in March the day after the Conservatives had a TV broadcast attacking Labour's withdrawal policy. In April the Tory Richard Simmonds attacked the BLG saying it needed a strategy on the unemployment that would ensue should Labour withdraw from the Community. After the election defeat things quietened down and normal business resumed. Both Clwyd and Enright later spoke of being fairly friendly with Tory Eric Forth, despite rough exchanges on the floor of the Parliament. The election itself took place in the middle of a Strasbourg session and many of the MEPs from both sides were at home campaigning.

An early warning sign was the loss by Labour of the safe working class seat of Bermondsey to Liberal Simon Hughes in February 1983. The saga surrounding this event fuelled Labour's splits. Right-wing and pro-market MP Bob Mellish had been in place since 1946 and was a Labour Chief Whip from 1969-76. He fell out with the left-wingers who progressively took over the constituency and were critical, not least due to his controversially taking up an unpaid position on the LDDC (London Dockland Development Council, then opposed by Labour in London). He decided not to stand again for Parliament, supporting right-winger John O'Grady, Leader of Southwark Council, to be his successor and leaving the party in August 1982. The constituency, highly controversially, selected young gay, left-wing activist Peter Tatchell instead, who was not supported by Michael Foot. Tatchell was supported by, but not part of Militant. After much argument and a second selection with the same result, Mellish took the Chiltern Hundreds, precipitating the by-election and supporting O'Grady as "Real Bermondsey Labour". (Mellish later joined the SDP and accepted a life Peerage in 1985. Tatchell was much later expelled from the Labour Party.)

The 1983 general election manifesto spoke about being "committed to withdrawal in an amicable and orderly way." It was a ghastly election just a month after local elections, with even Tony Benn losing his seat (he was to return to Parliament in March 1984 in the Chesterfield by-election.) Astonishingly, afterwards, Heffer in the Queen's Speech debate insisted that Labour Party policy in the general election had been correct. Two Militant MPs were elected – Terry Fields in Liverpool and David Nellist from

Coventry. Labour's manifesto has been famously characterised (originally by Gerald Kaufman) as being "the longest suicide note in history". The SDP Liberal Alliance won twenty-three seats and the SDP another six and Labour's share of the vote was even less than in 1979. Afterwards Foot resigned and Kinnock won the Leadership election against Heffer, Shore, and others. Hattersley won the Deputy post against Dunwoody, Davies and Meacher. Patricia Hewitt was the Leader's press secretary and Charles Clarke chief of staff, both later becoming government Ministers. Much has been written about this election in numerous other books and it will not be repeated here. It marked a turning point in morale and the beginnings of isolation for the far left. Kinnock scathingly referred to the policies at that time as "revolutionary pessimism".

Caborn, Rogers and Boyes were elected to the House of Commons; Clwyd followed in 1984 in a by-election. Rogers had also been due to fight a by-election following the death of an MP, but the election was called on the same date.

In the European Parliament the Conservative MEPs rubbed in their election victory. Sir Henry Plumb said that the British people wanted the Community to be a success, and Lady Elles claimed that over 70% of the British population had voted to remain in Europe.

At party conference that year Castle used her Leader's speech to warn of the European move to federalism, but also rounded on local parties who were not bothering to select candidates, saying "you had better get interested" because what was happening in Europe was affecting all our lives. She also pointed out the relevance to the home political situation, saying: "If… this party is forced into third place in terms of votes that could be a mortal blow for us, because we have become a third party instead of the alternative government… I beg you to wake up before it's too late and turn out and win next June." She acknowledged that some of the BLG were more in favour of the EEC than others, but were united in denouncing scandals and exposing the need for change.

The National Executive Report to conference in 1983 noted that "the EEC Study Group has been in abeyance over the year. Work on the specific implications of EEC withdrawal has been conducted by other sub committees and it was intended before the election that the study group would meet subsequently to draw these together. The EEC Liaison Committee recently began meeting again to assist in the coordination of the campaign for the 1984 elections." The MEPs' Report said: "The result of the general election means that Britain will remain a member of the EC for the next few years. This makes it all the more vital that Labour should have a bigger voice in the EP."

After Neil Kinnock became Leader the position on Europe slowly began to soften, Kinnock having put support for the EC in his election manifesto for the leadership. The defeat of Benn for the Deputy Leadership split the left and this is when the Campaign Group was formed, as a harder line faction than the Tribune Group. It was to play a large part in the splits in the BLG in the next electoral period.

Moving on

Kinnock recognized that the 1983 election was the last that Labour could fight on an anti- EEC platform. He wanted to demonstrate that the inward looking and self-obsessed past was not good and that the party should look at the way comrades did things on the continent. The thrust of his policy was that Labour should fit Britain to the world of 2010 and not that of 1945. He was also aware that talk of exchange controls could not work in the face of international technological advances. A party campaign briefing (Number 31) in November 1983 said: "The European elections next year give socialists the chance to offer common solutions to the problems we share. Action by individual governments will not be enough. We must work with our allies in a Europe-wide crusade for jobs." Peace and justice were also seen as areas for cooperation. An NEC statement at the 1983 autumn conference said Britain had to remain in the EEC for the term of the next Parliament and fight within it "for the best deal for Britain" and "to retain the option of withdrawal." Clwyd claims some credit for working on Kinnock to change his earlier opposition to the EEC when she spoke to him at a miners' rally in Cardiff, as does Castle in private chats. However any formal attempt to reverse the withdrawal policy at the 1983 conference was bound to fail as most of the large unions were still bound by withdrawal policies, so the officials did their best to keep the subject off the agenda.

When the Socialist Group met in Paris in late 1983, David Lowe arranged a side meeting between Kinnock and Charles Clarke and Lionel Jospin and Axel Queval of the French Socialist Party secretariat. They had rugby in common. Kinnock is said to have assured Jospin: "If I have one clear ambition as Leader of the Labour Party it is to drag it out of fifteen years of isolationism and put it back in the mainstream of European politics". Kinnock, as the new Labour Party Leader, spoke to the Group meeting and stressed his commitment to "a genuine dialogue between the British Labour and the other Socialist parties of Europe". This was received happily by the continentals and was seen as having put down a marker for a future change of policy. It was also a relief to the Labour staff in Europe. Gupwell enthused that this first speech was "a breath of fresh air. It was refreshing and wonderful". Clarke says that Kinnock believed that engagement was the right course.

A modification in the NEC's post general election stocktaking statement "Campaigning for a Fairer Britain" said:

> "Britain will remain a member of the EEC for the term of the next European Parliament, and Labour will fight to get the best deal for Britain within it. At the end of that time Britain will have been a member of the EEC for 15 years – and this will be reflected in our pattern of trade, the way our economy works and our political relations overseas. But we also recognize the fundamental nature of the changes we wish to see made in the EEC and that its rules may stand in the way of a Labour government when it acts to cut unemployment. It is in this context that we believe that Britain, like all member states, must retain the option of withdrawal from the EEC."

This was accepted by conference as part of a large document, with no specific discussion on this section of the text. David Wilkinson, a pro-European academic working at the Labour Party during the European election campaign, says that the document's phrasing proved remarkably effective in preventing the party from tearing itself apart during the election campaign. Only Bob Cryer in Sheffield and Les Huckfield in Merseyside

East disputed the status of the new formulation and issued their own anti-market leaflets.

The Socialist Group organized a conference in Strasbourg in September 1983 entitled National-Socialism and Resistance. The aim was to make a public stand against the right-wing parties that were gathering strength for the next election campaign. Whilst the conference focused on Nazism and the Second World War, it also included a contribution from former British trade union leader Jack Jones on the Spanish Civil War. There was a good attendance from socialist parties all over Europe. The British Labour Party sent a solid delegation – Joan Lestor, former MP, Dan Jones from the trades councils, Saiyad Shah, a lawyer, Frank Ward from the Fabian Society and its General Secretary Ian Martin, plus Virendra Sharma, Susan Reeves and David Ward from the Labour Party. From the BLG there were Buchan and Castle – an unlikely partnership. Is not at all clear how this choice of representation came about. Obviously Castle was Leader. Collins as Deputy may have been busy with environmental work, while Rogers as Secretary was by that time an MP, as was the Chair, Caborn. Buchan had a strong history of opposition to fascism and was keen to be the representative. This was a policy area on which there was no disagreement across borders and a clear feeling that socialist co-operation and a show of solidarity was a good thing.

Early in 1983 a cross-party group on the right formed the Kangaroo Group, so named because it supported the notion of the Single Market – hopping over borders. The main characters behind this were Basil de Ferranti for the Conservatives and Karl von Wogau of the EPP. Labour MEPs were not generally seen in this grouping in the early days as it was largely seen as a big business mouthpiece.

One of the many public rows about MEPs' expenses surfaced during 1983. There had been allegations of rules being bent by some Irish Members and President Dankert, operating on the Socialist ticket of transparency, demanded a review of the system, saying the Parliament had a "chaotic accountancy system". Under this impetus the Bureau agreed that MEPs would have to attend half the sessions or forfeit secretarial allowances.

Castle always felt that it would be a good thing to make comparisons between the UK and various aspects of life in the Common Market and in February 1984 the BLG took an advertisement in *New Socialist* showing a batch of unfavourable comparisons between the UK and most EC countries in all sorts of subjects, not least VAT. Certainly the comparisons existed, but it is mystifying clear why Castle felt this would be a good start to an election campaign.

In March 1984 Labour MEPs held a lengthy meeting in Luxembourg at the time of the Group and Confederation Congress, about a document offering a range of options on reorganization of the staff, emanating from Castle's working party on the Socialist Group Bureau. That paper had been taken to a subcommittee of the Labour NEC's International Committee by Caborn and a further paper had been prepared by Gupwell and Harris from the staff for debate. The proposal included plans to increase staff working for the BLG and for these staffers to be paid for by the Group out of its general budget. The thinking was that this group of employees would operate separately to other national groups and that it should be decided by the newly-elected BLG after June. There was, however, concern about there being one

[handwritten margin note: EP CP/ EP Group staffing]

set of staff on European pay rates and another on Labour Party scales. The view was that new staff could be managed by BLG officers and would be able to help MEPs with their work in Brussels and Strasbourg where they currently felt the Socialist Group staff was not sufficiently supportive of their special needs. Castle always felt the BLG "were being robbed" in terms of lack of support by staffers of other nationalities and other opinions on the EEC. The reality was that the Socialist Group staff worked on committee lines, rather than in support of specific national delegations. Collins disagreed with Castle's proposals that Socialist Group staff should be reorganized to service national groups. The general principles of the new system of extra support were finally agreed, as ever by a small margin and this was to be the precursor of a more formal and better-funded BLG office.

Meanwhile back in the Parliament

Parliament offered Members a subsidy to bring groups of visitors from their constituencies to Strasbourg or Brussels once or twice a year. It slowly caught on and MEPs would ask colleagues from other countries to give talks to them. Once she had seen it in operation, Castle eschewed the opportunity to avail herself of the system, saying "As soon as the visitors return home they are pro-market". Buchan was another who was opposed to these visits. Hume was a particularly effective and inspirational speaker to such groups, outlining why the EEC was such an important institution in building and maintaining peace in Europe. A Labour-friendly Irishman, Niall O'Neill, was the Parliament official in charge and he, too, made witty and informative speeches supporting Members.

Claude Cheysson, venerable former Commissioner, had become Foreign Minister in the French government and would attend many parliamentary sessions for the Presidency. He had been friends with Buchan's husband Norman and Janey Buchan recalls that he came across the floor and gave her a hug on his first appearance for the Council. He was to come back to the Socialist Group as an MEP in 1989.

In February 1984 Gallagher made a rare explanation of vote on the preliminary draft Treaty on European Union. He said that "as the only representative of the UK Social Democrat-Liberal Alliance I will vote in favour." He cited an opinion poll in the UK that week revealing the majority of voters would like this Parliament to have more control over Community affairs.

There was a fairly acrimonious debate in March 1984 about the parental leave directive. Conservatives hated the fact that Europe was producing equalities legislation that was binding in the UK and flew in the face of Thatcherism. Shelagh Roberts was the rapporteur and steered a tricky line between the enthusiastic support from committee and her own party's opposition. Unsurprisingly, the Conservatives voted against the proposals, thus offering Labour a useful campaigning point for the June elections.

In April Castle was battling again opposing milk proposals, harmonization of taxation on wine and attempts to put VAT on food. A deal was struck to cut milk production but she was unconvinced that it was sufficient to solve the problems and was goaded by Conservative Commissioner Christopher Tugendhat, who said that "Mrs Castle was getting up a fine head of steam for the elections and the contest should be worth watching".

She was doubly furious at having stayed until midnight in expectation of a vote that did not take place until the Friday by which point she had given up and caught the plane home.

In May, the final month before the European election, very few Labour Members were present, mostly having gone home to campaign, but a reasonable bunch of Tories remained on deck for some reports including a directive on equal treatment of women. Castle felt it was important to be seen there right to the end, and Enright managed a characteristically brave comment saying he would retable a request for urgency on a motion to enable miners' families to receive subventions from the surplus food stocks when he returned in July as the new Member for Kent East. It was not, of course, to be the case. Quin was making demands about the crisis in the ship building industry right up to the last. The final BLG speaker of the parliament was industrious Adam, on energy and procurement issues in the budget.

There was not a lot of report-writing by the BLG Members during this term, probably due to the ambivalent position of the Group. Adam produced some opinions from the Energy and Research Committee for the budget, Boyes reported on workers' democracy and unemployment, Enright on Spanish and Portuguese accession, Namibia and development food aid, Griffiths on regional funding, Quin on New Zealand butter, several on fisheries and on economic matters, Collins on seal pups and lead in petrol, Rogers on gas and Megahy wrote an opinion on competition policy. Key did a report in the early days for Budget Control on the Commission's expenses and allowances, and an opinion on air transport deregulation, Clwyd an opinion on accession of Spain and Portugal. The others, whilst all vocal in debates and tablers of questions and amendments, did not take part in the formal amending of legislation.

After hours

Labour Members were held back to some extent by their lack of linguistic ability, and tended to socialise mostly amongst themselves, with some fraternizing with the English interpreters and only a minority venturing to spend time with other nationalities. Joyce Quin speaks of a Francophone "Amigo group" run by Jacques Delors where she and Enright, being linguists, felt amongst friends. Rogers, who spoke a little French and Italian, found friendship with some of the German members.

The historic Metropole Hotel in Brussels, which had been the headquarters for the Nazis during WWII, was the staging post of a number of the Labour Group, and Members such as gregarious raconteur Megahy would hold court in the bar in the early evenings surrounded by friends such as Seal and Lomas, and often MEPs from other countries.

It was not only language that caused some problems for our merry band, but currency exchange rates also managed to create some confusion. Francs in Strasbourg and francs in Brussels were very different in value. Megahy and Enright recall drinking a fine bottle of Chateau d'Yquem one night in Brussels, and were bemused to be complimented on their taste by a passing Italian colleague. They had not realized its quality and they thought the cost was about £6 but were embarrassed and horrified when it turned out to be almost ten times that much.

In general, as an SPD staffer put it, "the Brits didn't socialise much with 'Europeans'". There was even a feeling that some BLG Members felt that a pro-European attitude might be catching should they be in too much contact with colleagues from across the Channel. It is impossible to underestimate the damage to good relations that was done over the years by the blunt and impolite approach of some of the Labour Members. On the continent colleagues greet each other politely and exchange pleasantries. Labour Members would often completely blank Socialist staff members as if they did not exist. This caused great offence and is still remembered decades later by some individuals.

Some of the Labour Members had been introduced by earlier Assembly members to an unpretentious restaurant in Strasbourg near the station where simple fare such as steak frites was served. *L'Orient*'s fortunes were transformed as its humble back room became a regular eating place for the left, largely the BLG plus Hume, interpreters, staff and friends. This became a convivial default eating place for those with no other engagement, including Castle whose hotel was within walking distance so that she could totter back on foot. After much red wine late at night, left-wing and Scottish folk songs and Irish rebel songs sometimes rang out at "Bang the Bells" (as the place became known). Collins' fine voice could be heard on many occasions and Hume was fond of singing "The Town I Love so Well" in a manner that could bring tears to the eyes. Some Dutch, Danish and Irish Members would also join in. Hume was amongst others who joined in the singing at a Socialist Group meeting in Venice when they celebrated Castle's birthday and he sang a beautiful song "You stole my heart away..."

Castle decided in 1982 that the time had come for the BLG to extend the hand of friendship more positively to the Socialist Group and she persuaded them to hold a Christmas party for friends in the Group. For a few years these were to become popular events, held in the house of a friendly member of the Socialist Group staff, Kriek Basile. Part of this was Castle's desire to showcase British food, so goods such as York ham and Norfolk turkey were brought over in a car from London by Jan Royall, who was effectively the BLG's general secretary. Irish smoked salmon was imported by Hume via the good offices of an Irish driver and carved expertly by Prescott who would come as a guest in his role as a former Leader. There was always plenty of whisky from the duty free, and some long term cross-border friendships were forged. This was before climate change, and British wine was not considered best to inflict on the comrades. On one occasion Royall and Castle's assistant Pollack had an event-filled and much-delayed journey home in a blizzard when the car broke down more than once and finally the windscreen wipers packed up. Their main concern was to get back to the office in Queen Anne's Gate before it closed on Friday evening so as to pack their papers for the following week's Strasbourg session. Sheer determination got them there in the nick of time.

Most of the Members took advantage of the generous parliamentary scheme for learning languages and often included an intensive week or two in their holidays, sometimes with families in tow. Marie Therese Schmidt was the main French teacher and Maria Jose Quintela Goncalves took Spanish. These provided good opportunities to begin to make friends with other MEPs, including those from other parties. Some benefitted rather more than others from these courses. Castle took both French and German courses and worked hard at her vocabulary. In particular she said she wanted to be "fluent enough in German to be able to swear at Rudi Arndt", being already fluent in French.

Political groups in the Parliament normally meet in Brussels, but once or twice a year the Socialist Group would embark on Study Days in another country, on the grounds that it was useful to better understand the various political systems, visit projects and sometimes coinciding with local, regional or national election campaigns. They were often timetabled in tandem with Congress meetings of the Confed, so that the Socialist Group could offer interpretation facilities for those meetings. These visits, lasting the best part of a week or more, offered better opportunities for socializing. There was normally at least one major dinner for the entire group, with speeches translated into French, English and German and visits to interesting projects. Attendance by the BLG at these events was variable, but some of the most anti-market Members were amongst those who thoroughly enjoyed the experience, and even the hangovers. Several Members mentioned a trip to Montpellier in September 1983 where there was a boat trip in glorious weather and Tom Megahy, Barbara Castle, Alf Lomas and Gordon Adam did their bit to drink the boat dry. One of the most ardent anti-marketeers later ventured that there was a lot of fun to be had during the days when Paolo Falcone was General Secretary of the Group, but that it was much more austere later on when Pauline Green took over.

One other traditional event was the "Asparagus Feast" held in May courtesy of the Chambers of Commerce of the Regional Councils in the tourist areas of the Bas-Rhin near Strasbourg. Famous for their excellent white asparagus, and seizing a good opportunity to flag up their local produce, they would transport busloads of Members, staff and journalists, to marquees in a picturesque village where seemingly limitless quantities of Riesling and asparagus were downed and dancing took place to the tune of local traditional brass bands in a spirit of great bonhomie. Barbara Castle always enjoyed a dance at these events even if the only partner she could find was a Tory.

Most of the Members report eventually becoming friendly with at least some colleagues on their parliamentary committees, particularly the Germans, Dutch and Greeks who could speak English.

Not a sisterhood

Labour's four women Members could not have been more different from one another. Nor were they a close band, all of them being in their own way to some extent loners. Castle managed to have poor relations with each of them except Quin, whilst Buchan succeeded in alienating them all at one time or another. Clwyd ploughed her own field with an eye to the home media and the future. They were all childless except Janey Buchan, whose son was an adult.

Ann Clwyd, a former *Guardian* and BBC journalist, who we have seen changed her mind on the EEC half way through, beat off criticism of her stance and still managed to get selected for a safe Westminster seat, winning a by-election just before the 1984 election, at much the same time as her friend

Roland Boyes, on whom she did a fairly good job of beginning to convert to a pro-market position. Clwyd had tried to win selection for the Rhondda; she was beaten by Allan Rogers, but was then successful for the Cynon Valley by-election. She remains an MP today and says she thoroughly enjoyed her years as an MEP and valued the international comradeship, though confesses she did not manage too well with languages. She enjoyed going on peace marches with friends from Greece and Italy. She says that Buchan did not speak to her for years after her change of stance on the EEC.

Barbara Castle always refused to have anything to do with women's committees but was nevertheless a powerful role model for women as the only MEP most people in Britain had heard of. As Secretary of State for Social Security she had been responsible for the Equal Pay Act and has been commemorated on a stamp of six famous socialist women for that achievement. Having been a Secretary of State during the Wilson governments and former MP for Blackburn she entered the Parliament at the age of nearly 70 and retired at just on 80 to the House of Lords where she continued to campaign, this time for pensioners. She spoke French and German and enjoyed the challenge of language courses. She was anti-market but softened her views in 1982.

Joyce Quin, the youngest, supported her North East constituency by working hard on "fish and ships". As the only female politician in the North East she was given fairly good media coverage in the region. A linguist and former lecturer, she took an active part in working on good relations with other Group Members, particularly the French. Always pro-market, she became a Europe Minister, then Agriculture Minister in the Blair government and then went into the House of Lords, having resigned her Commons seat in the hope of standing for the planned North East Regional Assembly but was thwarted by the failure of the referendum to set up such a body.

Janey Buchan, a Glaswegian socialist interested in working class culture, did not undertake any reports during her term of office. A woman of very strong views and high principles, she and Castle did not get on at all and often traded insults. Buchan maintained she was pro-Europe but anti-market. She was keenly aware of the need for the BLG to have a London office and maintain close relations with the party headquarters and Parliament. She was a strong supporter of the UK staff during her years as a Member and a long-term doughty campaigner against apartheid and for gay rights.

Their socialist colleague Marijke van Hemeldonck tells of a group of socialist feminists who went to Ireland during the election campaign in 1984 with suitcases full of contraceptives, though none of the British women were part of this crusade to try and break the ban on contraception in Ireland.

Despite the rise of the Women's Action Committee (WAC) in the Labour Party since 1981 and the struggle for power for the women's organization and women's conference, there was still an inbuilt tendency for selection bodies to vote for the male Leader of the Council rather than a woman. This under-representation was evident for some time to come. There was no such thing as an all-women shortlist at the time.

The supporting cast

Jan Royall was hired in January 1979 before the election as a coordinator of

the Group working in London out of the BLG office, becoming general secretary in all but name for the new Labour Group. Her stipend was paid out
of a monthly contribution by all the Members. Those from the North, who
almost never passed by London, constantly quibbled about this cost and
were always trying to have the post abolished. She recalls that every month
she was fearful of not having a job, but lasted until December 1985 before
leaving to work in Kinnock's private office. When Labour Party salaries
were increased Caborn was proud of his successful attempt at last to obtain
a pay rise to get her on the Labour Party pay scale and a proper contract and
pension. Jan spoke several European languages and was a fine behind-the-
scenes interlocutor for the BLG with their European comrades. She stoically
tolerated some MEPs who treated her as a personal assistant.

Members set up staffed offices in their constituencies in a variety of ways.
Some were offered offices in town halls, whilst others preferred Labour or
trade union premises and a few set up space in their homes or hired rooms.
Castle did not have a constituency office, preferring to use the Leader's privilege to make a base in the Parliament Information Office in London for herself and her researcher, together with a secretary who came in to her private
home at Hell Corner Farm in Buckinghamshire. Rates of pay for assistants
conformed to no particular scale and there were substantial discrepancies. It
was not until offices were more settled in Europe and parliamentary power
had increased to the extent that committee work became important that
MEPs started hiring staff in Brussels.

Michael Wood was the first Briton to be recruited to the Parliament by the
Open Competition system, joining in 1974. He had worked for Prescott
when he was Leader of the Labour Group in the Assembly; he took leave of
absence to work for the election and afterwards went to work in the
Parliament. David Lowe, who had worked at the Labour Party, joined the
Parliament in 1982 and went to work in the Cabinet of Piet Dankert, then
Socialist President of the Parliament. He also wrote a regular column in
Tribune about the French Socialist Party and remains on the staff.

In the Socialist Group, the British administrators had been recruited
before direct elections and were all pro-EEC. David Blackman, an academic
and former classics scholar, had been there some time and was a Deputy
General Secretary of the Socialist Group. It was not easy to find Labour staff
with the requisite language skills to become official staff members of the
Parliament. Dick Gupwell had been appointed in1976 during the time when
Gwyneth Dunwoody was active on Labour's NEC International Committee
and met her approval because of his entertainment industry trade union
background. He recalls on one occasion completely drying up when challenged by a group of young German and Irish visitors to explain Labour's
withdrawal policy on which he had strong reservations. Geoff Harris had to
await a later chance for recruitment because his strong federalist views were
strenuously opposed by the formidable Dunwoody, although he worked
closely with the Labour delegation in the former Parliamentary Assembly.
Carole Tongue, who served as an MEP from 1984-99, had started work as a
secretary to Blackman after an earlier parliamentary stagiaireship. Rather
less well known to Members was Roy Cattermole who was involved in the
general administration section. A senior Irish administrator with a keen
mind, Fionnulla Richardson, was also highly rated by many of the British.

She was always supportive of those Members keen to advance the aims of the Group.

Left-wingers in the BLG were constantly irritated by these pro-Europeans with their more centrist or right-wing views (not to mention the fact they were better paid than the Members) and spent some time grumbling in BLG meetings that the British members of the Socialist Group staff should work to them and not to the General Secretary of the Group. It was late in the second Parliament before this difficulty was quietly buried.

Julian Priestley, a long-standing Labour member and strong pro-European, began working in the Parliament in June 1973 originally on a temporary contract when the Parliament was looking for someone to assist a British rapporteur for the budget. By 1984 he was on the permanent staff and running the secretariat of the Energy, Research and Technology Committee, and later that of the Budgets and Internal Market. He was to become a senior figure in the Parliament in the ensuing twenty-five years and retired in 2007 with a knighthood.

The Socialist Group had set aside a staff member to look after the British Members, even during the Assembly times. Kriek Basile, a Belgian woman, had a large informal office-cum-lounge room in which they could come and take a cup of coffee, read the newspapers and receive advice about parliamentary procedures. Even more important, she offered help about how to deal with landlords, install TVs in apartments and the small details of life in a foreign country. She was popular, particularly with those whose French was not highly developed. It was at her private house that the BLG held its Christmas parties. She was particularly fond of Prescott from the former Assembly and Lomas, Megahy and Seal, who for some years would visit her for barbecues in the summer.

Socialist parties in Europe

What was clear after the difficulties of developing a platform for the first European Parliament election in 1979 was that the national parties were just that and were set on fighting elections on the basis of national issues. In June 1979 former Confed Secretary-General Michel suggested that the parties must ask themselves whether they were prepared to give the Confederation greater powers. In 1980 the theme of the Congress was "Socialists against the Right". However it was clear that the Confed at that stage had no intention of becoming a European super-party.

The next two years saw four special conferences: in London in March 1981 on energy, in Paris in March on security and disarmament, in Madrid in November on enlargement, and in Marseilles in June 1982 on Mediterranean policy. Much support was given to Felipe Gonzalez in recognition of his contribution to freedom and democracy in Spain. The Greek, Spanish and Portuguese socialist parties had been involved in the work of the Confederation from the end of the 1970s. The congress in November that year in Paris was on the theme "Socialists and European Revival". The idea was to develop a theme for the 1984 elections on a European economic recovery plan. Lessons were learned from 1979 and national parties were left to organize their own campaign conferences.

Labour MEPs were not normally considered by the NEC to be delegates to the Confederation meetings, in contrast to the position of many of the other parties. It was seen very much as the province of the International Committee of the NEC and the International Department of the Labour Party. There was very little continuity of elected MPs attending and the British did not have any Member on the Bureau until 1985. There was also virtually no linkage about topics, debates, or results of the deliberations between the European wing of the party and its bureaucracy at home.

Reselection battles

Such was the divided state of the Labour Party that talk of reselections and deselections for MEPs was already on the agenda at the beginning of 1983 for an election that was not due until the middle of 1984. The disunity and sheer bitterness between the pro and anti-EEC factions in the party frequently spilled over into the press during these eighteen months, inevitably adding to the negative image of Labour as a party at war with itself.

Even before the general election there had been a stormy meeting of the BLG over policy. In January Seal supported a Lomas resolution calling for all candidates to support the Labour Party manifesto promise of withdrawal. The vote tied 8-8. Caborn in the Chair, having voted for the resolution, did not give it a casting vote and it fell. Enright said: "My actions, my attendance and my work rate are the true proof of my loyalty to the party", and it was the case that he was constantly present and active in the Parliament.

At the same meeting Collins managed to have a proposal carried saying that "as far as possible candidates should be selected using the same procedures as those for the Westminster Parliament." There was copious coverage in the Scottish and Sheffield press and rumours began to circulate that anti-marketeers in the party were seeking to unseat as many as nine of the seventeen MEPs. The *Sheffield Morning Telegraph* in January criticized Key and suggested the NUM were organizing to ditch him, which was the case. The second safest Labour European seat was a plum target for a miners' candidate.

Kelvingrove Labour Party (in Buchan's constituency) passed a resolution demanding that panels of candidates should be loyal to conference decisions and the party's NEC. This went to Labour's Scottish Conference in March. Easter's Co-operative Party Conference in 1983 also passed a withdrawal motion from their Women's Guild. Pressure was building. In February Collins' CLP called on him to support Labour Party policy on withdrawal, the request being moved by Adam Ingram, who was a candidate for Parliament. Collins promised them a speech and in due course gave a good and detailed argument and won support. (Ingram did not win a seat that time but was elected to Parliament for East Kilbride in June 1987, was for a time PPS to Neil Kinnock and became a government Minister.)

Janey Buchan was so vociferous in her criticism of the EEC that the Head of the European Commission office in Edinburgh early in 1983 refused to allow his staff to take part in a media programme with her. This then occasioned another row in the press.

Some Labour MEPs organized a series of rallies during 1983 against continuing Common Market membership. The first was held in London on

March 22, supported by trade unions, the Co-op and leading anti-marke-teers.

The NEC held off opening the European selection process until after the 1983 general election. With Militant still active in many constituencies, and the right/left, pro-and anti-market positions still dividing local Labour par-ties, arguments were rife throughout the autumn of 1983 as reselection came uppermost in the minds of some activists. Selections were due to commence in September, and European selection organizations were constituted, but because of delays in completing boundary reviews, they did not begin work until December. There were even some late boundary decisions, with can-didates having to be re-allocated in eleven constituencies.

Reselections for Labour MEPs were to be made even more complicated by boundary changes necessitated by aligning with the earlier changes in boundaries of Westminster seats. Only six constituencies were totally unchanged, with another seven slightly changed. For the rest there was fairly substantial redrawing of boundaries and seat re-naming. Barbara Castle was dismayed to find her own constituency borders were changing and unnerved that she had to fight to be selected for Greater Manchester West, a seat containing only part of her former constituency, against some opposition from party members who were not happy with her perceived softening on Europe. She had attempted to be selected for that seat for the 1979 election but not been short-listed and it had been won by Conservative William Hopper with the tiny majority of 302 over Labour's candidate. In her former seat she was again opposed by Glyn Ford, who publicized her earlier promise only to stand for one term. She was spared having to con-front him for selection by winning the other seat first. The fact that she did not visit her constituency very often was apparent when she told party workers she wanted to visit every factory in her constituency and was shocked to be told that "there are none left."

Derek Enright had originally won his selection by only one vote from John Gunnell (who later succeeded Merlyn Rees as MP for Morley and South Leeds). His agent in 1979 had been Geoff Hoon. Enright's wife Jane believes that there were Militants in some of the constituencies, but McGowan says he does not believe they were present amongst the 110 del-egates at the selection meeting and that he was not in contact with them. Enright found himself squeezed between McGowan on the one hand and Colin Bergen (also now a Labour MP) on the other and was eliminated in the first ballot. McGowan had served as a Leeds City Councillor, a member of the Area Health Authority and Chair of the Community Health Council, had worked as Secretary of the Leeds Co-operative Party and development officer at the HQ of the Industrial Common Ownership Movement, was an active campaigner with CND and West Yorkshire coordinator for END.

Jane Enright suggests that in retrospect it may have not been the best tactic for Derek to have employed two ambitious Labour Councillors, who were busy with Council work rather than with the task of promoting the MEP. One of those, John Battle, was very talented and later went on himself to Westminster. There was no doubt that Labour lost a colourful character in Europe when Enright was deposed. A classic scholar whose ready wit and erudite puns and quotations often caused difficulties for the inter-preters, he became known as the man who sang *Yellow Submarine* in Latin.

There appeared to have been little kudos for him in having obtained substantial ESF funds for his area and for being actively involved in persuading the Commission to set up a form of help for redundant mineworkers. Enright was asked to fight what was seen as a hopeless seat in Kent. With typical chutzpa, he gave it a vigorous campaign and managed to finish second behind the Tories, bucking the local and national trend and helping build up the party for victory a few years later.

Balfe's reselection suffered a slight hiccup when in January 1984 it was forced to begin again. In the re-run he won easily.

Brian Key was deselected in Yorkshire. Arthur Scargill's NUM had a large number of local union branches affiliated to displace Key in favour of his close confidant Norman West. Key, formerly Chair of Barnsley Labour Group, had originally beaten Martin Redmond in the selection in 1978. At that meeting, another NUM hopeful, Sir Jack Leyden, seen as the front runner, lost at the first ballot and saw that his votes transferred to Key rather than Redmond because of animosity to Scargill. This time Key's supporters were outnumbered and the NUM had its way. Key was out.

Michael Gallagher deselected himself by joining the SDP prior to the 1984 election. One of the main concerns of the Labour Group was the fact that he was entitled to several thousands of pounds from the Socialist Group once he was outside the Labour delegation, and that he could use that for electoral purposes. Castle unhesitatingly slammed him (inaccurately) in the press and to the NEC as a "poor attender".

Another four of the Labour MEPs had been elected in 1983 to the House of Commons and did not stand again: Ann Clwyd, Roland Boyes, Richard Caborn and Allan Rogers. Selected when anti-EU sentiment was still strong in the winter of 1983-84, all of their successors were anti-marketeers. This swung the balance in the BLG against what was becoming the prevailing pragmatic wind and was to cause trouble in the period ahead.

Key and Enright, with typical dedication, were working and speaking in plenary sessions right up to the last, defending their Leader and continuing to speak up for progressive policies. Castle said about Enright and Key that "though hardworking and conscientious MEPs, they had fallen victim to the manoeuvrings of the hard left."

PART II

1984-89

Trouble and strife

The scene

This second electoral period was one of Labour's most publicly and privately divi-sive times, with bitter in-fights and four changes of European Leader in five years that destined the British Labour Group to punch below its weight. The miners' strike dominated the early period with demonstrations in and out of the Chamber. One Labour MEP died and a further three became MPs. Budgetary battles began to die down. Struggles against Thatcherism continued, and campaigns against racism and fascism were waged. Jacques Delors spoke to the TUC. More Labour MEPs changed their mind on the EEC. Labour lost another general election, the first under Neil Kinnock's leadership. The Single European Act came into force in 1987. Barbara Castle retired 1989.

Rocky road to a manifesto

Preparations leading up to the 1984 European elections, beginning with a more conciliatory tone from the new leadership on EEC policy, were dogged by policy rifts and bureaucratic difficulties. Labour Party staff had internal disagreements and relations between staff, the NEC, the party and its MEPs were fraught. Given the divisions, the better-than-expected Labour result can probably best be attributed to the growing unpopularity of the Conservatives and a proportion of their vote staying at home.

Labour conference in 1983 did not debate Europe for the reasons outlined earlier. The policy that was to be the mainstay of the European election was set out in the NEC's post-general election stocktaking statement "Campaigning for a Fairer Britain", quoted on p. 58. This was accepted by conference as part of a broader document, without discussion and managed to be acceptable enough for the purposes of the election campaign. Some CLPs and MEPs preferred to adhere to the withdrawal policy laid down in the general election manifesto early in 1983 and previous conference resolutions.

A Campaign Strategy Group including Castle was established at the end of October 1983 under the day-to-day management of Robin Cook MP. Some heads of department felt it was something of a Trojan horse with the new leadership trying to assert itself in contrast to the NEC. It led to a com-plaint from General Secretary Jim Mortimer (anti-market) that he had to take instructions both from this group and the NEC. Some officials were still of the view that the elections should not be contested at all. Relations were bound to be strained. The lines of command in headquarters with existing heads of department were far from smooth and eventually the unit was wound up before the campaign launch in May 1984.

Adding to the plethora of internal committees, a separate EEC Unit was set up in late 1983 at Walworth Road headed by anti-market Jim Parish who was, according to some in the unit at the time, not the world's most natural team builder. The main aim of the staff for the election was to put down a marker against the Conservatives and build towards the next general election, having done so badly earlier that year. Parish in November produced an internal paper for the NEC, saying the election should be about the Labour Party versus Thatcherism, not about Europe. Winning European seats was not seen as particularly important, but the party desperately wanted to increase the total Labour vote across the country so as to be seen as a viable opposition and in particular to beat the SDP. That was of some help to candidates in terms of mobilising voters in marginal areas to vote Labour rather than voting for the Liberal/SDP Alliance as an alternative to the Tories.

Castle, Seal and Rogers were part of the European Campaign Group which met weekly. Others on this committee were Kinnock, Hattersley, Heffer, Hadden, Dunwoody, Cook, Kitson, McCluskie, Hoyle, Hughes, Foulkes, and Booth – a very mixed bag of views on Europe. In early November 1983 Castle wrote to Joyce Gould, assistant National Agent, who acted as Secretary to the Campaign Committee, protesting at Parish's view of the campaign.

> "The campaign unit argues that the elections should be fought purely as an expression of domestic policies and that we should keep European issues and the work of the BLG out of it. I strongly disagree… once this strategy is known it will be used against us as proof that we cannot be trusted to take the work of the EP seriously, and that therefore people should not bother to vote for us…"

The Campaign team was set up before Christmas, partly to ensure the selection process was a bit more organized than in 1979. There is not a great deal of evidence to suggest that this aim was achieved. Most CLPs remained firmly anti-market and their delegates to European Constituency Parties selected their candidates accordingly.

Robin Cook, the Labour front bench spokesman on Europe and unofficial campaign manager, set out electoral objectives on campaign strategy in a December 1983 paper "The European Campaign: Political Strategy". They were:

> "To establish Labour as the clear political alternative to the Tories. This can only be achieved by beating the Alliance into a poor third place.
>
> To recapture to Labour as many as possible of the defectors of the June election.
>
> To project Labour as a competent party conducting a well-managed and competent campaign".

Kinnock was not prepared to exclude a European dimension; he believed in the value of European Socialist co-operation, having friends in the left movement in Italy where there was enthusiasm for European project, so in January the following campaign crucial aim was added:

> "To secure the return of as many Labour candidates as possible".

This was by no means the main goal of the MPs on the NEC, who agreed the aim should be to maximize the total number of Labour votes rather than of seats. The party was still smarting from the successes of the SDP-Liberal Alliance in the 1983 general election, where it almost succeeded in ousting Labour as the principal opposition party and where Labour's proportion of the vote was the lowest since 1918.

The view was that the issues to be campaigned on should be those likely to gain most public support (i.e. unemployment and health). According to an insider at HQ, some officers argued that the development of the EEC, activities of the Socialist Group and the work of Labour MEPs should play virtually no part in the campaign. However Cook argued that both domestic and European issues should figure: food prices and CAP, deployment of Cruise missiles, a common strategy to tackle unemployment, third world, regional and industrial regeneration. To some extent this mollified the MEPs.

Labour sent representatives to manifesto meetings of the Confederation of Socialist Parties, whose campaign committee, chaired by Karel Van Miert, was set up by February 1983, and a manifesto working group chaired by a French Socialist, a text going to the congress in Luxembourg on 8-9 March 1984. Under Kinnock's leadership there was a slightly more positive attitude, of necessity tempered by the official Labour position on Europe (still for withdrawal), the composition of the NEC which remained predominantly anti-market, and the fact that these negotiations were the preserve of the NEC's International and Home Policy Committees. Following a *Sunday Times* piece in November 1983 picturing Cook under the heading "Kinnock woos his European comrades", an attempt to send Cook to a meeting of the manifesto drafting committee in January was blocked by Jenny Little, International Secretary and Alex Kitson, Chair of the NEC's International Committee. Bish and Little attended, while most of the manifesto meetings had been attended by Sigler and Parish – they were anti-marketeers all.

For the congress in March Labour's delegation again consisted predominantly of anti-marketeers apart from Hattersley and Clwyd. They were Dunwoody, Hoyle, Wise, Mortimer, Bish, Little, Sigler plus pro-EEC Wilkinson from the EEC Unit. Bish had suggested Labour formally dissociate itself from those sections of the text calling for greater European integration and more powers for the Parliament. By the second day there was a threat that Labour would torpedo the Socialist manifesto altogether. This did not please Kinnock back in London, who phoned Dunwoody and emphasized the importance of agreeing a text. Despite the problems, agreement was finally reached on what was the first European Socialist manifesto, with some footnotes expressing Labour reservations. The paper was more ambitious than the short common declaration of 1979, majoring on an economic plan for a "European Way out of the Crisis". Not only the British but also the Danes opposed the sections on monetary policy coordination and increased power for the European Parliament, whilst the Italians stressed that they would campaign on the draft European Treaty which proposed precisely those points. The Leaders' meeting in Brussels on 31 May-1 June was attended by Kinnock and Little.

But back home the NEC agreed only to endorse a text with a foreword by Jim Mortimer setting out Labour reservations and as before it hardly featured in Labour's campaign. Its slogan was "Jobs - Peace - Freedom" and it laid down three reservations where Labour was unable to reach agreement with its European partners, outlined as: "The European Monetary System (of which Britain is not a member); the powers of the European Parliament; and a proposal to increase the community's 'own resources'." There were a number of other caveats on policy details. A reference in the European manifesto for "reconversion in the coal-producing regions" was rejected. The Foreword said that there must be no detraction from our policy for a major increase in investment in coal. Given the volatile situation in the coal industry in the UK, this was hardly surprising. Support was, however, given to the notion of achieving a new deal for the people of Europe.

Labour's manifesto, "A Fair deal for Britain and a new deal for Europe", was drafted for a small committee drawn from the Campaign Strategy

Committee (CSC) and the NEC by Bish. There were confusingly two committees. The first was an EEC election Manifesto drafting Committee, consisting
of Heffer, Castle (with Caborn as alternate), Cook, Dunwoody, Hoyle, Kitson,
Bish and Little. The second was dubbed the EEC Manifesto Committee consisting of Heffer, Booth, Castle, Hadden, Hattersley, Hoyle, Kinnock, Kitson,
Seal, Mortimer, Bish and Little. The text, adopted by the NEC on 9 May and
launched on the 21st, said Labour should seek to get the best deal for Britain
within the EEC whilst maintaining the option of withdrawal. It included support for joint action in the EEC on regional policy, industrial democracy in
multinational companies and a 35-hour week. The final version was translated into journalese by *Daily Mirror* writer Joe Haines focusing on jobs, food,
social justice, peace and security. Skinner and Maynard on the NEC tried to
get the draft rejected and were only narrowly defeated by seven votes to five.
The resulting text was necessarily a classic fudge. The section entitled
"Britain's role in the Community" reiterated the relatively pragmatic statement on membership of the EEC agreed at the conference of 1983. But by the
time the NEC finished with it this statement was completely contradictory,
also saying: "We stand by the arguments we presented in our election manifesto" (meaning that of the general election in 1983, i.e. withdrawal). It ended
with "The new beginning", saying Labour believed it was time for a fresh
start and that "We can help create a new Europe". The text was a hostage to
fortune, giving succour to both sides of the withdrawal argument, and would
dog the Labour MEPs during the whole of the next term.

Campaigning

This time at least there was a formal commitment to contest the elections
and it was put to the party as being an important first test for its new Leader.
In terms of electioneering, MEPs were sidelined and relations between the
EEC Unit and the BLG were sensitive. Money from the Confed was spent
centrally and its deployment in the first instance had been negotiated by the
BLG representatives on the Socialist Group Bureau (Castle and Rogers).
This, too, was a source of complaint from the anti-marketeers, who reckoned
it amounted to £4,000 per constituency that could have been used for local
anti-market literature. This was an unrealistic pipe dream because of the
rules governing such funding.

Strings attached to the European funding meant that temporary staff had to
be identifiably engaged in the campaign. The EEC Unit was always under-
staffed (HQ being reluctant to lose control of staff by seconding them) and
money was inevitably wasted on consultants and freelancers. The BLG
wanted a broadsheet produced to inform about their work but were ignored.
Attempts to hold conferences on the steel industry or alternatives to arms
manufacture were stonewalled, despite there being separate funding on offer
from the Socialist Group for such events. "In these circumstances", says one
of the temporary staff involved in the campaign, "MEPs' attitudes to Party
HQ could be depicted as a grievance looking for a suitable issue." After a campaign meeting of the BLG in February in Strasbourg a stiffly worded letter of
protest was sent to Kinnock and leaked to *The Guardian* on 18 February, thus
having some effect. Rogers was the BLG representative on the Campaign
Committee, supposed to be always the same person so as to ensure continu-

ity. Although there was in theory a useful link, the reality was that Rogers had been elected to the House of Commons in 1983, was running a dual mandate and had little spare time to attend meetings; he did not attend the daily meetings at all once the campaign started.

There was sometimes lack of liaison between MEPs. Caborn (who also had a dual mandate) flew back from Strasbourg in May for an ITN interview, to find Boyes doing it, as the broadcaster had been told that he could not make it. Staff had not checked each other's diaries. Caborn was then asked if he would attend the Campaign Committee meeting on 24 May, since Rogers could not attend and refused, on the grounds the whole point was to have only one BLG representative. It didn't help put European issues to the forefront of the campaign.

All MEPs had European funds which were meant to be for information purposes about their work rather than party political propaganda and to be spent before the campaign began. Areas without a Labour MEP did not have this luxury on their side and the BLG pooled their resources to commission a film on their work to show at Euro CLP meetings titled "EEC Elections – the next round against Thatcher". To some extent this was sabotaged, because a planned showing at the candidates' conference became impossible when party organizers "forgot" to ensure the availability of the equipment necessary to play it. It was also a problem at constituency party level. Most meetings were in dingy halls with no TV on which to play a video, so they tended to remain unseen unless an MEP sponsored an event at which a video could be shown.

Most of the income for the election, just over £700,000, came from the European Socialists. The NEC report to conference after the election ungratefully complained that the party had sustained a net loss on the campaign which was largely due to the failure of the European Socialist Group to meet its commitments on the funding of a number of mutually agreed special projects, leaving £50,000 still in dispute.

There was dissent within the BLG about how to use the MEPs' money. Lomas suggested (*The Guardian* 19 February 1984) that each MEP should conduct their own campaign in their own way in their own constituencies, the implication being that there was no confidence in Walworth Road. The BLG set up its own campaign office for the last three weeks at Queen Anne's Gate (the European Parliament's Information Office), staffed by some volunteers from Brussels (including Geoff Harris and Tony Robinson from the Socialist Group), issued press releases and launched a telephone enquiry service on Euro-jargon. There was little co-ordination between this unit and the EEC Unit at Walworth Road, where the "Today" team wrote campaign briefings almost exclusively on domestic issues. The Socialist Group supplied pens and balloons rather late in the day and some material allegedly did not even arrive until after the election. A complaint from the grass roots was that people did not know what material to expect and could not plan its most effective use. Poor relations between BLG Members and party HQ cost money. Individual Members produced briefing leaflets that could have been part of a more co-ordinated information package. Carole Tongue was fortunate in being young, attractive and female and attracted a good degree of media attention. Martin Linton of *The Guardian* (now Labour MP for Battersea) wrote a half page profile of her, forecasting, correctly, a win in London East.

A well-received Labour campaign bus was launched on 12 March, touring parts of the country with Prescott and others. A video "Victory Bells" was produced, in which various MPs, Benn, Hattersley, Blunkett and Livingstone, exhorted activists "to deliver a verdict on Thatcher". No MEPs featured, and it suffered from a shortage of viewing opportunities. There was a successful pensioners' rally in April amidst grumbles that understaffing of the EEC Unit meant freelance press work cost an unnecessary £1,600. A series of regional "Eurofests" were held even with an attendance charge in Manchester, London, Edinburgh and Leeds and an eve of poll rally in Cardiff with Kinnock and Willy Brandt. These attempted to be a mixture of policy and showbiz in order to enthuse campaigners and had a total attendance of eight thousand. Again because of the lack of press staff, there was a feeling that they had been undersold to the media. One of the headquarters officials later wrote that "far from bringing members of the BLG and the rest of the party together... the ... campaign provided them with fresh sources of grievance... It served notice on the rest of the party that its relationships with the BLG could now no longer be kept off Labour's agenda."

Formal commitment to campaigning did not always filter down to the grass-roots. It was often the case that if a pro-European candidate had been selected the anti-market party members would not do any work, and vice versa. Hoon recalls that Bolsover in his constituency refused even to nominate a candidate for the selection process and remained supremely indifferent to the campaign. In their case the miners' strike was king. There was little any local agent could do about this, having to work with whatever strengths there were on the ground. Leaflet coverage and certainly anything more dynamic, such as canvassing, could be extremely patchy and bore little relationship to the winability of any seat. Hallam remembers one horror of campaigning, travelling all the way to a branch meeting, a round trip of fifty miles, all self-funded, giving a speech and then the Chair accepting a motion that "whilst appreciating the enthusiasm of the candidate this branch will not take part in the elections to the European Assembly". In 1994 he was still standing with half an eye on Westminster but was finally successful.

The influential Labour Co-Ordinating Committee (LCC – the left of centre activist-oriented body opposed to Militant and Trotskyism with a member-ship by then approaching that of the Fabians) was changing both its mem-bership and its policy. After the 1983 election defeat it argued for change along the lines that Kinnock was pursuing. Some of the more prominent hard-liners left its executive. It was now chaired by Harriet Harman MP (who had won the Peckham by-election in October 1982), executive mem-bers including Peter Hain, John Denham, Barbara Roche, and Caroline Flint (all later to become Labour government Ministers); Cherie Booth (married to Tony Blair, who was elected to Parliament in 1983), who sometimes brought her baby and breastfed him at meetings; Alan Haworth (later Secretary of the PLP and subsequently Lord Haworth), and Anita Pollack (at that time working for Barbara Castle). It was run with wit and strategic intelligence by Nigel Stanley, a researcher for initially Bryan Gould and later Robin Cook and now at the TUC. A London section was active in organizing cam-paigning events. Pollack's own campaign centred on the VAT issue that was also top of Castle's agenda. Her Kingston and Surbiton parties (held by Conservatives) featured a rally with Tony Benn as the speaker. Whilst popu-lar in the local parties as a high-profile event attended by four hundred, since he was strongly anti-market, it probably only confused people as to the virtues of bothering to vote.

London LCC set up an EEC Working Group in July 1983 "to put some heart and fresh ideas into Labour's campaign" and by December had produced a series of a dozen detailed information papers on the EEC in advance of the election campaign, circulated to Labour activists and supplemented by a speakers' list offered for CLPs. It organized a well-attended European conference on 18 February 1984, addressed by Cook and other top names, some from across the water courtesy of the Friedrich Ebert Stiftung. The bulk of these fact sheets had been drafted by Castle's assistant, some academics and David Ward, later assistant to John Smith. They were couched in fairly neutral language, attempting to interest local Labour members enough to campaign in the elections with solid information about a range of subject areas dealt with at the European level and were a clear departure from LCC's anti-EEC position of five years before. The paper on employment, for instance, took the lead from Stuart Holland's policies on promoting co-ordinated economic reflation at a European level, rather than the Alternative Economic Strategy. These fact sheets proved useful to the party in preparing election literature, since only a couple of the sitting MEPs had provided policy briefings to central staff. All this activity may have encouraged more campaigning in London, leading to the higher than average swing to Labour in the capital.

For candidates, the metropolitan district elections held in May meant activists had little energy for further campaigning, so again there was not a great deal of activity apart from leaflet distribution. Canvassing records were used from the earlier election. Those Labour seats considered "safe" saw minimalist activity, whilst the ones on the target list made a bit more effort. Turnouts were highly variable.

The Conservatives ran a fairly low key campaign with the slogan "The Strong Voice in Europe", not wanting to wake up the Labour vote. It may have been a lack of confidence in their ability to persuade their own supporters to turn out, since there were opponents of Thatcher's policies internally even at that time. For them Europe had become a subject to be kept off the doorsteps.

Election gains

Voting for the elections on 14 June took place twelve weeks into the miners' strike and many Labour minds were on that struggle rather than the electoral one. Local Labour Party members were far more interested in holding benefits, stalls, and petitions in support of the miners than in campaigning for potential European MPs. Candidates were expected to be present on stalls in high streets campaigning in favour of the miners even in non-mining areas such as London. There was still massive grass-roots lack of interest in the European Parliament, including in the hapless candidates, but generally outright opposition had reduced.

The pitiful UK turnout of 1979 was only fractionally surpassed and at 32.57% was still the lowest in the European Community. *The Times 1984 European Election Guide* called it a "nationwide display of stupendous indifference". Hughes said that in Sunderland in one ward there was only a 1%

turnout. Despite its internal differences, Labour presented a relatively coherent front and avoided too many public splits. By defusing withdrawal as an issue it wrong-footed the Conservatives, set the agenda successfully on jobs, peace and food and also managed to convey that the European Liberals were on the right of the political spectrum. As far as the NEC was concerned, the most important aspect was that Labour had replaced the SDP-Liberal Alliance as the second party in seventeen seats.

The Conservatives won most votes – 5,426,866 – giving them forty-five seats for 40.8% of the vote, but still lost fifteen with a 5.3% swing against them since the 1983 general election. Labour's target was twenty-five to thirty seats and it won thirty-two (nearly double its previous effort), receiving 4,865,224 votes, 36.5% of the total. The SDP-Liberal Alliance scored 2,591,659, still with no seats at 18.5% of the vote. Again they registered unhappiness with the first-past-the-post electoral system, as did the Ecology Party which received 71,000 votes across the country but no seats. In a gratifyingly large number of seats Labour came from behind to replace the Alliance as second party, especially across the South and East of England containing a high number of key Westminster marginals. In doing so it fulfilled one of the key election aims. The Tory lead of 15.2% in the general election was cut to 3.25% with the Alliance pushed into third place. As the first electoral test for the new Leader Neil Kinnock, it was a success.

In London, as in most other parts of the country, there were late boundary changes and an above-average swing to Labour of 8.5%, not least due to the threatened abolition of the GLC now under left-winger Ken Livingstone. There was also a big swing to Labour in its strongholds in the regions heavily hit by unemployment as a result of recession and Thatcherite economic policies. In South Yorkshire the swing was 10.3%, Wales 9.2% and Durham 9.1%.

Twenty-two of the Labour Members were new, outnumbering the old guard by more than two-to-one. Three were left-wing former MPs who had lost their House of Commons seats in the 1983 general election: Bob Cryer, Stan Newens and Les Huckfield (boundary change). These three all sought selection again as MPs, but only Cryer returned to the House of Commons (in 1987). A fourth former MP was John Tomlinson, a former Foreign Office Minister on the right of the party. He had lost his seat in 1979 and had been lecturing at Solihull College of Technology in the interim. Three Labour MEPs had been deselected: Enright, Key and Gallagher. Gallagher's seat was lost to the Conservatives after he defected to the SDP and fought the election in Lancashire Central instead of his home town. Four of Labour's first intake had departed to the House of Commons: Boyes, Caborn, Clwyd (at a by-election on 3 May) and Rogers.

Whilst the Labour Party under Kinnock was moving to a more pragmatic position on the European Community, the constituency grass roots sent an almost totally anti-market addition to the European team. The Labour Group during this term was often evenly divided and decisions could depend on one vote changing sides (with Balfe often the swing vote). It was a lasting recipe for trouble and strife.

Twelve women were returned from the UK but only five of these were Labour of whom only two were new. The Conservatives had their biggest female contingent in twenty-five years. The Labour women were: Janey Buchan, Barbara Castle, Christine Crawley, Carole Tongue and Joyce Quin.

Having almost doubled its total representation, there was embarrassingly only one more woman on the Labour team than in 1979. This disappointingly small number reflected the lack of any all-women shortlists at that time. It was not until 1988 that Labour Women's Network was set up, campaigning for more female political representation under the guidance of Val Price and Hilary de Lyon. In the entire country there were only ten Labour women candidates, local party instinct still being to select the male Leader of the Labour Group on the Council. However the two new Labour women did inject some refreshing feminism into the group.

There had been a large number of boundary changes and new seat names. Castle's seat had changed substantially and this time she fought Greater Manchester West, ostensibly marginal but won with a thumping 37,689 majority over Conservative William Hopper. A by-election was held in Portsmouth South on the same day where the SDP won the seat from the Conservatives. Once again there had been only one minority ethnic candidate for Labour – Keith Vaz, who came third in Surrey West but later went on to become an MP and briefly a Europe Minister.

Labour's mixed team

The remaining old hands were: Adam, Balfe, Buchan, Castle, Collins, Griffiths, Lomas, Megahy, Quin, and Seal.

The twenty-two new recruits were:

Christine Crawley, Irish (the first British non-national to be elected to the EP), a former drama teacher and Oxfordshire Councillor, in Birmingham East, a re-drawn boundary, defeating Norvella Forster. She had tried for Westminster in 1983 in South East Staffordshire.

Bob Cryer, former MP and junior Minister, sponsored by the National Union of Mineworkers, a former lecturer and Councillor described as hard left and strongly anti-market; he replaced Richard Caborn in Sheffield.

Michael Elliott, former food chemist, an LCC and Fabian member and Ealing Councillor, won London West from Conservative Brian Hord with a comparatively high turnout of 37.7%. He had stood for Westminster in 1964, 1966 and 1970, and for Europe in 1979 and was rewarded at last for his tenacity, having won the selection by only one vote from Keith Vaz. Elliott's successful tactic was to maximize the Southall Asian vote for Labour and persuade Labour supporters in Richmond (often in the habit of voting Liberal to defeat the Conservatives) that their best bet was Labour because of the larger constituency including strong Labour areas, flooding these areas with special leaflets. He was pro-Europe.

Alex Falconer, left-wing senior convenor for the T&GWU in Rosyth dockyards and former stoker, won Mid Scotland and Fife from Conservative John Purvis with a turnout of 35.5%. Purvis returned to the Parliament in 1999.

Glyn Ford, a research academic, marine geologist, lecturer and Japan expert, Tameside Councillor, a left-wing internationalist, ex-ILP, speaking French, won Greater Manchester East, a boundary change seat, against a non-sitting Conservative. As did some others, he held his Council seat until the next local elections a year later.

Michael Hindley, a Council Leader, trade union tutor and academic with experience in East Germany and Poland, hard-left, speaking German, French and some Polish, won Lancashire East from Conservative Edward Kellett-Bowman. (The latter returned at the Hampshire by-election in 1988 following the death of Basil de Ferranti. The other half of that family team, Elaine Kellett-Bowman, lost out in a boundary redistribution, the victorious Tory candidate being Sheila Faith in Cumbria and Lancashire North.) Hindley had fought Blackpool North in the general election of 1983.

Geoff Hoon, a barrister, who had been Enright's agent in 1979, was surprised to win Derbyshire from Conservative Tom Spencer, who famously said it was "the first time a Conservative loss to Labour is a shift to the right". He was only 29, a good speaker, and won the nomination against a much-nominated Co-op candidate.

Les Huckfield was a former lecturer and Director of Transport for the GLC, MP and junior Minister at the DTI, strongly anti-market, whose constituency of Nuneaton had ceased to exist thus forcing his retirement from the House of Commons. He had been on Labour's NEC and had tried unsuccessfully to be selected for Sedgefield for the 1983 general election, being beaten by Tony Blair. He won Merseyside East, also a boundary change seat, with a low turnout. He spoke some French and German.

Stephen Hughes, a local government researcher replaced Roland Boyes in Durham with a massive majority in a renamed seat, having won a tough selection contest against Ossie O'Brien, a former MP.

Michael McGowan, BBC TV and radio producer, Leeds City Councillor, broad left and committed anti-nuclear campaigner, green socialist vegetarian and internationalist, replaced deselected Enright in Leeds. He had been a parliamentary candidate in Ripon 1966 and Brighouse and Spenborough in 1979.

Hugh McMahon, a deputy headmaster and Fabian, defeated Conservative Jacqui Lait in Strathclyde West. The seat in 1979 had been held by Adam Fergusson, who decamped to London Central. Lait became an MP in 1997 and a member of the Conservative Shadow Cabinet.

David Martin, a young Councillor, former economics lecturer and Fabian, won Lothians from a new Conservative in a boundary change seat.

David Morris, a Methodist lay preacher and peace campaigner, former foundry worker and education advisor, replaced Ann Clwyd in Mid and West Wales with a comparatively large turnout of 40.2%. He had contested Brecon and Radnor in the general election of 1983.

Stan Newens, former MP, former coalminer and history teacher and Co-operative sponsored, defeated Conservative Adam Fergusson in London Central, with Ernest Wistrich of the European Movement coming third for the SDP-Liberal Alliance. He had attempted to win back Harlow in the general election.

Edward Newman, a local Councillor, regional executive member and a Militant supporter for much of the 1970s, a trades union activist working for the post office, won Greater Manchester Central. This was also a boundary change where the Conservative party had deselected Harmar-Nicholls. He was one of the ten youngest Members of the Parliament.

Terry Pitt, former head of the Labour Party research office 1964-70, Fabian, reputedly author of Harold Wilson's famous "White Heat of Technology" paper, won Midlands West. There had been a boundary change here and the previous Conservative incumbent, Richard Simmonds, moved to a safer southern seat.

Llewellyn Smith, an anti-market anti-nuclear campaigner, former Militant supporter and WEA tutor in South East Wales took over from Labour's Allan Rogers who had gone to Westminster.

George Stevenson, a former miner and bus driver, a local Councillor, won Staffordshire East from Conservative Robert Moreland in a boundary change. He was anti-market but pro-Europe.

Ken Stewart, veteran left-wing Liverpool former Chair of Housing, supported by Militant (but not a member); strong trades unionist sponsored by the Co-operative Party, decorated WWII paratrooper and building worker sponsored by UCATT won Merseyside West in a boundary change from Conservative Gloria Hooper. The Liverpool Labour vote had been galvanized in the May local elections because of the battles over tactics on a deficit budget.

John Tomlinson, former MP, Minister and PPS to Harold Wilson, on the right of the party, a lecturer; pro-European, Co-operative Party sponsored, won Birmingham West where there had also been a boundary change. As a Minister he had responsibility for Europe and overseas development.

Carole Tongue, a 28 year old pro-European administrator in the Socialist Group, fluent in French, with some Italian, Spanish and German, won London East from Alan Tyrell, turning a 13,000 Conservative majority into 13,000 for Labour following considerable media interest.

Norman West, a miner sponsored by the NUM, close associate of Arthur Scargill and strongly anti-market, replaced deselected Key in Yorkshire South. He was Chair of the Highways Committee of South Yorkshire County Council but felt it was proper to resign and a by-election for the Council had to be held once he was elected.

In addition, John Bird, a moderate pro-European Black Country Council Leader, was elected in a by-election in 1987 after Terry Pitt died.

Once again a majority had local authority backgrounds, trades union or Co-operative sponsorships or both and were members of CND and the Anti-Apartheid Movement as were huge numbers of party members at the time. And again a good number had been candidates for the House of Commons and still wished for another opportunity to go there. The European Parliament was still not seen as a top career move. The difference in this intake was that several of those who formed the Campaign Group had strong working class roots and did not ever feel comfortable either socially or politically with their "soft left" and centre-right university educated middle-class comrades. It added to the tensions that lasted for over a decade. Some battles in the coming period were to be between the Tribunite left and the Campaign Group, rather than simply a left-right axis. At that time even the right-wingers were probably to the left of some of today's New Labourites.

This made the balance of opinion on the Common Market at the time of their election (though some were to change as time went on) as follows:

Pro-marketeers: Adam, Collins, Elliott, Griffiths, Hoon, McGowan, Newens, Tomlinson, Tongue and Quin. Of these the old guard were on the right of the party and some were committed members of the European Movement, and some but not many were also supporters of Solidarity or the Manifesto Group. In contrast, the new Members were much more of a mixed bag politically, mostly being on the left except for Hoon, Tomlinson and Stevenson. Many were Tribune and some even Campaign Group supporters and opposed to NATO. Newens and McGowan would describe themselves as pro-European internationalists rather than pro-marketeers, as would Hindley and Pitt. After Pitt died his replacement, John Bird, was a pragmatic right-winger and pro-market.

Anti-marketeers: Buchan, Crawley, Cryer, Falconer, Ford, Hindley, Huckfield, Hughes, Lomas, Martin, Megahy, Morris, Newman, Pitt, Seal, Smith, Stevenson, West and Stewart. About half of these were Campaign Group and the other half Tribune and they did not all see eye to eye. These differences were to sharpen as time went on. Many of these would also describe themselves as pro-Europe, but anti-market.

Pragmatic middle: Castle (though she would have hated to be labeled thus), Balfe, who managed simultaneously to support federalism and suggest that he was anti-market (about whom it was once said by a senior Labour figure that he was not political), McMahon (who became more in favour).

Soon, however, Martin and Hughes saw the benefits of positive engagement in the EEC and within a couple of years they and Ford, Morris, and Crawley shifted their position in line with the leadership support for the EEC. A feeling that the workers needed Europe began to surface. Even Newman and Stewart became more pragmatic as time wore on. Stevenson, on the contrary, says the more he discovered about how the system worked the more anti he became, though he was very much in favour of European co-operation. By the end of this electoral term the solid anti-market crew were again in a minority: Buchan, Cryer, Falconer, Huckfield, Lomas, Megahy, and Seal. Even this group was not cohesive, supporting as they did different factions of the left of the party.

And those who lost

There were quite a lot of characters who were to attain prominence at a later date.

Deselected Leeds MEP Derek Enright made a valiant attempt in strongly Conservative Kent East against Christopher Jackson, squeezing the Tory vote a little, invigorating the local parties and being proud of keeping the SDP-Liberal Alliance in third place.

Keith Vaz, to become MP for Leicester East 1987 and one of Labour's many Europe Ministers, came third in Surrey West against the Marquess of Douro.

Castle's assistant Anita Pollack lost an attempt to defeat Dame Shelagh Roberts in London South West but further reduced the majority. There was a last-minute boundary change in this seat, making it in principle less winnable for Labour than it had been at the time of her selection. The tide was swinging against the Conservatives in this seat and it was finally won in 1989.

Jan Royall, enthusiastic European and former BLG administrator soon to be working in Neil Kinnock's private office, valiantly campaigned often in isolation in her home patch of the Cotswolds, coming third against Sir Henry Plumb after the SDP-Liberal Alliance.

Mike Gapes, an official in Labour's International Department, and MP for Ilford South from 1992, had hoped to be selected in London East, but despite having the most nominations was trumped by Tongue's barnstorming pro-market speech at the selection meeting and was not a candidate.

David Blackman, Deputy General Secretary of the Socialist Group, a

Quaker and Co-op sponsored, fought Midlands Central and came second to Conservative John de Courcy Ling.

Peter Crampton, finally elected in 1989, battled unsuccessfully against Conservative Robert (Bob) Battersby in Humberside but massively reduced the majority.

Ken Coates, well-known peace activist and polemicist, also to be elected in 1989, fought Gallagher's old seat of Nottingham with a boundary change, where the Labour vote was split and Conservatives won. He had fought the parliamentary seat of Nottingham South in the 1983 general election.

Roger Liddle, standing for the SDP, lost Oxford and Buckinghamshire to Conservative James Elles (son of Baroness Elles). He was later an adviser to both Tony Blair and Labour Commissioner Peter Mandelson.

David Hallam, finally elected in 1994, lost to Christopher Prout in Shropshire.

Helen Jones in Lancashire Central pushed Gallagher for the SDP-Alliance into third place and became MP for Warrington North in 1997.

Douglas Herbison, nephew of former Labour MP Peggy Herbison, came fourth in Strathclyde West for the SDP.

Andrew MacKinlay was defeated by Pollack in a closely fought London South West selection and fought London South and Surrey East, coming second. After applying for numerous seats he became MP for Thurrock in 1992.

Sarah Ludford, later Baroness, came second for the SDP-Liberal Alliance to Conservative Richard Simmonds in Wight and Hampshire East. She gained a seat on the South East regional list in 1999.

Pat Healy, a left-wing specialist correspondent on *The Times*, fought London North West, failing to win it from Lord Bethell, but managing a large swing to Labour of 12.3%. This campaign was not without controversy. Pat, with joint Irish nationality, held a meeting in Brent (an area with a significant Irish community) with Sinn Fein on the platform with Ken Livingstone. Kinnock as Leader condemned the meeting, as Sinn Fein were standing against Labour's sister party, the SDLP, in Northern Ireland. At that time of the Troubles in Northern Ireland it was anathema to mainstream politics to give Sinn Fein any kind of platform. Healy said the campaign was like trying to kick-start a jumbo jet.

Roger Berry for Bristol became MP for Kingswood in 1992.

Frank Doran in North East Scotland became MP for Aberdeen North in 1987-92 and 1997.

David Hanson in Cheshire West became MP for Delyn in 1992 and was to become a Minister in the Blair government.

Tony McWalter in Hertfordshire was MP for Hemel Hempstead from 1997-2005.

Peter Soulsby came close in Leicester, was knighted in 1999 and became MP for Leicester South in 2005.

Gavin Rees, an economist in West Sussex, later worked for Pollack on her submission against Terminal 5 at London Heathrow.

Three other seats were lost with majorities less than 5,000: Paul Tinnion in Cleveland and Yorkshire North, Ernest Large in London North and Robin Stewart in Scotland South. For the Conservatives, Neil Balfour, formerly a Yorkshire MEP, lost out in the selection race and lost again in the Ryedale by-election in May 1986 when the Conservatives lost the seat to a Liberal and Labour's Shirley Haines came third. There were only two other Labour women candidates: Shirley Haines in York and Jane Linden in Somerset and Dorset West.

Europe's election

Over 40% of this 434-strong Parliament was completely new. In France, with the Socialists in government, there was a fall in the Socialist and Communist vote. Disturbingly, the National Front gained 11% of the vote, all but overtaking the Communist Party, with Le Pen and nine other fascists joining the Parliament where they formed the Group of the European Right with Members from Italy and one Greek. The fall-out led to a change of French Prime Minister from Pierre Mauroy to Laurent Fabius. In Belgium an anti-immigrant independent won a seat. These results provided Labour Members with fuel against proportional representation. In Germany the Greens (anti-EEC) took 8% of the vote and up to 14% in some cities, winning seven seats, joining with Dutch and Belgian Greens and anti-Europeans to form a new group, Arc en Ciel (Rainbow). The main parties in Germany lost seats, blamed on a low turn-out of 56.8%. Left-wing PASOK was down in Greece but still the winner, whilst Labour, in government in Ireland, lost four. In Italy the Communists won more votes than the Christian Democrats, perhaps with a sympathy vote since their popular leader, Enrico Berlinguer, died during the campaign. There was a slight swing to the left in Luxembourg. Labour was the winner in the Netherlands, where Cruise missiles were an issue. Conservatives did well in Denmark. Women were still only 16% of the Parliament.

The Socialist Group, slightly increased to 130 despite French losses, remained the largest, within which only the German SPD with thirty-three members was larger than Labour. This meant a shift in the balance of power, with the senior and pragmatic German Rudi Arndt defeating the more left-wing Ernest Glinne for the Presidency (the BLG supporting Glinne again). Castle and Arndt were both strong characters and went head to head fairly frequently in debates. Arndt was held in deep respect as someone whose father had been an enemy of the Hitler regime, whose aunt had been executed by the Nazis and who himself had been a courier for the Resistance.

The improved UK election results were the reason the Socialists remained the biggest group and it meant more parliamentary positions for the BLG. Castle was still senior Vice-President of the Socialist Group.

Some of the famous names such as Willy Brandt had moved on, but there were important new faces. Lionel Jospin later became Prime Minister of France; Paraskevas Avgerinos was a founder member of PASOK and had been a Greek Minister since 1981; Grigoris Varfis was a Secretary of State for Foreign Affairs (who had been a player in the unfortunate Greek Presidency where the British rebate had not been settled); Alain Bombard was a world famous French seafarer; Ove Fich from Denmark was a nuclear physicist and former Foreign Minister; Vincenzo Mattina was Secretary of the socialist Italian Labour Union (UIL); Jannis Sakellariou was Germany's only Turkish member; Heinz Oskar Vetter from Germany was President of the European Trade Union Confederation; Kurt Vittinghof was Secretary of the powerful IG-Metal trade union. Vera Squarcialupi, an Italian Communist, had been a member of the Italian Senate and became friendly with several of the Labour Members including Tongue.

Former heads of state or government in the Parliament were fewer than the time before and none were Socialists: Pierre Pflimlin from France, Leopoldo Calvo Sotelo from Spain, Maria de Lourdes Pintasilgo and Francisco Balsemao from Portugal. Only Pflimlin took up his place, the others disappearing before the proceedings began, having been simply figureheads on lists.

The Conservatives maintained their largely British EDG Group, with Sir Henry Plumb as Leader. Only one Conservative MEP retained a dual mandate – Sir Tom Normanton. They were preparing for future expansion of the Group after the accession of Spain and Portugal. Plumb had led a small delegation to Spain in the early part of 1984 to sound out members of the right-wing Alianza Popular. This was tactically difficult since the founder of that party, Manuel Fraga, had been a minister under Franco's dictatorship. Plumb was not deterred by this, and as he records in his book (Plumb, 2001) they simply agreed to put another controversial matter, Gibraltar "in the fridge". Stanley Johnson for the Conservatives had lost out in the boundary battles and returned to the European Commission's environment directorate.

A new start in team Labour

The BLG's AGM was held in London on 19 June. Many had to wind up jobs or had holiday commitments but thirty managed to be present, with apologies from Hughes and McGowan. Front-bench MPs Robin Cook, George Foulkes and Eric Heffer attended. Present also was Tony Robinson, a Northern Irishman who was by then the English-speaking Press Officer of the Socialist Group. A photo call was held with Neil Kinnock during the afternoon.

A left caucus had been held the night before organized by Buchan and others, agreeing to cast their votes openly and support Lomas for Deputy Leader. At the AGM Collins and Adam were furious at the disciplined left voting slate defeating the right at every vote. Castle was re-elected Leader to acclaim. For Deputy there was a contest between Lomas and Collins (the incumbent), repeating the contest of the year before. This time Lomas won 20 – 9. For the post of Chair, previously held by Caborn who was now an MP, the contest was between Megahy and Griffiths, with Megahy the victor on the same numbers. Megahy proved to be a popular Chair, with his dry wit and sense of fair play. Adam contested Buchan for Secretary (the previous incumbent Rogers also having become an MP) and lost by 21 – 8 with Elliott changing sides. Whip and Socialist Bureau member was Seal. There had been a successful motion put by Pitt to separate the posts of Secretary and Whip and it was agreed that the Whip should go on the Bureau. It had also been agreed to have a Treasurer and not a Press Officer (now that Tony Robinson was in place in the Socialist Group to be the conduit to press). Balfe became Treasurer unopposed. This line-up gave a largely anti-market set of officers to liaise with Kinnock's Labour Party at a time when he was in the process of taking a more positive line on the EEC. There was bound to be trouble ahead.

Lomas proposed a resolution in support of the National Union of Mineworkers and contributions were invited for the fighting fund.

Members paid £12 a week to that cause for the next year, some much more. Members were also paying into the fund to employ Royall as Secretary to the Group on a paper from Caborn. Falconer proposed a review of standing orders. The fairly bland press release issued after the meeting gave no indication of the debate that had been held about its wording. It had taken some time to agree that it was tactically unsuitable to include a commitment to withdrawal from the EEC.

Cryer set the scene for disputes to come in an article in *Tribune* on 27 July where he complained about that press release and the election campaign. He wrote at length about the lack of money for constituencies to do their own thing, the use of the wording "European Parliament" instead of "consultative assembly" on literature, and complained that regional officers did not see the wording of the election address until it was printed and delivered, having only 50 words per candidate and 150 words on policy to add from a local angle.

The left divided amongst itself from an early stage. A set were from a variety of sections of the harder left and Cryer organized them as the Campaign Group – Falconer, Cryer, Huckfield, Lomas, Stewart, Newman, and McGowan with Hindley as a central character. Llew Smith normally aligned himself with the Campaign Group but was apparently not a member. Some Members outside this group were suspicious of Hindley, because he had worked for some years in a university in East Germany. The Campaign Group was an interesting grouping, some of whom had Trotskyist backgrounds and others not. Falconer describes himself as a syndicalist and says he stood for election for the money – not for himself, but for the Labour movement and that he gave over £30,000 to the miners, using his salary and surplus travel and subsistence allowances as far as possible for the good of the party and trades union movement. McGowan claims to believe in "unity of the left", was never a Trot and was in favour of European co-operation but did not support the EU as an economic arm of NATO. He was the only one to be a member of both Tribune and Campaign groups. Hughes never joined the Campaign Group, although he was friends with individuals and frequently voted on their slate. Seal had had run-ins with Pat Wall of Militant in his Bradford constituency and was not considered one of them. Years later he said he was considered to be on the right in Bradford but on the left in Europe. Newman and Stewart were thought to be Militant supporters, though neither were Militant members and had ceased to support that organization some years before. Huckfield was often accused of being a Militant, but this also was not the case. He was militant and a tad anarchistic in his approach, certainly, but not a supporter of the Trotskyist Militant Tendency. Professor Michael Crick in his book, *Militant* (Crick, 1984) asserts that Huckfield had "a long history of vehement opposition to the tendency".

Ford became convenor of a Broad Left grouping and at that stage, in sharp contrast to his position a couple of years later, felt it was important to be tough on withdrawal. By 1987 he had moved from this point of view. Cryer demanded that everyone had to sign an anti-Common Market pledge. Newens would not join under this restriction and was not the only one for whom this was a step too far. Morris, McMahon and Hughes were also not prepared to sign up to this stricture.

Newens set up a Tribune Group numbering amongst its members Ford,

Crawley, Morris, Martin, Elliott, McGowan, McMahon and Seal. He had been a member of the Tribune Group in the House of Commons along with Janey Buchan's husband Norman and says he was considered somewhat of a renegade by the hard left, being in favour of Europe, particularly as a catalyst for peace. It was a sign of Labour's continuing internal divisions that some of its MEPs were happy to form themselves into three groups on the left, all with regular monthly meetings on top of all the other demands during busy Strasbourg weeks.

Rough landing

The first obstacle to a smooth landing for the enlarged BLG was that the Socialist Group organized its first meeting in Florence. It was in part a gesture to the General Secretary, Paolo Falcone and a tactical error from the British point of view, alienating some of the new anti-marketeers on two counts. First, new Members really needed to get acquainted with travel to Brussels and find their way around since once again many of them were financially stretched with little experience of foreign travel. Finding the cash for flights to Florence rather than Brussels put an even heavier strain on their limited cash flow, bearing in mind that this was before the days of cheap airlines and many of them had no credit cards with which to defer costs. Newman was not alone in being shocked to find that they were not MEPs from the date of the election results as is normally the case in the UK, but had to wait until the second week of official meetings, the middle of the July plenary session before their role formally began – with a salary not paid until the end of that month. Many had already taken unpaid leave from jobs for the election campaign and then had to resign, suffering a period with no income at all but lots of expenses in beginning to set up an office, travel to meetings and hire staff, not to mention keeping their families.

Second, in those days the Socialist Group tended to enjoy receptions in town halls and dinners in grand houses or palaces run by the left in Europe during such meetings. This went down very badly with Labour's more austere contingent, some of whom believed that MEPs should only take "a worker's wage". It was seen as indicative of EEC elitism and not for the working class. Mauro Guillambardo, another Italian, who some of the British mistrusted, was General Secretary of the Confed at that time and the feeling was that the continentals did not understand the pressures of the British tabloid media about gravy train stories. There was bad blood from the outset, and not a few lost tempers (not least that of Newman whose luggage failed to materialise). Hoon, Huckfield and Cryer did not attend.

It astonished the Socialist comrades that Labour Members cast their votes in the Group for posts both there and in the Parliament, openly in front of each other. This Stalinist manoeuvre, agreed in the left caucus meeting before the Labour AGM, was seen as a demonstration of lack of trust and in the fullness of time fell into disuse.

Many new MEPs saw the Socialist Group as another platform for resolutions, a favourite pastime of the hard left in Council and constituency politics of the last decade at home. Stewart, a veteran left-wing Liverpudlian and war-time paratrooper, found it difficult to accept that in order to table a resolution he had to speak to a German staff member. "The last time I saw a German it was at the point of a gun", he complained, bursting in the door of a Labour Group meeting, to be received with stunned silence. The administrator in charge of resolutions was Gisela Neumann, a close friend of Tongue and Pollack. Diplomacy was not a feature of the new intake and it set a rather uncomfortable tone.

This was soon compounded by another incident. In the UK there was an on-going struggle against Councillors who were members of the Masonic League and sometimes seen to be corrupt, particularly following a case in the north east of England. Much effort from the left was going into shaming masons out of public life. There had also been some problems in the Parliament concerning an official (appropriately named Monsieur le Compte) dealing with Members' cash payments and freemasons had rallied round to save him temporarily from being fired. One of the new Members, who most remember as being Ford, but some think was Huckfield, put down a resolution in the Socialist Group demanding masons be identified. It was based on a resolution Ford had successfully tabled in Tameside Council with the effect of excluding masons from committees. This caused absolute uproar. The British had no idea that in the war, freemasons in Europe had been active in the Resistance, saving socialists and trade unionists from the Nazis, and the continental left held an entirely different perception of this organization.

A Belgian Jewish Member, Marijke van Hemeldonck, had herself been saved in this way and she launched an immediate attack. A furious row ensued and the Brits had to retreat. Some attempted to take their names off the resolution, but Huckfield saw it as maintaining a consistent position, so he and Falconer kept their names on it and attempted to recruit more signatories. Newman, while Jewish, did not withdraw, resolutely keeping in mind the British left's attitude to the masons. Ford took his name off the resolution but still believes that secret societies in a democracy are not justified. It took some time to smooth the ruffled feathers (Griffiths' moderate reputation and efforts helped here) and indeed some people were never forgiven. Henri Saby, leader of the French delegation, was incensed, saying the behaviour of the British Group was a disgrace. He was charged with chairing an emergency meeting to resolve the matter. The British insensitivity and ignorance was even more problematic because at that time there were pre-accession negotiations being undertaken by the Socialist Group leaders with the Spanish and Portuguese parties where both party leaders were said to be masons and had spent part of their exile time in France. The British comrades did not know their history and were chastened by this experience.

A new parliament begins

At the July inaugural plenary of the Parliament in Strasbourg, 77 year-old French Christian Democrat Pierre Pflimlin, a former Prime Minister of France was elected President. He was also a former long-time Mayor of Strasbourg, putting paid to hopes of reducing parliamentary sessions in that town during his tenure. Indeed he began work on the building extensions in Strasbourg so that Members would have their own offices. He won against Socialist Dankert (who had attempted to buck the prevailing system of alternating right and left for the Presidencies) on a second ballot with the support of the (still largely British) EDG, but also, controversially, with the votes of the French National Front. This scandalized the Socialists, who, together with much of the rest of the left, wore white roses as a protest against fascism. Castle raised a point of order specifically asking Pflimin if he accepted the endorsement of Le Pen, to which he had no straight answer. The Conservatives had done a behind-the-scenes deal with the Christian Democrats (EPP) to give them their support in return for the latter to support an EDG President the next time around. Plumb, in his book *The Plumb Line* (Plumb, 2001) wrote that this was a written assurance from Egon Klepsch, the EPP leader.

The way the d'Hondt system worked for elections to committee posts reminded one of the new Labour MEPs of local government, with everything fixed before entering the Chamber. Griffiths became a popular Labour Vice-President of Parliament and held that post until the half-way point at the end of 1986. Seal became Chair of the influential Economic and Monetary Committee, Adam earned his spot as Vice-Chair of Energy and Research, Crawley became Vice-Chair of Women's Rights, Martin Vice-Chair of Budgetary Control, Hindley Vice-Chair of REX, Hoon Vice-Chair of Credentials, Huckfield Vice-Chair of Transport and Tourism, Newman Vice-Chair of Regional Affairs and Simpson Vice-Chair for the Yugoslavia delegation, a post he was to keep until 1999. Castle became Vice-Chair of the Malta delegation from February 1985 at the same time as Lomas became Vice-Chair of Central America, Newens Vice-Chair for the Gulf States, Stevenson for SAARC, Tomlinson Chair for the Nordic Council, Quin Vice-Chair of Australia and New Zealand and Hindley Vice-Chair for Eastern Europe. To his annoyance, Collins lost his bid for Chair of Environment, the BLG having changed its priorities.

The main debate in July, with Ireland in the Presidency, was on the Fontainebleau Summit held in June, offering a solution at last to the long-running dispute on the British rebate. Castle deplored the failure to launch a co-ordinated programme of economic recovery, saying Thatcher had come away with half a loaf, agreeing to increase the Community's own resources before any long-term budgetary solution had been agreed. Thatcher had won a 66% rebate but Castle said the UK government was having to provide the money to pay its own rebate back to itself. Whilst trying to sound conciliatory to the Socialist Group, the BLG nevertheless did not accept the Socialist Group motion on the Summit. Conservative Michael Welsh could not resist pointing out that none of her BLG colleagues were in the Chamber to listen to her impassioned speech.

The first the Parliament heard of Les Huckfield was when Ford raised a point of order at the end of the July plenary week pointing out that Huckfield had been arrested and charged with obstruction of the highway on a demonstration in support of the striking miners in the UK, and seeking to claim parliamentary immunity. It was decreed that this was not in pursuance of his parliamentary duties and immunity was ruled out.

Once the MEPs found their way to Brussels and Strasbourg they discovered they had offices in both places, with chauffeur-driven cars to bring them from their airports and hotels to work. In Brussels many of the offices were shared as the parliamentary buildings were only just beginning to expand and be refurbished. In Strasbourg they were mostly shared spaces in the Council of Europe building, unaccustomed luxury for our Members.

They were able to set up staffed offices in their constituencies to assist with election campaigning for Labour. Some combined with MPs, who were happy to see the money put to use to their benefit. Falconer speaks of sharing an office with Gordon Brown. Before too long the parliamentary allowances for staff were substantially increased (creating some jealousy from MPs). It was not until after the Single European Act that committee work became more important as the powers of the Parliament grew and not until the next Parliament that it became common for the Labour Members also to employ specialist staff in Brussels to assist them with this work.

Disruption time

By the end of the Strasbourg session in September, ten of the new BLG Members had managed a few words in the plenary. Their presence was to be felt with great frequency for the next five years, not least in prolific tabling of questions on an enormous range of subjects and intervening as additional speakers on questions tabled by others. Two new Labour Members featured most noisily in this period, Huckfield and Cryer. With their House of Commons experience they were masters of points of order and almost no session was to pass without interventions from them. In addition to the miners' strike in the UK the dockers were also on strike, and right-left tensions were high.

Cryer complained about proportional representation, objecting to accept-ance of the French National Front Members. There was the first of what was to be many demonstrations outside, this one featuring Chilean protestors about the murder of President Allende eleven years earlier. Cryer and Huckfield supported the demonstrators and Smith spoke on human rights in Chile. Cryer enquired how much of the EEC's information budget was spent on explaining the CAP; Morris complained that some parts of his con-stituency were being robbed of development area status by the British gov-ernment. Pitt battered away on agriculture and the budget and as a strong opponent of PR, made disparaging points about other Members being elec-ted on lists. Huckfield argued points of procedure, saying that as one of his colleagues had had a constituent killed the previous night as a result of the miners' dispute there should be an urgent resolution. Balfe was continuing a campaign from the previous year against the use of plastic bullets in Northern Ireland, now joined by Irish Christine Crawley. Tomlinson put down a question on youth unemployment and Hughes asked for the Commissioners to visit the North of England. Right from the outset he was beginning to realize there was some use for this organization. Cryer made another attempt to make some points concerning the British rebate.

On Wednesday 10 October, almost at the start of the session, Huckfield rose on a point of order, cutting across speakers on the UK rebate; he said the miners' dispute was now seven months long, with five people dead and that he had tried unsuccessfully to raise it under three different rules of procedure. Smith and West unfurled a large banner bearing the inscription "Blaenau Gwent National Union of Mineworkers" at the back of the hemicycle. Castle was amongst some of the BLG on their feet and clapping. Amidst complaints from Conservatives (Curry insisting that this was the face of left-wing totali-tarianism) the sitting was suspended in uproar after Otto Habsburg grabbed the banner and tried to pull it down, tussling with Huckfield. The British press pounced on it. *The Times* on the 11th wrote of a "British MEPs' demonstration taking over the floor of the House in Strasbourg." It reported on Huckfield "leaping through gaps in the rules to introduce the miners' strike to the debate", saying "the French benches groaned as he carried on to Socialist cheers". (The £475 million British rebate was agreed.)

Two weeks later, on 24 October, Huckfield was in action again. He had tabled a Socialist Group resolution on the miners' strike for the "urgencies" debate and it had not been selected for the agenda. He and Ford complained about this and when Huckfield's microphone was cut off, he whipped out a battery-powered megaphone and began shouting. Once again the sitting was suspended amidst bedlam and vigorous applause from parts of the left including Ford and Morris. Later in the day Castle managed to win a fairly divided vote in favour of scheduling a debate on the miners the next day. She was furious about the appalling behaviour of her fellow Labour MEP, but felt obliged as Leader to try and make some kind of effort. The main areas of support came from the Greens and the Communists. *The Times* on the 25th wrote: "British pit violence moves to Strasbourg". With a photo of Huckfield and the megaphone, the story led off: "The violence of the British miners' strike erupted in the staid chamber of the European Parliament yesterday, with Labour and Conservative MEPs being dragged physically apart...."

The next day Cryer was involved in a demonstration on nuclear expenditure and Trident. Huckfield spoke in the debate on the miners, saying it was the most important industrial struggle that we shall witness in the whole of our lifetime, that there was much suffering and the Conservative government was using the apparatus of the state to smash the NUM. West made his first speech, describing himself as "a striking miner", saying it was the longest strike of its kind in the history of British trade unionism, that the right to free association had been taken away and using the slogan from demonstrations, that "the miners of Britain united will never be defeated". He welcomed a delegation of miners' wives in the visitors' gallery. Plumb for the Conservatives was quick to demand a national ballot on the strike, pointing out that 70% of the miners in Nottingham had voted against the strike, leading to an attack from Buchan that he was a wealthy English landowner. Conservatives tabled a bunch of amendments to the BLG motion and despite support from Socialists and Communists, it was rejected in a roll call vote by 150 – 115 with 5 abstentions. Of the Labour Members, Collins was present that day but did not take part in the vote. Griffiths as a Vice-President was in the Chair. The Tories of course voted against the motion. Later in the day West interrupted debates to say that the British courts had ordered the sequestration of the funds of the NUM at which news the EDG applauded. Class war was being fought out on the floor of the Strasbourg Parliament at the same time as on the picket lines in the UK.

There were numerous points of order and protests from Huckfield and Cryer during the November session, but no further outbursts necessitating a suspension of proceedings. There was, however, a heated public argument between Thomas von der Vring, a Socialist Budget Committee member, Newens and Cryer.

December being the season of goodwill, the BLG set up a collection for the striking miners' children outside the hemicycle. There was by now serious hardship in the coalfields communities and the Labour movement every-where was fundraising. They erected a Christmas tree, and Falconer, Smith and others were energetically shaking collection buckets asking for funds from all-comers in the lobby area. Nothing like this had ever taken place before in the staid halls of the Conseil de l'Europe. Conservative Paul Howell began shouting aggressively and tried to pull down the Christmas tree and a fracas ensued between him and Smith, necessitating the inter-vention of others to calm down the protagonists. There were complaints from the right that the collection was a demonstration (some of the EDG called it a circus) and as such not permitted, and it was referred to the Quaestors (the parliamentary management committee), but the collections continued throughout the day, raising substantial funds for the cause.

La lutte continue

January 1985 saw a changeover of Commissioners. The UK's Ivor Richard departed, being replaced by Stanley Clinton Davis for Labour (himself for-merly an anti-marketeer but who had become more pragmatic over time); he became popular with the BLG but was in turn replaced by the Conservative government in 1988. Also new was Lord Cockfield, seen as a rather sourpuss mathematician with a scrupulous eye for detail and with a mission to create the Single Market, replacing Christopher Tugendhat for the Conservatives. Seal protested on 18 October about Cockfield, saying that the Treaty required Commissioners to be of proven independence but that he took the Conservative Whip in the Lords.

Carlo Ripa di Meana, a former Italian Socialist MEP, was now Commis-sioner for environment and another former Italian Socialist MEP, Gianni di Michelis, was President of the Council. Jacques Delors, who as an MEP had been chair of the Economic and Monetary Affairs Committee (EMAC), began his influential ten-year term as President of the Commission. Parliament had blocked the budget again and provisional twelfths were once more in oper-ation with the usual problems of spending restrictions that came with this system.

Labour Members were active sponsors of resolutions under the regular "Urgencies" section of the agenda. Proud of being internationalists, rarely did a session pass without Labour speakers on foreign affairs, human rights and development policies. Such matters were often raised by party mem-bers back home at constituency meetings, so it was a useful way to be able to demonstrate some kind of action in Parliament. Newens was a regular speaker on international affairs in this slot. Question Times were utilized as opportunities to press the Commission or Council about matters on which they were being secretive, attempts to embarrass the government at home, or raise constituency issues. They would attempt to catch the eye of the Chair for supplementary questions if one of their own was not called. Any attempts to curtail the length of time allocated to this agenda item were always vociferously opposed.

Cryer complained endlessly about the word "Europe" being used instead of "Common Market". He also insisted on using the term "consultative assem-bly" for the Parliament and styled himself on his personal letterhead, not as MEP, but as "Labour Party Representative in the Common Market Assembly".

Collins was to work with Environment and Transport Commissioner Clinton Davis on many environment matters between now and 1989. One such was a framework directive on emissions from industrial plants using a principle called BATNEEC – Best Available Technology Not Entailing Excessive Cost – which had been agreed. It was, however, not greeted with enthusiasm, particularly by the Conservative government, leading Clinton Davis to warn that it had been replaced by another acronym, invented by Jim Murphy, CATNIP – the Cheapest Available Technology Not Involving Prosecution.

Huckfield continued his demands for a Committee of Inquiry into police behaviour in the UK during the miners' strike. It was being quietly resisted by officialdom, being considered a national issue. Thatcher and others had protested in the House of Commons about the European Parliament's potential interference in the policing of the miners' strike. Huckfield had obtained the required number of signatures on a formal request for such a committee, and on 11 February 1985 the Bureau said this could consist of one Member per political group. Another Committee of Inquiry into drugs was also agreed. Huckfield had a spat with short-fused Conservative Howell in March, describing him as an "agricultural oaf", which led to a confrontation outside the Chamber. It is unclear precisely what triggered this little upset apart from the fact that they were both fairly belligerent characters and the history Howell had of publicly attacking Labour's left-wingers.

By March 1985, Cryer had settled in to what would become an on-going campaign about food aid, largely for hungry parts of Africa such as Ethiopia, wanting EEC food mountains to be shipped off there. He pursued this month in and month out under the *Suite donnée* procedure (the report on Commission's actions each month) until Commissioners must have dreaded appearing in the plenary altogether. His other area of concern was with border controls, maintaining that any loosening of restrictions would increase drug trafficking and the spread of rabies. He was militantly vigilant, too, about any reduction of Question Time due to agenda pressures. In December that year he made an interesting point in a debate on the Luxembourg Summit. Whereas most were critical of the meagre results, Cryer pointed out to Parliament that while they might disagree with the Council, those Ministers were democratically elected representatives accountable to their national parliaments.

There were numerous other interventions from the comrades about events or media coverage in the UK. In April, Falconer raised a point of order regarding that day's *Glasgow Herald* report that twelve members of the European Parliament's security staff were allegedly being trained by special police in France to deal with "possible unruly British members".

President Reagan of the United States visited the Parliament in May 1985, to substantial opposition from the left. Balfe was one of the first to complain in the months before the visit about plans to restrict access to the public gallery, and that the President's bodyguards would be carrying weapons. He followed this up again in May saying that Reagan was not a welcome visitor and that his speech should not become part of the minutes of proceedings. Falconer and Huckfield added their complaints about the armed guards. When Reagan spoke on Wednesday 8 May, an assortment of banners was displayed by the left ("nuclear freeze now", "Star Wars No"). At

the point when he attacked Nicaragua for being communist, he was subjected to barracking from the left and cries of "Nicaragua, Nicaragua".
Socialists including BLG Members held up "Hands off Nicaragua" posters.
(The US was at that time giving military support to "contra" guerrillas
opposed to the leftist Nicaraguan government and BLG Members had
tabled numerous questions on the subject in previous months.) The BLG
joined much of the left in staging a walk out. Crawley had earlier had a fall
and was limping, needing to be helped up by Cryer. Reagan managed a
fairly humorous response to the heckling and received a standing ovation
from the right and centre. The Socialists' resolution on the event was lost by
three votes. The same day had also seen a formal sitting to commemorate
the 40th anniversary of the end of World War Two.

Huckfield continued to pursue his call for a Committee of Inquiry, with
support from Lomas, Castle, Arndt and others, but it was stonewalled by
the right-wing political groups. Instead of simply arguing that it was not a
European issue, this slippery approach from the establishment enraged
Huckfield, Smith and West but relieved some others. By this time the strike
itself had become a source of embarrassment for some Labour MEPs,
although their sympathy for the plight of miners and their families was
undiminished. There was a strong feeling that Scargill had made a major
tactical error by not taking a national ballot of NUM members on the strike.
In the face of the heavy-handed and often brutal crack-downs on picketers
by government and police, and the use of scab labour in the mines, however,
Members did not feel able to attack the NUM, with its huge support
amongst party members. Indeed much of the Labour movement including
the MEPs was still raising money to alleviate hardship in decimated mining
communities.

A separate occasion for a bad-tempered contretemps was when Lomas discovered that posters advertising a French National Front meeting had been
put up on the walls of a room in which the Socialist Group were meeting.
Lomas rushed about the place taking down the posters and was punched by
one of the French Members. Although slight in stature, Lomas was no weak-
ling and had been an amateur boxer at one time. He retaliated enthusiastically, having to be dragged off by John Hume.

Before too long both Lomas and Seal bought apartments in Brussels,
admitting to colleagues the inevitability of continued membership of the
EEC for Britain, whilst still campaigning for withdrawal.

In July 1985 Parliament held what was to be its last plenary session in
Luxembourg. In a midnight debate on the Thursday of that session Crawley
spoke for Castle (who had returned home) on animal welfare, supporting
what was to be another very long campaign to stop the export of live calves.
The slogan "on the hook, not on the hoof" was born. Animal welfare did not
top the list of official Labour election priorities, but it was strongly supported
by the BLG and a priority with many of their constituents and marginal
voters. Most at one time or another raised a question on this wide-ranging
topic.

A Committee of Inquiry into the Drugs Problem was set up in 1985 and
ran until October 1986. Tongue was a member, writing a minority report
supporting the Dutch "harm reduction" approach, with Heinke Salisch and
Hedy d'Ancona, both Socialist Group MEPs. The final debate exposed

strong differences in opinion across the political spectrum. There was little Labour support for the minority view which was strongly opposed by Newman, who backed the "war on drugs" approach. There was unsurprisingly interest in the subject in various Member States, and out of it came a legal base in the Maastricht Treaty on co-operation in this field.

The Anglo-Irish Agreement was signed in November 1985 and the Ulster Unionists were so totally opposed that they resigned from the House of Commons. Mary Robinson, a future Irish President, also resigned from the Irish Labour Party, saying it would not achieve peace and stability because it was unacceptable to the Unionists. Labour, Conservatives and SDLP at home voted for the agreement but some in the Labour Party, led by Benn, opposed it on the grounds that Britain should withdraw from Northern Ireland. In Strasbourg Paisley attacked Hume saying that he was caught up in arms charges. The BLG, supporting Hume, were in favour of the Agreement.

Labour continued to vote to reject budgets. The 1985 draft budget had been rejected by Parliament because it only made available ten months funding for agriculture. The next budget did not include sufficient funds to cope with the accession of Spain and Portugal, and was sent to the European Court. In November Tomlinson, who worked tirelessly in committee, observed:

> "Parliament has an obsessive preoccupation with its demands for more powers... Gutless reaction to gross provocation by the Council and it shows an inability to use its existing powers effectively. 70% of the budget is still spent on wasteful agriculture policy".

Castle complained of rejection of an amendment she had tabled against export refunds that took up over one third of all agriculture spending. "It will spend 50% more in 1986 on export refunds for cereals than it did in 85... it is an inadequate and cowardly budget." Cryer observed that Bob Geldof had come and talked to us about food mountains and received a gold medal, but 2.4 billion ECU would be spent on just storing it; he demanded again that we "get the UK out of the Common Market".

In the farm price debate Collins for the Environment Committee continued his campaign to cut tobacco subsidies. Castle as usual was vitriolic, pointing out that a co-responsibility levy was an inefficient substitute for a price reduction and that the Provan (Conservative) report was shameful, accusing the Agriculture Committee of "bigoted obduracy" and the Commission of using co-responsibility levy money to promote butter sales "when our doctors are urging us to eat less of it." Once again she went down fighting. Reform was still some way ahead.

Mikhail Gorbachev came to power in the Soviet Union in March 1985 and the Cold War started to melt. He had visited London in December 1984 at which time he described Europe as "our common home" and visited France in October 1985. Thatcher had said that she liked him and they could do business together. The Socialist Group was supportive of the change in Soviet politics and sent a delegation including Castle to Moscow. On their return Arndt persuaded other groups of the need for parliamentary exchanges with the Soviet Union (which officially recognized the EEC in 1988).

Geoff Hoon was active on two fronts during 1985 in his Legal Affairs Committee work. He began to become quite vigilant on subsidiarity. He also proposed that the vote be extended to residents from other European countries, a change that was made following the Maastricht Treaty.

Labour continued to hold collections at Christmas, and in December 1985 collected for Oxfam, to the derision of Conservatives, particularly Howell. He made an astonishing attack about this

> "demonstration outside this Chamber which was banned by the Bureau in which the Labour Party once again sought to raise funds by rattling tins... the collection was entirely under false pretences in that they had not approached the charity organization and asked its permission... the monies that have been collected are not destined for Oxfam...[interruptions]. As I understand it there is going to be no correct audit of the monies and none of that money will see its way to Oxfam..."

Falconer defended the collection and explained a connection to Oxfam. Outside the hemicycle there was a punch-up between Howell, Smith and Huckfield that Seal had to calm down. It made the press the next day as "MEPs vote with their fists". On Thursday 12th Cryer criticized Howell, saying the Labour collection for Oxfam was under the title "moving mountains to get rid of the food mountains", that Howell received CAP money as a wealthy farmer, had intervention stores and a direct financial interest and should have declared it. Lady Elles, in the chair, promptly deplored Cryer for attacking Howell without giving him prior notice, saying that was unconstitutional and discourteous. Lomas demanded that Howell withdraw his statement, which he did in a grudging fashion. The affair was a potent demonstration of the mistrust the right had of the Labour Members even when trying to do a bit of seasonal good.

Castle toppled

Without Caborn and Boyes to mind her back Castle found herself in trouble as Leader. She continued to be rather a loner, not making huge efforts to endear herself to the enlarged BLG and suddenly she was under attack. She intimated that she might step down as Leader, but in the end decided she wanted to give it another year on the grounds of her involvement in reforming both the CAP and organization of the Socialist Group. Tomlinson said she had thought she could rely on the votes of the Manifesto Group, but it was not enough. That in itself indicated how skewed the politics of the BLG had become, since Castle was still seen as a heroine of the left at home. The Campaign Group had been tactically astute. Things started to go wrong at a meeting before Christmas when Tomlinson had agreed with Newens on some issue making Castle furious. That evening when she saw him she swore violently at him, but calmed down the next day, saying "I only insult people whose opinions I value".

The left were keen to make their mark and so in a very bad tempered AGM on 11 June 1985 in Strasbourg, Castle was thrown out. The voting for Leader was Castle 14, Lomas 18. The *Daily Mirror* wrote it up in its editorial on 13 June as "Big Castle, little man".

> "It is sad when a glittering career ends. Sadder still when a celebrity is replaced by a nonentity. Mrs Barbara Castle, the most formidable woman

the Labour Party ever produced, has just been beaten for the leadership of the Labour group in the European Parliament. True, she is 74 and would have stood down next year. True, she has had a splendid innings since she burst into politics red-headed and radical, 40 years ago. But she deserved better than defeat by Mr Alf Lomas. Mr Lomas is one of the hard-line London Left, which says buckets about him. Immediately after his victory, he depressingly declared: 'As a committed anti-marketeer, I shall continue to campaign for Britain's withdrawal.' Like others in his Labour group, Mr Lomas hasn't noticed events have passed him by. Britain is not going to withdraw from Europe. Labour is not going to withdraw from Europe. Labour is not going to fight the next election by campaigning to withdraw from Europe. Mr Lomas and his followers are outcasts in the real world of politics, cut off from reality and not knowing Napoleon is dead. Mrs Castle herself was once a fervent anti-marketeer. But she knew that times had changed. Even while she led them, Labour's Euro-group counted for little. Without her, they will count for less."

Lomas says the editorial was written by Robert Maxwell, who had been a buddy of the Castles.

The Scotsman on 21 June headlined the event as "Victory for Labour's anti-marketeers marks new threat to Kinnock". The *Yorkshire Post* the next day quoted Foreign Secretary Sir Geoffrey Howe as saying "Mr Alf Lomas, who recently ousted Mrs Barbara Castle for the job, made the Militant Tendency look like rabid anti-Communists."

Castle was shocked at her defeat as she had not seen it coming, but Lomas recalls she got up, walked around the table and shook hands with him in a dignified manner before leaving the meeting. Back in her office she was both angry and not far from tears that they had done her down. Lomas immediately put out an anti-market press release couched as supporting Labour Party policy against that of the Socialist Group, making Tomlinson livid. Lomas was surprised at the anger, since he felt he was supporting official party policy.

All BLG voting was recorded at the time, and those for Castle were: Adam, Castle, Collins, Crawley, Griffiths, Hoon, McMahon, Morris, Newens, Smith, Stevenson, Tomlinson, Tongue and Quin. Those for Lomas were: Balfe, Buchan, Cryer, Elliott, Falconer, Ford, Hindley, Huckfield, Hughes, Lomas, Martin, McGowan, Megahy, Newman, Pitt, Seal, Stewart and West. Smith was the odd one out for Castle and Martin was a surprise vote against.

Stan Newens had moved Castle for Leader. She had told him she just wanted one more year and then would step down, and he accepted that but says Ford wanted her out of the way, pushing Lomas to stand. Ford says he initially approached Newens to stand against her, recalling that in her selection conference for 1979 she had said she would only stay for one term and believing that the Leader's role needed to be passed over to someone new. Castle had stuck her neck out in plenary supporting the more disruptive elements of her team on issues such as the miners' strike but that clearly held no water. Lomas maintains he only reluctantly stood against her, and continues to admire her for her passion, charisma and hard work. The post of Leader had been discussed in the pre-AGM meeting of the Broad Left where the feeling was that she had sold out on her previous position as an anti-marketeer. More feeble criticisms were that she did not stay in the Group meetings for the full time and Lomas said she did not consult him on anything as Deputy Leader. They complained that she never went to the Members' bar to be convivial, only the press bar.

Lomas says there was a debate in the Broad Left as to what to do and he voted against opposing her but the majority said she had to go. Then they decided that he should be the one to stand against her, so he says he went with the flow. Yet more than twenty years later he said that she was an outstanding politician and head and shoulders above the rest. Elliott said he felt no rancour to Castle but thought it was time to bring in someone else as she had been Leader since 1979. Although Lomas would not have been his first choice, he had known him for many years being a Londoner, and was the only alternative put forward. Martin likewise felt it was time for change and had found Lomas friendly when they were on the Latin American delegation together. His change of heart on Europe was in embryonic form at this stage, but fast developing. There appears to have been little or no concern that Castle was the only MEP the British public had heard of. They had shot down their only star, Labour's Red Queen.

Many years later McGowan proffered the understatement that "we probably under-rated Barbara". Seal now testifies to her impressive performances and says that in his opinion none of the big guns in the Socialist Group were a patch on her (including Mitterrand, Brandt etc). He was impressed with her ability to analyse events and facts quickly and get a grip on strategy. He recalls her professionalism and propensity to be swearing and cursing right up to the last second before a TV show and then instantly turn on the charm for the cameras. However this touch of regret did not stop him voting for change at the time.

At that AGM there was a clean sweep for the Broad Left slate except for Chair, where West was beaten by Newens. Buchan and Elliott changed sides and supported Newens. The new officers were: Lomas as Leader, Newens as Chair, Megahy as Deputy Leader, Buchan as Secretary (defeating Hindley by 24 – 7), Balfe as Treasurer, McGowan as Whip. There was then a problem with the two places for Socialist Group Bureau. Lomas proposed Castle and Seal, but this was not possible, as one place was earmarked for the Leader. It was eventually agreed that Castle should keep her place until the end of the year because she was working on reorganizing the Group and Seal withdrew. It was also agreed to elect an Executive to consist of the officers plus three lay members. This took two ballots before finally electing Seal, Martin and Hindley. Tongue lost an attempt for elections to be taken by secret ballot by 25 – 5 and a resolution was carried 21 – 9 to the effect that "No statement should be made by any Members of the BLG to the press about voting records of individual members".

The Socialists were horrified at the ousting of Castle by anti-market Lomas and the latter said that it was several months before they could bring themselves to move his name plate in the plenary down to the front (Leaders') row of seating. A Group press release from Leader Arndt was sternly critical:

> "Alf Lomas has overlooked that Labour Members... are members of the Socialist Group and not an independent group in the European Parliament.

> Lomas is wrong in his view that Labour Euro MPs are not bound by the
> common electoral manifesto of the European socialist parties. The Labour
> Party agreed upon this manifesto with the exception of only two points –
> institutional questions and the EMS. The Labour Members are therefore
> bound by the unanimous vote on the manifesto of Socialist Parties of 1984."

The wind went out of Barbara Castle's sails somewhat after she lost the
Leadership, but nothing could keep her down permanently. In *Labour
Weekly* on 14 June 1985 she wrote defiantly: "I shall welcome the lightening
of my load of work. I had already indicated to the group that I only wanted
to serve another 12 months in order to complete the restructuring of the
European Parliament's Socialist Group secretariat..." She held on to a
smaller office in the Queen Anne's Gate building in London simply by force
of personality until the summer of the following year.

In November Castle was still valiantly tabling amendments to reduce
spending on agricultural export refunds and direct income aids. She liked to
take a walk out of the Strasbourg building at lunch time to a small family
run restaurant for a salad and some fresh air and withdrew from socializing
so much with the BLG in the evenings. She continued her German lessons
with Gudrun Stahlschmidt, worked on her memoirs and became more
involved in animal welfare campaigning. Her main concerns were the fur
leghold trap and transport of live animals for slaughter, problems that
carried on for more than the next decade. In December 1986 she was grateful for a directive on animal experiments from Commissioner Clinton Davis,
the beginning of setting up a European Centre for Alternatives to Animal
Testing, followed to fruition by her assistant Pollack in the next Parliament.
In July 1988, together with the Eurogroup for Animal Welfare run then by
Seymour-Rouse, she mounted an exhibition in the Parliament, "Animal
Matters", about the fur trade, attended by the Prince Aga Khan (a strong
supporter of animal welfare) and opened by Clinton Davis of the Commis-
sion and President Plumb. This infuriated the Conservatives.

Castle also took the time to respond to an invitation to visit from former
colleague Derek Enright and his wife Jane. Despite their differences of
policy on the EEC, they had become firm friends and so she took herself off
to Guinea Bissau, where Enright had secured a post as European
Commission Delegate (akin to an Ambassadorship), and had an enjoyable
and interesting, if short sojourn.

Troubled times

A dispute arose when in October Tomlinson accepted a nomination for
Chief Whip of the Socialist Group. The BLG had decided not to nominate for
any post in the Group but some colleagues from other countries asked
Tomlinson to accept their nomination. He consulted the BLG and when they
opposed it he pointed out that he was not acting against their decision, since
that only precluded their own group making nominations. He was duly elected, feeling that the BLG decision was symptomatic of its self-imposed isolation and that members of the Socialist Group were trying to engage the
Labour Members, which should be welcomed. Following his election the BLG
engaged in a long drawn-out attempt to expel him. Voting was 15 – 15 with

two abstentions (himself and Crawley). Eventually a decision was taken instead simply to write to his Euro GC. That body supported him and the matter "ran into the sands".

The crisis in the UK coal industry was always on the minds of the BLG, many of whom came from coal mining areas. They financed an academic study into "Clean Coal" and commissioned some academics to prepare a report. Environmentalists in the Parliament were arguing against burning fossil fuels, but the BLG were still struggling against the closure of coal mines and consequent devastation of coalmining communities. They advanced an argument that there was a future for coal, and used this report as ammunition. The huge (465 page) report was entitled "The Defence of Coal – a Critical response to the EEC coal directorate's close-and-import plan as laid out in COM (85) 251 and COM (85 525)", by George Kereva of Edinburgh University, Richard Saville of St Andrews and Debra Percival of the Socialist Group. Its main point was that we needed domestic productive capacity kept intact. The BLG held a conference on coal to put this case and also raise concerns over imports of cheap coal from South Africa.

In 1986 the BLG produced a small pamphlet with its Information money for circulation in the Labour movement. Entitled "Actions of Solidarity During the Miners' Strike", it had a foreword by Arthur Scargill and Peter Heathfield. The BLG Treasurer had compiled a list of all the monies raised in support of the miners, including production of the Coal Report. It came to a grand total of £71,920.12.

The BLG's AGM on 10 June 1986 was again a bitter affair. By now its meetings had become a kind of grisly spectator sport for the British staff in the Socialist Group, and most of them attended as visitors. Many of the posts were still contested, but the Broad Left held sway again. Newens recalls that there was a move, only just defeated, to stop Westminster candidates becoming officers. It is not clear who was seeking to stave off whom with this proposal. Cryer, Griffiths and Quin were to go to Westminster in 1987. Perhaps it was an attempt to knock the inoffensive Griffiths out of his post as Vice-President of the Parliament. In any case he gave that up at the beginning of 1987.

Lomas, Megahy, Buchan and Newens were unopposed as Leader, Deputy, Secretary and Chair respectively, with conspicuous abstentions from the minority group. An attempt made by Pitt to oust Balfe as Treasurer was soundly defeated by 21 – 8 (Ford abstaining). McGowan beat off an attempt by Stevenson for Whip by 18 – 11. Once again Lomas suggested that Castle stay on as Socialist Group Bureau Member until the end of the year, as her work there on reorganization was just coming to fruition. There was then a vote on Seal versus Ford to succeed her, which Seal won by 16 – 14.

West registered concern at a proposal emanating from Larry Whitty during these years that some BLG funds should be diverted to help the Labour Party at home. He was not alone in believing that this would be against the funding rules and asked for his opposition to be recorded. There was never a chance that this use of monies would be permitted.

Permanent revolution and infantile behaviour

When Castle was Leader she had sought to have a policy paper on the EEC drawn up by the BLG, to influence the debate back home in the party.

Lomas took this up, seeking to ensure it favoured withdrawal. It boiled down to a contest about what held greater primacy, the 1983 election manifesto or subsequent policy developments. An anti-market policy paper from the MEPs would cut across the initiative of Kinnock as Leader working towards changing Labour's approach on Europe and pre-empt any attempt to change Conference decisions. It was not helpful to the leadership at home that the MEPs were digging themselves into a bunker.

Lomas produced an anti-EEC draft document, in his view in line with official party policy, hoping to get it signed off in advance of Labour conference in the autumn of 1986. In response to the challenge, the pro-marketeers in the BLG tabled over a hundred amendments, hoping partly to turn it into a less confrontational document, but mostly to delay it. Each mover and seconder of an amendment had, under the standing orders, an opportunity for several minutes of speaking time (movers five minutes and speakers three) and Collins recalls they used this filibuster time to great effect. Tomlinson said happily: "we talked it past another Party conference". McGowan later criticized the "ridiculous ganging up" that took place against this policy paper. West was critical of Newens' poor chairing of the lengthy meetings and the atmosphere was as bad as ever it had been. Newens and Falconer had a shouting match about it at one point and there were plenty of unhappy exchanges.

Throughout the middle of 1986 the BLG was in virtually continuous special meetings in Strasbourg whenever the plenary was not voting. Quin attests to the poisonous, hostile and angry atmosphere making it a highly unpleasant place to be, particularly with all votes being openly and tediously recorded. She said 1984-86 was a particular upsetting time in the Group. On the final vote she recalls most of her pro-market colleagues being absent and she recorded her vote on an amendment in a small voice: "against". Newman congratulated her, saying "at least there is an honest person". Some of the others had voted a sort of compromise position in favour of it being forwarded to the NEC. There was much acrimonious correspondence about suitable times for meetings. Collins was always cross when there were important debates on environmental legislation being held in the plenary at the same time as a planned BLG meeting.

Stan Newens as Chair had a difficult time keeping order and discipline, causing meetings to drag on, often for more than three hours. On one unfortunate occasion and goaded by Newman's sharp tongue, Newens lost some friends by unwisely calling Newman (a Jew), in the heat of the moment, "an ignorant pig". He was never anti-semitic however and Newman accepted his personal apology. Newens considers that some members of the Campaign Group deliberately disrupted meetings to make things difficult for him in the chair as he was "an errant left-winger". West, a principled stickler for rules, became known as "point of order Norman", which in its turn lengthened meetings interminably. Buchan at one point goaded Tongue to tears, and Castle and Buchan had several spats. Internecine factionalism ruled throughout 1985-87 and some Members openly despised others. Comrades they were not.

Eventually, with a large number of amendments still remaining on the "Lomas paper", the remainder was taken *en bloc*, just to get the thing finalized. As expected, many of the pro-market amendments had been defeated.

It was agreed that it would not be used until endorsed by the NEC, which Party General Secretary Whitty ensured never happened. Finally in October 1986 there was a vote 18 – 13 to submit the document to the NEC. This too, was subject to a row. There had been substantial leaking of the paper to the press before the vote took place, completely against standing orders. Collins complained in letters on 9 October to *The Independent* and *The Guardian* that they had reported something before it had happened, and copied his letters to Whitty. He also complained to Buchan, BLG Secretary, about comprehensive leaking of the paper, pointing out that there could be seen to be a split in party policy in the run up to the forthcoming general election and the Midlands by-election. "At present we have a widespread interpretation of it as being a revival of an old split in the party and even of an attack on Neil Kinnock...." Some were not bothered by such niceties. Whitty many years later said relations with the BLG were not close and that officers did not bother much with attending the NEC in this period.

There had been a gradual sea change in the opinions of some Members. Perhaps it was embarrassment at the dinosaur-like attitude of some throughout this acrimonious policy debate. Perhaps it was the result of active participation in real parliamentary work and seeing that things could be achieved at the European level, or perhaps for some it was simply loyalty to Kinnock. Ford had shifted his position at least partly as a result of attending a Monday dining club with Tongue and left colleagues from both the Socialist and other groups where discussions were wide-ranging. He also saw the power of Japan and felt there needed to be a European counter-balance. Whatever it was, Ford, Crawley, Morris and Martin had shifted their view, writing a strongly-worded article published in *Tribune* on 12 December 1986 headed "Kamikaze Politics or the Collective Madness that Grips Labour in Europe". Ford was a prolific writer for *Tribune* (being later on its editorial board) and the article has his stylistic stamp on it. In addition to some voting idiocy in plenary on Star Wars it was about the attempts to mobilize the financial resources of the MEPs to help the Labour Party win the next general election. Some in the BLG had been proposing to use some of the Group's "Information money" to publicise why the party should continue to be against the EEC, rather than positive examples of work achieved such as the anti-racism initiative. It criticized the lack of political direction at Walworth Road (Party headquarters) and said in part:

> "One of the barriers to changing these attitudes is the mouldy corpse of a long-dead debate on the Common Market whose decaying stench suffocates any attempt at fresh thinking... After nearly twelve months of deliberation, the British Labour Group of MEPs recently produced a discussion document on the EEC. This document, at best, made a reasonable case for not joining the Community in 1973, and at worst served as a collective comforter to be nursed against the threatened intrusion of the real world. What that document should have discussed was how socialists, working and co-operating together, could make use of the EEC to tackle the major international issues of our times, despite the Treaty of Rome... Yet our day-to-day activities in Europe are governed by a form of revolutionary nihilism whose legitimation is our 'imminent departure', whose practice is intimidatory, and whose forward vision is lemming-like... On at least

three occasions, on defence issues such as Star Wars and European security, BLG members have voted against the Socialist Group and Labour
Group whip because, in the classic style of what Lenin called Parliamentary cretinism, they have mistaken the trees for the wood and have aided
the Right in its enthusiasm for Reagan's Strategic Defence Initiatives
because of 'theoretical' objections to some obscure paragraph." (repro-
duced in *The Evolution of a European* by Glyn Ford, 1993)

This provoked a response in *Labour Weekly* in January by Lomas with several pages from the Common Market Safeguards Campaign including a half
page advertisement sending best wishes to that organization from the
undersigned, under the slogan: "We need the full support of all the Labour
movement to enable us to carry out conference decisions and party policy"
(the implication being the policy of withdrawal). The signatories to this
attempt to stem the tide of change were, highly confusingly: Balfe, Buchan,
Crawley, Cryer, Elliott, Falconer, Ford, Hindley, Hoon, Huckfield, Hughes,
Lomas, Martin, Megahy, Morris, Seal and Smith. Half of these were by then
not anti-market at all. Some say that the Safeguards Committee continued to
put names on publications without specific permission and this is likely to
have been what happened here.

After the exhausting and exhaustive battles over the policy paper and
faced with the loss of support of some previously anti-market MEPs, Lomas
decided at the 1987 AGM to stand down. He said this was because party
policy had changed to pro-EEC which he could not support and his constituency work was suffering "because of the many pointless meetings he
had to attend as Leader, such as the Socialist Group Bureau". There had also
been a badly handled event when Bob Geldof came to town in November
and when finally permitted to speak to the BLG meeting (the decision not
being without internal controversy), had come in with TV cameras and
promptly proceeded to attack Labour policy, whilst Cryer antagonized him
even more by ranting about food mountains.

The AGM opened up an opportunity for a complete change, giving a victory to the right and centre. McMahon remembers plotting on the part of the
soft left to get Martin elected. Martin had written an article in the autumn of
1986 in *Radical Scotland* quaintly titled "Whither the left in Europe" that
spoke about cooperating in Europe on environment, energy, aid and
research. The contest for the leadership this time was between Hindley,
Martin and Newens and finally Martin won with 16 votes to Hindley's 13,
with two abstentions (Buchan and Elliott). Deputy Leader went to
Tomlinson with 15 votes against Hindley with 13, Elliott, Buchan and
Newens abstaining. Kinnock was supportive of the new Leader and that
autumn Martin was the first BLG Leader to be given an automatic right to
speak at Labour Party conference, since then a regular slot on the agenda.
The Guardian, in the form of a piece by Palmer, on 17 June 1987, said "Labour
MEPs swing to the right". *Labour Weekly* on 26 June, reporting on the new
BLG Leader, spoke of "Dangers in the market. We must demand a campaign
for a real social policy in Europe." Martin then wrote a piece in September
raising the possibility of a rethink on Labour EEC policy.

The post of Chair at this AGM was contested between Newens, Stevenson
and West, with Stevenson winning 16 – 12 – 3. Balfe beat Falconer for

Secretary, 16 – 13 – 2 and Ford beat Newman for Treasurer, 18 -13. Elliott was elected Whip in a contest against Crawley and Stewart. For Socialist Group Bureau, Seal beat Collins by 16 – 14. There was some acrimony over this. Hoon and his colleagues had drawn up a voting slate to support Collins but Newens proclaimed himself a left-winger who felt that would be unprincipled as the slate had not supported him for Chair. Castle, who had no love for Seal, was furious with Newens, as were Griffiths, Adam and Collins. Elliott attempted unsuccessfully to insert an extra post of Vice-Chair. The Campaign Group's slate had clearly slipped up. There was a dispute over a ruling from Newens in the chair about whether changes in standing orders should be implemented immediately, with Newens saying they should. The challenge to the Chair was lost. Hoon was soundly defeated in an attempt to get a telephone vote for Crawley who was away ill. There was a three-part vote on a standing order change that no Group officer could simultaneously hold other posts in the Parliament. Hoon further attempted an amendment that the record on recorded ballots should only be read out after election. This was amended and partially carried in an emasculated form. This was the first AGM for moderate John Bird, who must have wondered what sort of organization he had become part of. The balance of power was now temporarily with the centre.

Labour at home and another lost election

After the 1983 general election defeat Neil Kinnock as new Leader knew the position on Europe must be softened and that anti-Europeanism was not an election winner. He wanted to build a forward-looking party but also had to contend with a strong left-wing caucus. Benn had won a seat back in Parliament in the Chesterfield by-election in March on the resignation of Eric Varley. The good news was Labour's victory for Nick Raynsford over the Conservative candidate at the Fulham by-election in April. Roger Liddle, who had popped up again for the SDP, came third.

At the 1984 party conference Castle in her Leader's speech had thanked activists for doubling the number of MEPs and the boost to morale, crowing that the SDP-Liberal Alliance had in her constituency lost their deposit. She said: "We dedicate ourselves in our new jobs to … using our platform, our resources, using our propaganda opportunities, to secure a victory for Labour at the next general election." But she continued: "please let us stop making MEPs feel like lepers or deserters; we are your colleagues in arms." She also reported to applause, with Arndt in the visitors' gallery, that staff of the European Parliament had raised £5,000 for the miners' fund and the Socialist Group another £2,000.

Several candidates spoke: Cryer complaining about the European election campaign unit not supporting withdrawal, Vaz about lack of support from the NEC and MacKinlay of paucity of support from the campaign unit. Conference was mainly dominated by discussions about OMOV (one member, one vote) for elections of Leader and Deputy Leader. The Parliamentary Labour Party's report to that conference "recognised the importance of the BLG within the European Parliament, especially after the doubling of its representation… A closer working relationship between the PLP and BLG has been enhanced by regular meetings of the Liaison

Committee and by the newly instituted series of meetings initiated by the Foreign Affairs Committee." Alan Hadden, Chair of the NEC in 1984-85, said the problems had been boundary changes and finance and that our objective was not to be in or out of the EEC (in response to Cryer), but to take the opportunity to vote against the Tories and establish that Labour was still a viable and credible alternative. Newens spoke as a CRS delegate in moving composite resolution 24 against Star Wars and missile deployment in Europe and calling for the simultaneous and mutual disbandment of NATO and the Warsaw Pact, which was carried.

Kinnock appointed Whitty General Secretary of the party in 1985. He had worked both at the TUC and GMB trades union and was more Europe-friendly than the anti-market Jim Mortimer. In 1984 Labour's NEC created ten joint policy committees to streamline policy making. Castle was a member of the policy review group dealing with agriculture but could not get them to accept her plan for reform of the CAP.

In January 1985 the NEC tightened its view on MEPs standing for Westminster. It ruled that:

> "no sitting MEP will be permitted to seek nomination for a Parliamentary seat represented by a Labour MP who is seeking re-selection and re-election in that seat and no MP will be permitted to seek nomination for a Euro Assembly seat represented by a Labour MEP seeking re-selection in that seat."

MEPs' office allowances went up during this year and they could increase their staffing and improve their visibility at home. Extension of the franchise for British people living abroad was brought in during the summer. The BLG decided to use some of its finances to have a presence at the party's regional conferences from November that year, so as to raise its profile. In the same year a BLG/PLP working party was set up.

Neil Kinnock made his famous stand against Militant at annual conference in Bournemouth in the autumn of 1985, making it a symbol of his leadership with expulsion of eight Militant members from Liverpool. He also scrapped his support for CND. There were no conference resolutions on Europe in 1985, 1986 or 1987, but Willy Brandt, as Chairman of the Socialist International, was a guest speaker in 1986. George Robertson MP, junior party spokesperson on foreign affairs in the early 1980s, characterized Labour policy on the EEC as "in a state of flux" and "pragmatic rather than theological". Newens as Chair of the BLG says he counselled Kinnock and Charles Clarke that Labour needed to drop its anti-Europe policy, but Kinnock was already well on the way to doing precisely this. Many years later Lomas, described by some as a Stalinist, referred to Newens without animosity as "an old Trot" – a slightly exaggerated portrayal of his position as a left-wing internationalist. Newens was also referred to by a former colleague as an unreconstructed Marxist, a description he regards as a compliment.

The Labour Party began to streamline its internal organization, and Peter Mandelson, a pro-marketeer, was made the party's first Director of Communications in 1985, around the time that Whitty, much more pragmatic on Europe, took over as General Secretary. Mandelson worked closely with Kinnock and Clarke to modernize the party, one aspect of which was changing its Europe policy. Part of the streamlining was to rationalize the plethora of internal committees. Philip Gould, with Deborah Mattinson (both pro-Europeans), formed the Shadow Communications Agency and began to supply polling information to the party. By 1993 he was also advising the Socialist Group on its election campaign. In *The Unfinished Revolution* (Gould, 1998), Philip Gould acknowledged that he was seen as a threat by the NEC. A campaign management team including Whitty, Joyce Gould, then Director of Organisation, Bish and Mandelson was by then in place. The red rose logo surfaced in the summer of 1986, utilizing the traditional social democracy symbol of the European Socialists in a modified form. Kinnock had held policy seminars in 1985 and 1986 with French and German Socialists, who both had representations in London from the mid-eighties, and strengthened ties with the Socialist International and the Confed. He also helped Felipe Gonzales in Spain where a referendum campaign was held in 1985 regarding Spain's entry into NATO.

Policy on Europe was still sensitive. Kinnock's book *Making Our Way* (Kinnock, 1986), did not debate the subject, concentrating on a critique of the ERM and the Single Market White Paper and suggesting a co-ordinated European attack on unemployment and a programme of reform.

The ruthless running down of Britain's mining and heavy industry base continued as did Thatcher's attacks on anything that smacked of socialism, particularly local government. At the end of March 1986 she abolished the Greater London Council whose left-wing policies under Ken Livingstone had been a thorn in her side. Socialists in Europe were incredulous, thinking this must surely be unconstitutional. The Prime Minister appeared to be able to do anything she wished.

Labour suffered an unhappy defeat in the Greenwich by-election in March 1987, with a controversial candidate, a marker to what was to come. By the time of the general election in June, the leadership was no longer talking about withdrawal from the Common Market: the priority was to beat the Tories. Unfortunately, yet again, it was not to be. There was still a mountain to climb. Nevertheless, Philip Gould reckoned the campaign a success because of the partial modernization that had taken place. Labour, more united than for some time, beat the SDP-Liberal Alliance and its share of the vote rose over that of the 1983 election. Its manifesto abandoned the withdrawal policy and spoke about working constructively with EEC partners. This time it said:

> "Labour's aim is to work constructively with our EEC partners to promote economic expansion and combat unemployment. However, we will stand up for British interests within the European Community and will seek to put an end to the abuses and scandals of the CAP. We shall, like other member countries, reject EEC interference with our policy for national recovery and renewal."

Once again the combative British MEPs from both parties attacked each other endlessly in Parliament, to the general irritation of other Members who objected that national politics should not be pursued there. Quin had a fisheries report on the agenda on one occasion, to be accused by Conservative Alasdair Hutton of hijacking the Parliament into supporting her election campaign in Gateshead East. She pointed out that constituency is not on the coast and not affected by fishing. Labour MEPs played an active part in the general election campaign in their constituencies.

Cryer, Quin and Griffiths were all elected to the House of Commons but Newens did not win back Harlow, which he had lost in 1983. The successful three stayed on in the European Parliament with a dual mandate until the 1989 election, since no-one wanted European by-elections. It curtailed their activities to some extent. They were all hard-working and still managed to attend as much as possible of the plenary sessions and some committee meetings and continued to table questions, but were no longer able to maintain a constant presence in the Parliament, the BLG or the Socialist Group. Joyce Quin and Win Griffiths were a loss because of their hard work, likeable personalities and European solidarity, but comrades in the Socialist Group and quite a few in the BLG were relieved to see less of Cryer whom they had always seen as obstructive. Despite being a difficult character, Cryer in his own way did his bit for Europe. As a railway enthusiast he put in a good effort on the Transport Committee and supported historic vehicles when there was any legislation that might affect them. He also persuaded the Commission to change the name of a Dutch cabbage from Niggerhead to Danish Red, perhaps a small thing in the greater perspective, but a blow against residual racism.

The International Committee of Labour's NEC considered a paper in February 1988 on relations with the BLG. It noted there had been marked improvement in the relations between the BLG and Walworth Road, "helped, for example, by more frequent contact between senior Party officials and BLG officers." (This was during the Martin leadership.) The proposals included: "A quarterly report from the BLG could be made to the International Committee... The BLG Leader (or Deputy...) could become an observer to the International Committee... The NEC could revive the idea of annual BLG/NEC meetings... We could encourage more intensive contacts between PLP frontbench teams and relevant BLG members... The BLG could be asked to produce a paper on how they feel our relations could be further improved." The policy review groups were set up after the election defeat. David Martin for the MEPs was a member of the Britain in the World group until he was unseated by Seal. Gapes at HQ acted as secretary to this group.

At the 1988 party conference Kinnock's leadership was dented somewhat when the delegates voted in favour of unilateral nuclear disarmament at the time when he was seeking to distance the party from this policy. The principle of having one woman on every shortlist was carried but this small step forward was to carry over into only marginally better representation of women at the 1989 European elections. Heightened support for women as candidates for office notwithstanding, it was not until the electoral system changed in 1999 that more equality prevailed for the European elections. The EPLP reported that they had donated money to the ANC and £26,000 for Medical Aid to Nicaragua had been raised.

Anti-racism

Glyn Ford, long a campaigning member of the Anti-Nazi League, began to make his mark by October 1984, becoming Chair of a Committee of Inquiry into the Rise of Fascism and Racism in Europe. The EPLP and Socialists had proposed the committee. No other BLG Member had full membership. "Rock against Racism" in the UK at the beginning of the decade had been a powerful tool in raising awareness. In France Harlem Desir's grass roots organization SOS Racisme was making a positive mark and he was one of the first witnesses before the committee, which ran until January 1986. Michael Wood, one of the British Labour members on the Parliament staff, was seconded to work on the secretariat for the committee, setting in train a vigorous programme of investigation, visits and public hearings in different locations including three in Brussels. Ford took on a stagiaire, Caroline Lasko, to help with the work, becoming one of the first of the BLG to have staff in Brussels.

The work of this committee was never going to be anything but confrontational, and inevitably the ultra-right withdrew. When it was set up, Ford recalls that Le Pen wrote to him saying he would use all means possible to disrupt its work. Drawing on the experience of his local authority background, Ford took the precaution of convening pre-committee meetings with all those on the left – Socialists, Communists and Greens. At first it was not self-evident that the committee would lead to anything. The rapporteur, by tradition from the other main group, was Greek Christian Democrat Dimitrious Evrigenis, with a formidable pedigree as a judge at the European Court of Human Rights, a member of the UN Committee on Racial Discrimination, and a prisoner during the regime of the Colonels. He died not long after the report was voted on. There was a debate on the committee's work in December 1985, with accusations from Lomas that the President wanted to shove it all under the carpet. When it came to the final vote on the report in committee, the opposition was split any number of ways and Ford was able to get a fairly hard-hitting report through. Nevertheless it was a struggle and the report was labelled "alarmist". There was another row in the plenary when it was scheduled, because Ford claimed the papers were mixed up and that Parliament was being called upon to vote on an incorrect text. Attempts at postponement failed and the result was a report missing its annexes. Ford called for an intra-Community forum and a European Year to combat fascism and racism.

Ford continued an energetic follow up, in January 1986 persuading Parliament, Council and Commission to adopt an Action Plan and Declaration against Racism and Xenophobia. The final vote in this round was in June and was one of the first items the new Spanish socialist delegation was able to vote for. A second Committee of Inquiry into Racism and Xenophobia was to be set up in October 1989 with Ford as rapporteur this time, reporting in October 1990. Its main purpose was to pursue the application of the joint declaration and make suggestions for further action including setting up the European Migrants' Forum.

Many Labour MEPs from inner city and multi-ethnic constituencies were involved in case work on race issues, though there was relief that individual immigration cases remained strictly the preserve of MPs. It was of considerable concern to them not only that the Parliament was almost entirely white (save for a Member or two from French Guadeloupe who almost never turned up). They were horrified at the presence of the far right. It was a time of huge membership at home for the Anti-Apartheid Movement (in

1984 there had been a demonstration seventy thousand strong in London protesting against the visit of P.W. Botha).

Under Elliott's initiative the BLG set up an Ethnic Minorities working group focusing on anti-racist activities at home. It was serviced by Castle's assistant, and met most months during the Strasbourg session for a number of years, taking up a wide range of issues affecting the black and Asian communities in Britain. Eventually it changed its name to become an anti-racist group. Continental colleagues were slightly bemused at the British interest in these matters, but the simple fact was that in their countries most of the non-white inhabitants did not possess the vote, whilst in the UK they did and that vote largely supported Labour.

The Single European Act

Parliament in 1984 had proposed to replace the European Community treaties with a new Treaty on European Union, setting off more than two decades of often difficult treaty reform. After the Fontainebleau Council in 1984 a joint committee of representatives of Heads of State and Government plus MEPs was set up, chaired by Irish Senator Dooge, coming up with a fairly similar proposal to that made earlier by the Parliament. There were three dissenters; Danish, Greek and for the UK, Malcolm Rifkind. In the parliamentary debate in April 1985, Cryer said there should be more time for debate, that it was an erosion of the veto and had not been endorsed by the House of Commons. Megahy said that the British people did not want a Europe united in this way, implying that it was a grand design to strengthen the Community institutions. Unsurprisingly, the BLG was against the proposal.

The Milan Council in June 1985 used a simple majority vote (forced by the Italians), to decide to convene an Intergovernmental Conference (IGC) to revise the treaties to implement the Dooge Committee proposals. It was tending towards support for more majority voting, which did not make Britain happy. Single Market ideas were the mainstay of the British position, and Jacques Delors, as President of the Commission, had seen that the Single Market was a good thing if it could include a social dimension, this also being the position of the Confed, which wanted EC social policy and health and safety legislation. There was some contradiction in the government line in that unanimity in Council was one of the reasons for slow progress towards the Single Market. Parliament held a rather complacent debate on the Italian Summit but Castle struck a discordant note in arguing that social problems should be dealt with rather than institutional change.

In opposition to the IGC, Labour and the Tory government were at one, although there were a few British MEPs on both sides of the House who were in favour. In a debate on the IGC in October, Lomas, opposing it on behalf of the BLG, said "let us have less of the Euro-drivel and some action... on behalf of the workers of Europe".

Progress was up and down and in December 1985 Megahy was gloating that the Luxembourg Summit under the chairmanship of then Prime Minister Jacques Santer had seen off the Parliament's draft treaty proposals. "The elephant has conceived a mouse". It was not to be the case. What was finally agreed was far-reaching in the development of the European Union. Thatcher was reluctantly persuaded by officials to agree to a text giving

Parliament a new co-operation procedure even though final decision remained with the Council. It endorsed the terminology "European Parliament" and included references to economic and monetary union not supported by Britain. Freedom of movement was included and Britain managed to include a separate General Declaration reserving some rights for Member States in terms of controlling immigration, and combating crime and drug trafficking. It included a compromise on encouraging improvements in the working environment, leaving the door open to future legislation on health and safety under Qualified Majority Voting. The acceptance of QMV for Single Market legislation and mention of the environment was a boon to Collins on the Environment Committee, and he spent the next few years to great effect pursuing environment legislation under "Article 100A", the Single Market legal base permitting the use of the co-operation procedure under QMV in the Council. He abstained rather than follow the BLG Whip to vote against the Treaty when it came to Parliament.

There was little involvement (but quite a lot of hot air) on the part of Parliament in the IGC, which reported in January 1986. The Single European Act (SEA) was signed in February. The BLG remained fairly solidly opposed to all this, in common with Labour in Parliament at home, although the text was a far cry from the more ambitious aims of the Parliament. Britain had insisted that the move towards a frontier-free Europe should not undermine its control as an island over drugs, immigration, plant and animal health. Delors described the pruning of ambition insisted on as being tantamount to a "Texas chain-saw massacre" (a popular film at the time), but called the end result "a compromise for change". During the debate in January Crawley attacked the Cockfield White Paper on creation of the Single Market as "reinforcement of rabid free marketry." The social dimension of the Single Market was still pretty shadowy at this time. Labour at home vigorously opposed the SEA in its passage through the Westminster parliamentary process which was led by Linda Chalker for the government. Former MEP Clwyd was active during the ratification debate.

Once this Act came into force in 1987, the European Parliament gained two additional powers: the co-operation procedure, which added a second reading to the legislative process for a number of areas and the assent procedure. This was an important development giving equal power with the Council of Ministers on association agreements with third countries and on treaties. It was not long before Parliament used this new power. In 1988, it initially refused to give its assent to three protocols for agreements with Israel because of unhappiness with conditions imposed on Palestine for exports to Europe. This was used as a delaying tactic and gained some concessions.

The consequence of the Single Act was a torrent of legislation constructing the Single Market, which kept parliamentarians busy right up to 1992. The Commission agreed a three-stage plan for moving towards full economic and monetary union in July 1990. It had produced a lengthy report by an eminent Italian economist, Cecchini in 1988 (1992: The European Challenge), giving the cost of the existing trading barriers (the cost of "non-Europe") as £140 billion in British money, and suggesting it could create five million jobs. It followed an earlier report (Efficiency, Stability and Equality 1987) by another eminent Italian economist, Padua-Scioppa, on the ostensible gains for the European economy of a Single Market, harmonising state aids and improving mobility of the labour market. Lord Cockfield was put in charge of the 285 directives needed to bring the Single Market into being. His White Paper also included proposals for VAT harmonization. Castle thought him a supercilious technocrat with few social charms, despite his having taken her to lunch a few times, and was vehemently opposed to an increase in VAT.

Parliament on 11 March 1987 set up a Temporary Committee on "Making a Success of the Single Act" which by this time was known as the "Delors package", chaired by Lord Plumb and including Megahy. The Committee reported quickly on 13 May, with Parliament rejecting a Megahy amendment to its text. The EDG demanded a roll call vote on the report, which was carried by 227 – 38 with 63 abstentions. Balfe was the only BLG Member to vote for it, together with most of the Socialists. Eleven of the BLG did not vote, a further seven abstained and seven voted against, including Castle. In the vote on the strategy for achieving European union and setting out Parliament's amendments on 17 June (the rapporteur being Herman from the EPP), no BLG Member voted in favour. Balfe, Bird, Ford and Tomlinson abstained. Collins appears not to have voted.

European socialist party leaders at a meeting in Paris decided that the SEA meant that EC decisions would directly affect European citizens and national party politics and to hold such summits twice a year in future so as to be closer in touch. Delors, as Socialist President of the European Commission actively participated in every major meeting of socialist leaders over the next five years.

Margaret Thatcher at the European Council in Brussels, after a year's arguing, agreed to a mixture of doubling the structural funds and tighter controls on the CAP, but remained strongly opposed to the social dimension of the Single Market. It was Spain and Portugal who insisted in Council that the Single Market should be accompanied by the major expansion of regional policies, and these were incidentally to benefit British regions.

Parliament produced several reports between 1987 and 1989 suggesting the constitutional system laid down in the Single Act was not sufficient, and arguing for more treaty amendments. In a debate in October 1988, Huckfield was at pains to say that he was not supporting European union, not because he was a little Englander (saying he was an Atlanticist) but that a Labour government should repeal Section 2 of the 1972 Act which would mean that directives or regulations would have to be agreed by the House of Commons. In contrast, Martin spoke in support of Delors but said he did not support all that was in the report before Members. Megahy voted against, saying: "I don't relish the prospect of Britain being sucked into a vast European superstate". He described the EDG Members, who he said were selected initially as European federalists and were "now beached, stranded and marooned on the benches of this house". This was shortly after Thatcher's Bruges speech. Just at the time of the 1989 elections, the Madrid Council agreed to a new Intergovernmental Conference on EMU and a parallel one on political union, to take shape around the end of 1990.

Labour policy changing

In 1986 the Fabian Society held a big meeting on Labour in Europe at the Courtauld Institute. The main speakers in what was a fine debate were Castle, Bryan Gould MP and passionate left-winger, Luciana Castellina from Italy who although being outside the Socialist Group, was a friend of Tongue and an Anglophile. Gould's anti-market views were starting to sound unrealistic and were clearly in the minority as far as that audience was concerned. Castle was hugely nervous before she spoke in this debate, wanting to ensure that she hit the right note.

After the 1987 general election, Martin, by this time BLG Leader, stated in his report to the party conference : "This conference has rightly called for a rethink on Labour policy. On Europe we need to prepare our new policies now because the next major test will be the 1989 Euro elections... You have to come to the conclusion that that policy has got to be a policy for working within the EC". In February 1988 the International Committee reported that relations with the BLG had improved considerably, past relations not having been good. In the same month Martin wrote a pamphlet for the Fabian Society on Europe, with a preface from Kinnock, arguing that Labour should work with other Socialist parties to bring "common sense to the common market" (Martin, 1988).

A new generation of trades union leaders began to work with their European colleagues and the position on the EEC began to soften there too as they found a common agenda for their members. When Delors spoke to the TUC Conference in September 1988 he enthused the unions with the idea that social Europe, required as a counterweight to the creation of the Single Market for business, could only be achieved with active participation in European institutions, and he was warmly hailed as "Frère Jacques". It was the beginning of a sea change in attitude. The unions saw there was something here for them and the term "social partners" came into use. There was a space and role for trades unions and voluntary organizations denied at home. In due course party members took this on board too. Castle (1993) described it in terms of the Frenchman "spellbinding his unsentimental audience with his passionate determination not to allow workers to be marginalized in the new people's Europe he was trying to build". Delors' attendance at this meeting may have been down to luck. Tongue recalls a meeting with him where he was tempted by an invitation to address a meeting in Australia instead, but said that she persuaded him of the importance of speaking to the TUC. She could not have been more right. It was not until the unions changed their mind (a slow process given that many of them only held policy conferences every two years) that it was possible to get an official change of policy through Labour Party conference.

The 1988 party conference, following a rousing speech from Kinnock in favour of a social Europe, voted for the Policy Review document Britain in the World, containing the pivotal change of policy on Europe. Composite 58 lengthily spelled out what was virtually an election manifesto:

> "Conference recognizes that Britain is politically and economically inte-
> grated into the European Community. Therefore, the Labour Party, in con-
> junction with other Socialist parties of the EC, must seek to use and adapt

Community institutions to promote democratic socialism. Conference recognizes the completion of the Single Market will present a major challenge to the Socialist parties of Europe. Unless the Community is committed to implementing social provisions and a complementary social programme … to ensure the benefits of the unified market are shared by all people in the EC, it will only benefit the business community. Conference recognizes the need to devise a strategy to overcome these problems. Just as the business sector will greatly benefit from the harmonization of technical standards and the removal of barriers to trade, this must go hand-in-hand with the upward harmonization of standards at work in respect to health and safety, the working week, the age of retirement, pensions, holidays and the social standards which benefit the less privileged of the EC. There must also be industrial and economic democracy…protection for all workers irrespective of the size of the firm they are employed in or the nature of their employment contract (particularly in the case of insecure employment conditions), social protection… the right to initial training and to further vocational training and … to occupational therapy. Conference endorses the new social agenda of Commission President Jacques Delors and instructs the NEC to co-ordinate and monitor progress through the socialist parties of Europe, the PLP and BLG. …calls for an increase in the resources available to the social fund of the EC, so that the marginalized regions of Europe can more readily receive assistance. … opposes the implementation of Community laws which would benefit multinational companies and harmonization of taxes which would result in the introduction of VAT on food, children's clothes, books and other publications. … mandates the NEC, in concert with other socialist parties within the Community, to formulate a socialist manifesto for the 1989 European Parliament elections which would bring EC socialist parties together in support of:

a)   a common EC economic strategy for eliminating unemployment, greater accountability and democracy in work, common and higher EC standards for socialist provision,

b)   a complete review of the CAP so that the limited resources of the EC can be utilized more effectively in all areas,

c)   the EC as a forum to campaign for peace and disarmament.

Conference therefore instructs the NEC to adopt all of the above into the party's EC policy and calls for the manifesto for the forthcoming elections to reflect these opinions."

A more negative resolution 496 was remitted to the NEC. A future MEP Mo O'Toole spoke on jobs, Mel Read from MSF and a candidate for the Leicestershire Euro seat spoke on the Single Market. Pollack, candidate for London South West, highlighted the democratic deficit leading to policy trade-offs. "In passing composite 58 you will be giving our Euro MPs a mandate to meet those challenges". Seal as Leader in his Parliamentary report said: "the most positive way to improve our working environment is not to rely on the Common Market but to throw out Thatcher and elect a Labour government." The right-wing were still in the majority in the Parliament and this could be eliminated if the number of Labour Members were increased: "I urge all of you to ensure that the members you represent are aware of the importance for the Labour movement of next June's European elections".

Whilst firmly a European, John Palmer of *The Guardian* had doubts about the EEC and its institutions. In his book *Europe Without America?* (Palmer, 1987), he voiced some concerns about Labour's change of position. He said: "Ironically, the British Labour Party is in danger of moving from a narrow-minded opposition to all things European to a superficial infatuation with the institutions of the EEC." Castle, too, had some concerns as to whether Kinnock was becoming too enthusiastically pro-European.

Tony Benn was back on form in 1988 making a challenge to Kinnock's leadership, but this was beaten off at conference. The left/right divisions were still far from over. Left Members from Europe were invited to party conference to put an acceptable case for European involvement, such as Italian MEP Pasqualina Napolitano, thanks to the efforts of David Lowe in Brussels. She was from the Berlinguer wing supported by Kinnock and the presence of people like this at fringe meetings helped to convince constituency delegates that change was a good thing.

Relations with the Socialist Group

Individual Labour MEPs found common cause with some of their comrades in the Socialist Group, largely on jobs and workers' rights and the peace campaign. But the bad behaviour of some had soured the relationship with many and after Castle was thrown out the BLG found it hard to win friends as a Group. There was no constructive engagement by most Labour Members with the European vision that others were developing, although Tongue, Quin and Hindley, with their gift for languages, made friends across the nationality and cultural divide.

Relations between individuals broke down on more than one occasion. Once when Lomas was Leader he spoke up in the Parliament for aid for Vietnam, supported by much of the left after what the Americans had done to that country. It infuriated both Ripa di Meana and Czech Jiri Pelikan, who were virulently anti-Communist and who confronted him so forcefully in the Chamber during his speech that the former felt the need came to Lomas's office the next day to apologise.

Lomas speaks proudly of his tenacious adherence to his anti-EEC position, particularly during his two year reign as Leader, saying that he would sometimes be taken to lunch by leaders of Socialist parties attempting to get him to change his mind and advancing all kinds of arguments against his position. But he held firm, which left the rest of the Socialist Group (and a good number of his own team) in despair and caused aggravation from time to time when Labour did not support the Socialist Group whip.

In the press room of the Socialist Group the Labour Members were viewed with some dismay during this period. Jan Kurlemann, a German working in that section at the time, recalls an occasion when a Labour Member marched off with his typewriter. After some of the more divisive attempts at press statements by our comrades the staff devised two versions of headed paper: "Press release from the Socialist Group", and "Statement by (name) Member of the Socialist Group" used as a code for the press corps to signal when something being put out was not sanctioned by the Group.

One of Seal's preoccupations was to propose a loose federal structure for the Socialist Group, so that the BLG could obtain more paid staff. This did not go down well with Kinnock, who according to Tomlinson called in the officers and read the riot act, saying Labour was a sister party of the Socialist International and they were full members of the Socialist Group and anyone who couldn't accept that would cease to be a member. There had to be a bit of backing down.

New comrades and other matters

Spain and Portugal joined the Community in January 1986, with sixty new MEPs bringing the size of the Parliament up to 518. Their accession expanded both the EDG and the Socialist Group, the latter benefiting by forty-two. Embracing Members from Spain, Portugal, and earlier, Greece into the European Community as new democracies that had emerged from fascist dictatorships so recently was important for all on the left, the BLG included. In a debate on ERDF and enlargement in November 1985, Newman was beginning to engage constructively, making an excellent speech analyzing two reports from the Regional Committee, supporting the Spanish socialist government's regional policy and a Europe of the regions. His views on the Common Market were beginning to soften, but it was not something he discussed with the Tribunites. Crawley, in that debate however, had an eye on her constituency. She worried that the entry of two new and poor countries might reduce the availability of ERDF funding in the West Midlands.

The BLG was often surprised when the new Spanish Members would side with the Germans on critical policy votes within the Group and it took a while before the BLG realized it was not all down to personalities. The SPD had championed Spanish socialists and sheltered refugees throughout the long years of the Franco dictatorship and the Spanish reciprocated that solidarity. Labour seemed to think that because some British socialists, communists and trades unionists had fought in the Civil War all would be sweetness and light. They had become used to having a fairly free rein on policy matters from the home front and were also astonished at how disciplined the Spanish were in taking their line from their party. One Labour Member believes those in the Spanish group were scared of the confrontational position Labour and Conservative MEPs adopted. Because Spain was still a fledgling democracy they had not accepted the British had the freedom to be so combative in Parliament. Lomas had taken the initiative as Leader of the BLG to set up a meeting with the Spanish, but it turned out simply to be their leader speaking to the BLG and did not take root as a regular occurrence, nor was it broadened out to the entire Spanish group, largely because of language difficulties (there being no translation facilities for delegation meetings and many of the Spanish speaking French rather than English). Gibraltar also was a sore point with the Spanish which raised its head from time to time.

Castle regularly attended the annual spring Green Week in Berlin to pursue her arguments against agriculture prices with a wider audience, always keen to hear the opposing point of view. The party at home left her alone to battle on CAP reform. In April 1986 she was at it again, attacking the farm price settlement: "… the annual farce of price fixing and I sniff appeasement in the air. All a co-responsibility levy does is tax a surplus once it has taken place. It is an inefficient substitute for a price reduction. The (Conservative) Provan report is shameful". Parliament rejected the Commission's Regulations on farm prices after voting on four hundred amendments. Castle was right: the farmers called the tune and were hindering the Commission's attempts to move towards reforms. Yet when a Committee of Inquiry into the problem of stocks in the agriculture sector was set up in November 1985-87, she was not part of this work. It is not clear whether the Socialist Group failed to nominate her as a member.

Collins crossed swords with Conservative Ben Patterson in January 1986, when he supported an environment matter being dealt with under the internal market procedure. Patterson opined that the BLG's position was eccentric. Collins retorted that as a British Conservative he was uniquely placed to recognize eccentricity when he saw it, and made a robust defence of environment needing common value limits and quality objectives.

On 3 October 1986, Terry Pitt died unexpectedly at the age of forty-nine. It was a shock to all. He had been trying to give up smoking as a remedial pre-condition to some cardiac surgery and apparently asphyxiated on his anti-smoking gum in a taxi returning from Birmingham airport. Tomlinson, who had known him for many years and who would normally have shared the cab, was on a visit to Norway and was very upset at the news. Pitt had devoted his life to politics, was hard-working and well-liked across the board. Hoon described him warmly as "a West Winger". Newens said: "he was a lovely man and was involved in the Co-op 1960 Committee in London". During his period in the Parliament he had been active both on budget and anti-fraud matters and had softened his position on the EEC, probably in part due to his friendship with Tomlinson. Castle keenly felt his loss as she had thought highly of him. A by-election had to be held to replace him in the West Midlands, and on 5 March 1987, moderate John Bird, a former policeman, previously leader of Wolverhampton Council and a pragmatist on the EEC was elected on a turnout of 28.2%.

Often in the run up to the farm prices debates, French farmers would demonstrate in Strasbourg in front of the Parliament. There was once an attempt to drive a tractor up the grand steps of the Palais de l'Europe. One snowy day in mid-winter 1986, French wine-growers and others stormed the route to Parliament and Castle said: "I must go and talk to them". Out she went with her trusty assistant, using her charm and her French, arguing the toss with the burly farmers. It was quite a sight, Castle at five foot nothing surrounded by these angry demonstrators and smoke from burning tyres, with snowflakes drifting down. Needless to say she enjoyed it hugely. It was during this harsh winter that the EEC decided to give some of the surplus stored food to charities and people on low incomes.

The BLG was still not subject to substantial policy strictures from the Labour Party. It also had little day-to-day contact with the UK government office (UKRep) in Brussels, which was then headed by David Hannay. Many in the BLG felt that it was a mouthpiece for the Conservative government, although in theory the officials were impartial civil servants. Relations tended to take the form of one formal meeting a year over frugal lunch time sandwiches, with occasional meetings between the Ambassador and offi-cers. The party in the UK was more concerned with elections than specific European policy matters and Kinnock did not feel able to intervene in the various leadership changes. Collins said that when he began pushing the use of Article 100A (Single Market – majority voting in Council) for envi-ronment legislation, no-one at home said we shouldn't use it.

British Presidency

It was again Britain's turn to hold the European Presidency in the latter half of 1986 and one of its first actions was to arrange for a temporary change in the timing of Question Time to the Council, so as to enable the relevant Minister to catch a plane home without having to stay overnight in Strasbourg. British Ministers of both political persuasions prefer to get their meetings in "Europe" over with and return to home base as quickly as poss-ible. Cryer of course complained. Sir Geoffrey Howe, Thatcher's pro-market Foreign Secretary, began with humour; he mentioned that the budget had been agreed at 4.15 am, that the government was in favour of the Single Market and there would be no Euro-pessimism from the British Presidency and that they wanted to see the end of apartheid in South Africa.

Enthusiasm for completing the Single Market and pressure for CAP reform dominated. Britain resolutely resisted the Commission proposal (supported by France) for an oils and fats tax and in this Labour was on the side of the government. Castle, Stevenson and others spoke out frequently against this proposal that was felt to be unwise and would not solve the problem. Tory MEPs did not say much about it now that Plumb was President of Parliament rather than active in the Agriculture Committee. This idea was a protectionist measure against overseas agricultural exports to the Community, and the BLG opposed it on the grounds it would put up food prices unnecessarily and had nothing to do with the much overdue reform of the CAP.

During the September session there was a hot exchange between Lord Bethell for the EDG and Castle, whom he accused of supporting the notori-ous "necklace" method of black-on-black killing in South Africa in a debate calling for sanctions. She was understandably incandescent at this inaccu-rate attack, saying that she and the Socialist Group were voting in line with the Bishops of the Church of England. Bethell again accused her of support-ing petrol-soaked tyre necklaces leading Winnie Ewing to stand up for the Socialist position and support Castle. Barbara was on planet rage when she stormed back to her office, spitting unprintable remarks about Bethell and the unscrupulous Conservatives. She was angrier that they were using any excuse to undermine the ANC and Mandela at a critical time in the struggle against apartheid than about the ludicrous slur against herself. She was a strong supporter of Mandela, having attended his notorious "freedom trial" when in Harold Wilson's government.

In a gesture of opposition during a detailed vote on the food aid section of the budget, Huckfield was found to be racing wooden woodpeckers up and down a stick, yet again causing some disruption in the hemicycle.

Margaret Thatcher wound up on 9 December for the Council. Lomas as

Leader pronounced the British Presidency a resounding flop, saying nothing had been done about the twin evils of agriculture policy and unemployment, and complaining about the debacle of South Africa sanctions. He also complained about VAT and an obsession with the internal market, going on a bit to heckling from the right with laughter and remarks of "when are you going to stop?"

Thatcher's speech was disrupted by the Reverend Paisley, by holding up an "Ulster says No" poster in front of her and saying: "This is our message to you... I would like to indict you, Mrs Thatcher, as a traitor to the loyalist people of Northern Ireland in denying them the right to vote on the Anglo-Irish Agreement." Paisley produced the protest banner from under his jacket; Otto Habsburg snatched it from him but Paisley produced another. The ushers, predominantly short, stocky men in tail coats, confiscated the poster at which Paisley produced yet another. Falconer recalls that the ushers looked like penguins jumping up and down in front of the big man. Thatcher kept ploughing on, to applause. Paisley continued interrupting despite warnings from President Pflimlin and was then removed. Thatcher thanked the President for his kindness and courtesy and continued with her speech without losing her cool.

A BSE outbreak in cattle began in November 1986 as a result of contaminated meat-and-bone meal. The idea that meat residues were being fed to vegetarian cattle horrified some and opened up issues related to intensive farming methods. Stevenson was the hapless Labour Member on the Agriculture Committee who had to help Castle speak up to restore confidence. This whole episode was the subject of intensive discussion in the Environment Committee under Collins, but more was to come in the next Parliamentary terms as the crisis deepened.

Active Members

During 1987 Parliament moved its night sitting from Thursdays of Strasbourg week to Tuesdays, and began to schedule more important debates at that time in preparation for Single Act voting on Wednesdays. It enabled more people to disappear on Thursday evenings although many of the British were proud to stay to the end of the week.

BLG Members set up regional groups that met at lunch time during the Strasbourg week. The biggest two were London and the North West and these also contained the most hostile splits. For London Members abolition of the GLC by Thatcher was an important impetus to keeping going. The MEPs were the only way London's Labour authorities could speak with one voice in Brussels and all felt this to be important. Under the chairmanship of Balfe (who was also a member of the executive of the London Labour Party until 1995) the group agreed that they would only deal with matters on which they could agree, leaving other areas out of discussions. This proved an effective operational compromise and the group became adept in putting the case for London in Europe. The North West group, in contrast, maintained a highly-charged internal antagonism, not least fuelled by Newman and Huckfield running their own agenda, Ford being a renegade and with Castle being against all of them. Ford and Newman each saw himself as the pre-eminent Manchester Member. There were quite a few big egos battling in there and meetings consequently were stressful and often inconclusive. Castle hated the meetings and saw no point in them.

Balfe, by then on the Foreign Affairs Committee, involved himself in questions related to Turkey. He had once worked in the Arabian Department at the Foreign Office and says that there he became interested in Muslim democracy. Following a coup in Turkey in 1980 relations between the Parliament and the Turkish Grand National Assembly were suspended and Parliament had voted to block funds for Turkey. He had been rapporteur in 1984 laying down a number of steps, including abolition of the death penalty, to be taken in Turkey prior to resuming relations. That question came up on 11 October and Parliament decided, after two suspensions of sitting, that the Joint Committee (delegation) to Turkey would not be set up until the Association Treaty was implemented once again and until Parliament had reconsidered the situation in Turkey. In October 1985 he was rapporteur on human rights in Turkey, saying there had been a reduction in executions and that human rights cases could now be raised in the Grand National Assembly. Against opposition from some in the BLG and Socialist Group he insisted his report was balanced. It resulted in a resumption of relations with the country. Balfe records that part of his discussions in Turkey included a verbal promise that Parliament would appoint Ludwig Fellermaier Chair of the delegation in a nod to continuity, the German having been its leader in the previous Parliament. After the Joint Committee recommenced its work Fellermaier was indeed reinstated as Chairman and Balfe continued as a member until he left Parliament in 2004. Inevitably this delegation became involved in the North Cyprus problem too. Most Socialists and the BLG were not happy about Turkey and its invasion of North Cyprus.

Turkey formally applied to join the EEC in April 1987 and the following month Crawley spoke out against it – something on which Labour Members remained split for many years. In December Parliament voted against Assent for the Association Agreement, largely on grounds of human rights abuses. Balfe voted in favour but said this did not amount to an endorsement of the human rights record.

One of Castle's other causes was a Europe-wide pensioner's pass. She went at this largely via question time and found a little more sympathy from the Commission once Greek Socialist Vassou Papandreou became the person responsible for social affairs, who finally, after some research, put forward a Recommendation. Castle was cross that it was not a more legally-binding Directive, but there was no legal basis under which that could happen and it was the best option available. She wanted it to come into existence by the time of the European Year of the Elderly, due in 1990.

Newman latched on to the issue of the food stores where CAP surpluses were kept at great expense. The high cost of storage was a problem in successive budgets, arousing high moral outrage on the left. He, Crawley and others were keen to expose the ridiculous nature of food stockpiling, particularly in a time of economic downturn. The locations of these stores were always kept secret and Newman battered away until he found a list of the UK stores and then organized local demonstrations protesting against this outrageous policy. Crawley recalls taking a group of Birmingham pensioners on a "lovely day out" around food stores, to raise awareness of the problem.

Most of the BLG had become involved in the work of their committees or their inter-parliamentary delegations, speaking and raising issues related to that work or to their constituencies, and also in a range of "intergroups" – cross-party groupings that met to consider specific matters of European interest. The Anti-Racism Intergroup was set up after the first Committee of Inquiry and is still meeting. Of particular interest to BLG Members was the newly-formed Animal Welfare Intergroup, also still continuing, but others were more specialized, such as one concerning itself with Gibraltar on which Lomas worked side by side with Lord Bethell. Castle became Chair of the Malta parliamentary delegation, and was a favourite with the Labour Party in Malta which remained anti-EEC. BLG Members also raised concerns about human rights and the need for development aid in various corners of the world.

A devastating famine in Ethiopia was causing widespread concern. Another point of contest was the political situation in various Central and South American countries such as Nicaragua. Labour spoke up for all these causes. The BLG also continuously launched attacks on the Conservative government in the UK and its many injustices perpetrated on their constituents. At that time the Poll Tax was high on the home agenda and there were vigorous local opposition campaigns.

During this period there were initiatives on equal treatment at work and on indirect discrimination against women. The Women's Rights Committee wanted legislative action to deal with inequalities. Tongue and Crawley worked alongside their Socialist colleagues particularly on parental leave, pro rata rights for part time workers and measures to mitigate violence against women and children, with support from women in the UK particularly in the trades unions and NGOs. They were often up against formidable Tory women capable of developing tricky and nuanced strategic positions, particularly Dame Shelagh Roberts.

Major pieces of European equalities legislation such as that for equal pay, and equal treatment and access to employment, training and working conditions were brought in towards the end of the 1970s, and during the 1980s included the Directive on equal treatment in occupational social security schemes and equal treatment in training and work promotion. The Socialist Group, with active participation from Crawley and Tongue, highlighted sexual violence against women and girls and instigated a parliamentary hearing, producing a brochure on the subject. Hedy D'Ancona, a Dutch Member from the Socialist Group (and later Minister for Social Affairs in the Dutch government) was the rapporteur in 1986 on a report on sexual violence, and was strongly supported by Crawley in her work. The right, particularly the UK Conservatives, tabled an avalanche of wrecking amendments.

Elliott also took a place on the Women's Committee where he was bemused to find that some right-wing women were also feminists, generally concerned with the world of work such as taxation matters. One such veteran was Marlene Lenz, a German Christian Democrat who was Vice-President of the European Women's Union, an organization somewhat to the right of the WI. He had hitherto thought that feminism was a preserve of the left. He relates that he travelled in cars to Frankfurt airport with some Conservative Members from time to time and was appalled at their sexist remarks about women.

Gordon Adam was not the only person to get involved in the Energy and Research Committee. Ford became a rapporteur on the Eureka research programme in 1987 and opposed participation of the EEC in the USA's Star Wars programme. His report was controversial and rejected by 176 – 174. He was furious because Falconer and Smith did not vote, hence his reference in a *Tribune* article to parliamentary cretinism. He was also pushing for a re-opening of dialogue with North Korea and for arms procurement at European level.

A British President

At half time, January 1987, there was a controversial election for President. Despite the unofficial agreement with the Christian Democrats that a Socialist should have the post in the second half of the parliamentary term, this was sabotaged. The Socialists put up Enrique Baron Crespo, of their Spanish delegation, the right put up Sir Henry Plumb. On the third ballot Plumb narrowly won with 241 votes against Baron Crespo's 236. Le Pen unhelpfully said that his Group of the European Right supported Plumb in the three rounds of voting.

Plumb says the EDG had originally wished Lady Elles to be their President but the Christian Democrats let it be known they did not support her and that over the Christmas holiday he was pressed into service. He shows no embarrassment about his support from the far right. In his book (Plumb, 2001) he reports on travelling to Paris to see Le Pen with the EDG Secretary-General, Robert Ramsay, aware that he needed those votes to secure his victory. He does acknowledge that it was an awkward mission and was concerned that news of it would leak out.

Immediately upon his election Socialists were on the attack about his support from Le Pen's group. Plumb stonewalled and simply insisted that he treated all legitimate groups in the Parliament according to the spirit and letter of the rules. Plumb was a strong pro-European and said upon election "I was born an Englishman, I will die a European". He clashed to some extent with Thatcher over policy, but was normally polite and friendly, though she insisted on calling the Parliament an Assembly and him the Speaker. She elevated him to the House of Lords in February of that year. A stickler for protocol, he controversially received the South African Ambassador in February, at the height of left attempts to ostracise that government for which Crawley and others vociferously attacked him.

The start of Plumb's tenure was to have coincided with the Single European Act coming into force and attendant new parliamentary powers, e.g. research policy becoming subject to the new co-decision procedure. However due to an Irish legal challenge, it did not come into force until the beginning of July. The new procedures enhanced the powers of committee chairmen who had to ensure that legislative proposals had agenda priority. It also meant that the Parliament had to muster 260 votes to win the necessary SEA majority. Here began a period of much closer co-operation between the two biggest groups, Socialists and Christian Democrats (both at the time led by large Germans – Rudi Arndt and Egon Klepsch).

Plumb said that during his time in the chair he was faced every day with British Labour Members and some others seeking to raise various points of order. He had to learn to deal with them without delaying the business of the House. Simone Veil was cross with him for putting up with it but he felt it was all part of the democratic process and was relatively tolerant. Deploying the correct rule could be difficult in the chair and in his book Plumb speaks of another President, Calvinist Piet Dankert, asking advice on rules from Enrico Vinci, the Sicilian Secretary-General of the Parliament, and stumbling on a cultural difference. Vinci would frustratingly whisper: "tell me the answer you want, Mr President, and I will find you a rule". In the face of a barrage of points of order at the beginning of the Strasbourg sessions, Plumb decided to permit a small mini debate on topical issues that came to be known as "Henry's happy half-hour".

There was a newsworthy event at the expense of the President when the Chief Minister of Gibraltar visited the cross-party but largely British Gibraltar Intergroup which demanded a meeting with Plumb. The latter was then in deep hot water with his Spanish colleagues, who threatened to withdraw from the EDG if the President acceded to a formal meeting. Plumb mollified them by agreeing to the meeting being unofficial and held at the residence of the British Consul-General. The event was a mess, however. The Gibraltarian had not been told of the change of venue and turned up at Plumb's parliamentary office, making a fuss. Gibraltar also caused a row between Tomlinson and Arndt in the Socialist Group when important visitors from the Gibraltar Labour Party were relegated to the visitors' room rather than the back seats in the Group meeting room as was normal for parliamentarians from sister parties. The shouting match was so bad that the meeting had to be closed. The Spanish were not happy with Labour and in an attempt to show that there was no hard feeling, staffer Dick Gupwell sat with the Spanish comrades that evening at a social event on a barge in Strasbourg. Not long after, however, the Socialists with Spanish support defeated a Labour attempt in the Group to win support to table an urgency motion criticizing the government on its handling of a strike at home. The BLG wondered why that was.

At the Copenhagen Summit in December 1987 Plumb took a step forward by asking that he submit Parliament's position paper to the European Council himself, instead of simply handing over a written paper. It was the first time the European Parliament had formally been present at a Council meeting. After a good deal of negotiating, this became an accepted practice and was the beginning of attempts to bring more transparency to Council meetings. It was also a step change for Parliament's image. (Much more has been written about this in Priestley, 2008.)

Constructive efforts

At the half-time change of parliamentary posts in January 1987, McGowan was elected President of the Development Committee. Being passionate about development policy, he took his role very seriously, working closely with colleagues from other nationalities whilst, as he says, "maintaining his left principles". Gerd Kramer from the Socialist Group staff assisted. McGowan is proud to have been the only British Member ever to have held this post, it being one normally coveted by the French. Other Presidents have since included Michel Rocard and Bernard Kouchner. During his term in charge of this committee he enjoyed a good relationship with Chris Patten, who was Minister for Overseas Development in the UK, having quarterly meetings with him and finding him professional and committed. Amongst other areas he worked on South Africa, Cuba, Western Sahara and Kashmir and pursued co-operative principles, peace and human rights.

The knock-on effect of this gain was that Seal lost control of his committee and became a Vice-Chair, and Collins remained without the Chair of Environment, which pleased him not at all though he remained Vice-Chair. Priorities for committee chairs were voted on in the BLG. Newman lost his position as Vice-Chair of the Regional Affairs Committee, but was the Socialist Group's Co-ordinator on the Petitions Committee, and then became a Vice-Chair of that. Crawley was still Vice-Chair of the Women's Rights Committee. Lomas says that as Leader he negotiated Vice-Chair of the Energy and Research Committee for Adam. Hoon was Chair of the China standing delegation. Adam was also Vice-Chair of the Budget Committee, Castle became Chair of the Malta delegation, Tomlinson Vice-Chair of Norway, now a separate delegation. Lomas had been for a short time a Vice-President of the Socialist Group, being succeeded by Martin and then Seal as the BLG's leadership changed.

Tom Megahy became Labour's Vice-President of Parliament, since Griffiths was a candidate for a safe seat at the general election. Megahy, being vociferously anti-market, was not asked to undertake many of the formal social duties of a Vice-President such as hosting dinners for important international guests, but he proved to have a good touch in the chair, as had his predecessor. He was often scheduled in late night slots but did not complain, and was loyally assisted by Jane Stowell who later went to work for the Socialist Group. He was congenial and popular and relished chairing, despite the pain he had to put up with due to a leg damaged by polio in his youth. He thoroughly enjoyed his two and a half years in the post, often socializing with his mates Lomas and Seal. Megahy did not do a great many reports during his time in the Parliament, but he did one on summer time in November 1987, suggesting that the change be made permanent.

Llewellyn Smith spent his entire period in the European Parliament raising concerns about nuclear energy, nuclear weapons and nuclear pollution and being an anti-establishment voice in the BLG. As a single-minded effort it was quite impressive and he had a highly expert academic advising him (Dr David Lowry). The Chernobyl disaster in April 1986 caused a certain amount of panic in European countries at risk from nuclear pollution and gave rise to debates about the safety of nuclear reactors and on their emergency plans and eventually to a directive on nuclear safety. Smith demanded a ban on trans-frontier shipment of nuclear fuels. A Committee of Inquiry on the handling and transport of nuclear material worked from January to July 1988 under the chairmanship of Conservative Alexander Sherlock, following alleged contraventions of law and maladministration by the Commission concerning handling of radioactive waste at the Mol plant and allegations of the supply of weapons grade nuclear material to Pakistan and Libya. The rapporteur was Schmid from the Socialist Group, who reported no infringement of Community law, but proposed a supervisory committee to exercise more control over Euratom. There was also a great deal of to and fro for months on end about an experiment at Trawsfynydd nuclear power station that had emerged following the publication of declassified Cabinet papers from 1957; this gave rise to many parliamentary questions and several resolutions.

Hughes became closely involved in the work of the Social Affairs and Employment Committee, specializing in health and safety policy (included in the Single Market measures under the SEA) and working towards a ban on asbestos. In 1987 he was proposing a five year ban on asbestos products where safe substitutes were available and a phase out of the rest on the grounds that it is a dangerous carcinogen, in the face of opposition from the right. In a report in March that year he complained the proposal did not go far enough. He worked on this consistently for years and had some victories. Stephen had quickly realized that the EEC could have a substantial effect on the lives of working people and resolved to take it seriously, becoming in favour of a reformed EEC and jettisoning his earlier anti-market position. He liked the cross party coalition approach and spurned invitations to stand for the House of Commons, feeling he could best contribute to the Labour movement where he was. Although often voting with the Campaign Group he tended to work constructively and without the rancour that some of his colleagues brought to their relations within the BLG. He says that Falconer and Lomas would ask him why he was doing parliamentary reports on legislation and he told them that there was a possibility to do things that were of benefit to working people.

Seal had made constructive remarks in November 1985 in a report on the Commission's annual economic report for the EEC. He continued to raise concerns about the state of the textile industry, fearing the loss of 90,000 jobs in the UK were the Multifibre Agreement (MFA) not to be extended. He opposed help for textile factories in Bavaria, saying that the UK local authorities could not access similar funds because the government had cut them off, supported by Hindley, who maintained that the UK textile industry could not survive unprotected. By January 1987, at the time of problems with the survival of British Leyland in the UK, Seal was also calling for a Community plan for the car industry. Although he maintains a Eurosceptic position to this day, in October that year he was in agreement with Delors that exchange controls and protectionism were not the answer to unemployment and saw the need for some action at European level. This led to a personal attack the following month by Conservative Welsh, resulting in the latter having to make a grudging public apology. During his first term Seal learned to fly and gained his pilot's licence in the mid 1980s. He was often to fly to Brussels and Strasbourg during his lengthy term of office and tells plenty of tales about his adventures in the air. He would sometimes fly other northern Labour MEPs to the regional airport, but it was not always uneventful. On one occasion he had to return to Strasbourg airport and negotiate an almost crash landing, with military planes scrambled, after his electrical system failed. Hughes, amongst his white-knuckled passengers, declined to travel that way again.

Carole Tongue was active with Collins on the Environment Committee in the battle against the Commission on infant formula follow-up milks, accusing the Commission of siding with the industry lobby. There was a campaign against Nestle's promotion of powdered milk in developing countries. She opposed the promotion of breast milk substitutes in violation of the WHO code. Collins and his committee Chair, Beate Weber, ably assisted by the secretariat headed by Lieven van der Perre, continued to push the Commission and Council on environment, public health and consumer protection matters. The committee pushed for heavy warnings on cigarette packs and Collins began a lengthy campaign to cut subsidies for tobacco farming in the budget. For many years it was untouchable, coming under the section ear-marked "compulsory expenditure", but his efforts were to bear fruit a decade or so later. He pointed out that there was still no clear cut commitment to environment policy in the Treaty and attempted to get 1987 declared a year of the environment.

The campaign to ban lead in petrol continued. Collins had led a cross-party group of Members to see the British Environment Minister back in 1983 only to be sent away with a negative response. However after publication of a report from the Royal Commission on Environmental Pollution highlighting the dangers of lead, the government had a change of heart prior to the 1983 election and Collins was asked to bring the colleagues back to Whitehall where the same Minister and civil servants who had opposed them earlier asked for their help. An agreement on lead-free petrol and on exhaust emissions was eventually reached in March 1985 but only after a titanic battle with the car manufacturers (including Ford in Tongue's constituency) who said they could not change over to lean burn engines until the late 1990s. When it was pointed out that Japan had already banned lead in petrol and were using catalytic converters, they caved in.

During these years the Environment, Economic and Monetary Affairs (EMAC) and Legal Affairs committees had several disputes about which should be responsible for undertaking reports on legislation, particularly in relation to controversial sectors. Collins' committee produced a report on protection of workers from exposure to benzene in September 1987 and after much pressure the Commission finally responded to parliamentary demands for an amending directive. It was not much to their liking, however, and without sufficient support from the Commission for its amendments after second reading on 12 October, Parliament rejected the common position on 14 November 1988 by 276 – 47 with 3 abstentions. According to Priestley, it was the first such rejection.

Following a vote in October 1985 to ban some growth promoters (a regulation having been proposed in 1984 for which Collins was rapporteur), two artificial hormones considered toxic and carcinogenic had been banned, but not three "natural" ones and the committee wanted them banned too since boys in Italy had been developing breasts. The ban led to threats from the Americans of a trade war, as Europe began refusing to permit imports of American meat treated with hormones. The committee ensured enough evidence was generated to endorse continuation of this policy despite the threat. Three proposals on veterinary medicinal products were produced in January 1989 by the Commission and Collins argued for a fourth hurdle for the licensing system, based on a socio-economic environmental impact assessment. It was never more than an idea raised in a speech to the pharmaceutical industry, but the idea took off and he once found the US Secretary of State for Agriculture knocking on his door wanting to talk about "the fourth criterion".

A Temporary Committee of Inquiry was set up in 1988-89 on hormones in meat after an inspector in Belgium was killed whilst investigating the use of illegal hormones. This battle moved over into the next Parliament where Collins and a Portuguese colleague Carlos Pimenta put forward a joint resolution calling for an equivalent to the US Food and Drug Administration. Eventually both the Medicines Agency and the Food Safety Agency came out of it.

Clinton Davis for the Commission had launched the fourth Environment Action Programme in 1987, containing initiatives on waste and chemicals. He also raised the problem of the greenhouse effect in 1988. Complaints about pollution of the Irish Sea from Sellafield caused difficulties for the UK government which the Labour Members were quick to exploit. There had also been on-going controversy about the UK's failure properly to implement the bathing water directive, and the Commissioner stopped just short of taking legal action against the UK during his term of office. His successor Ripa di Meana did so later on with respect to Blackpool, coinciding with a stint by Chris Patten as Environment Minister who belatedly announced a major change, that all sewage would require at least primary treatment before discharge.

Parliament urged better monitoring of environment directives at Collins' instigation and he also pushed through a report on the implementation of rules on water pollution. He worked closely with Delors for the development of a European Environment Agency, which took a great deal of time to get support from the Council of Ministers and then faced lengthy stalling about its location, eventually ending up in Copenhagen. Delors was able to announce in January 1989 that it would be set up, but it took some time before that was accomplished.

South Africa, the apartheid regime and support for Nelson Mandela were also focal points over many years. McGowan's Development Committee achieved a budget line for victims of apartheid, giving practical help delivered through NGOs. Another budget line was brought in to assist human rights and opposition groups in Pinochet's Chile.

By the late 1980s the Conservative government was preparing to privatize the water industry in the UK, to some concern. It was not at that stage happening on the continent. MEPs pointed out that the government was postponing compliance with European water quality and treatment directives even to the extent of warnings about being taken to the European Court of Justice. Collins, who by then was acting as an adviser to public sector trade union NALGO, wanted to know how water quality would be monitored. Clinton Davis suggested that privatization would be improper without proper monitoring and the government withdrew its early proposals and had to re-introduce them with the inclusion of a proposal to set up the National Rivers Authority. There was still a feeling that expensive implementation of improved water and sewage treatment plants was being held back until after privatization to enable costs to be passed on to the consumer. Being taken to the European Court only assisted this strategy and offered a good campaigning opportunity during the 1989 European elections. Public opinion was wary of privatization and there was deep concern about pollution of sea, river and drinking water.

Many of the BLG tabled questions and energetically opposed the sale of Royal Ordnance factories in the UK, particularly the lack of consultation with employees. Hoon was one with a factory in his constituency. Although this was not strictly a European matter, their actions forced a formal statement from the European Commission, made by Lord Cockfield. Labour Members expressed dissatisfaction and wanted a full debate. Castle, McMahon and Seal in November 1987 made accusations that the right-wingers were trying to suppress the rights of back-benchers and that Cockfield was dodging the issue. There was much fuss about the minutes appearing late. It transpired that the Wednesday minutes were so long that staff had worked until 7am, which caused Hughes to raise issues of health and safety on their behalf.

The steel industry was being reduced drastically in the UK and those from steel areas endlessly highlighted problems of the resulting unemployment. There was a knock-on effect of this on shipbuilding, and Quin put down a resolution in June 1986 about four thousand redundancies in the UK in this sector. By 1987 the UK had lost two-thirds of the steel workers it had in 1979 and employment in shipbuilding on Tyneside had halved from 1981. In addition, a clutch of Caterpillar plants closed in Glasgow and Gateshead. Collins was angry that there had been £62 million investment in Glasgow only the year before, and that there was still no Vredeling Directive to assist workers with advance information of plant closures. Quin and Collins brought workers from the Caterpillar factories to Brussels to visit French and Belgian workers, with the assistance of the Socialist Group. There were demands for help from the regional funds. Martin wrote a report for the Regional Committee demanding a new fund to deal with the problems and later, with the help of Bruce Millan, the RECHAR fund was developed, in theory enabling substantial funding to be delivered in stricken areas. It then suffered from the government refusing to input its share of the funds.

BLG swings again

At the AGM on 14 June 1988 the pendulum swung back to the left. Martin was defeated by Seal for the Leadership in a very close vote, 16 – 15 with Elliott abstaining, giving the BLG their fourth Leader in four years and another heap of bad publicity. Labour at home was trying to present a more unified face to the electorate but the European wing was doing the opposite. It did not go down well with Kinnock and the front bench. Elliott later said that he was not really in favour of Seal but although he thought Martin had the right ideas, he had been too young for the Leadership and that it had not been a success. Seal acknowledged that there was pressure from Kinnock not to change Leader again but he felt Martin was not being transparent and the left supported him. He thought it was unfortunate that it was made out to be a left-right split, but that is what it was. There had been a lot of pressure on Newens to support Martin (Kinnock had spoken to him when they were at a meeting on Rome), but finally he plumped for Seal. Adam was particularly angry at Newens this time because there had been some unfavourable publicity about Seal's personal doings.

The party at home and much of the Shadow Cabinet were moving cautiously closer to the policy approach of the Socialist Confederation, whilst the MEPs were led once more by anti-marketeers. Yet again the BLG was out of step. Castle was furious at what she saw as a spineless and (to her) insulting vote by Newens this time in favour of Seal rather than the more moderate Martin and made her views plainly known. Her priority was the image of the party, whilst she felt his behaviour was self-indulgent leftism. It all added to the years of poor publicity for the BLG at a time when Labour was trying unsuccessfully to win elections against the Tories.

Still at the 1988 AGM, Newens beat Tomlinson for Deputy Leader, 17 – 15, Buchan defeated Stevenson for Chair by 16 – 15 with Balfe abstaining. Balfe remained Secretary, winning 16 – 15 against Bird with Buchan in turn abstaining. An unresolved contest between Ford and Newman for Treasurer went to three ballots before it was decided to reconvene in July to resolve the matter. Elliott beat Crawley 17 – 15 for Whip and Hindley defeated Tongue 17 – 15 for Socialist Group Bureau member. The other change at that meeting was ratification of the Labour Party's request that MEPs pay 1% of their salaries to the party. This also applied to MPs, but it was a continual grouch over the years that the MPs'contributions were not policed as assiduously as those of their European counterparts.

The reconvened AGM on 5 July elected Newman 16 – 14 against Ford for Treasurer. No voters actually changed sides, but Crawley and Collins were absent (the latter coming in too late to vote). By this time Ford was being supported by the pro-marketeers; however alliances by this time were less about individuals and more about following a particular slate. Elliott voted for Newman. He says he did not always vote for slates but for individuals yet his record shows him voting fairly consistently with the hard left slate. No-one seemed to take any notice of what the outside world would make of this state of constant warfare.

Wayne David remembers a taste of the bitterness. He was visiting as a guest of Griffiths, and watched in amazement as Castle put up her hand to speak, to be ignored by Buchan in the Chair whereupon the pair of them entered into a slanging match using colourful unparliamentary language, the like of which he had not previously encountered in a Labour Party meeting.

This meeting also included a discussion on the position of Martin as Socialist Group Vice-President. Buchan as Chair called on the Leader to introduce it as an additional item on the agenda, which first of all instigated a challenge to the Chair from Martin as to whether it could be on the agenda. The challenge to Chair was lost 12 -17. The minutes of the meeting state the following:

> "The Leader reported on a meeting he and the Secretary had had that morning with the Chair of the Socialist Group concerning the position of David Martin as Vice President on the Bureau. Richard Balfe moved that this BLG instructs David Martin to resign his position as Vice Chairman of the Socialist Group immediately. Hugh McMahon moved an amendment to delete 'instructs' and substitute 'requests', which was accepted by Balfe. David Martin explained his position and there followed a discussion. The Leader replied to the discussion. Eddy Newman moved that there should be a recorded vote on Balfe's motion as amended and this was agreed with 18 votes for. The motion was carried by 22 votes in favour and seven abstentions."

Following the vote, Martin informed the meeting that he had posted a letter of resignation from his office in Edinburgh the previous Wednesday.

Relations between Martin and Seal were at an all-time low. Martin's relations with Jo Oxenbould had also not been good as she complained that he was giving all the political research aspects of the job to his own assistant, Greg Perry.

Astonishingly, the meeting then switched tone to welcome Labour Commissioner Clinton Davis to the meeting who spoke about his programme of visits to Members' constituencies. It then went on to discuss normal plenary business. Having totally exhausted everyone, there followed a report on funding the next European election campaign from the Leader saying that no allocation of money had been made as yet, and that he had met Whitty who had agreed with him on the need to resurrect the EEC Liaison Committee and to discuss preparations for the European elections. Deputy Leader Newens would be the BLG's representative on the Campaign Strategy Committee, the Leader would be the representative on the policy review, continue to attend weekly Shadow Foreign Affairs team meetings in the House of Commons and also keep in touch with Philip Gould on the information campaign finances. Gould, an advertising man running the Shadow Communications Agency, was to become famous for his focus group opinion polling and was actively involved in Labour's election campaigning. He was also working with the Socialist Group on "Information campaign" matters. There was a substantial budget for this coming from the Socialist Group and Gould's firm was benefiting from a contract and running various campaigns in 1987-88, with thousands of leaflets being produced and themed press launches under the banner of "Bringing common sense to the common market", fronted by Bryan Gould, with relevant BLG spokespersons. There was, as ever, some dispute about the substance of advertising. The left were opposed to Philip Gould and to central use of the funds which they maintained should be at the disposal of individual Members rather than being top-sliced.

Seal also reported on a meeting with Joyce Gould (now Baroness Gould), a senior Labour Party national official (and no relation to Philip Gould or indeed Bryan Gould), on the reselection process. This was now completed for all sitting Members except for Huckfield where the regional office were intervening. A list of target seats had also been agreed.

In campaigning mode

The 1988 draft budget was rejected by Parliament including BLG votes and the provisional twelfths were yet again in operation for 1988. There was some concern among British Members about the sudden withdrawal of subsidies for visitor groups. The Parliament became concerned that it had no power to prevent overspending being agreed by Council. Tomlinson was active in obtaining a new Inter-Institutional Agreement in 1988 to the effect that policy implementation could not precede suitable budget amendments. This was a step change. He was also putting the case for Objective One status for Birmingham late that year, probably with an eye to the high unemployment and the following year's election. There had been an agreement at the European Council in February 1988 to double the structural funds in real terms by 1993, in accordance with Delors' dream of helping to balance the effects of the internal market. The budget was in a mess by May because farm prices had been agreed that were higher than planned. Finally, in December, Labour voted to support the following year's budget for the first time ever. Tomlinson's announcement of support was greeted with applause and laughter.

All British Members received large mail bags from animal lovers voicing a plethora of concerns. Castle, a fervent animal lover, made a rousing speech in February 1989 in favour of banning the leghold trap for fur-bearing animals. She waved a trap in the Chamber, demanding fur labelling and saying there had been a nauseating alliance between Spanish bullfighters and Danish trappers to protect their vested interest and that she was bitterly disappointed at the lack of progress. She pointed out that the indigenous people who were complaining that this would end their way of life had in fact suffered that fate two centuries earlier at the hands of the Hudson Bay Company.

The Commission's attempts to abolish VAT derogations were taken as threatening the UK's zero rating on food, children's clothes, books, newspapers and funerals. Labour Members never lost any opportunity in sticking up for the zero VAT rate, and pursued the Commission with questions for years on end. Tomlinson was one of the most vociferous, backed up by Castle, McMahon and many of the others. It was one matter on which they were united that did tend to gain some favourable press coverage for the MEPs and the zero rates remain in place.

Peace, disarmament and military policy was often controversial, and Members tended to follow their conscience with no Group coherence. A year after Spain had voted in a referendum to stay in NATO, in March 1987 Morris called for the Warsaw Pact and NATO to be dissolved (a fairly popular line on the left at that time) but in November 1988, after Kinnock had changed the party line, Ford was saying that we must strengthen the European pillar in NATO.

In a debate on services for the elderly, Ken Stewart asked for the EEC to set minimum standards for heating homes on the grounds that such standards existed for places of work. Stewart mostly worked on maritime matters and undertook a report on seafarers on which he worked for twelve months. He was upset that it was so amended in committee that it was no longer recognisably his report and resigned as rapporteur. His work had concentrated on safety and conditions for seamen and he followed up that work assiduously. The sinking of the *Herald of Free Enterprise* gave rise to a great deal of concern and both Stewart and Huckfield and also Martin pursued safety at sea matters following this disaster.

The controversial espionage exposé *Spycatcher* by former MI5 secret service officer Peter Wright, was published in Australia by Heinemann in 1987 but banned in Britain because of its alleged sensitive content. This was still the pre-internet age and it was legally on sale in the USA but getting it into the UK was difficult. Ford staged an event to highlight the absurdity of the censorship in what was a threatening atmosphere, having imported some copies and sold them to colleagues. Crawley seized the opportunity to make fun of the British government. She rose in plenary in September to read out a section of the book, cheekily demanding that her excerpt be published in the minutes. Ford joined the fray as the week progressed. These two plus Cryer, McMahon, Hughes and Hoon made a fuss about whether written explanations of vote are published in the official record of debates, or in the minutes, to highlight the pointlessness of the UK ban. Questions were asked about whether the *Rainbow* (the daily verbatim report of proceedings) would be distributed by HMSO (as was normal). Tomlinson spoke about a resolution on human rights and the following month there was one. Ford suggested that a delay in production of the *Rainbow* was due to Plumb attempting to censure Parliament's record. It was more likely to have been the officials misguidedly acting in what they thought was the best interest of the establishment but it was of interest to the MEPs because journalist Palmer wanted to quote it by reporting the official record of Parliament.

When the big hurricane hit the UK in October 1987 British Members across the board were seeking aid. There was also sympathy from all sides when the Kings Cross fire in Newens' constituency killed thirty people in November 1987 and point-scoring across the political divide was temporarily put on hold. Likewise after the Manchester air disaster in 1985 Eddy Newman had pushed long and hard for better air safety.

Labour's passionate defence of human rights led the MEPs to support a Socialist Group proposal for the Parliament to set up an annual Sakharov Prize. The first prize was awarded in 1988 to Nelson Mandela, followed in 1989 by Alexander Dubcek and in 1990 Aung San Suu Kyi of Burma.

In the first six months of 1988 the EC took more decisions than in the ten years from 1974-84 and it kept noses to the grindstone in committees and plenary. The main driver of this was the log jam of legislation for the 1992 "deadline" for the Single Market.

Under the German Presidency in February 1988, agreement was reached in the budget to double the regional and social funds, shifting the balance and reducing somewhat the dominance of agriculture. This was the first "Delors package," long the aim of socialist leaders and seen as a substantial sea change. The new regulations included a partnership arrangement whereby additionality was legally written in to the rules. From this point, these funds became more useful in tackling unemployment and regional development. The Germans then pressed on with a further development and established a committee of national experts to write a report on the prospects of economic and monetary union (EMU). The Socialist Confed held a number of special meetings and conferences on this development, in January in Brussels, March in Paris.

The pressure of legislation led to more night sittings of the Parliament and the staff were not happy about the long hours. There was a strike in June that year in protest. Seal and Ford spoke in support of their right to take such action.

Socialist Group "study days" were held in Glasgow in September 1988, agreed when Martin was Leader, in an attempt to show that the UK could be welcoming to the Socialists. Buchan did everything she could to stop this happening, ostensibly because she feared bad publicity. It was even suggested the reason may have been that she normally took her holidays in September and would not have been able to be present as the local Member. She and Collins clashed over the meeting and there was a huge row, too, with Castle, culminating in Castle whispering loudly: "I never could cope with the fish wife tendency". The successful event took place when Seal was Leader, with Kinnock making a pro-European speech. Both Glasgow City

Council and Strathclyde Regional Council hosted receptions and dinners for the Group. Buchan organized a "culture" visit to meet the local Italian community. A visit to Tate & Lyle sugar refinery, a whisky distillery and a business centre was organized by McMahon and Collins led an energy and environment visit. At a social event Collins sang a folk song about the Spanish Civil War by Ewan McColl, dedicated to Spanish comrades, which went down well. Buchan printed some political posters from that time but accidentally chose those for a party that the Spanish were not happy about. She and Seal also organized a caucus meeting for the next round of election candidates, but only selected left-wingers were invited. When David Earnshaw (a pro-marketeer) got wind of it and turned up the gathering was hastily adjourned. Such was the bitterness about the whole event on the part of Buchan that, following the death of her widely-liked and respected MP husband Norman in 1990, Collins, Martin and McMahon received a letter from her telling them that they would not be welcome at his funeral.

Delors' important speech to the TUC in September 1988 invoking a vision of a social Europe, clinched Thatcher's opposition to the EEC and she responded with her famous Bruges speech at the College of Europe. She said: "We have not successfully rolled back the frontiers of the state in Britain only to see them re-imposed at a European level with a European super-state exercising a new dominance from Brussels." This was the culmination of a gradual drift of Conservative opinion away from support for the EEC, together with a similar swing towards it from Labour. Stephen Wall (Wall, 2008) says that this was dynamite and shock waves resonated around the EC. He said: "even Margaret Thatcher had not previously made such a frontal assault on the EC's institutions, the Commission in particular."

Following on from this, Labour conference in 1988 carried resolution 58 in favour of a social Europe. A further resolution, number 496, calling for an amendment to the 1972 European Communities Act (code for the anti-marketeers) was remitted to the NEC, there to be quietly ignored.

An official visit of Pope John Paul II took place in October 1988, giving the Reverend Paisley another opportunity for a loud disturbance in the Chamber. Plumb thought he had defused him in advance by allowing him to express his objections the previous day, but was nevertheless expecting a disturbance and had warned the Pope that something might happen. Continuing to protest, the Reverend was briskly removed. On a lighter note, Tongue wryly observed that any sculptures in the Parliament that featured nudes had been discreetly removed for the visit so as not to cause offence to His Holiness.

In 1988 the Parliament, using its new assent procedure, refused three trading agreements with Israel, unhappy with the conditions imposed on Palestinian producers wishing to export from the occupied territories to Europe. This was at the time of the Intifada in the West Bank and Gaza. Plumb points out that "a majority in Parliament were sympathetic to Palestinian complaints that their agricultural producers were being prevented from organizing a proper export trade because of bureaucratic harassment by the Israelis at the border crossing points. There had been considerable diplomatic activity, but by the time the vote was due to be taken it had not been resolved." There followed a ping pong between the Parliament and Council and Parliament postponed consideration of the agreements for several months. Once some concessions had been negotiated by the German

Presidency, Parliament finally gave its assent. The vote in October was 315 – 24 and 19 abstentions. Labour mostly went along with the flow on this confrontation but on this occasion nineteen of the BLG voted against, feeling that the concessions were not sufficient: Balfe, Buchan, Cryer, Falconer, Ford, Hindley, Huckfield, Hughes, Lomas, Martin, McMahon, Megahy, Morris, Newens, Seal, Smith, Stevenson, Stewart and West. A few voted with the Socialist Group in favour: Castle, Collins, Griffiths and Quin. The others are not recorded as voting on this occasion.

A more controversial visitor in September 1988 was Yasser Arafat, leader of the PLO, invited by the Socialist Group, then addressing various meetings. In addition to the attendant media scrum, this caused substantial problems because of Arafat's armed bodyguards. After much negotiation it was agreed that the French and Parliament security forces would take responsibility for the man's personal safety whilst he was in the building, and his bodyguards had to deposit their arms before entering the building. The Socialist Group put pressure on Plumb to meet him and the Labour MEPs were delighted to have put Plumb on the spot.

Hoon produced a report in July the same year for the Legal Affairs Committee in favour of prohibiting dual membership of the European Parliament and national parliaments. Members from countries such as France and Italy in particular often had dual mandates and this affected their attendance and work in the Parliament, which was starting to feel it had important work to undertake. He remembers having many discussions about this with John Hume, who held a dual mandate throughout his terms as a MEP and was not happy with the report's conclusions. This report, however, did not suggest attempting to ban dual mandates for regional authorities and that was the core of the French problem, as many Members were Mayors of towns and spent most of their time at home cultivating their local base rather than attending to committee work or Parliament. Before this principle was ever put into practice (for the 1994 election), Hoon himself was to run a dual mandate from 1992-94.

Huckfield in the Transport Committee wrote a report proposing an EU common transport fund to subsidise public transport but he says this was so heavily amended that it was eventually withdrawn before it saw light of day in plenary.

Parliament, conscious of pressure for more meetings in Brussels, began a programme of building in that city around rue Belliard, aided by the Belgian government. Derek Prag, Conservative, had proposed that a single seat for the Parliament was essential, but this was ignored by the governments. There were almost never any debates about building policy on the floor of the House, negotiations being confined to the Bureau and kept rather secret. The tendency was to present *faits accomplis*.

Nominations for new British members of the European Commission were Leon Brittan for the Conservatives and Bruce Millan for Labour. This had a problematic knock-on effect for Labour. Millan resigned his seat in the House of Commons (where he had been during the previous Labour government Secretary of State for Scotland), forcing a by-election on 10 November 1988. Glasgow Govan should have been a safe Labour seat but the public are never too happy about people running off to well-salaried positions in Europe and there was a shock upset for Labour, with the SNP's

Jim Sillars winning the seat against Labour's Bob Gillespie. The Labour vote was down 27.8% and SNP up 38.4%. Sillars lost the seat back to Labour at the next general election. Millan and Collins never completely saw eye to eye. The by-election for Richmond held the following February to replace Leon Brittain, was won for the Conservatives by William Hague.

In the bleak mid-winter of December 1988 another by-election was needed in Hampshire Central, following the death of Conservative MEP Basil de Ferranti. It was a safe seat, returning Edward Kellett-Bowman, who had been defeated in 1984, to the European scene. Labour's candidate, John Arnold, came second, due to a split SLD/SDP vote. The lack of public enthusiasm for this election was shown by the very poor turnout of 14.1%.

At last in January 1989 MEPs were able to apply for passes to the Westminster palace complex. It made life much easier when they needed to go to meetings, particularly if stopping off on the way to an airport, with a bag in tow.

In April 1989 the question of footballers and their contracts and transfer fees became a controversial issue and remained so in the BLG, Members taking different positions depending on the football lobbies at home. It was some years before the matter was resolved at the European level. There was more on football, including the identity card scheme for fans. Trials took place for twenty-six British football fans charged with involuntary manslaughter following the May 1985 Heysel stadium riot in Belgium, and some were found guilty with three year prison sentences.

Castle's last speech was, typically, on agricultural prices in April 1989, looking back with affection to Commissioner Gundelach who had died, supporting the Commission's latest proposals as realistic, hitting out at the Agriculture Committee that "characteristically" was asking for more, and insisting we must carry on with reforms. She had worked on CAP reform with Stevenson, Morris and Peter Smith, a British Commission official in the Agriculture Directorate whom she would call in to her office at all hours and grill mercilessly in order to get the best advice. They got on well because he would argue with her with wit and perception (she hated sycophants) and even visited her at home in the Chilterns to work on reform plans. Castle personally commissioned Professor Kenneth Thomson, an agricultural economist at the Aberdeen School of Agriculture to test whether a deficiency payment system would be viable. She felt his final report gave a positive result, vindicating her work, but the plan, she later said, "got lost in the flurry of the Euro elections in 89". It was a good many years more before the set aside system was approved. Although she did not reform the CAP, Castle had made a considerable contribution during her ten years in the European Parliament and made real her philosophy that "in politics, guts is all". The Germans later awarded Castle the Commander's Cross of Order of Merit and the English interpreters sent her a letter on her retirement and made a special presentation saying they would miss the challenge of interpreting her. She was sorely missed by many in the Socialist Group who admired her tenacity, dedication and stamina even when they disagreed with her political position. As she had once said to Eric Heffer: "We as socialists have always talked about international cooperation – here [in the Parliament] we are practising it."

One of the early opportunities for Parliament to flex its muscles with its

SEA powers came in May 1989, when MEPs voted to strengthen the terms of a Council position on a draft directive to control car emissions. There were no Labour speakers on this, the rapporteur being German, but they did support the vote. Both health and climate change considerations meant that car emissions remained a high priority for the next two decades.

Right at the end of the Parliament Collins managed to get through his report on nitrates and other pollutants in water, making a comprehensive speech very late at night on the Thursday of the May session "to a vast and no doubt appreciative audience" consisting mostly of the interpreters and a few officials. It was a triumph of tenacity over time-tabling strictures. The Tories hated it. He had wanted to get it through because at home they were in the process of privatizing drinking water and it was a useful piece of electoral propaganda. He, Pollack and Earnshaw with some others took advantage of this for a campaign photo opportunity, taking a petition to Downing Street.

The last BLG speaker before the election was Adam on the internal energy market on Friday 26 May 1989. It was the second time he had been the last Labour voice before an election.

Taking on rapporteurships was not an indication of the amount of work a Member was doing, particularly since little legislation passes through some committees and Parliament' powers on legislation were also still embryonic. Adam produced opinions for his committee on the budget, Balfe did a report on Turkey, Crawley on women and children in prison, Ford on research and on the arms trade, Hindley on trade with China, Hoon on consumer credit and on dual mandate, Huckfield on transport, Hughes on health and safety, McMahon on new technologies, Megahy on summertime, Seal on the MFA, Smith on Euratom safety and Tongue on hotel fire safety. The remainder did not produce reports in this parliamentary term. They all tabled dozens of questions and many resolutions.

Constructing a better future

Tomlinson, Deputy Leader for the brief period of Martin's Leadership, was a forward-thinking tactician and had early strategic talks with Jean-Pierre Cot about the future. Tomlinson felt this should be worked out with Kinnock. During a Labour Local Government Conference in Birmingham, he talked to Priestley, Kinnock and Clarke about how things might shape up. They thought there would be substantial gains in the 1989 elections, and this would entitle Labour to more posts in a range of European organizations. The challenge was what to do with it. Kinnock and Hattersley were keen to signal that Labour was finally on board for Europe. Together they hit on the idea of bargaining with the aim of a Brit taking a job in the package of posts that would be available.

The various top positions in the Socialist Group, Confederation of Socialist Parties, and those available in the Parliament had traditionally been agreed amongst the European parties on the basis of a deal and shared amongst different nationalities. Cot from France was keen to become President of the Group, Enrique Baron from Spain wanted to run again for President of Parliament, and the idea was floated of supporting Julian Priestley (far and away the most senior Labour Brit in the Parliament secretariat) for General Secretary of the Group with a view to having him in place as a springboard to a bigger post in the Parliament in due course when Vinci, Secretary-General of the Parliament, retired during the next decade. The other part of the equation was Axel Hanisch of the SPD for General Secretary of the Confederation.

This whole package was a bit of long-term strategy hitherto unknown by Labour and involving closer collaboration with the continentals than had taken place in the past. Mitterrand, Jospin, Rocard and Fabius all spoke to Kinnock about supporting Cot, and Priestley's support for the plan was sought. This deal then had to be negotiated with Bettino Craxi. To clinch the deal after the 1989 election the negotiations included phone calls from Ford to Priestley from a motorway café, and Tomlinson tracking him down on a walking holiday in Norway. Gwyneth Dunwoody, chair of the International Committee, wanted to support Blackman for Socialist Group General Secretary but the feeling was that he was only supported by the left and would not get sufficiently broad support across the Group. The deal was done.

By this time MEPs were contributing financially to regional party offices, in addition to their 1% of salary tithe to the national party, and this also gave them representation rights in the Regional Executive Committees, or Boards as they were later to become known.

The backstage crew

The EPLP benefited from a larger allowance from the Socialist Group as a result of its increased numbers and was able to afford more staff. Jan Royall departed by the end of 1985 to work in Neil Kinnock's private office. Being highly-educated, politically aware and fluent in several languages, she had not been over-excited by being expected to undertake a range of mundane tasks, including letters booking Lomas' hotel rooms and was keen to join the forward-looking team Kinnock had gathered around himself.

Jo Oxenbould, an Oxford graduate, was head of the London office in Queen Anne's Gate, being assisted in the later period by Kevin Flack, Richard Frost and eventually Ann Oldroyd. She worked long, thankless hours on preparation and tasks resulting from BLG meetings, such as tabling urgency resolutions, often having to make several hundred copies of resolutions the BLG wished to table in the dead of night to put on desks in the Socialist Group meeting room because its meeting ended after the Group's document deadline. Occasionally others were drafted in for temporary work as the 1989 election drew closer and thousands of leaflets were being distributed to MEPs' offices. There were problems in that the Group was split down the middle and it was often not clear whether staff should obey the dictates of the Leader or the Group Secretary or officers and some officers were not above shouting at the staff on occasions. Oxenbould recalls at one time having to choose between working at one officer's meeting called by Martin as Leader and another called at the same time by Balfe as Secretary, and chose the latter, believing she was supposed to work to the Group Secretary. It did not go down well with the Leader. The situation was quite untenable for the staff who attempted not to be drawn into one or other of the factions. The staffing arrangements had grown with no coherent plan and by the end of the parliamentary period the situation was less than perfect, although Oxenbould and Flack had been eventually put on to Labour Party pay scales.

There was one positive spin-off of Huckfield's period in the Labour group. He was a whiz at technology, always up to date with the latest gadgets (the first Member to use a laptop in the plenary) and persuaded the BLG to upgrade its equipment and begin to get into the IT age. He says that as a result of his impetus, Tony Robinson obtained BT Gold e-mail addresses for all the BLG.

Most MEPs still only had staff in their constituencies, employed on a range of salary and contractual scales, often without pension funds, although funding for assistants and offices was increased in 1985. Unlike Westminster, the European Parliament had no Members' staff pension scheme and indeed an Assistants' Statute was not voted until 2008. Castle's researcher set up an assistants' group and persuaded Members to fund meetings once or twice a year to compare conditions. It was only grudgingly supported by the Members, some of whom presided over very low rates of pay and rather stingy employment practices. The group was never a cosy bunch given their political differences, but the meetings helped some of the lower paid to better their conditions and served as a useful forum for exchanging campaigning ideas. A couple of the sensible stalwarts were Megahy's assistant, Kate Moore and Seal's assistant Ann Martin. In 1986 the UK's Parliamentary Labour Party agreed to negotiate with their assistants' trades unions for the purpose of discussing terms and conditions of employment, but MEPs still refused to recognize their assistants as a collective, not least as they were not all in the same union. There was some disgruntlement at this but not a lot was resolved.

In the Socialist Group the British administrators were by then David Blackman, one of the Deputy General Secretaries, Dick Gupwell, Geoff Harris and Roy Cattermole. Colin Kotz and Paulette Fuller were appointed during this parliament. Kotz was a clever linguist with a solid Labour background, his father having been a prominent GLC Councillor. He had a great sense of fun, and worked on the Women's Committee amongst other duties. A decade later he left to retrain as an interpreter. Fuller was young, gifted and black and helpful to Castle on Socialist Group business. Tessa Ryan, later to move to Kinnock's office at the Commission, joined in 1988 and was a staunchly loyal and dedicated Labour member, with a dry wit and quick brain. She returned to the Socialist Group secretariat after Kinnock ended his term in the Commission in 2004. Julie Owens, who left to fight (unsuccessfully) the UK parliamentary seat of Peterborough in 1992, also arrived during this term. These individuals did not work to Labour, but functioned for the Socialist Group on the various parliamentary committees, providing briefings, preparing voting lists and the like. There were also British secretaries, many of whom took an interest in the Labour Group's doings.

Nick Sigler from the Labour Party's research department was seconded to the Socialist Group for one year in 1985-86, partly to address British underrepresentation. Nick, who had been responsible for agriculture policy and Europe back in London, worked as British liaison officer to Castle as Vice-President of the Group. Castle tended to treat him as a personal researcher on agriculture and he did substantial work with her on CAP reform. Appointed in March 1985, he did not start work until much later in the year after she had lost the leadership to Lomas. Despite remaining a Eurosceptic, Sigler reports that Lomas was incapable of working with him as he saw him as a Labour headquarters' stooge and he felt his position was fairly untenable from the start. He observed that the BLG was rife with tensions and conspiracy theorists and it was impossible to build any coherence. When the Anglo-Irish Agreement was in the offing, Nick phoned Kinnock's office in London to find out what the party line was whereupon Lomas attacked him for being a lackey of the Leader's office. He reports that he did manage fairly good relations with Buchan who was Secretary of the BLG at the time. Whitty records that he, too, had fairly good relations with Buchan, probably because she always wanted the BLG to keep a close relationship to the party at home.

Tony Robinson was the Group's British press officer, with a keen news eye for sensational anti-European stories. Nevertheless he would not sanction any old rubbish, and on one occasion drew the line at a draft Stewart had produced, refusing to put it out. Stewart was incensed at this and in front of Ford and several members of the British press corps, punched Robinson in a restaurant in Strasbourg. The event was happily greeted in the *Liverpool Echo* as "Our Ken punches Europrat".

Castle struck up a particular friendship with an extremely competent Belgian administrator, Nadia van Hamme, in the Socialist Group during the time when she worked on the Bureau. Nadia, a close friend of Ernest Glinne, took Castle, Pollack and Castle's secretary from High Wycombe, Joan Woodman, on a trip to Bruges and her home village in the spring of 1984.

On the Energy and Research Committee Reinhold Hack of the SPD worked in the Socialist Group with Adam, in tandem with Gordon Lake on the Parliament side, who was possessed of a fine sense of humour and tactical intelligence. Lake died in very sad circumstances in Luxembourg in 2002. The Budget Committee benefited from the wisdom of Michael Shackleton who became one of the authors of textbooks on the Parliament with Corbett and Francis Jacobs, another talented administrator.

Many of the BLG did not take kindly to Socialist Group staff of any nationality, considering them to be right-wing pro-marketeers generally working against them. There was a grain of truth in this, but these were also passionate, able and hard working party members, no matter what their nationality, working for the common good. Reinhold Hack recalls that the BLG Members were largely allergic to the word "compromise", which was the mainstay of Group attempts to survive in a multinational and multiparty Parliament. They had to devise a form of words when developing strategy on legislation with BLG Members without talking about compromise, along the lines of "How can we find a way to go forward and yet retain as much as possible of what we believe in?" As a socialist political animal, SPD staffer Fritz Roll made friends with many of the Brits. Many of the staff from all nationalities were exceptionally talented and committed and most did their best to work constructively with the British.

There are numerous Labour Party members scattered around in offices of the European institutions, many of whom give strong support to the party at election times. Priestley and Chris Piening from the Parliament staff came and campaigned for Ford in his election campaign. Quite a few are active in the Brussels Labour Group which meets regularly, debates European political issues and sometimes fundraises. Some of its most active members at that time were Peter Wragg and Belinda Pyke, both Commission officials, and earlier, a British feminist Joanna Tachmintsis.

Not much togetherness

By now the BLG was far too fragmented to be socializing as a group and *L'Orient* had ceased to hold its former charm. It was not long before it closed down, its owner moving to another city. Similarly, the Christmas parties in Brussels had come to an end, partly due to increased size and partly lack of coherence.

The rigours of getting up very early on Mondays for planes to Strasbourg notwithstanding, this became a favourite evening for various dining groups. The pro-marketeers joined with some members of the staff and assistants and met in *L'Ogelgluk*, a restaurant within walking distance of the Parliament. Discussions were lively and generally focused on a particular topic, sometimes with a guest speaker from one of the other national groups. All had equal speaking rights, whether they were a Member or not. These dinners continued for many years. Ford also attended a different multi-national and multi-party Monday dinner club and recalls that on one occasion, Jesse Jackson came and spoke. This met in *L'oiseau de France* and it, too, continued for quite some years.

The Campaign Group kept to themselves and generally enjoyed their own company. McGowan stayed with a local family in Strasbourg and did not do much dining out. The rest of them frequented an Italian restaurant in Brussels where the proprietor named a pasta dish *à la Ken Stewart*. Stewart tended to order the same dish and professed to prefer quantity to quality, and endeared himself to this particular establishment. In Strasbourg they preferred a Chinese, *Le Mandarin* in the central district or *La Bodega*. There was little fraternizing with the rest of the Labour Group except for Hughes who was friendly with them.

Occasionally some sport was played and here cross-party or cross-faction considerations did not seem to matter. Seal played squash with Tongue. She was fairly active, and also played tennis with Collins. Five-a-side football matches were sometimes held between Members and staff or Labour and Socialist Group and so on.

The May asparagus feasts were still going strong, and attended by many of the Labour and Socialist Members, although the Campaign Group kept away. Castle organized a farewell lunch from the BLG for *The Guardian*'s left-wing European correspondent John Palmer during one of those more relaxed periods.

Preparing for election

At grass roots level, the influential Labour Co-Ordinating Committee organized a high-profile weekend European conference in London in November 1987 with a wide range of speakers, under the title "The Alternative to Trade Wars?" Key figures in the organization were Frances Morrell, a former assistant to Tony Benn, Tongue, and Pollack, assistant to Barbara Castle who was herself selected as a candidate the following week. The event was endorsed by the top ranks of the party, who felt it was never something that it would be able to organize itself at that time.

In the chair was Tom Sawyer, Deputy General Secretary of the trade union NUPE (and later Labour Party General Secretary) with keynote speakers Bryan Gould MP and top socialists from many European countries. All had agreed to come at their own expense. The agenda was wide-ranging and designed to stimulate ideas and debate. Tony Blair, then on Labour's Treasury Team, spoke on Europe and the World Financial System together with socialist economists from Germany, France and Spain. There was a session on Defending Workers' Rights in Multinational Europe, with Denis MacShane, then with the International Metal Workers in Geneva (later an MP and Europe Minister) and Michael Meacher MP, Labour spokesperson on Employment, as well as other speakers from Ireland, Finland, and Hedy D'Ancona as Chair of the Parliament Women's Committee. An important session on environment included Oskar Lafontaine from Germany, then a prominent figure in the SPD. Whitty summed up the first day as General Secretary of the Labour Party, together with Coates and an Italian woman MEP. He referred to the need for more effective co-operation between Socialist parties of Europe in approaching economic and industrial policy within the EEC.

The second day carried a session "Do we need a European Industrial Strategy?" chaired by John Lloyd of the *New Statesman*. Speakers included leading trade unionists, academics and politicians from the UK and abroad. A session on "Single Country Reflation – can it work?" was presided over by the charismatic Palmer of *The Guardian* with French, German and Danish politicians debating with Stuart Holland MP, author of *Out of Crisis*. A further session looked at trade and the CAP with Joan Lestor MP, Meghnad Desai from LSE and speakers from NGOs. Then a session on the Internal Market was conducted with another high flying range of Europeans plus Martin as Leader of the Labour Group of MEPs. The regional divide and inner cities was conducted by Pollack with Michael Ward and more eminent speakers from the UK, Italy and France plus Gerhard Stahl from the German SPD in the Socialist Group, now Secretary General of the Committee of the Regions in Brussels. Finally, the conference wound up with a session including Ford, Karsten Voigt, then SPD Foreign Affairs spokesperson, Whitty and Morrell.

The low-budget conference was a huge success, well-attended and written up constructively in the press. It had aired and openly debated contentious issues, presenting arguments that the EEC could be a force for progress. The message to the constituency parties was that they should think carefully about the candidates they selected next time. It was seen by many as a pivotal event in opening minds on the left towards the European agenda.

Selections

Labour put in place new rules for the selection bodies, European Assembly Joint Constituency Labour Parties, as they were called (known as "EuroGCs"). They did not always come up to their full permitted strength. The rules were adopted by the NEC in May 1986 and ratified by conference that October, to put in place reselections for sitting MEPs to take place between January 1987 and June 1988. The 1988 conference changed the party rules to demand one woman on every shortlist for selections to office, if any woman had been nominated.

New candidates had to be selected to replace Cryer, Griffiths and Quin who had gone to the House of Commons, and Castle who was retiring. In the case of Huckfield's seat of Merseyside East there was also a contest, won by right-winger Terry Wynn.

PART III

1989-94

Building a better Europe

The Scene

Golden years. Labour bigger than the Conservatives, working positively in Europe for the first time. A more tranquil and constructive term under new leadership. Fall of the Berlin Wall and enlargement ahead. EMU and Black Wednesday. Coal still a problem. Some CAP reform. Thatcher replaced but Labour loses general election against John Major. Kinnock bows out to John Smith. Hoon helps on Maastricht. Opt out for UK on Social Chapter. Maastricht Treaty increases powers of Parliament. Delors II. Labour in policy power bids. The Gulf War. Pensioners' parliaments. Motorbike rumbles. EFTA and the EEA. Three more MEPs to Westminster. The rise of Pauline Green.

Victory at last

On 15 June 1989 Labour won forty-five seats with 39% of the vote against the Conservatives' thirty-two with 33%, exactly reversing the 1984 result, and was for the first time the largest political delegation from Britain. Labour campaigned to great effect that the election was a mid-term referendum on the Thatcher government, delivering the first defeat for the Conservatives since 1974. The Poll Tax and state of the economy were unpopular and this line held resonance for grass-roots members. There were no Tories elected in Scotland or Wales, and Labour did particularly well in the North West, Midlands and London (the latter possibly due to anger at Thatcher's abolition of the GLC). The result, an 8.5% swing from the Conservatives, was better than expected, the highest since 1970 and some Members found themselves representing constituencies that had never been Labour before and whose activists were ecstatic. Optimism was in the air.

The Liberal Democrats on 6.2% of the vote were surprised to lose their place as third party to the Greens, who gained 14.5% – two million votes (more than in any other EC country), but also won no seat. The Greens said PR would have given them twelve, and their European Group put Jean Lambert from London on their Bureau, paying for her to attend meetings for several years. Lib-Dem policy on Europe was enthusiastically in favour, whilst the Greens were more critical. Turnout in the UK increased very slightly, to 36.2%, but was still low in comparison to other countries.

New professionalism in Labour headquarters proved effective. Key strategists were Peter Mandelson and Bryan Gould MP, the latter still anti-EEC, but strongly in favour of winning elections. Environment was an election issue, particularly acid rain, water quality and tropical rainforests. Labour successfully attacked Conservative Britain as "the dirty man of Europe" following the Commission taking the UK to court for non-implementation of European legislation. The Conservative line of "Don't Let Labour in by the back door" was a resounding flop and their internal state of war over Europe was exploited by Labour, for the first time enjoying relative peace on European policy. Seal, then Leader of the Labour Group, wrote publicly to all Conservative candidates asking them to make it clear which of the two Tory parties (pro or anti Europe) they were standing for. One of the off-shoots of the prominence of environment policy was Thatcher's Cabinet re-shuffle that summer, replacing Nicholas Ridley with greener Chris Patten as Environment Secretary.

Labour ran a well co-ordinated, eye catching and energetic campaign, "Meet the Challenge, Make the Change", with colourful broadsheets. There had been themed launches with leaflets for at least a year prior to the election. One leaflet in favour of the Social Charter proposed by Commission President Jacques Delors depicted Britain as a small island in the middle of the Atlantic. Members and candidates put forward a positive message, for the first time giving critical support to the EEC whereas the Conservatives were cooling. Kinnock promised that if he were in government he would reverse the rule whereby aid won from EC funds was deducted from government aid to the regions, a Conservative financial penalty that was deeply unpopular. Tongue organized a rock concert featuring Billy Bragg and other well-known artists. Labour supporters noticeably warmed to Europe during the campaign, realizing it was a stepping-stone in the fightback.

Seal and Balfe as Leader and Secretary of the BLG were on the Campaign Management Committee with Gould. In addition to the daily press conferences there was frequent communication with target constituencies via BT Gold – a technical innovation for the party. A Euro Briefing pack of 23 policy sheets was produced and twice-weekly briefings were sent to constituencies, some of which were even relevant to the EEC. Heartening by-election wins for Labour on 4 May in the Vale of Glamorgan and in mid-Staffordshire in March with a 21% swing from the Conservatives lent an upbeat beginning to the campaign. Until then Labour had been braced to lose seats to the Tories. The downside was that in many parts of the country activists were weary after campaigning for the local elections a month earlier. White recalls local Labour official David Gardner declaring that a Bristol City by-election in May was more important than the European election, although much later had to admit he was wrong.

The Conservatives were divided. At their conference in Scotland on 12 May Thatcher said that they were good Europeans but against a socialist superstate. Heseltine published a pro-European book saying we should join EMS and in late May European Parliament President Plumb gave a speech taking issue with Thatcher on virtually every aspect of the EC. Plumb had a substantial Green vote against him in the Cotswolds of 23.4% which kept Labour firmly in third place. Conservative MEPs were still more pro than anti.

Existing Members were at some advantage because of their Information money, for use as non-party-political information about their work. The Labour Party wanted to get its hands on this, but strict rules for its use prevented it being more equitably distributed, so financing for marginal seats remained tight as there was no spare cash at HQ. The Socialist Group produced the usual paraphernalia and money for the national campaign. Their very general leaflets were handy for street stalls. Some candidates had trades union or Co-operative sponsorship, often "in kind", such as a driver and car for the election period, or secondment of staff for campaigning. Local Labour parties with marginal Westminster seats were becoming aware of the useful financial benefits of having a Labour MEP where MEPs had been able to use their office allowances to rent rooms in Labour, trades union or Co-op premises and use their equipment, from photocopiers to telephones to reduce pressure on party fundraising. They had also been assiduous in putting solidarity advertisements in the socialist press at special times of the year, such as May Day, reminding the Labour movement of their existence.

Manifesto peace

Once Kinnock had persuaded the party to jettison EEC withdrawal as part of the Policy Review the next step had been a constructive message for the European elections. Officials and many MPs were still minded for yet another national referendum against the Tories, feeling that national issues had more resonance. This, too, was the case in many constituencies, where a hard job had to be done to persuade activists that the elections mattered. Whilst remaining split on EEC membership, most MEPs were keen to promote the work they had been involved in and to feature European policy in addition to bashing the Conservatives. The European Commission obligingly launched the Social Charter a month before the elections, giving candidates a useful campaigning tool.

After months of meetings, the party came up with a pragmatic approach, partly written by Nigel Stanley working for Bryan Gould. "Meeting the Challenge in Europe" set a tone that was both critical of the CAP and other excesses, but also visionary, characterized by the second part of the slogan, "Make the Change". The text spoke of reforms, the Single Market, a social Europe, a cleaner, safer Europe, and better childcare. For the first time Labour could say Thatcher was out of sympathy with the European agenda, and provide an assurance to work positively for change and progress. MEPs produced additional literature and in particular featured "Bringing common sense to the common market" as a way of highlighting practical work and Members in specific regions.

Developing the manifesto of the Confederation of Socialist Parties was not without some internal battles. According to Mike Gapes, then working in Labour's International Department, there was a row about who should attend a meeting in Berlin early in 1988. Charles Clarke (pro-European), in the Leader's office, instructed Bish, head of research, that Gapes had to attend in addition to Jenny Little as the International Secretary, on the grounds that his specialism was defence policy, a hot issue at the time. Pro-European Julian Eccles also worked in the International Department, specializing in European policy. The NEC saw a paper earlier that year suggesting that the Confed draft manifesto fitted fairly well with Labour policy in economic and industrial areas.

Socialist leaders had begun manifesto work in June 1988. More special conferences were held: on environment in Lisbon in June, on employment and social affairs including ETUC representatives in December, a meeting with the EFTA leaders in November in Berlin, on enlargement. The manifesto working party was chaired by Enrique Baron from Spain and on one occasion Gapes had to ask for an adjournment to phone London for clearance on some text. Finally he was able to go back in to the meeting and say "Bryan Gould says yes". It was an important turning point.

The Confed Congress met in Brussels on 10 February 1989 to adopt and launch the manifesto "For a Europe of Unity, Prosperity and Solidarity". Its six main planks were a united Europe, prosperity, solidarity through social standards, a Community fit to live in with policies on environment, democracy and common foreign policies via human rights, peace, security and disarmament. It was the first time ever that Labour recorded no formal objections to the final document. Gapes recalls that at a later European lecture at LSE, Baron jovially remarked to the audience: "I wonder if Mike Gapes today has 106 amendments in his back pocket?"

The Paris Leaders' summit of the Confed at the end of June to commemorate the 200th anniversary of the French Revolution, declared they "support the objectives of the Delors Report on the creation of economic and monetary union". *The History of the PES* (Hix and Lesse, 2002) records: "even the British Labour Party, which in all previous declarations had insisted on a footnote that it opposed EMU, signed up to this commitment." Labour had previously argued the conditions for joining EMU would be deflationary. The Leaders also "called upon the heads of state and government to decide definitely at the next meeting of the European Council, if necessary by a majority, a programme of action involving the adoption of a Charter for Fundamental Social Rights guaranteed by binding instruments." Peace had broken out at last amongst the European comrades.

Beating the Tories

A sense of change was in the air. Party members had a gritty awareness, two years from the last general election defeat, that they must make better progress against the Tory government. The European election offered a mid-term possibility to go on the attack and they were up for it. Much campaigning centred on sending a sharp message to the Tories. A London local leaflet said: "Use your Euro Vote to Protest", talking about roads, health service, Poll Tax and mortgages with no mention of Europe. Other literature targeted women concerned about childcare, trades unionists on employment conditions, and people concerned about environmental standards. Philip Gould (1998) writes that he suggested the title "New Labour" to Kinnock in February 1989, shortly before he left, but it was not in use during this campaign.

Election day schools, fundraisers and public meetings attempted to build interest and inform activists. In some areas leaflets were translated into other languages. Candidates' training meetings were held in the spring to consolidate contacts and exchange ideas. Although official campaigning was only the last few weeks before election day, candidates were working for more than six months before, speaking to local organizations and seeking publicity, not to mention helping campaign in local elections. During the campaign itself there was a daily press conference organized by Mandelson, normally with front-bench spokespersons rather than MEPs.

The Socialist Group held a women's conference in Milan in February 1989 with a view to building the left-wing women's movement and a special meeting in Paris in April for candidates and agents designed to build a sense of European solidarity. Not too many went to that, not least because the Labour Party organised a European rally in the Midlands on the same weekend. Many British staff in the Group took unpaid leave and came over to help campaign, often in their home towns, but some in Labour headquarters and the EPLP office. Jo Oxenbould headed up a campaign team of twelve in the London office.

Part of any candidate's work was to raise the interest-level of party members, who even if not antagonistic, still found the EEC completely eye-glazing. Often the best a candidate could hope for was to be active during the local election period, and the knocking up information was generally left over from earlier canvassing. Some personally produced regular "newsletters" to be circulated to members, with information about Europe tied in to local issues and national interests. White recalls driving a Labour campaign bus when not one party member had come out to help, so he was going round on his own. The Windmill Hill branch in his constituency had formally decided not to campaign and a member was astonished when her door was knocked on. Many branches took that line. Even with a more positive policy, many candidates still found one hand tied behind them.

Winners and losers

The existing Members were Adam, Balfe, Bird, Buchan, Collins, Crawley, Elliott, Falconer, Ford, Hindley, Hoon, Hughes, Lomas, Martin, McGowan, McMahon, Megahy, Morris, Newens, Newman, Seal, Llewellyn Smith, Stevenson, Stewart, Tomlinson, Tongue and West; a very varied crew in terms of their position on Europe and their political leanings, but slightly more by now in favour of the European Community. Only three women remained, due to the departure of Castle and Quin.

Eighteen new Labour Members were elected, of whom only four were female; yet again a pathetic result for women, highlighting the inadequacy of party rules to encourage more female politicians. They were a mixed batch politically, but the largest influx were pragmatic Kinnock supporters of the so-called soft or Tribunite left (ten of the group were now LCC members) Many felt that factionalism should be reduced bearing in mind the awful history of the previous five years. The new team were:

Roger Barton, an engineering fitter, trade unionist and Councillor, originally anti-market but now seeking democratic reform, took over from Cryer in Sheffield, where the latter had gone to Westminster. He had tried unsuccessfully for selection in 1984, was Secretary of the District Labour Party and Trades Council Labour Group.

David Bowe, a science teacher and former Middlesborough Councillor, pragmatic on Europe, comfortably won Cleveland and Yorkshire North from Sir Peter Vanneck.

Ken Coates, veteran Marxist academic, pro-European writer, peace campaigner, former miner, easily won Nottingham from Conservative Michael Kilby. He had fought the seat in 1984 and at the 1983 general election. He could speak French and some Italian. He was a founding member of the Movement for European Nuclear Disarmament and a member of the Bertrand Russell Peace Foundation.

Peter Crampton, a pro-European geography lecturer and former Chair of the European Nuclear Disarmament Campaign finally won Humberside from Bob Battersby, having fought it in 1984.

Wayne David, another WEA tutor-organiser, historian and an LCC member, replaced Griffiths, who had gone to the House of Commons, in rock solid Labour South Wales.

Alan Donnelly, GMB Deputy General Secretary and Councillor, now pro-Europe, replaced Joyce Quin in Labour Tyne and Wear after she, too, had left for Westminster. He had once been seconded to Denis Healey who recommended the European arena to him.

Pauline Green, a Co-operative official, pro-European former police-woman born in Malta, had a fine victory in marginal London North against a non-sitting Tory.

Lyndon Harrison, a pro-European Cheshire County Councillor and college administrator won convincingly in Cheshire West against Conservative Andrew Pearce.

Henry McCubbin, a film cameraman, left-wing strong pro-European and peace campaigner, took Scotland North East with a small margin in a three-way split where the Conservative incumbent, James Provan, came third to the SNP.

Christine Oddy, a French-speaking left-wing law lecturer specializing in trade union and employment law, EEC law and comparative law, pro-European, defeated John de Courcy Ling in Midlands Central. She had previously worked in the European Commission and in Paris.

Anita Pollack, an LCC executive member, formerly Castle's assistant and an Australian citizen (her parents came over for the election), scraped home after a recount in London South West, defeating Dame Shelagh Roberts by the tiniest majority in the country, a mere 518 votes. She had contested the safe Conservative seat of Woking in the general election and it was her second attempt at this European seat.

Imelda (Mel) Read, a pro-European MSF union National Executive Council member, lecturer and former Plessey laboratory technician, won Leicester by a good margin from Conservative Frederick (Fred) Tuckman. She had fought in both the 1979 and 1983 general elections and was Chair of the East Midlands TUC Women's Committee.

Brian Simpson, a pro-European since Delors, PE teacher and Councillor, narrowly won Cheshire East from veteran Conservative Sir Tom Normanton.

Alex Smith, a local authority gardener and anti-marketeer, had a good win in Scotland South from Conservative Alasdair Hutton and promptly joined the Campaign Group.

Gary Titley, a former teacher and pro-European County Councillor who had worked for both Terry Pitt and John Bird, took over from Castle in Greater Manchester West with a resounding 53.9% of the vote. He spoke Spanish and some French and had contested Dudley West in the 1987 general election.

Ian White, a lawyer and another strongly federalist pro-European, won Bristol from Conservative Richard Cottrell. He had contested a House of Commons seat, but said he always wanted to be in Europe; a German speaker.

Anthony (Joe) Wilson, a former PE teacher and Councillor, generally anti-market until Delors but a believer in the CAP because he felt it had stopped a large migration from rural to urban life, won Wales North from Conservative Beate Brookes. He had stood for the House of Commons in Montgomery in 1983.

Terry Wynn, a former marine engineer, Methodist lay preacher and Councillor on the right of the party supported by the electricians' union, took over from deselected Huckfield in Merseyside East. According to Wynn, Neil Kinnock greeted him enthusiastically at a candidates' photo call by saying "A Labour gain already, even before the election". Wynn was unpopular with the Campaign Group from the outset.

Notable Labour candidates who lost included: John Hutton in Cumbria and Lancashire North (later an MP and from 2005 a Cabinet Minister): David Earnshaw, who was Ken Collins' assistant and nearly won London South East; Robert Evans, who became an MEP in 1994, fought Moorhouse in London South and Surrey East; David Hallam tried again in Shropshire and Stafford, narrowing the gap against Christopher Prout but did not quite make it; Geoff Harris, pro-European official in the Socialist Group fought Caroline Jackson without much hope of success in Wiltshire. A couple of former Conservatives who had been defeated in 1984 tried again, and Malcolm Harbour, who later became a Tory MEP, fought Christine Crawley in Birmingham East. Brendan Donnelly, who worked for the Conservative MEPs in London, fought Michael Elliott. For the Lib-Dems, Sarah Ludford, who had fought Tory Richard Simmonds in Wight and Hampshire East in 1984, came fourth after the Conservatives and Greens against Newens in London Central. She was elected in 1999 under the list system.

The party's positive approach to the EEC was reflected in the make-up of the new Labour Group. However some anti-marketeers remained: Buchan, Falconer, Lomas, Megahy, Seal, Llew Smith, Stewart (becoming more pragmatic) and West. Of the new intake only Alex Smith was a committed anti-marketeer, although most remained critical of the CAP. Newman later said he did not argue with the party's positive manifesto. The terms "new" and "old" Labour were not yet in currency but the distinction was beginning to emerge. Vestiges of class differences remained present, and as yet undefined modernisers versus traditionalists tension was emerging. In the coming five years disputes were more concerned with the differences between right, centre-left and hard left than about policy for or against the EEC. Four of the newly-elected Members, all strong peace campaigners were in favour of a federalist Europe. Crampton, Coates and White became known as the "three musketeers" and soon made friends with Henry McCubbin to make the "federalist four".

The Campaign Group core was often supported by several "non-aligned" left-wingers, such as Oddy, Hughes, Megahy, Morris, Buchan, Seal, Elliott and Llew Smith. The Group was considered to be Falconer, Hindley, Lomas, McGowan, Newman, Alex Smith, Stewart and West. Newens would vote with them sometimes if it was against the right, and some of the Tribunites would occasionally break ranks to support the harder left, depending on the issue. The London *Evening Standard* in October 1991 quoted Socialist Campaign Group News as listing the above as members except for Alex Smith.

This five year term was much less strife-ridden. Some Members were strident performers in the Parliament against the Conservatives both in Europe and at home, and against the Commission. The "grand coalition" approach of Socialists and Christian Democrats continued because of the need to get 270 votes for legislation. Labour was uncomfortable with this cosy relationship, but most accepted it as an unpleasant necessity and the EPLP for the first time became mainstream in the political current of the Parliament. There was optimism in that some progress was being made on reforms in Europe and Labour was growing in popularity at home, at least until the

1992 election failure. The main campaigning position of the Labour Group, agreed at the AGM, was to argue for the Social Charter to be taken on board in the UK. It did not actually happen until 1997.

How Europe voted

In the Parliament now of 518 members the Socialist Group remained the largest, up from 165 to 180, largely thanks to Labour gains. Some have suggested Labour could have led the Group, but having done a deal to install Julian Priestley as General Secretary, they said they wished to concentrate on wining a general election at home and voted for Jean-Pierre Cot for Leader.

The EPP (Christian Democrats) under Klepsch went up from 113 to 121, at least partly because the Spanish Popular Party left the EDG group in frustration at Thatcher's anti-European stance. The EDG, now led by Christopher Prout (soon to be knighted), was a shrunken 34; the British plus two Danes. In Denmark the conservatives lost two to Social Democrats and Liberals. The Liberal Democrat and Reformist Group was led by senior French politician Valery Giscard d'Estaing with 49. The United Left, comprising Communists and friends, had 14. The Greens had done so well, increasing to 30, particularly with a good result in Belgium, that they formed their own group, les Verts, led by Maria Santos of Portugal. This left Birgit Bjornvig of Denmark to lead a much smaller Rainbow group, now including Winnie Ewing. German far-right Republicans worryingly gained six seats from the conservative CDU/CSU and joined with the 10 French Front National and one Belgian to form the Droits Européenes, 17 strong, led by France's Le Pen. There were several other groups. Half of the Parliament's Members were new.

The proportion of women MEPs was higher, with 103 elected (20%), compared with 75 in 1984 and 67 in 1979. Germany returned 25 women out of 81 compared with 16 before, at least in part due to the SPD's new quota system, the envy of Labour women. The percentage of women in the Socialist Group went down from 28% to 22%, but the SPD managed 12 out of their 31. The UK female total remained at 12, but the BLG went up only marginally from 5 to 7, despite the jump in their numbers, adding fuel to the demand for quotas for women as opposed to the patently failed "one woman on every shortlist" policy of 1988. There were more female Labour candidates for the 1989 European election than ever but few were successful. Yet again, it was the male Leader of the Council who won selections in safest seats. Labour brought in a quota system at its 1989 annual conference.

For the first time, apart from the French Dependent Territories, there was a black woman Member, Dacia Valent, for the Italian Communists and two French Arab women – Djida Tazdait in the Green Group and 25 year old Nora Zaidi with the Socialists. Other notables in the Socialist Group this time were: Claude Cheysson, who had been the French Commissioner 1973-81, Minister for Foreign Affairs 1981- 84 and a Commissioner again in 1985-89; Bettino Craxi, former Prime Minister of Italy; Laurent Fabius, former French Prime Minister; Catherine Trautmann, Mayor of Strasbourg; and Elio di Rupo from Belgium, later to become Prime Minister. There was also Irish Labour Barry Desmond, a former Minister in the Dail who later went on to be a member of the European Court of Auditors; Professor Leon Schwartzenberg, an eminent French doctor and environmentalist and former Health Minister, with huge moral authority; and Barbara Duhrkop Duhrkop, a courageous PSOE Member of Swedish/German extraction married to a Spanish politician who had been murdered in front of her family by ETA. She was always friendly to the British.

In Parliament as a whole some leading figures were: Emilio Colombo, former Prime Minister of Italy and President of the European Parliament 1977-79; Valery Giscard d'Estaing, former President of France; Leo Tindemans, former Prime Minister of Belgium; Willy de Clerq, former Commissioner and Deputy Prime Minister of Belgium; Arnaldo Forlani, another former Prime Minister of Italy; Otto Habsburg; and Giovanni Goria, another former Italian Prime Minister. Daniel Cohn-Bendit (Danny the Red of Paris 1968 fame) was elected as a German Green and was always surrounded by TV cameras. A number of other Members had been Ministers and mayors of cities, particularly in France and Italy. The line-up was not without its eccentrics too. One Karl Partsch, a German ecologist from the mountains, wore lederhosen, including suede shorts and hiking boots, to every session, even in the depths of winter.

A new European team

Kinnock was delighted with the result and both he and Priestley, now running the Socialist Group, encouraged the BLG to take a more responsible role. Ford, a survivor of the tormented power swings of the previous five years, having mellowed his views on Europe, with Donnelly organized a pre-AGM caucus to ensure Kinnock supporters took the officerships. On 20 June at the European Parliament office at Queen Anne's Gate, all Members except Stewart (ill in hospital) were present for the AGM. Blackman, Fuller, Gupwell and Ryan were there from Brussels, plus assistants Earnshaw, McKenzie-Grey, Perry, and staffers Oxenbould, Flack, Oldroyd and Frost. Earlier there was a lunch and presentation to Barbara Castle, and in the evening a reception on the House of Commons Terrace for women Labour MPs and MEPs – an effort at solidarity that failed to lead to very much lasting closeness between the groups.

On the day of the AGM Ford and Tongue wrote in the *Morning Star* (a paper then still read by a fairly substantial number of Labour activists): "Labour is now the Party of Europe... What the debate is now about is what kind of Europe we are going to build."

AGM business was conducted fairly briskly. Ford was elected Leader against Seal, 27 – 17. The political affiliations were plain to see. Voting for Ford were: Adam, Bird, Bowe, Coates, Collins, Crampton, Crawley, David, Donnelly, Ford, Green, Harrison, Hoon, McCubbin, McMahon, Martin, Morris, Pollack, Read, Simpson, Stevenson, Titley, Tomlinson, Tongue, White, Wilson and Wynn. Hindley later referred to this as "the Kinnock list", but there is no evidence that Kinnock was directing votes. Voting for Seal were: Balfe, Barton, Buchan, Elliott, Falconer, Hindley, Hughes, Lomas, McGowan, Megahy, Newens, Newman, Oddy, Seal, both Smiths and West. The odd one out here was Elliott, who was a pro-European Tribunite, but said that Seal had worked on him, using local government experience as an argument. This was odd, since Ford had more recent local government experience as a Chair of Education, was a Tribunite, and was now more pro-European. Ford said there had been some discussion about putting Stevenson forward as Leader, but he would not make a commitment to stay in the Parliament for the full term.

Christine Crawley was keen that the officers should include at least one woman. It was impossible to attempt anything more in the way of a quota, since there were so few. The same division as for Leader voted for Tongue as Deputy Leader against Newens, putting one woman in the team. This paved the way for Bird to be elected Chair by 25 – 19 against anti-market veteran Buchan. Voting was the same again except that Coates and Crampton changed sides. Both of these were on the left and Buchan had always been a peace campaigner, whereas Bird was on the right. For Secretary, Donnelly defeated Balfe by the same number and voting pattern except that Green stayed loyal to her Co-operative movement connection and voted for Balfe, whilst Donnelly attracted Coates' vote. Wayne David was elected Treasurer against Newman, 26 – 18. Voting for this post was as for Deputy Leader except that Crampton voted for Newman. Whip was won by Titley by 25 votes to Elliott's 19 with much the same division as before. When it came to the Socialist Group Bureau Member the contest was Tomlinson 25 versus Hindley 19, again with the same breakdown of votes. McMahon and Wynn were elected auditors. McCubbin was put forward for Socialist Group Chief Whip, in a move to give a clear signal that the reluctant attitude of previous Labour delegations to working with comrades in the Group was a thing of the past. His trades union background was helpful in the negotiations he was to undertake in that role.

Those who voted against Ford were excluded from posts. Many years later Hindley was still miffed about the ruthlessness of this "coup", saying that his local government experience and five years of work on the External Economic Relations Committee was ignored. He felt that he should have been rewarded for his talents, but that the slate was purely political. Hindley's abilities are undisputed but the officerships were about loyalty to Kinnock and as a member of the Campaign Group he was perceived as unsuitable. There was nothing new about such behaviour and the hard left had indulged in it when they were in control. Stevenson told him it was a pity he was left-wing because he was so talented. His SPD colleague Gerhard Schmid, on hearing he had been knocked off the Socialist Group Bureau, said "why can't we have Tomlinson AND Hindley – why must it always be one or the other?" Several of the Campaign Group observed that those outside the Ford clique were given no posts of any kind. There were never enough jobs to go around for the ambitious, the result being that those who lost out were from the opposing political faction to those who happened to be in control at any one time.

It was agreed the regional groups would continue to meet and elect their own officers. These maintained links with regional party organizations, arranging meetings with key figures in Europe such as Commissioners and raising matters of importance in their area, thus illustrating that Europe was working for people at home. MEPs set up their own methods of reporting back to their European constituency parties (ECLPs) and many also tried to get to General Committee Meetings of individual parliamentary constituencies (they normally had about eight of these) where they could. There was little pressure from the latter and those that met mid-week found it difficult to find suitable dates when MEPs were not abroad, often under the stricture of a Whip. In this Parliament the MEPs also organized themselves into trades union groups meeting regularly and often spoke at trades union conferences and training schools. Most Members belonged either to MSF, the GMB or T&GWU.

The Confed held a Party Leaders' meeting in Paris on 26-28 June, to which the Labour Party sent Hattersley, Dunwoody, Ford and Gapes. This was where deals were finalized on parliamentary and other posts.

When Kinnock met Ford and Tongue shortly after their election as officers, he looked forward to increased liaison between the MEPs, the Shadow Cabinet and the PLP. Tongue had to make this happen and soon Labour MEPs were in place, elected by their peers on each respective committee, as link Members. Tongue would chair liaison group meetings where controversial issues were flagged up and would then communicate with the Shadow Cabinet, but also to some extent regional parties, trades unions and even NGOs. There was by now a standing invitation for the Leader of the MEPs to attend and speak at PLP meetings, but this was not often taken up as the PLP met on Wednesday mornings, a day of the week when MEPs were guaranteed to have to be abroad. A former Secretary of the PLP, Alan Haworth (now Lord Haworth) opined: "there was never a huge desire to hear from colleagues in Europe".

Parliament resumes

The Parliament now of twelve nations, for the first time elected its President on the first ballot, Enrique Baron Crespo, an Anglophile Spanish Socialist, President of the European Movement since 1987. It was his second attempt, having been defeated by Lord Plumb previously. The result was due to another deal with the Christian Democrats (EPP), who were promised Socialist support next time round. Votes were exactly equal to the 180 Socialists and 121 EPP. All was not sweetness and light, however. The oldest Member, who by custom presides at the election of the President, was National Front, Mr Autant-Lara, and he used the opportunity of his introductory speech to advance his objectionable cause. The Socialists and Greens staged a walk-out, placing red roses on their desks, leaving the Member to make a lengthy speech to an almost empty Chamber. Even many of the Conservatives left.

David Martin was elected one of the Vice-Presidents and was to serve in this post until 1999. Tories won the chairmanship of the Committee on Budgetary Control with Wynn a Vice-Chair. Collins won back Chair of Environment (now a priority) and Crawley became Chair of Women's Rights. Ford secured a position as Vice-President of the Security and Defence subcommittee of Foreign Affairs for White who later said he was unhappy with this position, feeling completely out of his milieu in the company of former generals, some of whom would turn up in uniform to meetings. One had been in charge of the French secret service implicated in the sinking of the *Rainbow Warrior* in New Zealand. White said sadly "It was not a disarmament Committee" and he was certainly not popular with the

Chair of the Committee, Hans-Gert Pottering, or his colleague Balfe. Other Vice-Chairs were Crampton for Foreign Affairs, Adam for Energy and Research yet again and Harrison for Rules. By this time the work of the standing delegations to a range of parliaments in the world was also becoming important. Ford had tentatively suggested Seal for the prestigious USA delegation but was opposed by Tomlinson and Hoon so obtained it for Hoon. Stevenson chaired SAARC (South Asia), seen as relevant given the many South Asians living and voting in the UK, and Vice-Presidencies went to Donnelly for Japan, Megahy for Gulf, Hughes for Poland, Bird for Malta, McCubbin for SE Europe, McMahon for Norway and Elliott for Finland and the Nordic countries.

Labour, determined to take a more constructive role in the Socialist Group, was aided by the fact that its new President, Cot, a former French MP and Minister for Overseas Development, for whom they had voted, was another Anglophile. Priestley had by now replaced the Italian General Secretary and was seen by Kinnock as a safe pair of hands. (He was to remain in this post until 1994 when he moved to the President's department, subsequently becoming the Parliament's Secretary-General from 1997-2007.) Labour was now a substantial delegation in the Group with more say in its proceedings and policies but did not always get its own way. They complained to the press that the French Presidency had given a filofax to every MEP and promises of other largesse. This was seen as disloyalty to their comrade, the impressive Socialist MEP Catherine Trautmann, the Mayor of Strasbourg. The gifts, normal in France, were seen by Labour as a bribe to keep the Parliament in Strasbourg, when many wanted to move to Brussels.

Pauline Green was the first to make her mark on the first day, demanding an urgent debate on arrests on the Green line in Cyprus, backed up by Hugh McMahon who was to become an almost daily speaker in the Chamber. Green had a high proportion of Cypriots from both sides of the divide in her marginal North London constituency, both as voters and party members. She says she made an effort to research the subject and take into account human rights and respect issues, focusing on security and safety and felt it was necessary to draw a line under the past and find common ground for a settlement. Nevertheless she feels she was perceived as taking a pro-Greek line. She says she always paid her own way on visits that were not official parliamentary delegations and also never tabled draft resolutions drawn up by others. Her assistant and agent, Ray Collins, was later to marry a Greek Cypriot and settle in Cyprus. She also was an expert on consumer affairs, given her Co-operative Union background and spoke in the October session in a debate on food irradiation and again in a debate on completion of the internal market on consumer protection.

Kinnock visited Strasbourg during the first week for talks with the Presidents of Parliament (Baron) and the Commission (Delors). At a press conference he was careful to say he would not participate in any development that would be in conflict with the interests of Britain, that improved liaison between MEPs and MPs would be introduced and that Labour would be considering what part the delegation could play in a restructured Labour Party conference and NEC. He told the BLG they should not think they were rocking the boat if they were pro-EEC. Cot was invited to address

Labour conference in the autumn and received a standing ovation when he did so. Such had times changed.

Not all was peaceful for Labour in that first week. In a vote on EMU, several voted against and others abstained, insisting it was contrary to party policy although it had been agreed as part of the Confed manifesto. The resolution was on the Madrid Summit, but included a statement saying that the Parliament "backs the objectives of the Delors report on the establishment of monetary union" and welcoming the decision to convene an IGC. Those against were Megahy, Stevenson and West, and abstaining were Falconer, Hindley, Lomas, Newman and both Smiths.

Ford as Leader referred to Thatcher's Bruges speech the previous autumn and said the BLG now spoke for the British people had who voted for a social Europe. He said: "Labour Party Members of the Socialist Group are determined to play their part in fulfilling the role of setting the pace towards a new Europe." What a change from five years earlier.

Mel Read and others expressed some disappointment when they arrived as new Members, saying there was no inheritance from the previous terms, nothing to build on and no substantive policy briefings that could be carried as guidance into committee meetings. Given the dislocated and strife-ridden nature of the previous period for the Labour Group, this was not altogether unsurprising.

As before, most new Members were a bit surprised to find out just how much time they needed to spend "in Europe". In the constituencies many viewed trips abroad as junketing rather than day-to-day work. Plenary sessions were one week a month in Strasbourg, which continued to have its logistical difficulties of poor flight connections. The "parliamentary special" direct flight to London left around 1pm on Fridays and often debates continued right up to that time, necessitating frantic attempts to get the plane's departure put back, or having to re-book on much later flights with poor connections, arriving home utterly exhausted very late at night. Many had to catch onward flights to their regions. Some flew to Frankfurt where there was then a two-hour car journey to Strasbourg, or to Basle, where the journey was over an hour by car – often four or five Members of different parties jammed into one vehicle. Not fun when it was Reverend Paisley. Others had to change in Paris or Amsterdam. Political group meetings took up much of the week before that, either in Brussels or in other locations around the EEC, and the other two weeks of the month were timetabled for committee meetings, leaving only Fridays, some Mondays and weekends for appointments back home and getting around large areas, normally comprising eight parliamentary constituencies.

As Parliament's powers grew, more work was undertaken in committees and Members found themselves having to spend at least Tuesday to Thursday away, but often more, leaving little time for shoring up the party base and fulfilling engagements, not to mention a family life. Many rented or bought apartments in Brussels for convenience (hotels in Brussels rapidly filling up during the week) and this further fragmented social cohesion. There was a subtle shift in the culture of the Parliament too. What had been a French-speaking organization was slowly becoming an area where the common language (as SPD Member Gerhard Schmid put it) was bad English.

Some EPLP Members also became Socialist Group co-ordinators. It meant they organized the Socialist Members on their committee, bidding for rapporteurships, chairing the pre-meetings of Socialist Members, ironing out disputes and advising the Group on contentious items that might need to be debated in full Group. This was a substantial amount of work, largely unrecognized at home.

Members were permitted expenses if invited to speak about Europe at meetings anywhere in the world. This not only facilitated invitations to colleagues from other countries to speak at "Euro-GCs", but also meant they could travel to conferences or undertake investigative trips in pursuit of special interests separately from the overseas parliamentary delegation meetings. It was enormously useful and many made use of it, claiming that the Parliament was a terrific adult education course. These meetings provided a useful forum for party locals to meet cross-border and form bonds, and these would become particularly useful in building teams for campaigning in marginal parliamentary seats.

Relations were not always smooth with local MPs but MEPs were keen to foster good relations and to help win marginal parliamentary seats for Labour. Some MPs opportunistically saw a funding mechanism for an office that they were not prepared to pay for themselves but more MEPs ended up setting up their own offices than sharing with MPs or using local Labour rooms, the latter often being cramped, shabby and unfit for purpose. In the North there was some tradition of Labour Councils offering elected Members rooms to rent in the Town Hall. In other cases there were deals to be had with trades unions or Co-op buildings. Some rented premises in town centres and a few set up shop in their homes which was only viable if they had a sufficiently large house, because staff would come there to work.

New Members were keen to be seen as active as quickly as possible and during the September session Crawley, Pollack, Elliott, Titley, McCubbin, Donnelly, Wynn and Crampton found opportunities to break the ice, mostly during question time. Crawley attacked secrecy in Council meetings. Pollack had a question on border controls after 1992 and concerns about legal residents who were not citizens, being in that position herself. By the end of the first year she was concentrating on banning fur imports and campaigning to save tropical forests. (Twenty years later in 2009 the Commission brought forward proposals for their protection.) McCubbin, from northern Scotland where fishing was important, intervened on Norwegian salmon dumping. Titley jumped into a question by someone else on salmonella. Donnelly made a maiden speech about a delegation of young parliamentarians to Poland. Elliott took up age discrimination in Commission recruitment policies, a long-standing British cross-party complaint. Crampton got stuck in on human rights and the Soviet Union, welcoming democratization. Wynn, a strong anti-smoking campaigner, squeezed in on the Friday on banning smoking in public places. As he settled in to budget work he was to take up the cudgels on reducing subsidies to tobacco farmers.

A stronger presence of the far right in Parliament had an inevitable knock-on effect on official positions. According to the rules they were entitled to fair treatment and by 11 October there was a row concerning two parliamentary standing delegations. One of the holocaust-deniers, whom Ford denounced as a former member of the Waffen SS, had been put forward as

Vice-Chair of the delegation for Israel, this being promptly blocked by
Socialist members of that committee at its formative meeting. A shouting
match in Parliament followed, resulting in a suspension of the sitting for
over an hour. Voting for committee Chairs and Vice-Chairs was normally a
formality because of the D'Hondt system and this was a serious rocking of
the boat. A deal was eventually done behind closed doors to prevent this
particular appointment from being ratified and a replacement was found.

At the Madrid Council in June 1989 eleven countries encouraged the
Commission to prepare action on social rights for the December summit in
Strasbourg, Thatcher being opposed. A large demonstration in support of
the Social Charter took place on 18 October in Brussels attended by many
UK trades unionists. One said: "I can hardly hold back the tears. To think
we fought two wars and now we are all together, shoulder to shoulder, creating a better life…" There could be no better indication that the labour
movement in the UK had taken Europe on board. When at the Summit
heads of government overrode Britain and adopted the Social Charter (ultimately appended to the Maastricht Treaty as the Social Chapter) Thatcher
memorably commented: "If I am in a minority of one the other eleven must
be wrong". Such pig-headedness was to be her downfall within a year.
McMahon devoted himself to endless attacks on the UK government for its
opt out, raising it at every opportunity for years. Early in 1990 Pollack and
McMahon had a meeting in the House of Commons with Tony Blair, then
Shadow Employment Secretary, to discuss the Social Charter and Labour's
commitment to it and particularly the minimum wage, which Blair supported (and brought in shortly after his election in 1997).

President Mitterrand's speech as President of the Council in October
elicited a banner reading "No to nuclear" from the benches of the Green
Group (most Socialists not wishing to demonstrate against their own political family), to protests from the right. It was to be another matter in 1995
when Chirac was President.

Some of the UK political high-fliers were now happy to make contact.
Kinnock made efforts to bring about better communication, meeting with
the Labour Group in June 1990 in London. It was beginning to outlive its
past notorious reputation and gain some credence. Britain's Ambassador to
Europe, David Hannay, hosted a meeting with the group twice that year
and these became regular events as the UKRep office began making more of
an effort to be even-handed in its approach.

Stuart Holland, Labour MP for Vauxhall, resigned to take a post at the
European Institute in Florence in 1989. He was one of the intellectuals who
had been working with Kinnock in changing Labour's position on the EEC
and an economics adviser to Delors at the European Commission. It was he
who coined the phrase "beggar my neighbour economic policy" in opposition to nationalistic policies.

John Smith and Gordon Brown visited Brussels in October to attend a
meeting on monetary union, taking the opportunity to visit the Labour
Group, as part of a tour of Paris, Brussels, Frankfurt and Bonn exploring
policy on EMU and putting Labour on the European map.

A protracted strike of ambulance workers took place in the winter of 1989.
Labour wanted an "urgency" debate criticizing the government but Spanish
colleagues voted against it in Group, unhappy with Labour support for

Gibraltar. It was this sort of behaviour that governed whether some votes were won or lost. BLG Members gave financial support to the appeal over the winter, including a day's parliamentary attendance allowance and a ten pounds per week levy, presenting a cheque for £9,000 to the union just before Christmas. In January they managed to get a supportive resolution carried, seeking arbitration, with a delegation of the strikers in the audience. Donnelly, Ford, Pollack and Falconer spoke in support.

At party conference as winners

Reporting as Leader to party conference in Brighton in 1989, Ford said: "Labour is now the party of Europe... Every policy we discuss this week has a European dimension." Balfe, as a delegate for the Co-operative Wholesale Society (CWS), said:

> "We are now linked inextricably whether we like it or not, to the EC and its nations. We must not make the mistake of believing that this means we are somehow submerging ourselves. We are joining with other socialists in European countries who are profoundly dissatisfied with the EC and who want to change it as much as we do...The way in which that will be done is by a unified Labour movement in Europe comprised of British and other European socialists fighting together with an informed party behind it. We are all in this together. There is no future for us outside this Community but the Community will be what we shape it to be. That is the challenge of the 1990s."

Composite 51 over-enthusiastically called for the Parliament to have the power to legislate, and was defeated. The *Britain in the World* text on Europe was carried, on enlargement, European political co-operation, and EC institutions. It suggested greater scrutiny at Westminster with a Select Committee in the Commons similar to that in the Lords, and ended with: "Labour will use the EC as a means of facilitating successful European co-operation. Our approach will be pragmatic. The essential prerequisite remains the election of a Labour government in Britain". The European Charter of Worker's Rights was unveiled by Kinnock and Cot who gave a well-received fraternal address, saying "thanks to your splendid victory Britain is back in the European Parliament", and mentioning the efficient and respected British General Secretary of the Socialist Group.

Conference agreed that rules for 40% women quotas for the NEC, CLPs and branch officers and delegations should be brought forward the following year. It was not until 1993 that the policy was adopted that 50% of seats where Labour MPs are retiring should be reserved for women candidates. In 1994 there were several composites put forward to adopt women-only shortlists but that ran into difficulties when tested against the law.

MEPs were beginning to feature at fringe meetings. The Labour Movement for Europe featured Cot and Priestley, Ford spoke on Social Europe for the Campaign for Local Economic Strategies (CLES), Seal at the Common Market Safeguards Committee, Tongue at one *Tribune* meeting and Ford at another, Newens and Balfe at Co-op meetings, Newens again at Labour Heritage, and Pollack at an LCC meeting on women's quotas and on the floor of conference on the same matter. Ford, Barton and Pollack helped sponsor the LCC

Activists' Briefing. By this time the MEPs were paying for a stall at annual conference stocked with their literature, which was proving successful in raising awareness about their work.

Staff troubles

The new leader and his officers agreed the BLG office in London needed sorting out. It had grown like topsy over the previous decade with a lack of organization and there was a feeling that some staff were not ideologically supporting the new regime. An unhappy atmosphere and lack of mutual trust had prevailed for some time. There were unclear lines of responsibility, with both Leader and Secretary in the past seeking to give (often conflicting) orders to staff, and treating them as their personal assistants, with some ensuing crossed wires and not a little acrimony.

Jo Oxenbould was being treated as a simple administrator, found Ford unhappy about working with her and understandably felt disgruntled. Staff in Brussels took solidarity action at the first whiff of change, writing to the BLG officers at the beginning of July expressing their support should staff take industrial action. Matters came to a head when some MEPs wrote to the officers protesting about the establishment of an office in Brussels with two temporary staff, Jenny McKenzie-Grey and Greg Perry, who were closely identified with Tongue and Martin. This was probably a mistake as there had been no consultation and the staff went on strike about this and the lack of agreed job descriptions. This breakdown of confidence was embarrassing, particularly when a meeting at Queen Anne's Gate was picketed causing unwanted publicity for Labour. Oxenbould says that she was excluded from officers' meetings from this time.

Charles Clarke from Kinnock's office contacted John Carr, who had been a senior personnel manager in local government and in charge of personnel at the GLC, to ask if he would undertake an independent report and make recommendations about how to achieve a good administrative machine. The substantial cost of this had to be borne out of BLG funds and was the subject of some disagreement.

The exercise took about a year, during which most of the staff left (Flack went by the summer of 1990 to the League Against Cruel Sports and Oxenbould took voluntary severance with a year's pay in July). Perry and McKenzie-Grey had been temporary. Some in the Campaign Group felt it was a plot on the part of the party's central office to take control and install people of their own choice. Carr proposed a complete restructuring and replacement of staff. One of his messages to the Members was that they had to define their own agenda and make themselves indispensable to the party so that it would be impossible for the leadership to proceed on policy without consulting them. He felt this was their passport to the recognition they craved.

A bargaining agreement was reached on 14 July 1990, paving the way for employment of a new general secretary, Dianne Hayter, in October 1990. She had a high profile: a past General Secretary of the Fabian Society, she had worked in the media, and came from the right-wing pro-market tradition in the party, enjoying strong links to the NEC and some MPs. The Campaign Group remained suspicious of her. With a firm hand she ensured lines of communication were firmly in place so that policy in Brussels and

Strasbourg aligned with policy at home and campaigns to elect a Labour government. One of her early projects was to offer media training to the Members in April 1991, courtesy of journalist friend Veronica Crichton and media specialist Ivor Gabor. The age of "Folletting" (power dressing) was soon also in swing, Ford and Crawley being given the treatment.

There was a problem with Hayter's job title. The Carr report referred to "Head of Office" but as this didn't mean much in UK terms, she asked Ford if it could be Chief Executive, which is what it became. It was a bit of a sudden change and annoyed some who felt she was seeking self-aggrandisement. The first suggestion had been General Secretary, which was what more frequently was used in the union and Labour movement, but as there was a Secretary to the Group it was thought that wouldn't be right. Much later the title reverted to Secretary-General.

Angie Forrester (later to marry Larry Whitty) was already part of the team, having worked with Oxenbould and by January 1991 Stephen Brown and Cathy Burton had been recruited in Brussels, with Carol Rawlings as UK press officer from February and a finance officer in London. Setting up the Brussels office was a fraught business, since there was no entitlement for offices for national delegations within the Socialist Group and they had to camp, resulting in inevitable disputes, in the room Ford and Donnelly shared. Hayter was upset that there was nowhere suitable for staff to work, objected to Ford smoking and almost took them out on strike. The unsatisfactory arrangements were at the root of continuing poor relations. It was a good deal of time before separate space was negotiated out of the Socialist Group's allocation of rooms. At this time staff were expected to carry large amounts of photocopied papers from London to Brussels and Strasbourg for meetings, it being before the regular use of e-mails.

Leader and Chief Executive did not enjoy a good relationship. Ford felt her candidacy had been pushed by Donnelly and accuses her of calling officers' meetings at times he could not make. For her part Hayter always felt that Ford did not understand the needs of the staff, and felt undermined that she was not permitted to speak at EPLP meetings and by various other perceived slights. She felt the MEPs were rude and disrespectful of Shadow spokespersons and showed little social solidarity to her. Her view of the way things should operate hinged on judging decisions by what the Shadow Cabinet, the NEC, the press and the opposition would say about them and tried in vain to make the Group more like the PLP. They were different animals operating in different theatres, and it was an uphill struggle.

Fall of the Berlin Wall and German unification

In autumn 1989 the old Soviet Union and its dependencies were facing a new world. Some, such as Hungary and Poland, were "rejoining Europe" as a result of the easing of the Cold War. Massive demonstrations took place in Prague and elsewhere. There was much talk about the needs of the emerging democracies in finance, training, and solidarity. Dealing with the legacy of neglect, pollution and deprivation in the East were immense problems and ways to assist would have to be found. Tomlinson was vexed that support was demanded by Council for Romania and Bulgaria, but no extra money was forthcoming, necessitating cuts elsewhere.

On 9 November the Berlin Wall "fell", an event entirely unpredicted even a few months earlier. Socialist party leaders held a summit in Lisbon three days after, welcoming it and announcing the next congress of the Confederation of Socialist Parties would be held in Berlin, themed as "The Common Future of Europe". Brandt came to speak to the Group on the end of the "post-Stalinist period" but said he did not think that Germany would unite. Chancellor Kohl and President Mitterrand spoke at the November plenary in Strasbourg, necessitating much re-arranging of the agenda, not the least of which included keeping the Archbishop of Canterbury, who was visiting, waiting some hours.

The Socialist Group took advantage of this congress to meet in Berlin in February, visiting the Reichstag, making a ceremonial crossing as the first group of westerners through the Brandenburg Gate. They held an all-star public hearing in the Volksbuhne Theatre in East Berlin, attended by the socialist party leaders including Kinnock and Gro Harlem Brundtland. There was a feeling of renewal and that the times really were a'changing. Stewart, asked if he had been to Germany before, responded with a twinkle in his eye: "I dropped in as a paratrooper".

Raising the Iron Curtain led to a heartening moment in January 1990 when Alexander Dubcek from Czechoslovakia was able to attend Parliament to accept his Sakharov Prize. Coates had for some time run a campaign for a ground-breaking joint session between the European Parliament and the Supreme Soviet the following year with eventual support from the Socialist Group (the Germans were reluctant) and Christian Democrats, notably Klepsch and Habsburg. Coates says: "Gorbachev was most interested and assigned Zagladin to work with him to bring this about. Unfortunately, towards the end of that year events intervened. Gorbachev, who had won the Nobel Peace Prize in 1990, was kidnapped, Yeltsin was elevated, and the project was annulled". Coates today regrets these events, saying that "had Gorbachev survived in government it might have given a different perspective to Europe and we could have had disarmament and peace".

Parliament set up a Temporary Committee on Unification of Germany in February 1990 and Ford, sensing it would be something big, negotiated the rapporteurship for Donnelly. It made him an overnight star. He had already been prominently involved in work on EMU legislation. Gerhard Stahl from the Socialist Group staff, with a German Treasury background, was his right hand man, arranging an extensive programme of meetings in Germany and with the Commission; Arlene McCarthy, a stagiaire with Ford (and who became an MEP in 1994), also helped. It was chaired by a Spanish Christian Democrat, Fernandez Albor. The only other UK Member was Welsh for the Tories, and the main heavyweights were Elmar Brok (Christian Democrat), Claude Cheysson (Socialist) and Simone Veil (Liberal). In April the BLG held a four hour meeting on the subject.

Stahl and Donnelly's strategy was to win the support of the political elite to accept unification of Germany against a background of hostile right-wing establishment Cold War attitudes (not least in the UK) and to hold fast to Poland's western border, the Oder-Neisse line. As we have seen, in the beginning unification was not a foregone conclusion and the situation was of great political delicacy. Mitterrand had made a state visit to East Germany in an attempt to stabilise the regime. Delors proved visionary, saying that there had to be a European answer and monetary union was partly a consequence of that. He believed the new, bigger Germany had to be consolidated into the greater Europe and lose its own currency. It did not all happen at once. The East Germans had their own election in March and then in due course the Volkskammer decided to opt for unification. Donnelly and Stahl attended the historic meeting when it was agreed to close down, the tipping point for the decision being when Gorbachev said the Russians would not intervene. Political union with West Germany took place on 3 October 1990.

One aim for the work of the Temporary Committee was to raise the profile of the European Parliament, but it also opened up events inside Germany, exposing contradictions. Chancellor Kohl was receiving the EP committee at the same time as blocking the setting up of a similar one in the Bundestag. Donnelly moved quickly and by July, with Stahl's help, had produced an interim report on a range of transitional measures, debated in the presence of a delegation from the Volkskammer. He was supported by the Socialist Group which organized a conference on the economies of Central and Eastern Europe on 5 July 1990 and another on a single currency on 6 September when a further report came before Parliament, again with a delegation from the Volkskammer present in the gallery. This was second reading on a directive and a regulation pertaining to the technicalities of unification. Eddy Newman was concerned about Germany becoming the largest political and economic force in Europe, wanted all fascist organizations banned, and voted against this report.

East Germans were to have observer status in the EP from October or November. Donnelly's reports and speeches called for the full participation of Parliament, in particular by demanding transparency in the form of a management committee to oversee matters, rather than a regulatory committee as proposed by the Commission. The October parliamentary debate contained three separate reports on legislation. The final report was voted in November, when on the 20th Donnelly said that the "Council has broken ranks and ended the mood of compromise and solidarity…we have reached a poor compromise on implementing measures…" After holding out on this the Italian Presidency agreed to key amendments from Parliament and the necessary legal measures went through. It was a major achievement, not least because there were concerns from the Southern Member States that the whole thing might be a threat to their substantial European funding. Donnelly skilfully defused this problem by achieving guarantees for Portugal and Spain.

All-German elections were held on 2 December 1990. Donnelly, a non-German speaker, had found his trades union background stood him well and he proved to be an adroit negotiator, and apparently very good with the staff of the committee. His work was so appreciated that he was awarded a Knight Commander of the Order of Merit by the German government. There was a rare moment of support from the Conservatives when Welsh produced a limerick about Donnelly as an explanation of vote:

> "There was a young Member from Jarrow
> Whose views were, perforce, somewhat narrow
> But in special Committee
> He was charming and witty
> And his colleagues were thrilled to the marrow."

It was not the end of the project, because once unification took place there was the little matter of how many new MEPs Germany would be entitled to, to cope with its 16.7 million new citizens. There had traditionally been an agreed balance between Britain, France and Germany on numbers and now Germany would have a much larger representation if numbers were extended pro-rata. After much wrangling, with Donnelly insisting Parliament should be involved on equal terms, it was agreed by Council that Germany could have ninety-nine MEPs in total, anything over a hundred being seen as politically unacceptable. This would bring the Parliament's size up to 567. It was an accession of a new country without the normal years of negotiation.

In due course the Warsaw Pact was dissolved. Balfe supported a resolution from the Foreign Affairs Committee in favour of a nuclear weapons system, saying that the winding up of the Pact made the world less stable. Most of the comrades were not happy with this.

Getting stuck in

At the end of 1989, Donnelly had also been working on a report on co-operation between central banks of the Member States, demanding democratic control of financial institutions. The Commission rejected all his amendments requiring that the Chairman of the Committee of Central Bank Governors should appear before the parliamentary committee and the report was referred back to committee, which did not suit the French Presidency. Donnelly says Delors summoned Cot and himself to a meeting and put forward a new amendment which required the Chairman to appear before Parliament annually. This enabled Donnelly to tell plenary in February that a compromise had been found and to thank Delors. It was significant, because it meant that when the European Central Bank (ECB) was created a decade later its president had to be under parliamentary scrutiny.

By October the next year Labour Members were speaking up for an accountable Central Bank but Read argued that the BLG could not support fiscal harmonization. She abstained along with most of the BLG on this matter, but Falconer and Newens voted against. Martin was concerned that EMU might exacerbate regional disparities. Ford and Martin wrote in *Tribune* in November 1990 on our common European future, saying Tory policy on the single currency was a complete mess and that Labour was supporting EMU.

Much legislation was passing through in preparation for the Single Market, and Labour Members were actively absorbed in their committee work as scrutinisers and amenders. There was a learning curve as MEPs put more weight on proposals with the co-operation procedure realizing they needed the Commission on side to succeed. Enjoying closer communication with the party, they relished their role in constructing a better life for British people and using their work to illustrate the positive aspects of a future Labour government. They worked hard, harrying the Conservatives at every opportunity, attempting to reform and democratize the European institutions, take rearguard action against over-the-top Commission initiatives and agitate for improvements in human rights around the world. This was not without some difficulty. The Labour Party had a careful eye to potential press problems. This sometimes led to clashes with policy positions that the Socialist Group had negotiated when instructions to vote differently would arrive from the Leader's office. McCubbin, PES Whip for these five years, was unhappy with the EPLP having separate whips from the main group. The Labour Members did, however, in most cases present a unified front in plenary even if they disagreed in their own meetings.

Ford proved to be an active Leader and was normally present at the beginning of every plenary session to comment on the business in hand or attempt to make political capital at the expense of the Tories or the far right. On one occasion when Thatcher had referred to a "Mickey Mouse Parliament", he was quick to brandish a Mickey face mask, but generally his points were strongly political.

As a result of the Single European Act, Parliament's powers had increased with the co-operation procedure. It gave MEPs more power than backbench MPs, though there was little recognition or respect for this at home. For the first time they had a taste of power and by 1992 half of Parliament's amendments were being accepted into legislation, but still some important ones were being rejected. The co-operation procedure added a second reading for legislation but Parliament still needed support from the Commission for its amendments. There was substantial tension between the two institutions on the subject of comitology, the type of committee put in place to oversee implementation of legislation, with Parliament preferring consultative committees rather than advisory ones. (For a comprehensive discussion of comitology see Corbett, Jacobs and Shackleton, 2007.) At this stage Council deliberations remained behind closed doors. Some governments were more secretive than others and as it was difficult for UK Members to find out anything about their government's position they were sometimes helped by Dutch colleagues who received information from their government representation office, and German MEPs who were advised via their Länder offices.

A prominent Labour-friendly pro-European surfaced in Brussels in 1989. This was Charles Grant of *The Economist*, included in numerous discussions during these years with many of the Tribunites. In 1996 he was to found the influential "Centre for European Reform". Present, too, was Vincent Hanna who began his Channel 4 programme "The Week in Politics" in 1989. He was well-informed, witty and enjoyed the political arena, not to mention the good food in Strasbourg and took an interest in the activities of the Labour Members in the European Parliament, even reporting on their work.

Geoff Hoon on Legal Affairs was piloting various technical pieces of legislation through the system. In October 1989 he was working on second readings about consumer credit and insider dealings, both important parts of the single market jigsaw. He was rapporteur on a package of proposals on personal data protection where many problems were identified in the initial proposal at the first reading vote in March 1992; it was not until 1995 that the common position emerged from Council, by which time he was no longer a Member.

Tom Megahy reported in December 1989 on rights of residence in the EEC, concentrating on demanding rights for pensioners and cohabitees. Hughes pointed out that it was an incomplete Single Market where citizens did not have the right to live and work where they liked. Harrison suggested we must be generous in defining the family. Megahy also welcomed a directive on better facilities for people with disabilities on public transport in late 1991, spurred on by his own disability from polio. Today ramps on buses and places for push chairs and wheelchairs are taken for granted in Britain but at that time they were almost non-existent, and some good examples from the more progressive European countries were publicized in support of harmonized standards.

David Martin was working in the Regional Affairs Committee on a report in November 1989 that with the help of Socialist Detlev Samland in the Budget Committee led to the creation of the RECHAR fund, eventually bringing millions into hard-pressed areas of the UK suffering from the decline of coal and steel. It ran into problems when the UK government held back local authority spending, preventing eligible projects from proceeding. Labour's new Commissioner Bruce Millan took it up, saying this was not the only fund experiencing problems. Wayne David in the Regional Affairs Committee and McMahon on Social Affairs and Employment kept close watch on the various funding streams. David questioned whether the British government was breaking EU rules by not matching European money from the structural funds "pound for pound". He was also emerging as an environment-friendly voice. The funding issue came to a head when monies were held back from South Wales. At the beginning of 1992 Millan blocked RECHAR funds to the UK worth £115 million, pending cessation of government top-slicing and demanding proper additionality (which had been written into the reform of the structural funds in 1988). This high risk strategy led to improvements. It was the time of the Third Poverty Programme and a network of NGOs, the European Anti Poverty Network, was set up to provide the civil society side of the equation with the approval of Delors.

Adding to the general optimism there was elation on the left when Nelson Mandela was released from prison in February 1990. Ford promptly suggested 11 February be Mandela Day, and asked for him to be invited to visit the Parliament. The BLG, most of whom were members of the Anti-Apartheid movement and had spent decades going on marches, supported Mandela's request that sanctions should not be lifted until there was one-person-one-vote in South Africa and they remained in place until April of 1991. The Conservatives were split on the subject. In June 1990 Mandela was able to visit Strasbourg with his then wife Winnie, attended by Ford for two days, to receive the Sakharov Prize awarded to him in 1988 (the first of such prizes), an event that was the subject of much happy publicity by the left. Archbishop Desmond Tutu was another honoured guest in November. It was with a mixture of joy and nostalgia that Members marked the winding up of the Anti-Apartheid movement in 1994 after the first democratic elections in South Africa when Mandela was elected President. Several MEPs, including McGowan, went as observers to the elections.

Following on from the previous parliament, Collins was not going to let go without a fight on veterinary medicines and growth-promoting hormones. In a debate on 15 March 1990 he rejected the view of the Legal Affairs Committee. Bangemann for the Commission refused to endorse the Environment Committee's advocacy of the "fourth hurdle" (environmental impact assessment), but accepted some other amendments. A common position was produced in June but only one amendment at second reading obtained the necessary 260 votes. Two directives were adopted in December. Collins ensured that the fourth hurdle concept set the context of continuing discussions and finally the Commission began to develop proposals for a licensing procedure including impact assessment. Determined influence had important future repercussions.

Council prevarication for more than a year on the location of the new European Environment Agency infuriated Collins, who made it an item in his speech to the first East/West Ministerial meeting on environment in 1990. He was also becoming involved in resisting the marketing in the EU of genetically modified organisms (GMOs). The Commission had five different directorates dealing with it which he said was a recipe for disaster, demanding an internal task force to co-ordinate activity. In addition to the consumer matters being dealt with by Green, Collins was also engaged with the BSE problem, transport of nuclear waste, substances that deplete the ozone layer, nature conservation, import and export of harmful products, dangerous substances – and still with tobacco subsidies.

A debate on areas of the UK in Objective 2 took place on 15 May that year with speakers David, Smith, Bowe and Green on a resolution critical of the government's top slicing, noting that:

> "ERDF assistance is added to domestic public expenditure only at the national level and then allocated to all areas, including non-eligible areas, in clear breach not only of the spirit but the letter of ERDF regulations, according to which ERDF grants should be spent in addition to national budgets for regional development... Congratulates the Commission... by taking an unambiguous stand and freezing over 100 MECU available under the RECHAR programme, it has persuaded the UK to apply the principles of the structural funds."

The government eventually ended the impasse by providing more of its own money and changing its accountancy procedures.

When it became apparent that one of the Social Fund schemes, HORIZON (to help people with disabilities), had an eligibility list that excluded all parts of the UK except England, the EPLP used its influence and had the list modified. There was another structural fund problem building up. A new Objective 4 as part of the European Social Fund had been developed, the aim of which was to help re-train those in danger of redundancy *in situ*. The British government was tardy in taking this up and Tongue, mindful of the precarious nature of the Ford works in her constituency, was in full cry.

The UK's BSE problem was continuing to cause concern. A farcical attempt by the government to allay fears about the safety of British beef involved John Gummer, then Agriculture Minister, feeding his four year old daughter a hamburger in front of the television cameras in May 1990. Concerns about the possibility of CJD infection of humans began to spread and were taken up by Collins. A Commission statement on UK beef exports was debated on 12 June when Stevenson spoke of the "unfortunate saga" and demanded measures to restore confidence. There was much more to come later.

There was an almighty fuss in July 1990 when Cabinet Minister Nicholas Ridley was quoted in *The Spectator* making a grossly impolitic statement about Germany just before a visit to London by Karl Otto Pohl, the German central bank President, to promote European monetary union. Ridley, the Trade and Industry Secretary, said that West Germany was trying to take over Europe and giving up sovereignty to the European Community would be tantamount to surrendering to Hitler. The remarks caused outrage in Bonn, Strasbourg and London, caused the pound to weaken and he had to resign. In plenary Ford raised it on 12 July and Balfe, too, disowned the remarks.

Budget problems were rearing up again and a new financial perspective was being negotiated. Tomlinson, as the BLG's budget supremo, spoke of a "negative reserve" in October 1990 and the following month was furious about the Council not taking the problem seriously:

> "Council has once again reduced our budgetary argument to a level which would be a disgrace to a moderately well-run kindergarten... its integrity is about as valuable as Attila the Hun's contribution to diplomacy... Last week we had a compromise agreement worked out. This week the Council reneged and ratted on that compromise".

His complaint was that a raft of policy areas that had been agreed by Council could not be financed within the financial limits including LINGUA, Thermie, the environment fund, tropical forests, the fight against drugs, transport infrastructure and the social consequences of 1992, all dear to socialists' hearts. Lack of funding would be a recurring theme. Before too long he was also putting the case for modernization of Parliament's accounting practices to ensure greater accuracy and transparency; a lengthy battle and not always successful. Many of Tomlinson's speeches on budget matters were conducted in a form of jargon intelligible only to those who served on the Budget Committee but he pursued a strong line against corruption and secrecy. Stevenson joined in the debate on budget problems in May 1991, pointing out that there was also an unsustainable 32% increase in farm prices.

Labour Members made accusations about British Aerospace and the takeover of Austin Rover concerning a huge subsidy and debt write-off. Donnelly alleged an unofficial deal between the British government and Commission officials to reduce the financial penalty. There were months of demands from Donnelly and Ford for a statement from the Commission. Read insisted that EEC money had been misused and that the British government had given a financial bonanza to its privileged supporters. The BLG particularly wanted Sir Leon Brittan on toast, because he had been the responsible Minister at the time of the allegedly illegal subsidy. The Commission was being accused of misleading the House and was hiding behind the fact that it had not been officially informed by the British government of what had happened, despite it having been all over the press. Finally in March 1993 they had to tell BAe to repay £44 million in government aid, a victory of sorts for the European campaigners.

Gravy train accusations surfaced regularly in the press, and were occasionally justified. There were serious deficiencies in the parliamentary system of checking expenses. Labour MEPs always voted for reforms, but they were slow in coming because of resistance from some other national groupings. Although there had been some reforms in the way travel expenses were calculated, it was still possible for Members to buy cheap "back to back" air tickets and make a profit on the allowance. The changing timetable of the Parliament made cheap tickets risky, however, and it would often be necessary to dump a ticket and buy another. Hayter was furious when a Member inexcusably missed a vote because of "having" to leave to catch his cheap flight home.

A lengthy saga arose in 1989 when the Commission was amending a directive on cosmetic products against public revulsion that animals were tortured for beauty, sparking extensive lobbying. As a result of early influence from Pollack and Roth-Behrendt the proposals were re-drafted before they saw the light of day. The latter became rapporteur, assisted in her work by Armin Machmer, and her report was adopted in February 1992, but referred back to find a compromise with the Commission. In June a text was only acceptable in Council to Denmark and Germany whilst the big cosmetic manufacturing country was France. During the British Presidency a fudged compromise on banning testing subject to finding alternatives was carried. In April 1993 two amendments were overwhelmingly voted by Parliament including a European Centre for Validating Alternatives to Animal Testing to be set up for which in November Pollack secured a budget amendment. Council adopted the directive in June 1994. The Socialists were furious when the Commission, getting cold feet about a potential backlash via international trade rules, wanted to put off a ban for four years. It carried over into the next parliamentary term.

The BLG produced a pro-European publication in September 1990, "The New Europe", about using education and training to develop a skilled workforce – a European technology strategy, and proposed scaling down the CAP and developing a Good Food policy and a charter for the environment. During this term they put together a number of other excellent publications distributed via constituency offices. That same autumn London MEPs held a conference on East-West relations and another on Europe and quality of life.

Mindful of the Ford motor plant in her East London constituency, Tongue became rapporteur on the motor industry, producing her first report in June 1991, this highlighting overcapacity, potential job losses and environmental issues. The debate featured an argument about the desirability of Japanese car plants in Britain, with Donnelly supporting Nissan in the North East employing thirty thousand workers and Hoon attacking double standards on Japan. Hughes, Ford, Oddy, Elliott, Wynn and Stewart all entered the debate. Not all were in agreement on the Japanese question. Tongue followed this up in June 1992 with PQs on local content rules and organized the first EU automobile forum in 1994 bringing together representatives from all EU institutions, car industry leaders, trades unions and academics. This produced a report leading to ESF funds to support workers threatened with redundancy.

Environment Commissioner Ripa di Meana, following numerous complaints and Labour activity during the election campaign, announced infringement procedures against the UK on bathing water. It was an opportunity for the BLG to attack the government in the regional press, with the aid of helpful photos with the action group "Surfers Against Sewage". There were also problems in the UK with river water pollution and a formal letter of complaint had been sent from the Commission. The Commissioner, formerly a member of the Socialist Group, was happy to give the Conservative government a hard time and in October 1991 he also managed to block a number of UK transport projects on environmental grounds. These had been the subject of grass-roots campaigns and such actions went down well in the affected regions.

Before the 1989 election Collins was contacted from the Co-op in London (via Pauline Green), asking for a meeting to make a case for a food hygiene directive. Collins and his assistant Earnshaw explained how to frame the request to the Commission, on which Collins then exerted pressure. The Commission did put forward a number of proposals on food hygiene, particularly meat, but as Green pointed out, they were wildly inconsistent – rules relative to poultry were different to those for other meat. Freida Stack for the Co-op undertook a study of some of the problems, highlighting that if inspectors went into a big plant, they would have to change clothes three times because of the standards for different products. Collins decided the only way to inject sense into the system was to campaign for a wide-ranging food hygiene directive, which eventually was grudgingly produced. Green greeted this with excitement, saying she had campaigned for it for six years, three before she came to Parliament. She met frequently with Commission officials to work out what was achievable in an early example of close co-operation.

The Environment Committee proposed a ban on tobacco advertising as part of the Europe Against Cancer programme, with the support of Commission official Dr Bill Hunter. This proved to be highly controversial, uniting German Members across parties in opposition, arguing that if it was legal to sell tobacco it should be legal to advertise it.

Collins had cornered the veterinary issues and Green consumer matters, with Bowe, as a former science teacher, becoming involved in toxic waste and other subjects concerning the chemical industry. With an eye to her marginal, largely middle class constituency, Pollack pursued some of the animal welfare campaigns that she had worked on as Castle's assistant, including a protracted argument with the Commission about banning seal fur imports revolving around so-called "humane" trapping methods. She asked the Commission "how many minute a trapped muskrat should die in for the Commission to consider death humane?" She joined Tony Banks MP and others, courtesy of the International Fund for Animal Welfare (whose Brussels person, Lesley O'Donnell worked closely with many Labour Members), in Canada's Gulf of St Lawrence in March 1991 to attempt to stop the carnage of baby seals on the ice. This became a controversial subject once the Commission began to succumb to lobbies from Canada (which claimed that seals ate the cod stocks and that hunting was a way of life) and threats of WTO resistance to an import ban. Other Members were to follow on this annual trip as the campaign gained public attention. The slaughter on the ice stopped for a few years but has latterly begun again with Parliament again in 2009 voting on a seal products import ban and the same threats of WTO action.

There was much more on animal welfare. Morris became rapporteur for improved time limits on transport for live animals. This was the subject of much lobbying and it took years for progress to be made. He first reported in April 1990 and various reports and amendments carried on through May 1993, with many ups and downs in Parliament and outside. Cruel sow tethering was also tackled by Pollack, waving a medieval-looking trap in

Parliament and challenging the Agriculture Commissioner, leading eventually to some improvement in the rules. In July 1990, supported by the RSPCA, whose headquarters was in her constituency, she produced a report on the need for dog registration, aiming for free movement with proper registration and vaccination. This was uncontroversial except with some Conservatives who feared rabies crossing borders. With colleagues on the Agriculture Committee she also waged a campaign (continuing a decade later) for better treatment of live animals transported for slaughter. This was a huge issue in the UK and a petition with 1.5 million signatures was presented to the Council in April 1991.

Mel Read settled in to what would be her niche work on complicated and technical telecommunications issues, initially as rapporteur on telecom terminal equipment. She spoke up for the public interest, pushing for better rights of worker consultation and for harmonisation of type approval, saying that seventy more jobs were going at Plessey (where she had once worked and been an active trade unionist). These were important for the British economy, largely in competition with the USA, and because most of the Labour Group did not have much of a clue about the detail, she was given her head and worked for years on this area to great effect. It was generally too technical to enjoy press coverage at home.

Gary Titley, representing part of the North West's declining textile belt, joined the earlier efforts of Hindley and Seal in arguing for continuation of the MFA, in which he was strongly backed by the trades unions. His argument was that ending the social clause in the MFA would cost thirty-five thousand jobs in the UK. In June 1991 he was again expressing concern that the Commission might be prepared to sacrifice the textile industry in GATT negotiations for the sake of agriculture, saying one in four workers in West Yorkshire were in textiles. Alex Smith said fifty percent of the manufacturing in his constituency was in textiles and that there were no alternative jobs.

New proposals to build on an earlier shelved directive on workers' access to information, consultation and negotiation (Vredeling) were put forward by the Commission which would afford companies certain privileges in establishing and operating in other EC countries not available under existing national regulations. It came in the form of a regulation on a company law statute and a directive on the consultation part. Oddy was joint rapporteur with Socialist Rothley, aided by Group staffer Christian Lange. The main problem was the different way in which countries consulted workers. The West German Mitbestimmung model, with election of workers' representatives onto boards, was the preferred system unveiled in July 1989 by Commissioner Bangemann. A system of workers' councils was also used in Belgium, France and Netherlands, but the TUC did not want representatives who were not trade unionists. Spanish Members, not long out of the Franco era, were concerned about "yellow" unions and wanted independents. The Bureau paid for Oddy to visit Germany and Stockholm to study worker participation for this report. There were other sticking points such as tax. It was quite a technical dossier with a large number of amendments in January 1991 at first reading, and became stuck in Council for years. Finally after the efforts of a Committee of Wise Men, it reappeared at the end of the Parliament and Labour Members supported the compromise. Second reading was in September 1994 after the election.

The Commission produced a ground-breaking Green Paper on Urban Environment, brain-child of Nick Hanley and a marker for future action. Pollack took this up enthusiastically as rapporteur, travelling to Delft, Berlin, Vienna and elsewhere to look at best practice in urban environment management and traffic control. In undertaking this work long-lasting friends were made in the Commission including Liz Mills, a British expert and top networker passionately interested in furthering Commission action on urban environment. Following on from this she pressed for a tunnel for the high-speed rail link into Stratford, to save historic Oxleas Wood. Although stonewalled at the time, when the rail link was finally constructed in 2006-7, it was indeed a tunnel that was built and the wood remains a beautiful place for walkers and wildlife.

Ken Coates took an innovative step in using some of his resources to produce a quarterly journal, *European Labour Forum*, distributed via Spokesman Press. The first issue appeared in Summer 1990 and it ran up to the Winter of 1999, with thoughtful articles by MEPs, both British and other nationalities, academics, trades unionists and prominent left-wing and peace thinkers from all over Europe on a theme of socialism, peace, a social dimension to EMU and a greater Europe including a European Socialist Party. In the spirit of a think tank the journal raised many ideas that were not official Labour Party policy. The party mostly ignored the publication but the leadership was less than pleased when in the next parliamentary period it became the home of more vociferously oppositionist articles on subjects such as Clause IV. At that point the perception of Coates as a serial dissident became more embedded.

Gulf War

Saddam Hussein of Iraq invaded and annexed Kuwait in September 1990, triggering the first Gulf War. In the early stages the Labour Group supported sanctions and UN resolutions and criticised the "hawkish" UK Prime Minister. White demanded an emergency recall of Parliament should war break out. Coates insisted that the embargo must succeed and war should be avoided.

A small group from the Foreign Affairs Committee met jointly with the Council of Ministers in advance of their formal meeting. It was chaired by Crampton because the Italian chair (a motor racing driver) was unable to attend. They discussed funds for various countries and he held out for support for Jordan because they were coping with Iraqi refugees from the war and opposed funds for Egypt and Turkey. Because of good relations with Gianni di Michelis, a former Socialist MEP who was then President-in-Office of the Council, he was able to negotiate with him and Jordan's funding was agreed. A delegation, including Crampton, flew off to meet President Mubarak in Alexandria, King Faud and the Emirs of Kuwait in Jeddah, Foreign Minister Hassan in Amman, President Assad in Damascus and finally Yasser Arafat in Tunis on what was an exciting trip for a fairly new Member. They took a vote on whether to go to Baghdad and meet Saddam Hussein. He and Cheysson voted to go but were defeated.

By the following January the war was on. There was much hand-wringing about what to do, with suggestions that the Community was letting

Left to right: John Hume, Barbara Castle and Lord (Ted) Castle, July 1979. (*photo European Parliament*)

Roland Boyes in full flow in Strasbourg in the early 1980s. (*photo European Parliament*)

Les Huckfield defending the miners via megaphone in the European Parliament 24 October 1984. (*photo European Parliament*)

Derek Enright
(MEP 1979-1984)

Tom Megahy
(MEP 1979-1999)

Ann Clwyd
(MEP 1979-1984)

Bary Seal
(MEP 1979-1999)

Anita Pollack, Labour candidate for Woking 1987, with Labour Leader Neil Kinnock. David Ward in the background. (*photo Labour Party*)

Brian Key
(MEP 1979-1984)

Joyce Quin
(MEP 1979-1989)

Janey Buchan
(MEP 1979-1994)

MEPs handing over cheque to striking ambulance workers, December 1989. *Left to right:* Roger Poole, Anita Pollack, Pauline Green, Stan Newens and Wayne David. (*photo EPLP*)

Left to right: George Robertson, Shadow Europe Spokesperson, Neil Kinnock, Leader of the Labour Party and David Martin, Leader of the British Labour Group, Brussels, February 1988. (*photo European Parliament)*

Allan Rogers at a Socialist Group meeting. (*photo European Parliament*)

Dick Caborn
(MEP 1979-1984)

Michael Gallagher
(MEP 1979-1984)

Glyn Ford (*left*), Leader of the EPLP with Enrique
Baron, President of the European Parliament in
September 1990. (*photo European Parliament*)

Win Griffiths
(MEP 1979-1989)

Michael Hindley
(MEP 1984-1999)

Anita Pollack discussing tactics with Ken
Collins, Chair of the Committee on Environ-
ment, Public Health and Consumer
Protection, September 1991. (*photo EPLP*)

Norman West and Arthur Scargill in the European
Parliament, July 1985. (*photo European Parliament*)

Happy days at Hell Corner Farm, summer 1987.
Barbara Castle with Jan Royall (left) and Anita
Pollack and their children.

Alex Falconer
(MEP 1984-1999)

Hugh McMahon
(MEP 1984-1999)

Ken Stewart
(MEP 1984-1996)

Opening the Parliament's creche in Strasbourg, September 1992. *Left to right:* Mel Read, Christine Crawley, Hilary Moser, Anita Pollack, Carol Tongue. (*photo European Parliament*)

Michael McGowan
(MEP 1984-1999)

Llewellyn Smith
(MEP 1984-1994)

Meeting in the North East 1993. *Left to right:* Alan Donnelly, Gordon Adam, John Smith and Glyn Ford.

Geoff Hoon
(MEP 1984-1994)

Terence Pitt
(MEP 1984-1986)

Edward Newman
(MEP 1984-1999)

Bob Cryer
(MEP 1984-1989)

May 1994. The Sunday before John Smith died a group of distinguished Scottish politicians came together to launch the election campaign for Ken Collins. *Seated:* Peggy Herbison, Ken Collins; *standing left to right:* Jeremy Bray, Willie McKelvie, John Reid, John Smith, Tony McEvoy, Tom Clarke, Adam Ingram, George Robertson. (*photo Contrast Photography, Glasgow*)

Women Labour MEPs 1994 -1999. *Left to right:* Eluned Morgan, Pauline Green, Eryl McNally, Arlene McCarthy, Carole Tongue, Anita Pollack, Mel Read, Glenys Kinnock, Angela Billingham, Veronica Hardstaff. The three missing are Christine Crawley, Sue Waddington and Christine Oddy.
(*photo European Parliament*)

London Labour MEPs 1994-1999. *Left to right: seated* Richard Balfe, Carole Tongue, Alf Lomas, Pauline Green; *standing* Anita Pollack, Stan Newens, Michael Elliott, Shaun Spiers and Robert Evans. (*photo EPLP*)

Labour's team on the BSE follow-up Committee of Inquiry, July 1997. *Left to right:* Jack Cunningham (Secretary of State for Agriculture) and MEPs David Thomas, Phillip Whitehead and Anita Pollack. (*photo European Parliament*)

George Stevenson
(MEP 1984-1989)

John Tomlinson
(MEP 1984-1999)

Rev David (Dai) Morris
(MEP 1984-1999)

John Bird
(MEP 1987-1994)

Gary Titley
(MEP 1989-2009)

Ken Coates
(MEP 1989-1999)

Alex Smith
(MEP 1989-1999)

Henry McCubbin
(MEP 1989-1994)

Ian White
(MEP 1989-1999)

Anthony (Joe) Wilson
(MEP 1989-1999)

Victorious Labour MEPs after the sweeping success of the 1994 election, with Margaret Beckett and Jack Cunningham. Most but not all of the 62 are present. Most of the new intake were pro-European and only six remained of the original 1979 intake. (*photo Labour Party*)

Peter Crampton
(MEP 1989-1999)

David Bowe
(MEP 1989-2004)

Roger Barton and Anita Pollack on his Triumph, April 1994. (*photo European Parliament*)

Lyndon Harrison
(MEP 1989-1999)

Peter Skinner
(MEP 1994-)

Supporting fair trade Caribbean bananas. *Left to right:* Glenys Kinnock, Terry Wynn and David Thomas. (*photo European Parliament*)

Clive Needle
(MEP 1994-1999)

Hugh Kerr
(MEP 1994-1999)

Tony Cunningham
(MEP 1994-1999)

Peter Truscott
(MEP 1994-1999)

EPLP Chairs and other officers, January 1997. *Left to right:* Brian Simpson, Stephen Hughes, Anita Pollack, David Martin, Wayne David, Pauline Green, Richard Balfe, Ken Collins, Allan Donnelly (*photo European Parliament*)

EPLP officers in Autumn 1998 during the British Presidency. *Left to right:* Douglas Henderson (Europe Minister), Roger Barton, Phillip Whitehead, Wayne David (Leader EPLP), Veronica Hardstaff with Michael Tappin and Christine Crawley (barely seen) behind, Tony Blair, Simon Murphy, Eryl McNally, Shaun Spiers and Christine Oddy. (*photo European Parliament*)

Mark Hendrick
(MEP 1994-1999)

David Hallam
(MEP 1994-1999)

Bill Miller
(MEP 1994-2004)

Susan Waddington
(MEP 1994-1999)

Richard Howitt
(MEP 1994-)

Mark Watts
(MEP 1994-2004)

Richard Corbett
(MEP 1996-2009)

Linda McAvan
(MEP 1998-)

All photos not individually credited courtesy of Photo European Parliament

America do its dirty work. Coates made a rare speech about the temporary impotence of the European institutions and called for Members to attend a peace demonstration at the Cathedral in Strasbourg. Many of the group including Crawley, Tongue, Stewart, Newens, Lomas and Hughes spoke out for peace. This gave some lovely ammunition to Conservative Ben Patterson who said that Labour Members "systematically undermine the policies of their own party."

Labour in the House of Commons had decided to support the war, causing some problems for the more pacifist of the MEPs. The BLG voted for a cease-fire, cutting across Kinnock's carefully-crafted position at home and Hayter told the officers they had to find some way to repudiate their position. She recalls paging George Robertson, Europe spokesperson, about the vote and he was not happy. A form of words was grudgingly agreed with the officers for a press release to defuse the situation. Kinnock later said he had faced down his rebels at home, sacking two front-benchers and had not realized the vote was coming up in the European Parliament, but was not greatly worried about the haphazard voting.

The Socialist Confed held an extraordinary Leaders' strategy discussion on the war in Brussels on 20 January. With serious divisions amongst the member parties, a common declaration was not possible. There was also a row in Parliament as a Socialist Group resolution was emasculated by the right and withdrawn. A special session of the Parliament was held in Brussels on 30 January, with much speechifying. Collins demanded that the Geneva Convention should be altered to include forbidding environmental damage being used as a weapon of war. Ford said that the Labour Party that day endorsed the offer by USA and USSR for a cease fire.

European Labour Forum carried a piece in its May Day 1991 edition on matters arising from the Gulf War, looking at the arms trade, chemical and nuclear weapon proliferation and speaking of a New World Order. A second piece in the same edition expressed fears about an arms momentum and arguing for conversion of military R&D – a peace dividend.

What's in a name?

Stability was the order of the day for the AGM on 13 June 1990 in Strasbourg. There was a proposal from Coates, with the approval of the leadership at home, to change the name from British Labour Group to European Parliamentary Labour Party, and this was carried by 26 – 17. The feeling was that this would do more to formalize the group and put it on a footing more commensurate with that of the Parliamentary Labour Party. Coates argued that the title BLG was analogous to Labour Groups on County Councils whereas the PLP and EPLP were elected on a nationwide suffrage – though the following day he met Prescott in a conference in Nottingham who said "What's this then, a UDI?" It was formally ratified in a party rule change in 1991. Hayter was by now fostering a much closer relationship with the NEC and Leader's office and there was a joint parliamentary co-ordination committee chaired by George Robertson.

An attempt by White to scrap the recorded votes and substitute a secret ballot was lost by 18 – 22; however he was successful in proposing hustings statements in future for officerships, this being carried by 24 – 18. With party policy now that women should have forty percent of elected posts inside the party, there was difficulty achieving this given the paucity of female Members and it was agreed that it would have to remain an aspiration until after the next election.

Ford was re-elected Leader against another challenge by Seal, 25 – 19, Tongue beat off a challenge by Newens for Deputy Leader by the same margin and Read was elected Chair against Elliott by the same margin. (Bird stood down after having been away ill with a heart attack and Read had already acted as Chair quite often.) Donnelly was re-elected this time against Falconer for Secretary by 26 – 18. In this vote Balfe cast his vote for Donnelly – a switch of sides for him. David was Treasurer again, winning by 26 – 18 against Oddy. Titley retained the post of Whip against Simpson 25 – 18 and in a three-way contest for Socialist Group Bureau Member, Tomlinson was again successful with 23 votes, against Hindley 18 and White 4. White abstained in some of the votes, citing his principled position that the Labour members should belong to a European Socialist Party rather than to a separate national bloc.

Coates successfully proposed an amendment to standing orders (23 – 21) that made a significant change of tack in favour of a more European system and the implications of it must have escaped many of the Members at the time. It said:

> "It is the duty of members to act in pursuit of the policies of the Labour Party and the manifestos and decision of the Confederation of Socialist Parties of the EC and to assist in the harmonious development of relations between the Labour Party in Britain and our socialist colleagues in Europe."

Gillian Shepherd, the Undersecretary of State for Social Services, was visiting Strasbourg and met with the BLG, bravely facing demands for the government to implement the Social Charter.

At the end of the first year the EPLP published an upbeat "annual report" for the first time, entitled "A Year of Labour achievement in Europe". At conference in 1990, Crawley spoke about women and training, Spiers (to become an MEP in 1994) for the CWS about overseas aid and Eastern Europe, and Ford gave a strong Leader's speech:

> "Labour has a key role at the centre of European politics… This is a wonderful time to be a European… Our vision of a new Europe… is shared by millions…Britain is our country and we are proud of our identity, but we are Europeans too, and we know that the new Europe is our future."

Donnelly spoke on German unification and Tongue on electoral systems, pointing out that no other country in Western Europe used a first-past-the-post system.

Conference star was Barbara Castle, now eighty, who had been created a Life Peer in the Queen's Birthday Honours. She made a rousing socialist speech with no mention of Europe. Newens, as a CWS delegate, seconded an emergency resolution on Socialist Organiser, disagreeing with their line but supporting the right of dissent. Speakers at fringe meetings were Tomlinson at LME, Buchan at the Safeguards Committee, Tongue on electoral reform and Crawley for LCC. During 1991 the Electoral Systems Working Party visited the EPLP as did a number of front bench MPs – Kinnock, Robertson, Mowlam, David Clark, Ann Taylor and John Marek. Conference endorsed the report of the third Policy Review, Looking to the Future, that supported enlargement of the EU, institutional reform, the Social Charter and ERM. Resolution 63 recommended Labour support ERM membership in principle.

At the next AGM on 12 June 1991 the intimidatory recorded ballot system, in place since 1983, was finally disposed of. It was agreed that officers should produce written reports to AGMs. Voting for officers was not hugely different from the previous year. Ford this time beat Falconer for Leader by 27 – 14 with 3 abstentions (one of whom was Newens). Tongue stood down as Deputy Leader and Crawley surprisingly lost to Hughes by 24 – 16 with one abstention. Some felt that committee chairs should not have EPLP posts as well and this affected her vote. Read was re-elected Chair versus West by 28 – 13 with 3 abstentions. There was always a little tension there and Read who had served on the national executive of one of the country's largest trades unions, was not one to take any nonsense. On a later occasion when West tabled a resolution, she briskly ruled it out of order as "pious", which annoyed the Campaign Group.

Still at the 1991 AGM, Harrison became Secretary with 23 votes versus 20 for Elliott and one abstention. Donnelly did not stand on this occasion as he wanted to concentrate on legislative work. This time Balfe stood against Wayne David for Treasurer and won 24 – 20. Simpson won against Titley to become Whip. The Socialist Group Bureau position was a three way contest again. In the first ballot the votes were: Tomlinson 21, Megahy 20 and White 3. Second ballot was Tomlinson and Megahy even on 22 and a re-ballot was put off until a reconvened AGM on 10 July, when Tomlinson won by 24 to Megahy's 18. Now there were Hughes and Balfe on the hitherto tight Kinnockite officer group making it slightly more unpredictable.

The power of the Whip was negligible in comparison to that in Westminster, because there were no effective sanctions. There was also sometimes conflict between an EPLP policy position and that of the Socialist Group where McCubbin was Chief Whip. The main task was to advise the latter how many votes the EPLP would be able to deliver for legislative proposals requiring the minimum 260 votes in Parliament.

A belief that individuals should not hold more than one position prompted a couple of attempts to change standing orders. Elliott and Lomas lost a proposal that "All nominations for positions within the Socialist Group and Parliament, including changes or filling vacancies in Committee memberships and EPLP places on Committees of Inquiry must be first approved by the EPLP". Hoon and Read then proposed that "all nominations for positions within the Socialist Group and Parliament must be approved in the first instance by the EPLP" which was overwhelmingly lost. Finally the majority voted for the less restrictive: "no member of the EPLP, having been entitled to serve as a member of the Socialist Group Bureau, shall simultaneously hold a position in the Parliament." This was probably designed to stop Tomlinson becoming Chair of the Budget Committee at the half-way changeover in parliamentary positions at the end of the year.

Labour was delighted when the EPP rejected a proposal of marriage from the EDG made by John Major and Chris Patten, a factor being Major's refusal to back the Social Charter. In April 1991 Donnelly highlighted the failed marriage, leading to a riposte by Socialist colleague Enrique Baron in the chair: "Mr Donnelly, you know as well as I do that pre-marital affairs are not one of the subjects our Parliament deals with". Within a year, however, the marriage took place.

Inter-governmental conferences

In autumn 1989 the Socialist Group was arguing for an IGC on EMU and insisting there must be democratic control of a European Bank. Martin was supporting this having moved on from his anti-European days of 1984. In an interim report endorsed by the BLG on 6 March 1990 he wanted the right to initiate legislative proposals and ratify treaties, control over the executive and over hiring and firing of the Commission and for the IGC to include twelve MEPs, including some women. In debate he thanked three Conservative Members "for ending their political careers in supporting a federal Europe". White took the opportunity to push the boat out:

> "it is increasingly necessary rapidly to transform the EC into an EU of the federal type and going beyond the single market and economic and monetary union. The British Labour Party has now crossed to the other side of the Channel."

This was never really the case. Monetary union was controversial at home, though Labour was beginning to suggest it might be acceptable under the right terms. In contrast to White's enthusiasm, Megahy said:

> "I intend to stick to my tradition of voting against any report that comes from the Committee on Institutional Affairs. The total package encapsulates the drive to European union to which I and my party are opposed. Support for federalism does not exist in the NEC or pubs and clubs of Yorkshire."

In June Martin welcomed Council support for a second IGC. His reports, produced with the assistance of Socialist Group administrator Richard Corbett, proposed pragmatic procedural reform, including election of the Commission President by Parliament and included the first draft of what would become the co-decision procedure. One suggestion was to introduce QMV for environment policy, and the EPLP and front bench supported that, saying environment was too important for there to be a national veto.

The Socialist Group held a conference on EMU in Brussels to input into the way the IGCs developed. Parliamentary Assizes (a conference of parliaments) were held in Rome in November (again an Italian Presidency acting against Thatcher's wishes) in advance of the IGC on 14 December, endorsing the main proposals of the Martin reports. Just before the Assize, Martin produced two more final reports, saying it was an historic moment and an opportunity to create a democratic Community. He wanted to abolish the distinction between the "compulsory" (largely CAP) and "non-compulsory" sections of the budget (for the latter section the Parliament had no control). The Commission was opposed to many of these proposals. The next month Balfe found it necessary to stand up and say that he had intended to vote for the federalist aspects of the Martin reports but was away in the UK.

The Confed also wanted the IGC not simply to be limited to a discussion of EMU but also to consider political and institutional changes, enlisting the support of both Delors and Mitterrand. At the Leaders' meeting in 1990 in Dublin the position taken was that EMU must be linked to socio-economic cohesion and political union should be accompanied by greater co-decision powers for the Parliament, plus more co-operation on foreign and security matters. A 14-point plan was outlined for the two IGCs. It was largely national parliaments represented at the Rome Assize in 1990 to finalise the agenda of the IGC and George Robertson was there for Labour. Corbett was loaned by the Socialist Group and the final resolution was largely his drafting.

Thatcher had caused a revolt by her Chancellor Nigel Lawson and Foreign Secretary Geoffrey Howe just before the Madrid summit meeting in June 1989 over her refusal to agree to Britain joining the ERM in preparation for monetary union. Howe eventually resigned in November 1990 as Deputy Prime Minister in protest at her European policy and she found herself losing in a leadership election. Rather than face a second round ballot, she resigned as Leader of the Conservative Party (and consequently Prime Minister) on 22 November. After all the opposition she had faced from the Labour movement, her downfall was her own. John Major, her Chancellor, won the contest to be her successor.

Socialists in Europe

Two concerns of the Confed at this time were its own internal reform plus the IGCs. At the Vienna meeting of socialist leaders in March 1990, EFTA leaders were also included and the idea of a European Economic and Social Space was agreed. It was also agreed to support establishment of democratic institutions and disarmament in the new Central and Eastern European countries. Standing working parties were set up and two conferences organized in 1991 – in Brussels on women and in Copenhagen on the environment.

The "Luxembourg Declaration" in June welcomed both the draft Treaty on European Union and enlargement. There was some progress on an idea that had been vetoed the year before, the beginning of turning the Socialist Group in the Parliament into a group of the Party of European Socialists. Later that year the Liberals proposed regular communication with the Socialists and the Christian Democrats. Several meetings of this kind were held during 1990-91 in the run up to the Maastricht Summit. By the end of that year most of the socialist parties in the EU had similar policies on European monetary and political union.

The Maastricht Treaty pleased the party leaders because it said: "Political Parties at the European level are an important factor for integration within the Union. They contribute to forming a European awareness and to expressing the political will of the citizens of the Union". In response the Confed's Bureau set up a working group on strengthening the organisation. Eventually a Statute of European Political Parties was developed and in October 1992 the Party of European Socialists (PES) was launched. Kinnock was not keen on the idea. Although the change was in reality not great, it was seen as important symbolically even though it simply involved automatic membership for national party members, most of whom knew nothing about it. The Socialist Group in the European Parliament was to become known as the "Group of" this Party. The first well-publicised Leaders' conference of the "new" European party was held during the Edinburgh Summit in December 1992 to begin work on the next election manifesto.

This change to a formal European party was of great interest to the "federalist four" (Crampton, Coates, White and McCubbin). White and McCubbin, on the occasion of Labour's first European conference, printed PES "membership" cards to suggest that Labour Party grass roots members should join the "European Party".

The Socialist Group was expanded by Italian Communists in 1993, the third political party from Italy to sit in the big group. They had long been friends with the Labour Party. By this time the Conservatives had joined the Christian Democrats.

The PES Brussels Congress in 1993 created a formal women's committee for the first time, with a voting representative on the Bureau. European and also international socialist women were at this time debating quotas for women. Later, in 1997, two representatives of ECOSY, the youth section, were also granted voting rights on the Bureau. From the UK, this sort of representation was filled from the NEC rather than from the ranks of the MEPs and there was not much in the way of exchange of information about activities.

Labour MEPs had no reservations about disagreeing in public, particularly in the Socialist Group. On one occasion the speakers were all British, all disagreeing, the subject matter now lost in the mists of time. Leading Spanish Socialist Luis Planas, astonished once more about the lack of discipline, remarked to Ford that "I can count on normally at least 23 of the 25 Members in my delegation, how many can you count on? Ford is said to have replied wryly: "Well, there's me..."

Still fighting racism

Glyn Ford coined the phrase "Europe's 13th state" for its 12 to 14 million immigrants, pushing for a further committee of inquiry into racism and xenophobia to be set up. When that was agreed he was at first thwarted because his opponents in the Campaign Group ensured that Elliott was put on the committee, making him a substitute. He had to do a deal with a Dutch colleague to win a place so as to become rapporteur. His report in October 1990 advanced seventy-seven recommendations to follow up his earlier committee's findings, including the European Migrants' Forum. During the preparation of this report he had to have bodyguards for a visit to Marseilles, hotbed of the French extreme right. He took delight in February 1992 in publicizing the mad call at the Young Conservatives' conference for Strasbourg to be bombed, an indicator that Labour had become pro-European, whilst the Tories had gone the other way.

Feelings continued to run high and Socialist van Hemeldonck, also on the committee, vigorously opposed a statement of Giscard d'Estaing that the French were fed up with immigrants. This escalated and led to the invocation of the dispute between Napoleon and Talleyrand when the former said "vous êtes de la merde dans un bas de soie" ("you are a shit in a silk stocking"). Ford had a run-in with Giscard over the report in the chamber but the next day walked across the floor and shook his hand to make up.

Mel Read wrote *Against a Rising Tide: Racism, Europe and 1992* with Alan Simpson MP in 1991, saying that "turning back the tide of racism will require support for the actions that the Ford Report calls for at the European level."

Labour MEPs often complained about border discrimination against black citizens, when coach loads of visitor groups were detained because of one or two with the wrong passports or colour of skin. One such example was when Oona King (later a high profile MP for Bethnal Green and Bow), who worked for Ford, was stopped in March 1994 at Gatwick on her way to Strasbourg by British Airways officials who demanded proof that she was not seeking to stay in France.

Le Pen's far-right group was indulging in serial junketing, which was exposed by Ford who accused them of going to Corfu for four days on expenses and only meeting for four hours. They had also gone to the Caribbean and wanted to travel to amongst other places Edinburgh, which roused Falconer furiously to assert that they would not be welcome in that city and that the trades unions would ensure they could not find hotels in which to stay. Ford addressed an anti-Le Pen rally in Edinburgh. It became pretty acrimonious for a time but eventually died out.

Builders at work

More of the BLG were now actively engaged in the legislative process, for instance Adam on the third research programme and Green on EHLASS, a new programme for consumers concerning home and leisure accidents. She first reported in July 1990 and it came back in June 1993. Bowe worked on the controversial landfill directive and despite only having consultative powers, the committee's amendments virtually rewrote the proposal, the bulk of which was accepted by the Commission in November 1990. Parliament wielded considerably more influence than its formal powers offered.

A Committee of Inquiry on the Spread of Organised Crime Linked to Drugs Trafficking, chaired by Bowe, was set up in January 1991. It reported in May the next year, alongside a report by Tory Sir Jack Stewart-Clark from the Education and Youth Committee about education to combat health and drugs misuse and a proposal to set up a European Drugs Monitoring Centre. Substantial differences of opinion in committee spilled over into the debate in plenary. One recommendation was that possession of small quantities of illicit drugs for personal use should not be considered a criminal offence. Some felt this flew in the face of UN Conventions and saw it as a drug pusher's charter. Bowe made a careful non-committal speech saying there were no simple solutions, and called for measures to coordinate policies to tackle the threat, saying "we were not all able to put our names to the majority recommendations". Barry Desmond, an Irish Member of the Socialist Group, said an heroic effort was made by Bowe as Chair to find a compromise but it was voted down.

By February 1991 Parliament was debating what became a contentious issue, that of working time, or "never on Sundays". A German rapporteur for the Socialist Group, Heincke Salisch, demanded a thirty-five hour week without loss of pay, also supported by the French Rocardians, and the EDG (Tories) accused the Socialists of being unwilling to negotiate, claiming that Parliament was exceeding its powers. Conservative Lord O'Hagan spoke of "the tyranny of the temporary majority". Green was in support, as her backing by the shop workers' union USDAW meant she was opposed to Sunday working. The first Working Time Directive was agreed in November 1993 with the help of Hughes, giving three weeks holiday to the countries covered by the Social Chapter, and offering Labour a welcome publicity opportunity at home. Arguments for shorter working hours to reduce unemployment carried over into the next parliament and indeed the next decade.

In March there was a controversial proposal for a European police force, with many amendments. Following the cautious Labour approach on this from the UK, there were abstentions from the majority of the EPLP but a smallish group voted in favour: Balfe, Billingham, Coates, Crampton, Green, Hughes, Morgan, Tomlinson, Tongue, White and Whitehead. There is no record of there being a fuss over a lapsed whip.

The EPLP began to organize its own events, holding a conference on Europe in December of that year in London, at which Blair and Brown spoke. Recognition also came from the unions – Ford was invited to speak as Leader to the TUC as well as Labour conference. Denis Healey came to the Socialist Group on 13 February 1991 with Millan giving a reception in evening in his honour. Smith came out again to Brussels on 18 October and in November the EPLP held a conference on environment and food in London. By this time there was a steady trail of Labour's Shadow spokespersons to Brussels or Strasbourg, organized by Hayter and her staff. MEPs engineered helpful meetings and photo opportunities with Socialist Commissioners, also offering the MEPs good news stories, since MPs, particularly Shadow Cabinet Members, were always more newsworthy. Amongst others, Pollack, as the BLG's non-voting representative on the NEC Women's Committee, hosted Joan Lestor, Labour women's spokesperson in April, arranging visits to Belgian nurseries in both language sectors to learn about their excellent provision in contrast to that in the UK. Hattersley came out in April of that year to the BLG, having replaced Gwyneth Dunwoody MP as Labour's member of the Confed Bureau, serving there from March 1990 to November 1992.

Similarly, Members invited Socialist MEPs home to meet their Euro GCs or speak at local conferences and to their visitor groups to Strasbourg, providing an opportunity for the continentals to cement in the minds of the grassroots members the idea of a social Europe and working together. One of the best speakers was always John Hume with his excellent story about the importance of the European Parliament for peace, whilst referring to Northern Ireland. It always went down very well.

Lyndon Harrison absorbed himself in rules changes and trying to reduce the plethora of urgency resolutions into a coherent system of subject grouping. He also joined in the chorus of protests about job losses in the UK recession when over two thousand jobs were about to be lost at Cammell Laird shipyard in his constituency. He pioneered an important development for the Parliament, of giving opinions on Commission Green Papers (often pre-cursors to legislation), hitherto not part of the elected Members' input.

Christine Oddy took part in an unofficial delegation to Sri Lanka early on with two lawyers, Belgian and Dutch, at the invitation of a former Sri Lankan MA student. From that point on both Oddy and also Alex Smith raised the problems of human rights and Tamils in that country on a regular basis and this was to be pursued in the next parliament also by Robert Evans.

New buildings in Strasbourg extending office space were delivered in 1990-91, not without a lot of pressure from Tomlinson and Prag for the Bureau to be more open about plans and financing, none of which was ever transparent. They maintained it had exceeded its mandate. For those who wished to do away with the monthly Strasbourg trek, it was a disappoint-ment, cementing the commitment to that city. This modernization put TV sets in Members' rooms, but failed to give them information about what was going on in the hemicycle, giving Tomlinson more room for complaint. There was also expansion in the office and meeting room space in Brussels, all causing pressure on the budget. The Strasbourg extensions included a new media centre, giving rise to a brief but unrealized hope that the British media might take a more constructive and interested line on Parliament, given the amount of legislation being passed. The reality was that British journalists based in Brussels were and still are mostly interested in the Council and to some extent the Commission, confining their observations of the Parliament to expenses scams or photo stunts. Regional journalists, when they visited, had not the slightest understanding of what they were seeing and tended to write uninformed pieces about trunks of documents in corridors, sparse attendance of MEPs in plenary (given the lack of oppor-tunity for unscheduled interventions they tended to be there only if taking part in a debate or voting) or food and drink. The long legislative process remains media-unfriendly, with two or more readings over a period of sometimes years. Journalists must decide at what stage to focus on a story, so they tend to take the easy route and wait for the Council decision. It all adds to the invisibility of MEPs.

One of the European obsessions was competition with Japan and the USA, with an emphasis on the need to create European jobs. Manufacturing investment from Japan into Britain was viewed with suspicion with accusa-tions such as "Britain is Japan's aircraft carrier". A problem arose for the British firm ICL, with headquarters in Putney on Pollack's turf employing two thousand people and one of its manufacturing centres in Ford's con-stituency employing another thousand. Following purchase of eighty per-cent of the company by Fujitsu, the Commission decreed it was no longer a European company, with major implications, since it was heavily involved in the research programme and the European Round Table of industrialists. After much pressure, a Pollack amendment arguing that ICL had European staff and sourcing policy and met the required article (58) of the Treaty was grudgingly accepted in a resolution on the Commission statement and the latter had to back down, permitting it to remain in ESPRIT (the research fund).There were other instances of difficulties and Donnelly supported Toyota who had a factory in the North East.

As seen by the above, by no means all the work took place in the European institutions. MEPs became involved when there were large-scale redundancies proposed in their areas and would try every avenue, together with trades unions and Labour MPs, either to halt the sackings or plant closure, or to find European help for regeneration or retraining. Such an event took place over a year or more when British Aerospace (BAe) in Kingston-upon-Thames sought to close their aircraft factory manufacturing Harrier Jets with a loss of over three thousand jobs as an unhelpful spin-off of the so-called "peace dividend". McMahon complained about a potential loss of a hundred thousand jobs in the defence industry in Scotland at risk because of cuts in military spending at the same time.

The unions at BAe were fairly hard left and the shop stewards' committee could not get face time with the local MP, Conservative Norman Lamont, the then Chancellor of the Exchequer, who refused to admit there was a crisis. Pollack was mobilized to organize meetings for them at the Treasury to put their case, the first of which was on 21 December 1990. Leading a bunch of tough shop stewards through the lofty Treasury corridors to sip tea from dainty china cups would have been a comedy scene had it not been such a serious matter.

In the face of company intransigence and government indifference, she worked with the unions and others for a funding package to produce an alternative economic plan for the company. The aircraft workers maintained they could happily switch from producing Harrier jets to civil aircraft and keep in production the plant that had provided jobs in Kingston for decades, but BAe had separated out their civil and military production companies and were not about to negotiate. The alternative plan was jointly funded by the unions and BAe and produced by Kingston Polytechnic, the unions and the local training organization, AZTEC. It suggested a "Skypark", including leisure facilities and production of civil aircraft and was presented to BAe management. Pollack also raised the problem in Parliament and led a delegation of MEPs to the Commission. Meetings, marches, a twenty-six thousand strong petition, lobbying and speeches all failed and a year or so later BAe closed the plant, but as a result of the high-profile campaign they did at least transfer around a thousand of their technical staff to Farnborough, lessening the number of jobs lost. The huge plot of prime land on the banks of the Thames was sold off to developers for luxury housing. This effort galvanized the local Labour Party that had operated in a Tory seat since time immemorial, and eventually a Liberal Democrat became MP and Labour gained a few more seats on the Council. There was never much hope it could go to Labour but getting rid of Lamont was satisfying.

There was a bit of cross-party togetherness in April 1991 when both Barton and Conservative Ben Patterson strongly opposed a proposal from the Commission to outlaw cast iron boilers. This was supposed to be an energy efficiency measure but Donnelly said it would put thousands of jobs at risk in the UK.

Boris Yeltsin was a visitor to Parliament during 1991. He spoke to the Socialist Group, where he was received coolly. Buchan had strongly opposed his visit, as had others. Cot had been distressed at his rise and gave him short shrift and Labour Members had mixed reactions. In the plenary, he was seated next to Cot who subjected him to a strong speech on democracy that had Yeltsin heckling and complaining. There was a strong exchange of words between the two, captured on film by the Parliament's TV.

Women's work

The Women's Rights Committee chaired by Crawley was concerned about the effects of the Single Market on women. Trades unions in the UK were also watching progress and proclaiming the need for a social Europe in meetings such as the TUC conference "Women Across Europe – Impact of 1992" at the start of May 1990. Townswomen's Guilds were also getting involved and in November that year the National Federation of Women's Institutes held a conference in London on "the 1990s – opportunity for change". Pollack commissioned a research paper by Jane Goldsmith on the effect of 1992 on ethnic minority women, which fed into a report by van Hemeldonck and was published separately for home use. The concerns were that in the Single Market black and ethnic minority women would be among the least mobile sections of the community and in the most vulnerable sectors without adequate legal protection. In the Commission Odile Quintin was a strong ally for those working on equality issues.

A proposed directive to protect pregnant women in the workplace was dealt with in the Social Affairs Committee under the Single Market legal base, meaning majority voting in the Council. It was bitterly fought by the Conservatives and the UK government attempted to persuade Council to split the proposal into two parts, each under a different legal base. Crawley persuaded the Commission to stand firm against Council and pointed out that in the UK maternity pay was linked to sick pay, which was not good enough as pregnant women were not sick. The British government was unhappy that this directive was put through under health and safety rules meaning they could not veto it, and maintained, unsuccessfully, that it should be seen as social legislation. Tongue enjoyed publicizing the directive with her assistant dressed up as clown with the slogan "bang the drum for mum" in one of her constituency's high streets.

Crawley arranged for the Women's Rights Committee to hold its November meeting in Birmingham, her constituency, which attracted favourable publicity, with the City Council taking part in the ceremonial aspects. In addition to being vigorous exponents of the Social Charter, Crawley and Pollack pursued with some success the need for ESF (European Social Fund) training schemes to pay to provide child care facilities for those taking part in courses. The committee pressed for a creche in Parliament, but lost a vote on providing child care facilities in October 1990. After much work by Read as Quaestor it opened in September 1992. A feminist academic, Jane Pillinger from Northern College was also of enormous help on women's rights issues. Improving child care was of major concern as part of Labour's election manifesto. In April 1991 Pollack, with the aid of expert Catherine O'Donnell, a stagiaire in her office, produced a report demanding a directive on child care, after studying the wide disparities in quality and quantity of provision in different Member States, showing Britain to be near the bottom of the league just above Portugal. It was followed up by another in November the same year putting amendments to the Recommendation that the Commission had brought forward as a result of the earlier pressure.

One of Crawley's campaigning efforts was the treatment of women in the struggles in former Yugoslavia, and attempting to have rape treated as a war crime. She visited Bosnia during the war there as part of a parliamentary delegation. The Women's Committee held a public hearing on the subject in February 1993.

Labour loses again – Smith takes the helm

Thatcher's government introduced the Community Charge (Poll Tax) in 1989. Seen as a tax shift from rich to poor it was massively unpopular and culminated in a demonstration of over two hundred thousand people which turned into a riot in Trafalgar Square on 31 March 1990. It became instrumental in the downfall of Thatcher and her replacement by John Major. This deflated Labour a little as she was a rallying point as an enemy, whereas Major appeared more conciliatory.

In the local elections of May 1991 Labour enjoyed a thirteen percent swing from the Conservatives and won the Monmouth by-election. Such was the optimism that activists thought Labour could win the next general election.

Kinnock's speech at the 1991 Labour conference determined to put Labour into Europe's first division. The AEU put forward a resolution supportive of the Single Market and change was in the air. The party's economic sub-committee came out in favour of economic and monetary union. Conference passed a rule change including MEPs as part of the PLP section of the electoral college for leadership posts. It also supported co-decision powers for the European Parliament and a democratically accountable central bank, giving MEPs much more space to support emerging policy in their line of work. The final Policy Review document, *Opportunity Britain*, was supported.

Constitutional changes gave the EPLP five seats on the policy forum, one on regional executives, a regular European conference and input into the preparation of an election manifesto, but banned MEPs from seeking election to the Commons whilst holding their European seats. This evened up the ban on MPs standing for European positions, but effectively trapped MEPs from moving into government, seen by some as cutting off a potential line of promotion. Ford supported it because he said half the EPLP was trying to get selected for Westminster. Experience gained in the European arena was used by colleagues from other countries, who often moved in and out of government into and out of the European Parliament. Labour was not about to open that particular door. There were some that the leadership did not want migrating into the House of Commons such as Llew Smith, but it came too late to stop his selection. At this time an electoral reform working party was set up (June 1991) under academic Ben Pimlott.

The EPLP held a fringe meeting entitled "Making Europe Work for Labour" with Read, George Robertson MP, Ford and Enrique Baron. The conference fringe was growing exponentially with now hundreds of meetings, and MEPs attempted to make their mark in front of party delegations. There was a bumper crop of speakers: the MEPs were becoming more visible.

Blair as Shadow Employment Minister made himself initially popular on a visit to Brussels in April 1992 just before the election, telling the Commission that the next Labour government would immediately accede to the Social Chapter and this was part of the general election manifesto that year. It was not until 1997 that he was able to fulfil his promise.

Despite the ditching of Thatcher by her own party and recession reaching the South of England, Labour's growing popularity and high hopes were not sufficient to win the general election of 19 April 1992. It did gain seats from the Conservatives but the electorate voted to give the new Prime Minister, Major, a chance. He had abolished the hated Poll Tax and put a softer face on Thatcherism. It was a tough campaign featuring plans John Smith as Shadow Chancellor floated for a higher rate of taxation which the Tories used as a stick against Labour. After the triumphalist Sheffield pre-election rally it was said that "Labour snatched defeat from the jaws of victory".

Members, along with the Labour movement, were shattered by this failure to win the election despite all the modernizing that had taken place, even though party officials now say they knew Labour would lose. Three days later Kinnock resigned, followed by his deputy, Hattersley. He had made great progress in modernizing the party and opening the door to Europe and handed it over in a far better position to win than when he had started.

Three Labour MEPS went to Westminster and retained dual mandates until the 1994 Euro election: Geoff Hoon for Ashfield, Llewellyn Smith for Blaenau Gwent and George Stevenson for Stoke-on-Trent South. Gordon Adam unsuccessfully fought Berwick-upon-Tweed again with a good swing to Labour but it was held by a Liberal Democrat; Balfe was unsuccessful in Southwark and Bermondsey in attempting to regain the seat from the Liberal Democrat Simon Hughes. Stevenson did not contribute in the Chamber after the election, and Llewellyn Smith's interventions became rare and confined to his usual interest of nuclear waste. He had never been particularly congenial and was consistently anti-EEC so there were some who were not unhappy to see him go. Kinnock, however, was distinctly unhappy to see him as MP for the famous Welsh seat whose previous incumbents had been those heroes of the Labour movement Aneurin Bevan and Michael Foot. Hoon continued to take part a little more than the others because of the nature of the legislation going through his committee.

Hugh McMahon uncovered a bit of Tory skulduggery in May concerning the election, accusing Sir Leon Brittan of having written a letter to thirteen hundred British electors in Belgium urging them to vote Conservative and appealing for money. This was of course improper (since Commissioners were not supposed to engage in party political activity), but somehow Brittan managed to emerge unscathed. Parliament had voted against having a debate on the subject, a cop-out on the part of the right.

Ford was campaign manager in the EPLP for John Smith, working with John Cunningham and Mo Mowlam. Smith and Bryan Gould came to the EPLP on 8 June 1992 to seek support in the leadership contest, which at a special conference in July was resoundingly won by Smith. He was a pro-European, one of the few Labour MPs to vote for entry into Europe back in 1969, and had the support of the majority of the MEPs. A three way Deputy contest of Beckett, Prescott and Gould was won by Margaret Beckett with more than fifty percent of the vote.

Selections for the European elections of 1994 began shortly after the general election and in the period from August to December 1992 MEPs were not permitted to contact the Labour Party members in their constituencies. This was some disquiet about this and it was never clear whether the local members were told this was the case. Conference in 1992 carried NEC documents *Agenda for Change* and *Europe*. Resolution 69 was also carried, being in line with the NEC's objectives laid down in these and previous papers.

At conference in 1993 Smith's victory was followed by approval of more modernisation, a system of one-member-one-vote for internal party elections and selections, helped by the support of Prescott. Emphasis in the party was now on new Labour. Anything that smacked of higher taxes, an overpowering state, being soft on crime or weak on defence, anti-family or being under undue trades union influence was to be avoided. Not all the comrades took this new turn on board. This conference also adopted a policy of all-women shortlists in half of all vacant Labour-held and marginal seats (this was short-lived and declared illegal by an industrial relations tribunal in January 1996). There was a report from the National Policy Forum which first met in May.

Henry McCubbin saw the arrival of Smith as a sea change. He says he met with him as PES Chief Whip and they had a straightforward relationship. Smith understood that the EPLP might, due to the operational needs of a Parliament without a majority party, have to support texts that were less than perfect from the point of view of the front bench, because the struggle was often Parliament versus Council or Parliament versus Commission. McCubbin says that all Smith asked was to be forewarned of possible conflicts prior to them surfacing during a vote. Coates was also an admirer of Smith, years later wondering how different things might have been had he lived longer.

Arch anti-marketeer and ex-leadership contender Bryan Gould MP stood down in 1994 to return to academia in his native New Zealand. In his resignation speech he conceded that the EC was needed for environment policy, to the satisfaction of Collins.

Before long Kinnock was set to become President of the Party of European Socialists. He says that when the Danes voted "No" in the referendum on the Maastricht Treaty he was concerned about being seen to argue in favour of it at home because he had a position, so at the last minute withdrew. The Europeans tried to persuade him to remain a candidate but he felt it was correct to pull out. Willy Claes from Belgium was elected, the second in a row from that country, following Guy Spitaels.

Bill Clinton had become Democratic President in the United States in 1992 and some high-ranking Labour Party officials including Margaret McDonagh worked in his campaign team. "It's the economy, stupid" became an important slogan and work began on the long march to electoral victory in 1997. The message spread throughout Labour's elected Members, some of whom had been at the convention in Chicago when Clinton was nominated to be the Democratic Party candidate.

Maastricht Treaty and the Social Chapter

Following his earlier work, Martin had the task of drawing up proposals to the IGCs which negotiated the Maastricht Treaty. The notion of a Committee of the Regions was put forward in his report, although at first there was a feeling that there were already too many European institutions. Delors, however, was not happy that responsibility for regional opinions on policy should be in the hands of ECOSOC and favoured special input from local and regional authorities, so that body was set up in 1994.

Helped in the Socialist Group by Corbett, who later became a prominent MEP, Martin visited every head of state and government in advance of the negotiations on the new treaty. Mitterrand was concerned about procedural matters. The Greek Prime Minister was asked why he was against co-decision and at that point backed down and agreed to it, and the same occurred with Major in the UK. Martin says he did get lectured by Kinnock and rapped over the knuckles about his policy stance at a Labour Scottish conference in Dunoon at a time when George Robertson (prominently pro-Europe) was European spokesperson. He maintained he was putting forward the views in his report as Socialist Group rapporteur and for the Parliament, not on behalf of the EPLP and that he was not against party policy, simply a little in advance of it.

In negotiations Major's government refused to share any details with the opposition. Governments play things close to the chest when engaged in international negotiations. Chris Smith (now a Lord, then MP) says this made life difficult for the Labour opposition, where he was part of the Shadow Treasury team. However because of Labour's close relationship with the Socialist parties, he was able to find out what was going on from colleagues across the water. The German government was content to share information with the SDP on what they were doing, and also on other governments' positions, and they passed the information on to their sister party. Smith recalls appreciatively that Priestley efficiently fostered such discussions and would often be there at the meetings, helping the Chair.

The Maastricht Treaty was signed on 7 February 1992, the UK opting out of the Social Chapter. Labour pledged to revoke the social opt-out. The UK took a reserved position on EMU with no firm commitment to join. Collins was happy that the Treaty recognized sustainability for the first time and gave the Parliament substantially more power. The Treaty proved controversial in France, largely because of opposition to agriculture reform, but it scraped through. (Irish Commissioner Ray MacSharry had introduced his CAP reform proposals at this time.) It put in place a "pillar" system for a common foreign and security policy and for justice and home affairs, keeping both these subjects on an inter-governmental level, this being marketed in the UK as a great success against a centralized Europe – "Game, set and match to the UK" said Major.

The plan was that the Treaty would come into force on 1 January 1993, together with the Single Market, but events delayed it. Ireland approved it in their referendum but the Danish people by a tiny majority rejected it in a referendum in June 1992. A year later, after negotiating four opt-outs at the Edinburgh Summit, on defence and security, home affairs and the euro, Denmark voted "yes" in May. (A full account of the Treaty and its tortuous ratification can be found in *The Treaty of Maastricht* (Corbett, 1993).)

When Major was re-elected in the general election of 9 April 1992 he had only a narrow majority which left him vulnerable to growing anti-Maastricht rebellions from both parties. Labour abstained at second reading of the Maastricht Bill on 21 May, because of the social Protocol, but Major suspended the committee stage after the Danish "No" vote.

A "Labour Campaign for a Social Europe" took a full page in the summer

1992 edition of *European Labour Forum*, supporting the Treaty despite its shortcomings and saying the call for a referendum must be rejected. This was signed by twenty-nine Labour MEPs plus Priestley, leaving sixteen potentially opposing the Treaty. Those who did not sign this were: Barton, Buchan, Falconer, Hindley, Lomas, McGowan, Megahy, Newman, Oddy, Seal, Simpson, A. Smith and L. Smith, Stevenson, Stewart and West.

As early as August 1992 the EPLP noted that "Labour Euro MPs believe that their colleagues in Westminster must not vote against the Bill when it returns to the Commons..." They acknowledged the Treaty was far from perfect, but believed it was a step forward. Furthermore, the Socialist Confed had agreed that each Socialist party leader should support the ratification of the Treaty.

Major, with a smaller majority than before the election, faced a campaign for a referendum from Thatcher and some of her heavyweight supporters. The ratification process also posed some problems for Labour, which was minded to oppose ratification because of the Social Chapter opt-out, even though it was in favour of the Treaty. There was a strong opposition campaign from the grass roots on these grounds, supported by some MPs such as Gould and Shore, as another sign of Europe's capitalist bias. Quite a few MEPs put together leaflets or pamphlets for their constituents on the Treaty such as "Maastricht in a Minute". The majority were along the lines that the Treaty was necessary, but imperfect in social terms. There was no vetting of these from the Labour Party. Labour's conference in the autumn supported the Treaty as "the best agreement that can currently be achieved", after which Gould resigned from the Shadow Cabinet.

The government introduced a "paving" motion in the Commons in November and Labour voted against, making it plain their beef was lack of a social chapter. To have voted in favour would have been a de facto vote of support for the government, says Corbett. Smith during the debate on 6 November said: "The old idea of British sovereignty must be seen for what it is – a proud and honourable relic of our past but not a positive means of future progress." It scraped through at this stage with Liberal support with a government majority of three, after an agreement to postpone till the Danes held their second referendum. After the deal was struck with Denmark the Bill was back in the Commons in January 1993 taking up hours of time. One victory in this protracted process for Labour was that members of the new Committee of the Regions should be elected local authority members.

Cot begged Labour not to defeat the Treaty (at the first European conference in Brighton in November 1992 he said: "don't play Russian roulette with the Maastricht Treaty"), but it took serious negotiating behind the scenes and was a big challenge for the new Leader, Smith. In January the PLP voted by 112 – 46 not to press wrecking amendments. Hoon was by this time in the House of Commons as well as the European Parliament, and in a canny move during the ratification process in July 1993 drafted an astute procedural amendment on the Social Chapter that became known as the "time bomb", proposing that the Act should only come into force (and therefore the Treaty ratified) after each House of Parliament had come to a resolution on the question of the Social Protocol.

Back in the House of Commons on 22 July after the Lords, Labour's amendment on the Social Protocol, after a dramatic debate, almost defeated the government. Votes were 317 – 317, with fifteen Tory rebels voting with Labour and only the casting vote of the Speaker caused the amendment to fall. Hoon's efforts won him the accolade of joint Parliamentarian of the Year together with Labour's George Robertson. A government "taking note" amendment during this process had ashen-faced Conservatives losing by 324 – 316 votes. Robertson wrote about this in *Tribune* on 30 July saying Major only finally managed to get the Treaty ratified by dint of narrowly winning a confidence vote in the Commons the next day. Labour's efforts had been carefully organized to win changes to the legislation but not wreck the Treaty. He crowed: "Labour won the argument, and the sheer dishonesty of the Tory case against minimum employment standards has produced a clear moral division between the parties." The EPLP were split on the Treaty (quite a few supporting the line, espoused by amongst others Peter Hain, that it should be renegotiated) as were the Conservatives but the majority were this time in favour.

There was no doubt the Treaty was controversial. Stephen Tindale, a former Fabian Society researcher later to become an influential environmentalist and Labour government adviser, criticised the Social Chapter as a fig leaf. Some said it marked the shift of the Labour Party from British socialism to European social democracy. Oddy was not alone in producing a leaflet in her constituency saying the social provisions were weak and inadequate and that the Treaty needed to be renegotiated. Megahy and Falconer opposed Ford and Martin in parliamentary debates on the Maastricht resolution, and Alex Smith also said he was not convinced. Megahy said: "Trying to deal with the problem of unemployment by use of the convergence criteria under Maastricht is like trying to put out the fire with the aid of a petrol pump." Stefano Fella, writing in *Democratising the European Union* (Hoskyns and Newman eds, 2000), suggested that some of the Labour opposition was not about the principle of European integration, but rather its undemocratic character.

Most of the left-wing Campaign Group in the House of Commons opposed Maastricht from the outset. The PLP Tribune Group published "The Left and Europe" which came out in favour of "no ratification without re-negotiation". However in March 1993 the Tribune Group of MEPs took a different line, using some of their own resources to publish a 23-page pamphlet: "Building on Maastricht: a Left Agenda for Europe", written by Wayne David and signed by 24 MEPs and 14 MPs. Hoon signed in both of his roles, and Kinnock put his name to it, as did Green, then Leader of the EPLP. Other notable signatories included Donald Anderson MP (Labour's Foreign Affairs spokesman) and Peter Mandelson MP. Although critical of some aspects of the Treaty, its main thrust was to support it and argue for improvements at the next IGC. It pointed out to Labour doubters that renegotiation would need to take into account that the majority of Europe's governments were right of centre and the political balance was moving away, thus risking a less radical treaty. The MEPs ensured it circulated around the constituencies. Ford's line was to say that Major was offering "Maastricht minus" with the opt-outs – Maastricht had to be built on rather than demolished and we had to start building for a "Maastricht plus".

The Treaty came into force on 1 November 1993. Its main provisions included a co-decision procedure including a conciliation process. This substantial increase in Parliament's power was to be used to great advantage in the coming years. It also provided the eighteen extra seats for Germany, and six for other big Member States, putting Parliament's size up to 567. There were other measures such as involving Parliament in the appointment of the Commission by means of a veto. The Commission's term would coincide with that of the Parliament and more closely reflect its political complexion. It extended the areas of qualified majority voting in Council and paved the way for the introduction of the euro. Its other main provisions were creating a "third pillar" covering co-operation in Justice and Home Affairs, outside the Community legal framework, a Common Foreign and Security Policy largely on an inter-governmental basis, and a timetable and procedure for monetary union. New areas came within the scope of the Parliament: education, culture, consumer protection, public health, trans-European networks, industry and European citizenship. The Treaty also permitted nationals of Member States resident in another to vote and stand in European elections where they lived.

Given the new pillar on Justice and Home Affairs, Elliott joined others who believed Parliament should have a means of monitoring events. He successfully lobbied Cot, leader of the Socialists, to suggest a new Committee on Civil Liberties be set up at the half-way parliamentary review at the end of 1991. A new Article 130s on environment policy, for some time gave rise to arguments about whether particular bits of environmental legislation should be put forward under the Single Market articles or this one. A further new Article 129 laid the basis for a European health policy and Collins' committee held a public hearing on the need to exchange ideas about best practices. He produced an authoritative leaflet on public health, entitled "How to keep both feet out of the grave", for wide circulation.

The British opt-out from the Social Chapter gave rise to a debate as to whether MEPs from the UK could vote on social legislation that would not apply in the UK. It was all very hot for a while, but they were never stopped from such voting on the grounds that it was hoped that in the future the UK would come on board.

Pensioners' and disabled people's parliaments

Labour Members continued the campaign to introduce a Europe-wide pensioner's concession card and tabled a petition with four thousand signatures in July 1990. Members were finding there was little European news of interest to pensioners' groups, who often invited them to speak. Revelations that the UK's state pension was one of the lowest in Europe were used to gain the support of the grey brigade at home (many of whom tended to be anti-Europe).

Coates, who played a leading role in the Institute for Workers' Control, the Bertrand Russell Peace Foundation and many other organizations, was keen to develop a European civil society in which people would have a stronger discourse than via formal European institutions. With European Year of the Elderly planned for 1993, Coates and the EPLP pushed hard in the Socialist Group to sponsor a Pensioners' Parliament. It was held at the beginning of April 1992 in Luxembourg and was a marvellous achievement. The old favourites spoke: Brandt, Delors, Castle. Each Socialist Member was permitted to bring a delegate. The unions, particularly the T&GWU Retired Members' section led by the redoubtable Jack Jones, also joined in. It was wonderful to see over five hundred men and women of the generation that had lived through the World War, able to talk to each other via interpreters, and discover many things in common such as health care, social services, peace and pensions. There was a great positive buzz and many cross-border links were made. It was of course, hugely expensive, and the Group did not feel able to run it again despite its obvious success, but there was support for the European Pensioners' Charter and a glossy brochure was produced. Labour produced a document on comparative pensions and benefits in Europe launched at the start of the Year of the Elderly and also held a well-received "Health for All" seminar in London.

Following this triumph, Coates and others agitated for an all-party parliament for pensioners during their special year. After a great deal of negotiating, this was held in November 1993. It was a bit more formal and suffered from serious logistical difficulties such as late tickets for participants and crises with hotel bookings. It was subjected to pompous speeches from group leaders and bigwigs in general and opened by the Parliament's EPP President Klepsch, so that there was much less time for debate. After this event there were no more. The organization and expense of the event were just too much. The legacy was an increasingly well-attended but badly named Ageing Intergroup, funded by the British NGO EuroLinkAge, the meetings of which were attended by many of the Labour and Conservative MEPs.

The next project was a successful Parliament of Disabled People, launched on the initiative of disability organizations with help from Coates. They put a staff member into his office and his own assistant made strenuous efforts to get this off the ground. There were initial problems when the President ruled that the event could not have access to the parliamentary hemicycle in Brussels, but this was eventually overturned after much lobbying of MEPs by the disability organizations and the President put in an appearance at the opening on 3 December 1993.

After the half-way waltz

True to the agreement, the EPP's Egon Klepsch was elected President of Parliament in January 1992, with Martin retaining his Vice-Presidency. The President was not loved by Labour, as more than one comrade claimed to have caught him misusing voting cards over the years. Collins remained Chair of Environment, Health and Consumer Protection having beaten off an attempt by Cot to split it into two. Ford had supported splitting it on the grounds that Collins had often remarked how busy the committee was with all the legislation for which it was responsible. Crawley kept her position as Chair of Women's Rights and Coates was Chair of the Human Rights Subcommittee of Foreign Affairs. Read was elected a Quaestor (one of the Members responsible for dealing with the management of Parliament) with the support of the Socialist Group. It was not a post that the EPLP had included on its wish-list and she was put forward via some individual women for Socialist Group support. Vice-Chairs went to Adam again on Energy and Research, Crampton on Foreign Affairs, McMahon on Social

Affairs and Employment, David on Regional Affairs and Balfe took over from White as a Vice-Chair on the Security Subcommittee of Foreign Affairs. On delegations, Donnelly succeeded Hoon as Chair of USA (this generally being seen as a British post), Pollack took Chair of SAARC (the countries of South Asia) from Stevenson, (those two now being pre-occupied with their work in the House of Commons) and Titley became Chair of Finland. There were several Vice-Chairs too: Elliott on Norway, White on Switzerland, Simpson on Yugoslavia, Ford on Japan and Wilson on Canada.

New committees covering Civil Liberties and Petitions were set up. All-party intergroups proliferated and Labour Members were involved in a range of these, including animal welfare of which Pollack became Chair, having been given an award by the Eurogroup for Animal Welfare (by then run by a British vet, David Wilkins) for her animal welfare activities in December. Other intergroups, of which there were many, covered peace, ageing, health (in which Read was active), anti-racism and trades unions to name just a few.

After co-decision came into force the Environment, Public Health and Consumer Protection Committee became a much more powerful arena, reflected in the large number of lobbyists who followed its work. Meetings of committees were normally open to the public and this one had to be held in the largest committee room because of the crowds it attracted, mostly from business.

Members of the Security Subcommittee had been seeking (in the face of opposition from the Socialist Group) since before 1989 to establish relations with the North Atlantic Assembly, the parliamentary wing of NATO. On the invitation of the Assembly some Members used their parliamentary allowance to attend meetings on a semi-official basis. An observer delegation of three (two Dutch: Jan-Willem Bertens, Liberal and Arie Oostlander, Christian Democrat; and Richard Balfe) were sent to meetings from 1990-94, alternating on giving a speech to the plenary of that body. It was outside the d'Hondt system at that stage. Over the years they regularly attended the twice yearly Assemblies which were held in different NATO member states. After 1994 the delegation was put on a more formal footing and is now a fully fledged parliamentary delegation. NATO as a body was still viewed with less than enthusiasm by many of the EPLP, which preferred to ignore this relationship.

A Temporary Committee "From Single Act to Maastricht and Beyond" was set up on 10 February 1992 on the Delors II package, which marked a substantial increase in the structural funds. Adam and Collins were members of this as were two Conservatives, Cassidy and Kellett-Bowman. The rapporteur was Socialist budget expert Thomas Von der Vring. It reported in June, with Adam in his Opinion saying that cohesion and economic convergence could not be achieved unless research funding was strengthened. The package put forward after the Maastricht Summit included the creation of a Cohesion Fund, and proposals that "own resources" be raised from 1.20% of GDP in 1993 to 1.37% in 1997. The contention was whether to push for the higher rate, or something marginally more modest, at 1.3%. Tomlinson, in contact with the front bench, was not in favour of the larger sum, leading to some dissent within the Group. The Edinburgh Summit finally agreed rather stingily that 1.27% would come into play in 1999.

Commissioner Ray MacSharry announced his long-awaited CAP reform package to Parliament on 12 June 1992, surprisingly scheduled on a Friday. Wilson congratulated him for the effort, Morris supported the set-aside idea and Alex Smith worried about US farm subsidies. As these reforms were going through Alex made efforts to sort out problems faced by the black-faced sheep breeders' association, by inviting MacSharry over to Scotland. The Commission was proposing a maximum flock size of 750 but the Scots were able to persuade him they needed 1,000 ewes to be viable. MacSharry brought in partial reform in the teeth of opposition from both some parts of the Council and even Parliament's Agriculture Committee. The reforms were unpopular with French farmers, almost derailing that country's ratification of Maastricht. The Agriculture Committee was still stuffed with farmers who vigorously continued to press the case for high farm prices and limited reforms. Some elements of market support were reduced and there was some direct grant compensation. It was either seen as radical or minimalist, depending from what side of the argument the commentator came but it did mark the beginning of the end of financially unsustainable and publicly unpopular food mountains.

The first delegation from the Russian Parliament came to Strasbourg in March 1992 and a debate was held on the effects of the Chernobyl nuclear disaster. Her Majesty the Queen made her first appearance and spoke to Parliament in May, partly in French, mentioning with well-received humour that British Members brought a vigorous and confrontational style as in Westminster debate, but that we were part of the Community of Europe. There were no interruptions or demonstrations. This was a signal that the Parliament was becoming important in the eyes of the British establishment, and before too long Prince Charles also paid a visit to Strasbourg.

German beer and the question of sweeteners caused Parliament to stamp its foot in May 1992. Conservative Caroline Jackson was the rapporteur. At first reading in March 1991 the committee wanted to make the approval process more transparent and Green pointed out that a significant sector was left out, snacks and cyclamates. It was hijacked in Council, however and the common position came back with a footnote designed to protect small "traditional" brewers in Germany. This was denounced by non-Germans as a particularly clumsy attempt at national protectionism. (Jackson called it a "poor little footnote".) Parliament had to ask for an extra month to deliberate and in plenary there was a mix-up on votes, with a motion for rejection first falling two votes short of the necessary absolute majority, and a second vote being held where the common position was then rejected (286 – 58 – 7) and the Commission withdrew the proposal. There was some confusion because COREPER continued to debate it but finally, because there had only been a slender majority in the Council in the first place, the Commission felt they would have first to bring a directive on traditional products before they could re-introduce legislation on sweeteners. The modification of the food additives directive was adopted in January 1996.

Many battles took a long time. Read as Quaestor attempted to improve the lot of Members' assistants. In a debate in May 1992 she said the present employment status and insecurity of the assistants was unsatisfactory. The resolution called for sufficient funding in the next budget for Members to be able to employ at least two full time members of staff.

In June Parliament attempted to reduce voting time by switching explanations of vote from before votes to afterwards, enabling most Members to leave the Chamber or submit something in writing without being held captive for lengthy periods of time. Falconer was incensed by this and spent months raising points of order, disputing rules and complaining about the shift, saying it was undemocratic and trampled on Members' rights. Whatever the rights and wrongs, the idea that anyone's explanation of a vote before they made it would serve to change a voting list was pie in the sky as the lists were compiled by political groups before MEPs entered the Chamber. His complaints fell on the deaf ears of the establishment.

MEPs being organized

The AGM of 1992 was firmly under Hayter's control. The election defeat had strengthened the resolve to step up discipline and unity. A system of written annual reports from officers on Hughes' initiative as Deputy had been introduced and new staff appointed. The Secretary reported about links with the PLP and front bench and a briefing document on procedures and contacts, entitled "The Knowledge" had been produced for use by Members and their staff.

Ford was the only nominee for Leader and was elected by 26 – 8 with 8 abstentions. Stewart was again away ill. Hughes was re-elected Deputy by 41 – 1. Wynn replaced Read as Chair, with 32 votes for, 8 against and one abstention, since Mel Read had taken the post of Quaestor at the beginning of the year. Harrison defeated Elliott for Secretary by 23 – 19, pretty much the same balance as the previous year. Balfe defeated Adam for Treasurer by 24 – 17 with one abstention. Simpson became Whip with 21 votes to Bowe's 19 with two spoilt papers. There was a contest for Socialist Group Bureau between Coates, Hindley and Tomlinson. On the first ballot votes were Coates 9, Hindley 15 and Tomlinson 18. The second ballot gave it to Tomlinson with 22 to Hindley's 16, and four abstentions.

Conference that year was the first for the new leadership. Ford enthused about Europe being our economic future and referred to the referendum on Maastricht in Denmark. Ireland and France were opposing demands for a referendum on the Treaty and Ford was in agreement with that, saying

> "The Commonwealth will not return, EFTA countries are queuing up to join the Community, Maastricht and all, along with Central and Eastern Europe… we want more… we want Maastricht plus [the Social Chapter]."

Hayter, a delegate from Holborn and St Pancras, opposed demands for a referendum and pointed out that the Treaty provided for the rights of EC citizens to vote in local and European elections. The Socialist fraternal guest speaker at Blackpool was Antonio Gutierres from Portugal, an excellent communicator, later to become Prime Minister. The NEC statement "Europe our Economic Future" was carried. It was a sea-change from ten years earlier.

Back in Parliament

In July Parliament had a chance to vote for the proposed President of the Commission, the nominee being Delors. The term of office for the

Commission ended at the end of 1993 but was extended until after the European elections of 1994 to begin the process of aligning the terms with those of Parliament. The Socialists were asking for a public election of the President but were of course happy to support Delors.

Chris Smith MP was Shadow Environment spokesperson between 1992-94, and set to work to produce a comprehensive environment policy for the Labour Party, working very closely with Collins, the argument being that environment issues could not be tackled on a one-country basis. In the production of what today remains a relevant policy document "In Trust for Tomorrow", he says that Collins was particularly helpful with ideas and information.

Donnelly was seen as a dynamic personality in the Socialist Group, full of ideas. Economic Committee staffer Derek Reed remembers that he was instrumental in getting the Group to set up an expert group on macro-economic policies and a horizontal structure covering several committees to better co-ordinate the policy mix. Jean-Pierre Fournier, a laid-back but astute Frenchman, was the team leader.

British Presidency and Black Wednesday

The second half of 1992 was again Britain's Presidency, an awkward time because of the slow ratification process on Maastricht. Plenary in July was over-shadowed by a massive blockade by French lorry drivers of bridges between Germany and France surrounding Strasbourg. McMahon complained that ten Questions tabled by Labour Members were not on the agenda, and accused the UKRep head, now Sir John Kerr, whom he undiplomatically referred to as "Sir Jock-have-a-cocktail-party-Kerr", of leaning on President Klepsch to avoid British domination of Question Time. The Labour senior Vice-President was not scheduled to chair this session and some smelled a plot. The following day McMahon complained that seventeen PQs on the Social Charter submitted by Labour were being ruled out and that "minions of Douglas Hurd have been running about the corridors saying there is a great deal of politicking taking place over the order of questions." This time he was supported by Tomlinson, Wynn, Ford, Crawley and Wilson.

Tristan Garel Jones for the government made himself unpopular with the EPLP by saying the UK was the first and only Member State to have implemented all twenty-two social directives. He regretted that the Labour Party had sought to introduce a note of controversy "by bringing our domestic disputes into the Parliament" and noted that his government had been recently returned with the largest popular vote in British history, observing (to Tory delight): "I think that the increasing irrelevance of the Labour Party in my country is perhaps matched by its increasing discourtesy in this House, for which I apologise". He was quite combative for a government Minister in this setting, and attacked Oddy when she went on about travel passes for elderly people not existing in the UK, observing: "If she wishes to discuss and take a close interest in free travel in Britain, perhaps she should attempt to become an MP in the UK and not in this House."

Lord O'Hagan enjoyed the attacks on Labour and joined in, saying McMahon "shows everyone here why the Labour Party lost the last election", describing him allegedly as "a verbally incontinent haggis" (an opinion also shared by some of his own colleagues). Labour was enjoying the general parliamentary fracas, which was all too rare in Strasbourg.

The Presidency was marred by Black Wednesday on 16 September when interest rates rocketed out of control and Britain crashed out of the European exchange rate mechanism (ERM) which it had joined in 1990. Thatcher had wished to stay out but had caved in when threatened with resignations by her Foreign Secretary and Chancellor. Now, with recession in full swing, Lamont as Chancellor had refused to devalue sterling and the Bundesbank refused to cut interest rates. It was an interesting lesson in European economic inter-connectedness and there was an atmosphere of shock in the Parliament. Donnelly initiated a short late-night debate in which successive Labour MEPs berated the government.

Parliament held a special session on 14 October to discuss the financial crisis, when Labour expressed disappointment that Major was not in attendance. The aim was to comment on a special Heads of Government meeting in Birmingham. Lamont, the Chancellor, was accused by Donnelly of being a "phantom ECOFIN President" because he did not come before Parliament. Lamont had blown German support at an ECOFIN in Bath in September because of his uncompromising anti-Europeanism.

The fall in value of the pound had a knock-on effect on some assistants' wages. Many Members paid their Brussels assistants via British bank accounts, and paid British social security. But the hapless staff had to transfer funds to Brussels in order to live and when the currency went down, so did their income. MEPs, meanwhile, benefitted from higher office allowances because funds were transferring in to their offices from Luxembourg. Salaries and office expenses came out of different funds, but a good number were too stingy to compensate their staff and some assistants left and moved to other Members who were prepared to pay more equitably.

Labour was arguing internally about whether a single currency was the way forward after Black Wednesday. Chris Smith MP was on the Shadow Treasury team and John Smith was Shadow Chancellor just before the leadership election and these two pro-Europeans were supportive of the idea of a single currency, but met an undercurrent of resistance from other influential elements of the party. Bryan Gould MP took the opportunity to write in the *New Statesman* daily Labour conference briefing in September that "the collapse of the ERM laid bare the delusion of the European super state".

The frozen Association Agreement with Turkey rumbled on and in the debate on whether to release this on 17 November 1992, Balfe said although Turkey still featured in Amnesty reports, so did many other countries. He argued that in 1985 we had promised to reinstate the protocol when parliamentary democracy was restored and that it was time "to do today what we agreed to do many years ago".

The Edinburgh Summit in December 1992 decided that Parliament would have to meet twelve times a year in Strasbourg, a blow for those who sought to move the travelling circus to Brussels. It was doubly difficult, in that there had been a gradual reduction in sessions to eleven per year, given streamlining of budget voting; with August being a time-honoured holiday month, it now meant that MEPs would have to shlep to Strasbourg twice each October to fulfil their obligations. In due course Parliament scheduled eleven Strasbourg sessions per year but was taken to the Court of Justice by the French government, and lost, the ECJ ruling in October 1997 that it had acted illegally in reducing the number of sessions. *European Voice* quoted Dutch Socialist Dankert, a former President of Parliament and chairman of the "one Seat" parliamentary working group:

> "We have got to respect the court, but it is a political problem which has to be dealt with in a political way. However everywhere else in Europe parliaments decide for themselves when and where they should meet".

The problem remains unsolved, but after 2000 Parliament shortened the Strasbourg weeks by cutting out Fridays. This possibly hit the local economy in terms of lost hotel nights more than losing one session per year would have done.

Black marks on coal

Proposals surfaced in the UK in September 1992 for closure of more than thirty collieries in the UK, opening up the sore spot of the mining problems of the 1980s. Up to thirty thousand jobs were at risk and it would finally break the back of the mining industry. It was the beginning of the government's "dash for gas" strategy to avoid reliance on coal and was hotly contested in the House of Commons. In October Arthur Scargill, General Secretary of the National Union of Mineworkers, was invited to speak to the Socialist Group. During the debate on the Birmingham Council, Ford for the Socialists attacked the proposed closures, supported by Adam and West who made the point that to close thirty-one pits would sterilize hundreds of millions of tonnes of coal, that these were Community reserves and that increased reliance on gas would deplete indigenous supplies and create a dependency on imports. David accused the government of rigging the energy market to the detriment of coal and advantage of gas; Coates observed that he had once worked at a mine on the hit list and that the plan contravened the directive on collective redundancies. Read lamented the prospective loss of two thousand jobs in North Warwickshire, Llew Smith complained about the small financial investment in coal compared with the huge sums going to nuclear and Hughes said the proposal was a disgrace because these mines were the lowest cost producing mines in Europe.

Labour then blew it. The Socialist Group put forward a procedural request for "an early vote" by Roll Call on the Oral Question with Debate, which took place around 9 pm, on Tuesday 27 October. Simpson, EPLP Whip, had issued a whip for all to be there, sending round a letter saying he suspected a Conservative ambush. It was the sort of thing that both sides did from time to time. It happened. The Conservatives packed the Chamber for this unscheduled vote and it was rejected by 63 – 62, a huge loss of face for the EPLP in the presence of the gloating British Presidency. Maggie Coulthard, a staunch Labour member soon to head the EPLP's Brussels office, was in the gallery at the time as were Scargill and Norman Willis of the TUC. Their perception was that some Labour Members had been more interested in going off to dinner than staying for a vote. The observers were furious with those who were not there for such an important moment.

Some of the EPLP were legitimately not in Parliament on that day:

Tongue was on maternity leave; Tomlinson, Hoon and Morris were out of town on official business; and McMahon had the Whip's permission to return home for an official engagement back in his Scottish constituency. (On his arrival in Greenock he was asked about a BBC radio broadcast covering the debacle and says he was shocked at the result and never again took a return trip home in the middle of a Strasbourg session.) Hindley was at a dinner with a visiting Chinese delegation. These events were very formal and unfortunately tended to start early at venues outside the building. International visitors were never tolerant of MEPs turning up late. White, as Vice-President of the Swiss delegation, was at a dinner with the Swiss Ambassador discussing a forthcoming referendum on Swiss membership of EEA. Neither had any idea there was likely to be a vote. Given the variable geometry of the European Parliament it has never been possible to put in place any kind of pairing system for voting.

Both Bowe and Collins were amongst those missing from the voting list and the next day Wynn on behalf of Collins and Bowe, then Collins himself, raised points of order insisting that they had been there and their votes had not been recorded. Bowe recalled standing clutching his coat ready to leave, and Collins pointed out that his grandfather was a coal miner and insists he definitely stayed to vote. This was never resolved, but rumbled on for some months with considerable bad temper. There was a Chemical Industries dinner in Strasbourg at which their presence was expected that night and they had made themselves late for that. Crampton remembers having a party of constituency Councillors and Council officers in town with an exhibition about Hull and also went to the Chemical Industries dinner to talk about a dioxide problem in the Humber and says he did not know about the coal vote until later.

Buchan and Stevenson were signed in but absent from the vote, as were Lomas, Seal and Balfe. Lomas said he was "absolutely mortified" at having missed the vote, as he was a huge supporter of the miners and it led to an exchange of letters between him and Scargill, with the latter saying he could not believe what had happened. Lomas is adamant that they did not know of the vote and went off to dinner, he thinks with Balfe and Seal, thinking that any vote would be at the normal scheduled voting time the next day. It was the responsibility of MEPs to check their pigeon holes for mail regularly, but not everyone did this more than once a day, generally in the mornings and the whip may have simply been missed. It would have been announced at the earlier Socialist Group meeting, but again, attendance at that tended to be patchy. Adam, Barton, Bird, Coates, Crawley, David, Donnelly, Elliott, Falconer, Ford, Green, Harrison, Hughes, McCubbin, McGowan, Martin, Megahy, Newens, Newman, Oddy, Pollack, Read, Simpson, both Smiths, Stewart, Titley, West, Wilson and Wynn all recorded their votes for the procedural request, along with those few of their Socialist colleagues who were present at that hour. The Tories, who had all voted against, were cock-a-hoop at Labour's misery.

Brian Simpson confirms that the officers of the EPLP were summoned to the House of Commons to see the very cross Leader. He accepted responsibility for the apparent inadequate whipping, saying that although Members had been informed they needed to be in the chamber the buck stopped with him and apologised. He says Smith's response was: "Brian I thank you for your statement and frankly you are the only one who has accepted any responsibility in this debacle and spoken with honesty on the matter."

It did not do the MEPs' reputation any good. The fiasco over the vote may have been the result of confusion and nothing more but the feeling, however misplaced, that they were too concerned about their dinner to vote for coal miners persists to this day. Next month Labour managed to facilitate a debate on coal. This time a fairly anodyne resolution calling for consultations "on the plan to close coal mines in the United Kingdom and coal policy and energy strategy in the European Community" was carried on 19 November with support even from the Conservatives by 157 – 74 – 19.

GLOBE

At the initiative of a Belgian Green and Dutch Socialist, an inter-parliamentary organization was set up, "Global Legislators Organised for a Balanced Environment" (GLOBE). This was a voluntary organization, funded in Europe by a combination of Members themselves (paying their travel costs), and the European Commission, enabling it to run a tiny office in Brussels. Parliamentarians in the international wing were from Europe, the USA, Japan and Russia and there were plenary meetings one year in Europe and the next year in another country. Al Gore from the USA was its president. A separate European organization grew up to co-ordinate more closely members in national parliaments in Europe both West and East and offer briefings to parliamentarians on environment matters.

Pollack and Bowe threw themselves enthusiastically into this organization and in 1995 were to join the executive committee, together with Roth-Behrendt, Socialist Group co-ordinator on the Environment Committee. One of the other key players was Tory Tom Spencer, who suggested that hurricanes should be named after oil companies. The main concern was climate change, closely followed by preserving tropical rainforests. Carlos Pimenta from Portugal and Hemmo Muntingh, a Dutch Socialist (and expert on tropical forests) were key players, joined in the next term by Socialist Ilona Graenitz from Austria and Doeke Eisma, a Dutch Liberal.

Members of GLOBE shared information on environment legislation with their colleagues from other countries, compared best practice and attempted to influence the text at international environment negotiations such as those at the UN. All sorts of actions found their inspiration under the GLOBE umbrella. In September 1992 Pollack, on an ASEAN delegation in Jakarta, took a side trip to Sarawak with a Dutch MEP, Mathilde van den Brink, at the invitation of a local MP, to visit a village where illegal logging was taking place to see its damaging effects. Pressure was then exerted on the European Commission to fund pilot projects to protect rainforests. Whilst in Jakarta she also took off alone to the bird market, taking photos of endangered species being sold there.

GLOBE had a considerable amount of success for very small outlay. Dealing with the Japanese and Russians was not without its frustrations, though their MPs were often better attenders at the meetings than the US delegates.

Eventually, via Joan Ruddock MP, UK Shadow Environment spokesperson and later an Environment Minister, a House of Commons GLOBE group was formed which continues today. She and David Chaytor MP have been amongst the active members, pushing many important environmental policies and hosting meetings on climate change. The GLOBE-EU network of parliamentarians is today more active than the international group, but they are both functioning.

Pauline Green ousts Ford

By the time of the 1993 AGM on 24 June there was growing support for a woman as Leader. Tomlinson and Hindley had been having discussions and there had been soundings about whether Tomlinson would stand. They said many were keen to eject Ford, who had lost some support because of his perceived cliquishness. Hindley insists that the left wanted Ford out of the way because with the anticipated good results for Labour in 1994, he could become President of the Socialist Group and a potential later contender for President of Parliament and they did not find this palatable. As is often the case in the Labour Party, the right and hard left can find it opportune to gang up against the centre (or squishy centre as Hindley puts it). David recalls that there had been a row about Ford's decision to allocate some of the group finance to the Campaign Group to fund an anti-EU pamphlet in a spirit of excessive even-handedness. A number of his key supporters saw this as an attempt to buy votes from that group and he lost their support. Crawley was keen to keep her position as Chair of the Women's Rights Committee and was not in the running. Green did not like the way Ford was leading the EPLP, feeling he was secretive about what went on at Socialist Group Bureau and did not treat staff well. Hayter, a strong supporter of a woman as Leader, was not happy with him, saying that he constantly undermined her. Despite not having a vote, she had ways of making her views known to Members.

Several people approached Green to stand as Leader. After consulting her Euro GC she agreed to run and had the support not only of some of the former "Kinnockites", but also much of the Campaign Group. Hindley says he tried to persuade Hughes not to stand for fear of splitting the anti-Ford vote. McGowan asked Pollack whether she would be interested in standing, to be told bluntly: "no, but Pauline Green is". Green says that because of her background, coming into the party later in life and being part of a modernizing process in her local party, Chipping Barnet, she "did not buy into the faction thing". Her views did not follow trends but she had good relations with the trades unions. She had continued in membership of CND after the Kinnock leadership had given up on it, and was strongly associated with the Co-operative Party, so her credentials looked pretty good to a broad spectrum. Newman takes some credit for getting support for her. The short period of stability in EPLP leadership was over again.

Voting for Leader took two ballots: on the first one the results were Green 19, Ford 15 and Hughes 11, and on second ballot Green won by 22 to Ford's 19, with 4 abstentions. Deputy Leader too, took two ballots: on the first Ford won 21, Hughes 19 and Tomlinson 5, on the second ballot Ford won by 23 to Hughes 21. Someone abstained. Wynn kept his position as Chair with an overwhelming vote and Harrison had a substantial vote of confidence as Secretary. Alex Smith was elected Whip by 26 to Bowe 18. Hindley said this was part of the deal with the Campaign Group to vote for Pauline Green. Balfe hung on as Treasurer by 24 votes to Adam's 21. Ford was also elected to the Socialist Group's Bureau, with Tomlinson losing. There was some rivalry between these two senior figures, and some felt they both had their eye on possibly leading the Socialist Group after the following elections. There was not a great deal of love lost between Ford and Green either. Even though they were both on the Group Bureau, he said that they never managed to have dinner together during the course of this year.

The written officers' reports were useful as a record, but also in speeding up tedious meetings. It was agreed to have a formal Liaison Group consisting of the Chair, Leader, Secretary and three back benchers. The election of this was deferred to the next meeting. An attempt to have a similar code of conduct to the PLP did not sit lightly. By January 1993 there was a discussion for the EPLP to have its own Code of Conduct, and matters pertaining to this rumbled on with substantial consequences in the next parliament.

Conservatives have often remarked that their Leaders invariably receive knighthoods or peerages for their services, but Labour is particularly niggardly in doling out "gongs". Castle's peerage reflected her distinguished career as a Cabinet Minister before her stint in Europe, and later Pauline Green was awarded a DBE but the others have been unrewarded. There was some talk that Ford hankered after a Privy Councillorship, as Conservative Leader Prout had been one, but nothing came his way

Labour at home

The first of the party's European conferences, with a thousand delegates, was held in Brighton in November 1992 (in the middle of Remembrance Day services) with Smith, Cot and Robertson as the main speakers.

Even given the much warmer attitude in the party to Europe, local parties remained grudging with opportunities for MEPs to report back to their members. Apart from the Euro GC meetings that MEPs organized, getting a hearing elsewhere was not easy. Crawley ruefully recounts that she was normally timetabled at the end of General Committee meetings after the raffle and she was not alone in this. A few minutes under "any other business" when delegates were keen to get to the pub was the norm. White describes a CLP meeting following a dispute in the Bristol Labour Group when a Councillor had thrown tea over one of the active women members, Pam Tatlow, and having to wait for over an hour whilst the tea incident was argued out before he was able to make his European report for which he had flown in specially. Given the plethora of complex policy matters being dealt with in Europe this was a disappointment and meant it was hard to educate the grass roots about the importance of European work.

At conference the new parliamentary selection procedure of one member one vote (OMOV), with a branch ballot to determine the trigger for reselection, went through, though not without some opposition. It marked the end of the trades union block vote and introduced party-wide voting in Leader and Deputy contests. PLP and EPLP members had a vote in one section, with constituency parties, socialist societies and trades unions also part of the electoral college. It meant that some members had more than one vote, but was seen as more transparent and democratic than what had gone before. The MEPs' own reselections had taken place astonishingly early, during the autumn of 1992 and were unaffected by this change, although there were difficulties to be faced with new boundaries. In the light of boundary changes affecting selections, a procedure for re-allocation of Euro candidates was agreed.

John Carr recalls working for Smith in the campaign running up to this conference and that one piece of campaigning was to have an advertisement in *Tribune* signed by important individuals; he says that Green (by this time Leader of EPLP) declined to sign. Cherie Blair in her book *Speaking for Myself* (Blair, 2009) records what a struggle it was to get this through conference and how helpful Prescott's sway with the unions was.

In the Europe debate, Green made a rousing speech:

> "Let us take democracy into the Community...We can give the lie to the Tory fantasy that Britain can go it alone. We believe in prosperity through co-operation, a policy for Europe which is firmly rooted in a policy for Britain... June 9 next year [European elections] will deliver John Major a knock out bloody nose..."

The 1993 conference report from the NEC reported that the EPLP had agreed to institute the 40% women's quota for key posts after the next election. Clare Short, Shadow Minister for Women, had floated the idea earlier in the year for all-women shortlists. An attempt was made the following year to introduce this, but after a few selections it was challenged in the courts and had to stop until the Labour government was able to change the law some years later. This conference settled for supporting fifty percent women shortlists in half of all vacant and marginal Labour seats.

Electoral reform was on the horizon as the report of the Plant Working Party on electoral reform had shown a majority of CLPs in favour of change for elections of MEPs, most favouring a regional list. A special EPLP meeting had been held on the subject on 18 May 1993. A few years later this subject would cause problems.

The EPLP report to conference listed visitors for the past year as Margaret Beckett, Tony Clarke, Europe and Foreign Affairs spokespersons, frontbenchers from the Treasury, Agriculture, Welsh, Industry, Development and Scottish teams and various backbenchers, plus Lord Plant, a sacked GCHQ trades unionist, nuclear test veterans and a representative of the Maxwell pensioners. It mentioned a raft of new publications, conferences by London MEPs on health and on post-16 education, a Welsh pensioners' event, and more. Jack Cunningham was by now a Vice-President of the PES and training programmes for key seats in the 1994 Euro elections were in progress for agents and key workers.

Gordon Brown produced a thirty page economic report which included a chapter on Britain in the European economy, saying that Labour endorsed Commissioner Flynn's Framework for Employment and a review of competitiveness. Brown went to Brussels on 1 March 1994, for meetings with Delors, making a submission on economic renewal plus seeing Millan and the EPLP. Writing in *European Labor Forum*'s New Year 1996 edition, Coates said that Brown "delivered a sermon" to the EPLP.

By February 1994 the party had merged the European and local government conferences as a cost-saver. It was held in Glasgow to launch the two election campaigns of May and June that year. Speakers included John Smith and Rudolf Scharping, Leader of the SPD. In her speech as Leader of the EPLP Green said "Labour leads for Britain... Europe is now part and parcel of our domestic policy..." It was true that many matters dealt with in Europe were also of interest to local government, not least the structural funds. Sally Morgan (National Agent and later to be a powerful figure in Blair's office) and Rex Osborn spoke of the party strategy to run the local and European elections as one campaign. Osborn spoke about polling concerns about Europe, outlining a provisional communications strategy. London Labour MEPs held a European conference on 19 March.

Former MEP Joyce Quin, who had a good rapport with the EPLP, was Shadow Europe spokesperson from November. At the Labour Party David Hill was director of publicity, Roland Wales was the new policy director and Peter Coleman in charge of structure and organization. There was some discussion that the Conservatives might ditch Major and replace him with Kenneth Clarke to have a spring general election. Emphasis for the European election would be the economy and democracy as building blocks for a future general election campaign.

The party had set up a Campaign Strategy Group as long ago as May 1992 which met monthly until transformed into the Campaign Management Team for the local elections. There was also a staff task force after 1993 conference to lead in to the elections. Walworth Road honchos with power point presentations on polling and strategies would occasionally visit the MEPs, irritatingly never leaving any hard copies of the information.

Barton's bikes

The Commission, under pressure from German manufacturer BMW, had put forward an ill-judged proposal on speed, torque and power of motorcycles, which would ban motorcycles over 100 brake horse power, allegedly on the grounds that big bikes were dangerous. Roger Barton, a motorbike enthusiast, found common cause with Tory Peter Beazley who became the rapporteur. Together they waged a battle opposing the restriction over a period of years to stop the Commission. Barton maintains that his trades union background made seeking a consensus second nature to him rather than scoring points. Thousands of bikers demonstrated in Brussels in September 1992 and when the Commission rejected Parliament's amendment against the power restriction in October, Members referred it back to committee for further negotiation.

No compromise was reached and in February 1993 Barton appeared in the Chamber resplendent in white full biker's leathers, saying he rode a Triumph motorcycle to Strasbourg that would be illegal if the Commission had its way. Martin in the President's chair, to laughter, remarked that: "given the new trend you have set, I am looking forward to seeing how you turn up when we discuss the nude bathing directive!" Read quickly joined in, saying that she represented the area where Triumph motorcycles were made and demanding that the ban proposal be withdrawn, arguing the Commissioner's information was inaccurate on at least three counts. Barton was making a serious point. The effect of the Commission's proposal would be to pretty much wipe out the UK industry and he raged about the idea of "banning the very product where we can compete successfully with non-European manufacturers". Parliament supported the amendment to delete the power restriction.

There followed frequent public demonstrations. Motorcyclists lobbied Councils in each country whilst the matter became a game of poker. In June 1993 Council agreed a common position with the UK abstaining. In September EMAC voted to reject that on the grounds of inadequate evidence for the proposal. Back in plenary on 27 October, Barton said this had become a constitutional matter and that it was "about who makes laws in today's Europe – democratically elected Parliament or secret so-called experts." The plenary vote as an "intention to reject under Article 189b (2) (c) of the Maastricht Treaty" was carried by 262 – 76 – 8 . The Maastricht Treaty, giving Parliament co-decision power, came into force on 1 November. After the proposal had spent some time in Council the Beazley report was back before Parliament in February 1994 when Barton invited Commissioner Bangemann to ride pillion on his superbike and MEPs voted overwhelmingly to confirm their position by 300 – 23 – 13 as a result of cross-party support.

After a period of informal negotiation in Council with EMAC demanding a comprehensive study, in April 1994 it came back to Parliament to be rejected by 252 – 25 – 2, the vote falling just short of the necessary absolute majority. Council then delayed sufficiently for it to continue over into the new Parliament. The Commission official in charge of this dossier had never expected such problems and was not at all aware that there would be such a strong opposition. The motorbike fraternity had engaged in a highly organized and constructive lobby of Brussels and they continued their protests against a series of further damaging proposals concerning bikes on noise and on components for some years.

The rise of Pauline Green

Green was becoming known as a forceful character. She continued to push for a directive on consumer protection and supported a ban on tobacco advertising. She was shadow rapporteur for the Socialists on a controversial general product safety directive, being piloted by Conservative Caroline Jackson. The debate went on for two and a half years and the original text was unpicked line by line by the Environment Committee. She also supported the idea of Cyprus joining the Community, as a possible solution to the long-standing division of that island.

By the time she became EPLP Leader in 1993 Green had become fairly well-known in the party at home. She always took a firm line in the Parliament against racism and in attacking the Conservative government. Her straight back, clear speech and high moral tone as a former policewoman gave her an automatic authority when she took up an issue. She could raise a fine tone in righteous indignation against injustices and did not pull any punches in debates against the right. Her battle for consumer rights had resonance and gained favourable publicity. Once she was leading the EPLP she automatically became a senior Vice-President of the Socialist Group and was often called in debates to speak if its head, Cot, was unavailable.

When she was having her regular Leaders' meetings with Smith, she was preparing him to decide what Labour should want in terms of posts after the 1994 election when the party was expected to do well. There were two key positions: Leader of the Socialist Group, which was the more powerful political position, and President of the Parliament, which is a more personally powerful placement. Green says she recommended to Smith that the party should set its sights on the Group leadership and thought that both Tomlinson and Ford wanted this. She recalls that at a meeting in December with Smith, Murray Elder (later Lord Elder) and her assistant Ray Collins, the others were sent out and she says Smith suggested that Tomlinson was yesterday's man, that he did not entirely trust Ford and had asked other Socialist leaders, who recommended her. There was a growing feeling that it should be a woman and with Smith's negotiating powers it was soon on the way to being a "done deal". At Labour's European conference in Glasgow the following February Tomlinson, Smith, Priestley and Green had a breakfast meeting to confirm the proposal made to the EPLP at his meeting with them during that conference. Smith then came to an EPLP meeting in Brussels that month where more election tactics were discussed.

Mostly construction

Our team continued to make a noise at every opportunity about job losses, economic policy and parts of British industry at risk of shutting down: DAF, Metal Box, coal mines, public services, the steel industry and shipbuilding. They worked on structural funds and their implementation, lots on environment, BSE and the need for tagging of animals, the price of sugar and its adverse effect on Uncle Joe's mint balls (Titley and Wynn) and plenty more. They stood up for protection of workers (Hughes battling against asbestos and McCubbin for improving health and safety in the offshore oil industry), animal welfare, health and safety, preventing pollution, consumer protection including that for time share property purchasers, much on food policy, new measures on radio paging, renewable energy, human rights and development aid, child labour, fishing and marginal farming and recognition of qualifications of doctors educated outside the Community in places such as India.

There was much opposition to the arms trade. Ford seized every opportunity to expose the extreme right and their doings both in and out of Parliament. Tongue was working on trades unions to set up Brussels offices because of the importance of European legislation for them. Others condemned various IRA bombings in the UK when they occurred. Wynn co-authored with Parliament staffer Richard Kitt a booklet "A Guide to the Community Budget" published by the Local Government International Bureau in 1994. Harrison championed short sea shipping and with Donnelly demanded an integrated maritime strategy. (More than a decade later this appeared – things work slowly in Europe.) Overall there was more input from Labour than it would be possible to mention. Members were active in more than one area and had remarkable staying power. On one occasion Titley was holding forth on the textile industry and complaining that the relevant Commissioner had left the Chamber (it was 11.56 pm).

Falconer undertook one report during his fifteen years in Parliament. He was on the Legal Affairs Committee when a Commission proposal concerned with transmission of confidential documents was about to be passed over without comment, and leapt in to become rapporteur. The staff association was concerned about the proposal and he felt it was tantamount to an official secrets act. It came up for debate in February 1993 and in the face of Socialist opposition the Commission withdrew the proposal, so he felt he had scored a victory over the system at both ends of the procedure.

Speaking in the plenary was by no means the measure of the activity of a Member. Most of the work and careful negotiations took place in the committees and Labour Members became both rapporteurs and shadow rapporteurs which also entailed a considerable effort, largely invisible to the public. Some committees dealt with more legislation than others. In particular Environment, Social Affairs and Employment, Legal Affairs and to some extent the Economic and Monetary Committee had the heaviest workload. Regional Affairs dealt with the structural funds undergoing their periodic renewals in this term. David Martin and Wayne David pushed for the PERIFRA II and RECHAR II funds and McCubbin introduced development funding for fishing regions. The Foreign Affairs Committee, to some known as "hot air and travel", had no remit for legislation but was the favourite of former prime ministers and others keen to strut the world stage and meet important world politicians.

Collins specialized in bone-crunching tackles on hapless Commission officials who had the misfortune to be responsible for a dossier before his committee. He was the first to invite government Ministers, in the early stages of each Presidency, to speak to the committee and take questions and was careful to ensure that the Minister replied individually to each question. Some other chairs simply let the Minister make their speech followed by Members' rambling and then a general wind-up from the Minister. The Collins approach certainly sharpened up some of the acts and let the Presidencies know what they were in for. He could be very moody and on more than one occasion stormed out of the room, leaving a Vice-Chair to preside. His key assistant, David Earnshaw, was often left to smooth ruffled feathers.

After some rule changes the Conference of Committee Chairpersons was formally recognized and Collins was elected Chair of that for a number of years, where he was able to exercise considerable power over setting the agenda. In this role he was also able to attend meetings of the Conference of Presidents (political group leaders); able to advise if not to vote, he used the opportunity to great advantage.

There was still a degree of freedom from the party at home in terms of policy but closer relations with front bench spokespersons had been put in place. There was always very limited speaking time and Labour MEPs were adept at tabling questions, both oral and written, chipping in on other people's questions, and raising points of order to keep the Commission and Council on their toes. Freedom from the strictures of Westminster party politics had to be negotiated on occasion, and sometimes sparks did fly.

Elliott, not normally a boat-rocker, went on the Today programme supporting free movement of people as it was Socialist Group policy. But he had not reckoned on just how contentious it was at home and Jack Straw, Shadow Home Secretary, unhesitatingly disputed his statement on radio. Straw then came out to Brussels for a meeting with the EPLP where after a strong exchange of views there was grudging agreement not to disagree publicly. The Europeans were not convinced of the Shadow Cabinet's line and the frank exchanges left Hayter aghast at what she felt was the rudeness of her brood. The MEPs did not perceive that they had been impolite and had simply put their points of view, feeling they had a right to input into policy that was passing through the European institutions.

Yet another shipping disaster, this time off the Shetlands, provided ammunition for several Labour Members to campaign for better maritime safety. Martin, Collins, McCubbin and Stewart all pushed for stronger ship design. When a ship with a dangerous cargo caught fire off Teesside, Bowe also campaigned against "floating bombs". Stewart demanded legislation to enforce IMO rules in the Community and was rapporteur in March 1994 on safety at sea.

The battle over food colourings saw Labour and Conservatives clash, with Green and Collins opposed by Caroline Jackson and Spencer. Much emotional posturing (with election time approaching) led to Jackson putting out a press release talking about "grey socialist cocktail cherries" and "food fascists", leading to a complaint from Danish leader Kirsten Jensen. Labour also took umbrage, the term "fascist", of course being highly sensitive in a European arena. Lord Inglewood complained that Blackpool rock would be banned; Jackson and Spencer accused Labour of wanting to ban some colourings not on grounds of safety, but because they could mislead the consumer, whereas Green was indignantly convinced of the need to prevent some colourings being used to imitate freshness. At second reading Jackson accused the Socialists of changing their tune, but was solidly stamped on by Green, having a go at the "grey" British Prime Minister and saying: "It never fails to amaze me how a British Conservative can take credit for other people's ideas... Jackson is full of praise for the Common position but it reflects many of Parliament's amendments from the Socialist Group..."

The Environment Committee was also considering the SAVE and ALTERNER energy programmes and Pollack was so rough with a Commission official, Malachy Hardagon, during the committee debate, that he remembered his bruising encounter a decade after she had left the Parliament. In the plenary debate in January 1994 she said the White Paper on Sustainable Mobility was depressing reading, with no legislative proposals to fulfil its aims.

Simpson and Newman fought the best delaying tactic they could on a single market for postal services, correctly seeing it as the thin end of the wedge of privatization and pointing out the number of jobs at stake in the UK. This battle, as many others, carried on for more than a decade.

Crawley continued her attempts to whip up some action about the appalling events in Bosnia following the break-up of Yugoslavia. Parliament sent a delegation to war-ravaged Sarajevo early in 1993 of which she was a part and in the ensuing debate she pointed out that time and again the Members were asked why the EC did not support intervention. "The people of former Yugoslavia... are walking the road to hell, their lives smashed...we have only been able to stand on the sideline and throw them some humanitarian aid and a map called the Vance/Owens Plan". In December an attempted visit to Parliament by a Bosnian delegation was squashed as a result of pressure from the Belgrade government.

Pollack as Chair of the SAARC delegation had to tread a delicate line between India and Pakistan on the long-standing Kashmir dispute and often had to fight off overly-partisan resolutions which were tabled by Members with large Pakistani constituencies such as Seal. On one occasion she was left raging mad when George Galloway, then a Glasgow MP, fronted up with a pro-"Azad" Kashmir demonstration, without having the courtesy to inform her. In October 1993 with Gupwell of the Socialist Group, she hosted a roundtable on Kashmir to air the various points of view but it caused some unwelcome publicity when the Belgian government arrested one of the Kashmiri speakers, Amunallah Khan. One of the other countries covered by SAARC was the Maldives, and her able and supportive Parliament officials Alberto Rossetti and Raymond Herdies were keen to organize a visit there, on the grounds of its risk of inundation due to climate change, but Pollack resisted, fearing the inevitable tropical island "junket" publicity.

Enlargement and blocking minority

Once the Maastricht Treaty was eventually ratified, the EU settled down to negotiations about enlargement. Delors had been keen to find a way to bring the EFTA countries into the Single Market, as they were not in a position to join the EU politically, and the European Economic Area (EEA) was born. The Socialist Group was enthusiastic about this marriage of two trading blocks, seeing it as a precursor to enlargement in the wake of the fall of the Berlin Wall. At that time the political objections of some disappeared, and Austria, Sweden, Finland and Norway applied to join (the latter ultimately rejecting accession in a referendum), with Switzerland deciding to remain separate, as did Iceland and Liechtenstein. Labour was in favour of enlargement and Titley became chair of the Finland Joint Parliamentary Committee. During the course of accession negotiations he became somewhat of a star in that country, and his work later earned him an honour of the Grand Commander of the Order of the White Rose. (The other countries had non-Labour rapporteurs.)

Part of the accession debate was over whether various parties supported "widening" or "deepening", occupying hours of debate amongst intellectuals and politicians. Problems at the inter-governmental level were money (Parliament demanding a reform of the financial perspective), weighting of votes in Council and also the number of Commissioners and number of MEPs, which gave rise to big-state/small-state arguments. Titley was vigilant in the lead up to accession, raising questions about structural funds, remote areas with small populations and ensuring democracy in the process, and fearing that decisions were being made very quickly. Green welcomed the applicant countries as bringing a long and proud history and tradition of social democracy.

By spring 1994 the policy matters had been ironed out, but Major decided to make an issue of the "blocking minority" question in Council. An account of this process can be found in Butler and Westlake (1995), and will not be repeated here. Labour MEPs voted solidly for accession on 4 May, just before the elections, in line with official Labour policy. The government's virtual blackmailing of the accession process had made few friends. Its relations with "Europe" were not helped by an argument about whether

Chancellor Kohl would be invited to D-Day celebrations, but this was resolved on the occasion of Kohl's visit to England on 27 April.

Even before the accession of the Nordic countries and Austria had been settled, negotiations were opening on the next round – that of the former communist Central and Eastern European countries. The Socialist Group, as well as Labour, was keen to embrace these countries in order to consolidate democracy.

Onwards for Europe and Labour

The first Brussels plenary in the brand new building was held in September 1993 and heralded as a marker for change. However the entire saga of buildings and expansion was fraught with secrecy, setting Tomlinson onto a trail attempting to bring transparency to the process. He insisted that the Strasbourg buildings contract should not be signed in its present form and that the Financial Controller had exceeded his mandate. He discovered that the minutes of Quaestors' meetings where some of these decisions were being made were not available to Members, and insisted at every opportunity that this be remedied. The buildings were not the only matters being dealt with by the Quaestors and he also felt there was some tacit approval of claims for expenses on the part of staff that were not justified.

Drugs policy raised its head again in February 1994 with accusations from the Conservative Home Secretary on BBC radio that Labour was voting to legalise drugs. Green protested this was absolutely not true, but they did abstain on a resolution with an objection to one particular paragraph. It was carefully crafted, but then Ford made a written explanation of vote saying he thought that possession of small amounts of soft drugs for personal use should be decriminalised, but that this was not the same as legalization. With the party at home taking an increasingly tough line for the benefit of the press, this highlighted what was seen from the British end as an embarrassing misalignment of policy. The next reading of the Action Plan on Drugs took place in January 1995 and the same cautions were in place.

As might be expected the BMW take-over of Rover, after all the rows about Rover and BAe earlier, was controversial with uneven application of competition policy by the Commission. In February 1994 an acrimonious exchange took place with Tomlinson and Read versus Anthony Simpson for the Conservatives on whether or not Rover was undervalued when it was sold. Tomlinson said workers who, in Birmingham, Oxford and the components industry had invested their lives and their families' livelihoods, were completely subordinated in the decision-making process to the interest of people who represented those who had merely invested their money. Honda was in negotiation to increase their share and BAe sold their 80%. BMW's £800 million cash injection put into BAe had not been invested in the car industry. Commissioner Bangemann did another of his masterful whitewashes, suggesting to Read that she should regard the takeover from the viewpoint of European industrial policy. This did not go down well. Donnelly asked whether he felt that "in the spirit of the EU it was appropriate for workers in Rover in the UK to find out about the sale of their company via the local press?" Tongue spoke of a hidden UK government interest free loan to Austin Rover of £1.29 billion prior to the sale to BAe which was a debt never repaid.

Labour MEPs held a series of public hearings in Britain about the structural funds and Community Initiatives (other sorts of funds) during the spring of 1994 and there was a major debate on all of them in the Parliament in May. The funds were hugely valued, but the way the UK government administered them came in for a large degree of criticism.

A directive on patenting biotechnological inventions was put forward and proved immensely controversial due to ethical considerations, questions of potential cures for diseases and animal welfare issues. It was subject to substantial and passionate lobbying from all sides. A large number of amendments were put forward and the Green group proposed to reject but was defeated 55 – 211 – 3 on 4 May. Voting on amendments continued on the 5th and then the deadline was extended to the July session, taking the matter over into the next Parliament.

The Tribune Group of MEPs published a pro-European "discussion pamphlet", *Going Forward in Europe* in March 1994 designed to inform the election campaign. Its officers at that time were Newens Chair, David Secretary and Bowe Treasurer. Chapters were contributed by David on employment, Donnelly on industry, Ford on science and technology, David again on regions, Hughes on the Social Chapter, Crawley on women, Oddy and Ford on race, Pollack on consumer protection, Elliott on education, Bowe on environment, Titley on enlargement and Newens on foreign policy.

By this time most of the Labour MEPs had been a rapporteur for something, even if it was not necessarily legislation. It was a pretty good record in terms of parliamentary activity. Adam had concentrated on energy and research budgets and safety standards for East European nuclear reactors. Balfe worked on the Conference on Security and Cooperation, Barton on motorbike standards, Bowe on pollution control, Coates on human rights, Collins on a range of subjects, Crawley on women, David on structural funds, Donnelly on banks, shipbuilding and Germany, Elliott on education, Falconer on official secrets, Ford on race, science and arms exports, Green on food and consumers, Harrison on a range of subjects, Hindley on Asia and trade, Hoon on a range of subjects, Hughes on health and safety, McCubbin on fishing, funds and health and safety, Martin on the IGCs, Megahy on rights of residence, Morris on animal welfare, Newman on human rights, Oddy on company statute, Pollack on urban, energy and transport, animal welfare and child care, Read on telecoms and on Rover, Seal on technology, Alex Smith on regional development, Llew Smith on nuclear fuel, Stevenson on rural development, Stewart on safety at sea, Titley on trade and on enlargement, Tomlinson on budget, Tongue on cars and on funds, White on subsidiarity, Wilson on agriculture, Wynn on budget related matters and on animal protection. Those who did not undertake any reports in this term were Bird, Buchan, Crampton, Lomas, McGowan, McMahon, Newens and West. Once again all contributed in debates such as urgencies and current events and tabled endless questions. The Group as a whole had made a positive mark during these five years.

The last speaker for the EPLP was Newman as rapporteur on human rights in the Community. Because it was critical, the EPP tabled a huge number of amendments and it was sabotaged by the right, who postponed a vote. It was not to come back until May 1995, when the right again sabotaged it, saying it was too broad, despite the support of Green and the Socialist Group and a good intervention from Newman in support of his text.

The feminist team

Given the under-represented Labour female contingent in this third elected parliament some of them made a fair amount of noise. Three of the women were from London, providing a strong and active voice for Labour in that city. The feminist positions they took were not always supported by some of their less progressive male colleagues.

Christine Crawley as Chair of the Women's Committee, following on from her work in the previous parliament pushed for the Social Charter, for equal rights for part-time workers, and for special treatment for pregnant women at work. A strong feminist with an eye to a quotable quote ("women are the keyboard coolies of the new technology" was one of them), she could be a formidable presence when debating. She had three children, the youngest of whom, twins, were only nine when she was first elected.

Carole Tongue, feminist, Francophile and linguist, had more confidence in this parliamentary term and was well connected into the Brussels networks. She had originally lived in Brussels with Huguette Vos, a motherly French Group staff member; now she shared an apartment with Eva Eberhardt, a Hungarian feminist Commission expert and they had a good social life with cosmopolitan friends. Coming from a Quaker tradition she focused her work on women's rights, peace, culture and media and economic and monetary policy. As Deputy Leader of the BLG for some of that time, she worked closely with the Labour front bench. Tongue became a founder board member of the Westminster Foundation for Democracy in March 1992. In December that year she had a baby daughter and was then the only female Labour Member apart from Pollack with a young child, though their friend the Leader of the Danish Social Democrats, Kirsten Jensen, had given birth about the same time. There was a battle with Parliament's authorities to accept the notion of maternity leave and that this was not sickness.

Janey Buchan, the Scottish veteran who had been in Parliament since the first elections, had an eye to the media and was strongly involved in supporting Nelson Mandela in South Africa. As an opponent of the EC, she made critical interventions on her rare speaking occasions, had nothing to do with the Women's Committee and did not take on reports. On development matters and the ACP, and on culture and education, however, she was passionately engaged at committee level. In later years she suffered from an inner ear problem that made travelling increasingly unpleasant.

Pauline Green worked pro-actively on consumer affairs and Cyprus and building strong links with the party leadership. A forceful speaker, by 1993 she had been voted to lead the Labour MEPs. Together with Tomlinson, Newens and Balfe, she represented the Co-operative Party and organization, though there was some rivalry with the section of the Co-op where Balfe had his roots. She, too, had children still at home, in their teens. In Brussels she shared a flat with Crawley.

Christine Oddy, a feminist with a fine legal brain, was involved in some very technical legislative reports and was EPLP liaison person for Legal Affairs. She was a founder member of Emily's List (set up in the UK with the dynamism of Barbara Follett to help more women become members of Parliament) and was Vice-President of the Financial Services Intergroup. Oddy teamed up with Alex Smith for various campaigns on Guatemala and Sri Lanka. As the only woman who was close to the Campaign Group, she was largely outwith the social circle of the others. She was subject to some discrimination on the part of ushers who often challenged her right to enter the Members' Bar, possibly, she believes, because she was young and they thought she was an administrator.

Anita Pollack was a feminist on the Women's Rights Committee as well as Environment and South Asia. She worked on child care, animal welfare and social and environmental issues. As the only mother of a young child in the group at first (her only daughter was three when she was elected), she was run fairly ragged trying to keep up with the pace in addition to nursing her highly marginal constituency and did not seek either EPLP or major parliamentary posts. For a time she set up a Tuesday night women's dinner where a few of the Labour women and some invited Socialist Group women enjoyed political discussions. It became difficult to sustain these when the Parliament's late Tuesday night sessions increasingly featured environment legislation, making it impossible to get away. She shared a house with two German Socialist colleagues – Dagmar Roth-Behrendt and Lissy Gruner. She was another founder member of Emily's List. Pollack was for the second half of the term Chair of the Animal Welfare Intergroup and of the delegation to the countries of South Asia, where on a diplomatic learning-curve she grappled with the twin problems of Kashmir and the Tamils, strong interests in her London constituency.

Mel Read, a strong trade unionist from ASTMS, a feminist, and a beekeeper in her spare time, enthusiastically tackled technical issues on her committee and was involved wherever possible in plenary attacks on the British government. During her term as Quaestor she broke ground by supporting gays and lesbians, particularly in relation to Parliament staff matters. She became active on the Health Intergroup, correctly judging this to be an area into which the Community was expanding, and on the USA delegation, where the EU's backwardness in technological developments caused concern. Her life partner, Mike Teague, was also her assistant and they found a flat, so kept pretty much to themselves.

After much campaigning a creche was opened in the Parliament in September 1992. The opening featured Crawley, Read, Tongue, Pollack and her assistant Hilary Moser (a Strasbourg resident), whose baby daughter was an early customer.

Out of hours

Following on from the tradition of making collections at Christmas for good causes that had earned so much ire from the Conservatives, the EPLP hit on the idea of holding an annual Christmas Review, consisting of sketches and a dinner, during the annual December Strasbourg session. Admission was charged, the profits going to a charity agreed by the group. The first of these in December 1990 was a roaring success, attended not only by British MEPs and staff, but other socialists from Denmark, Germany and the Netherlands who in following years also joined in with politically satirical cabaret turns as did, in due course, some of the assistants. A good amount of talent was unearthed: Collins could sing, McGowan and Tongue were pianists, and all sorts of sketches were developed, Megahy and Titley amongst others proving to be excellent comics. One hilarious and hugely popular act was Simpson and Barton doing "synchronized Olympic swimming" upside down on their hands, legs waving above a blue cloth denoting the water.

There was some strain on Labour and Socialist Group staff, because during the week-long Strasbourg sessions everyone was away from home and there was, as one put it "no boundary between work and social life, meaning that they were on duty the whole time including the evenings." Members did not often bring their UK staff with them to Brussels or Strasbourg, but assistants in Brussels offices were sometimes expected to be in Strasbourg, depending on the work load of the Member at the particular time. Sometimes they were given meagre funds to cover the cost of their travel, accommodation and food and the hours were long, hardly compensated for by occasional good dinners.

Collins began to organize Christmas parties for all the Members and staff of the Environment Committee. This cross-party event became very popular and each national delegation was encouraged to sing something, usually kicked off by the Germans with *Tannenbaum*. The assistants would put on a pantomime. Given the amount of legislation that went through this committee it was also important in building a sense of working together, since it was not possible to succeed in amending legislation without a cross-party majority in Parliament, so this was a canny move, but abandoned after Caroline Jackson took over the chair when Collins left in 1999.

The frequent travel saw off a few marriages during this parliament, and resulted in several divorces and re-marriages. Christine Crawley married Jim Murphy who was Stanley Clinton Davis's adviser, Glyn Ford married Daniela Zanelli, an Italian interpreter and Stephen Hughes married Cyndi Beaver who was at that time working as an assistant. There may have been others that were less noticeable.

The Monday Labour dinners continued in Strasbourg as a forum for pro-Europeans and became popular with the growing band of Members and assistants, and Labour staffers on the Socialist Group. Tribune dinners continued with occasional guest speakers, and for the rest most people socialized either with people close to them regionally, politically, or in their committees, or those befriended during language courses.

Slowly some Members also made friends across the ideological divide. Sometimes it was because they were initially thrown together on delegations or language courses. Bryan Cassidy, a right-wing but personable Conservative Member generally travelled with his wife Gillian who was also his assistant. He was Vice-Chair of the USA delegation when Hoon was Chair, and they struck up a friendship, and the two wives also were friendly. Cassidy said that he and his wife made a conscious effort to cross the political barrier. They also struck up a friendship with Oddy whilst on a Spanish course.

Kitty O'Shea's bar in Brussels near the Commission's Berlaymont building

became a late night drinking hole for those, generally male, with strong con-
stitutions. Although a fair amount of alcohol was drunk by many, most of
the Labour team were not outstandingly known for regular inebriation. In
Strasbourg the late-night haunt was known as the *Perestroika*.

One of the problems of the peripatetic life was missing important radio and
TV broadcasts. In Brussels the Today programme on Radio 4 is only available
on long wave, and in any case because the continent is an hour ahead in time
the crucial 8 am – 9 am slot is missed since meetings begin at 9am or earlier.
When the cricket is on Today disappears altogether on long wave. Those with
cable TV can receive the BBC in that town, but not ITV. In Strasbourg, the TV
is confined to channels such as CNN or Canal rather than BBC.

The strain of running three offices and getting on and off airplanes several
times a week, with speaking engagements on multiple subjects and attempting to be pro-active kept most Members in a state of permanent exhaustion.
Hayter was astonished on her first trip to Brussels that Pollack and Tongue,
on the same early morning plane out of London City Airport, did not sit and
chat in the way that perhaps good feminists ought. These Members do not
recall any slight in this, simply that they had a mere fifty minutes to scan the
newspapers before their punishing daily schedule would kick in. Members
were probably less attentive to EPLP and indeed Socialist Group staff than
they should have been for just this reason. Always running from one commitment to another tended to leave little space for a coffee and making
human contact with non-MEP colleagues.

By this time Stewart had diabetes and bad legs and Megahy's disability
from polio was also causing him difficulty in walking. They were both provided with electric scooters with which they whizzed around the Parliament
buildings and were also transported around the long corridors of Brussels
airport.

Staffers

It was an expanded British band in the Socialist Group under General
Secretary Priestley and, with the UK's larger entitlement, Derek Reed joined
in 1990 when they wanted someone with science, economic and industrial
relations policy knowledge. He was one of the few people around with that
background as well as several languages. A lawyer, Frazer Clarke, arrived
in 1992, proving to be an invaluable asset and great Labour loyalist. Peter
Brown joined, working in the Chairman's office and Morag Donaldson was
Priestley's trusted senior secretary staying with him for many years.
Paulette Fuller worked on Budget Control and Julie Owens on Social Policy
before leaving to fight as a candidate for Peterborough in the general election. Colin Kotz worked on the Women's Committee, Dick Gupwell was
still head of the sessions unit and Tessa Ryan was working on environment.
Tom Lines joined as an administrator on external relations. Nick Crook
joined in 1993 after having worked for both McMahon and Tomlinson.
Gareth Williams from Wales worked for the PES with Frenchman Jean-
Francois Vallin for a period before returning home. Geoff Harris moved
across to the Parliament staff. David Blackman was still there with his secretary Valerie Bryce, Roy Cattermole too. Richard Corbett was on the Group
staff as a constitutional expert and collaborated with Francis Jacobs and

Michael Shackleton on the Parliament staff to produce an important text book on the European Parliament. Its first edition was published in 1990 and there were to be many more. Tony Robinson was the stalwart in the press office with Eirwen Butland as secretary.

There were by then lots of British secretaries in the Group: Patricia Cardwell, Ludivine Weech, Mary Platts and Majella McCone, later joined by Patricia Furneaux, Pam Stewart and Wendy Stuart-Smith. Jane Stowell was back after having been Megahy's secretary when he was Vice-President. Elisabeth Smith worked as David Martin's secretary in his Vice-President role.

The EPLP staff now consisted of Hayter as Chief Executive, assisted in London by Angie Forrester and Carol Rawlings as press officer plus Mary Alexander and Foluke Ogunewu looking after the finances. Hayter was not hugely happy in her time with the group and once cried to Hindley that "they treat me worse than you". The Brussels and Strasbourg team included Stephen Brown and Cathy Burton. After 1992 the chief Brussels linchpin was the hugely competent loyalist Maggie Coulthard whose work particularly involved the Liaison group and ensuring good communications between the EPLP and the Socialist Group on voting.

At home, the assistants' group still met, with Kay Baxter being active. Those who were related to MEPs tended not to attend, so there were some gaps.

Boundary changes

There were substantial and late boundary changes before the 1994 election as a result of the increased number of UK seats, although there had been a boundary review taking place since half way through the previous year. France was still refusing to ratify the extra seats as late as January because of a row over the seat of the Parliament and construction of a new, much larger hemicycle in Strasbourg. The compromise was President Klepsch signing an agreement that Parliament would rent a new hemicycle for twenty years. Labour was strongly opposed to this deal. Parliament was to increase to 626 Members, and the UK's entitlement, including Northern Ireland, was increased from 81 to 87. Considerable uncertainty existed as to whether the new proposals would be ratified in time.

In some cases Labour Members were pitted against each other in the res-election process. Members were able to contest the selection in any seat where their old constituency was a substantial part of any new one. Probably the most difficult such dispute took place between Oddy and Read, and Read and Coates. Read's seat, primarily consisting of Leicester, was carved into a three-way split, with the original bit becoming a Conservative marginal. During a run-off between Read and Oddy for the latter's reconstituted seat, a letter ostensibly emanating from Coates was circulated saying he would be putting in for Derbyshire. Oddy won selection for the seat containing North Warwickshire and Nuneaton, but not until after the contest had to be re-run. Read then gained what had been Coates' Nottingham seat with North-West Leicestershire, in an ambitious parachuting move, with Coates moving to Derbyshire, now known as North

Nottingham and Chesterfield. Sue Waddington was then selected for the new, marginal Leicester seat.

Most sitting MEPs had no trouble passing their trigger ballots under the OMOV selection procedure and this process began early. Only three were challenged. One was Newens, who was challenged by amongst others former MEP assistant Oona King, later to become an MP; he accused Hayter of working against him. Balfe was "triggered" by a one-vote margin and was also opposed by Oona King. McGowan, too, faced opposition, but all three won without too much trouble in the full reselection process. The old pro- and anti-European divide had almost entirely disappeared as a selection consideration at the grass roots. Because of the uncertain situation about the number of seats, it was not clear until the last minute on which boundaries candidates were going to fight.

PART IV

1994-99

An adventure playground

The Scene

Interrupted election campaign due to death of John Smith. Labour sweeps to victory and leads the Socialists in the European Parliament. Neil Kinnock becomes a Commissioner. Tony Blair revises Clause IV. Three more countries join the EU. Mitterrand's last stand. Three by-elections. More BSE. New Labour landslide in 1997. Socialist governments lead Europe. Amsterdam Treaty and the Social Chapter. Agreement on single currency. After five years of relative harmony Labour's large group falls apart with expulsions, resignations and a new electoral system leading to bitter selections. Five peerages. Expenses and Members' Statute. Pro-European Conservatives. Fraud and resignation of the Santer Commission. Election losses.

A sad beginning

It was a strange election. Labour set off with a positive campaign strategy and was dealt a major blow. Four days before the official campaign was due to start, the party held a glitzy fund-raising dinner in London with French Socialist leader Michel Rocard alongside John Smith. He had just happily told Pauline Green the French party would vote for her to be Leader of the Socialist Group. The next morning, 12 May 1994, Smith was dead. Not only Labour but the nation was in shock and mourning for its potential Prime Minister. Election campaigning was postponed as a mark of respect until after his funeral, Margaret Beckett temporarily taking over as Labour Leader. Although the party decreed that the leadership election would be held off until after the election, press speculation took precedence over European matters.

Huge victory

Labour swept the board with sixty-two out of a UK total of eighty-seven seats, on 42.6% of the poll. Earlier the internal prediction had been a possible loss of thirteen of its forty-five seats. The Conservatives on 27% were slashed to eighteen, almost a complete reversal of the 1979 result. Liberal Democrats at last won two with 16.1% and the SNP also won two, one of which was Labour's only loss. The Green vote melted down to 3.1%. Some Labour Members were "unexpected" by the party hierarchy (i.e. unwanted). The electorate had woken up to the fact that even with a different Prime Minister they still had a Tory government and were ready for change. Turnout remained low at 36.4%, but for the first time was not the lowest, that "honour" going jointly to the Dutch and Portuguese with 35.6% each. Paradoxically, whilst the Parliament's power had grown substantially with the Maastricht Treaty, turnout fell in most countries.

Manifesto reservations return

The first draft of the European Socialist manifesto appeared in March 1993 and party leaders agreed in Copenhagen that June to a theme of tackling unemployment and racial discrimination. The manifesto was presented to the PES Congress on 5-6 November in Brussels and signed by John Smith just after the Maastricht Treaty had entered into force. Seven main areas covered jobs, equality, environment, peace and security, regulating immigration and fighting racism, fighting organized crime and working for democracy. The British footnote reared its head again. PES support for a 35-hour week was repudiated by Smith, mainly, says Sigler, because it was considered unachievable. Difficulties on this had gone back to when Kinnock was Leader when the EPLP had supported a manifesto call for full employment, leading to concern from Kinnock and Clarke. The other objection was the veto. The Europeans wanted majority voting to be the rule, but Labour was more nuanced about which bits of the veto it wished to preserve. The emblem of the red rose surrounded by twelve stars was adopted, replacing the star man. At the same congress the Larssen policy report on "The European Employment Initiative" was adopted. Nevertheless, many of the parties, where they were in opposition, fought on the performance of national governments rather than on Europe.

It was no different in Britain, where beating the Tories was uppermost in Labour minds. The pro-European policy was definitely the country cousin. Labour's rather unexciting manifesto adopted by the NEC on 27 April, entitled "Make Europe Work for You", spoke about prosperity and building a Europe of freedom and social justice, highlighted reforming the CAP, supporting enlargement, a clean environment and tackling waste and fraud. It emphasized the importance of economies converging before a single currency could come into force and indicated that the party would offer a referendum on the subject.

This time the manifesto had been the subject of consultation with the forty-five MEPs via Green who sat on the drafting sub-committee and it for once mentioned their work and that they had worked closely with Labour in Westminster. With a careful eye to Britain's aggressive press and headed "Europe for all the People", it said "we will not introduce a 35-hour week" and would protect the veto. It attacked the Tory government, particularly on the missing Social Chapter. The main themes were unemployment, fairness, the Social Chapter, environment, reform and "our future". Greg Cook, the party's leading strategist, recalls that the main strategy at head office was "don't wake up the Tories".

Party conference in 1993 had endorsed an NEC document "Prosperity Through Co-operation" and resolution 50. These texts, reflected in the manifesto, included support for an EU industrial policy, progress towards EMU, reform of the CAP, an EU environment charter, workers' rights and the Social Chapter, movement towards a common foreign and security policy, and democratising decision-making by Finance Ministers.

At the launch in Transport House Jack Straw told the press: "this election is about the leadership of Britain", putting the MEPs firmly back in their corner. He had reckoned without the enthusiasm of Green on Europe. The backdrop was the Socialist rose and a large union flag and slogan "Make Britain Work for You". During the last week this changed to "Tell the Tories you've had enough". "Key campaigners", i.e. Shadow Cabinet members, concentrated on marginal seats.

Although he was not yet a candidate for the leadership, Blair set a careful tone on Europe. A Federal Trust paper (Batory, 2000) wrote that he was "pandering to the eurosceptic, formerly Tory-supporting tabloids which now backed Labour" and that:

> "Blair occasionally seemed to adopt a tone reminiscent of John Major, or even his predecessor, Margaret Thatcher. He pledged to 'see off the Euro-dragons' in the *Sun* and suggested in an interview in the *Independent on Sunday*: 'It is important that we recognize that the people of Europe want co-operation between independent nation states...You must always be prepared to be isolated if it is in the national interest to be so'."

Burdensome boundaries

In December 1992 the Edinburgh Summit agreed six extra seats for the UK as part of the deal to give Germany more seats to cope with unification. It then took months for Parliament to decide on distribution. Scotland was left as it was and there was a rushed process of boundary reviews in thirteen English constituencies and three in Wales. The biggest changes were in the North West, the Midlands and in London which often meant new selections had to be held. A few Labour MEPs were challenged under the re-selection procedures and this has been covered in Part Three.

Double election campaign

The campaign aim was a smooth transition from local elections to the European, always with the fear that Labour voters would tire and not bother. The idea of a "double referendum" on the government did not entirely enthral party volunteers, who were expected to be active for at least ten weeks without a break. There was also some dissent from across the water. Members' assistants tend to be dedicated and intelligent creatures but priorities at home were often different from those of those cocooned in Brussels. The latter advocated campaigns run on European policy issues, whilst those on the home front were more in tune with plans based on national or regional concerns.

The opinion polling committee included Sally Morgan and Rex Osborn and in the run up to the elections, polls were giving Labour a comfortable lead with the Conservatives and Liberal Democrats fighting it out for second place. However because Labour had done well in the 1990 local elections at the height of the Poll Tax controversy, it was expecting to lose seats. In the end, Labour did well in the local elections, as did the Liberal Democrats, with the Tories in serious disarray.

A clutch of five by-elections also took place on polling day, 9 June, and much of the organizing attention was on those. Four were won and Eastleigh went from Conservatives to Liberal Democrats in a large swing, with Labour second. Labour held Bradford South, where the vacancy had been caused by the death of Bob Cryer. The Channel Tunnel was opened on 6 May; Thatcher and Mitterrand took the glory and Major was wrong-footed in the publicity as he was also by Michael Portillo breaking the government line and saying the UK should not join a single currency.

Margaret Beckett and Shadow Foreign Secretary Jack Cunningham (by now a Vice-President of the PES) were involved in election campaign planning. Candidates met at a 1993 conference sponsored by the EPLP and again in January, and schools for agents were run. For the first time an official "rapid rebuttal" team was set up and a European-side rapid response unit with two British members of the secretariat was set up in Brussels to deal with queries and "Euro myths". These were the ridiculous stories that surfaced frequently in the Murdoch press such as hairnets for fishermen and standardizing condom sizes. Several other British staff from the secretariat worked in the UK for the campaign. George Robertson was now Shadow Minister for Scotland and Joyce Quin, former MEP, was the party's Europe spokesperson. Beckett, rather less enthusiastic about Europe than Smith, was active in the campaign and acknowledged as doing an excellent job as stand-in Leader.

Daily press conferences were attended by Green as Leader and often an EPLP spokesperson on specific subjects, with Straw as conductor. Media monitoring was undertaken under the auspices of David Hill and Jo Moore at HQ. Sigler was International Secretary. Hayter was horrified at attempts by Green to float her own ideas including harmonizing electric plugs, potentially wildly expensive. The old chestnut of Brussels raising VAT on food and children's clothing was raised by the Tories but Labour was always firmly opposed too. Despite the fact that Green was Leader-elect of the Socialist Group, and therefore to be a powerful European politician, she complained that she was only once on TV.

Labour fought a quiet, pro-European campaign reduced to two-and-a-half weeks, largely focused on the short-comings of the government and more polite than usual because of the death of Smith. The short time-scale, coming after local election weariness, meant that there was not a hugely active campaign on the ground except in some highly-marginal seats. Labour was up-beat because of the good local election results, but yet again party members did not see Europe as something to get excited about.

Labour's leadership campaign was not supposed to take place until after the election but within a short time it was unofficially in full swing. Blair made a well-covered speech in Eastleigh on 2 June, the day after Brown had announced he was withdrawing from the contest that had not yet started. There was massive media coverage of the 50th anniversary of D-Day and a tragic major helicopter crash to keep the press interest away from European issues. Conservatives did not wish to draw much attention to Europe because that would simply highlight how divided they were, so they, too, were rather subdued and rarely, if ever, attended hustings meetings. Even election day was fairly dull, with parts of the BBC on strike.

A fun element was provided by the Natural Law Party, who stood candidates in all constituencies and enjoyed attending hustings meetings speaking in favour of Yogic flying, though generally without demonstrating the technique. Their TV broadcast did show such entertaining images. The other item pounced on by Labour was a Conservative Minister complaining he had to step over beggars on the way to the opera.

Many Labour MEPs were resentful that the public face of the campaign was dominated by MPs who, they felt, knew little about European issues. Several candidates had notably active and lengthy local campaigns that clearly paid off, including Eryl McNally, Veronica Hardstaff, Robert Evans, Mel Read and David Hallam. For once the literature from the PES was gratefully received and quite well used, even the PES manifesto. The NEC grumped that there were still financial contributions outstanding from constituencies from the last European election and that in future they would have to be self-supporting.

The London MEPs' manifesto attempted to reflect the PES emphasis on environment, a bigger issue in the capital than some other areas. This, plus the added attention from three by-elections, meant London recorded some of the highest swings to Labour, winning nine out of ten seats. Green's vote almost doubled and Pollack, highly marginal in 1989, won almost fifty percent of the vote, also benefiting from a boundary change. Labour had all seats in the North West, North East, Wales and East Midlands. Scotland was a Conservative-free zone and Labour won seven out of eight in Yorkshire and the Humber, eight out of nine in West Midlands and six out of eight in East of England. Only in the South East (two out of eleven) and South West (one out of seven with Liberal Democrats two) was Labour seriously outnumbered.

Biggest of the biggest

Labour had become the largest delegation in the largest group of Parliament. They were walking on air. There were still only thirteen women, though up from seven. Rules demanded at least one woman on every short list, but most of the sitting MEPs were re-selected without contests so even this meagre quota did not often kick in. Labour fielded more female candidates at twenty-two than the Conservatives at twelve, but not in enough winnable seats. Of the twenty-two new Labour Members still only seven were women. Buchan had retired, as had Bird. Hoon, Stevenson and Llew Smith had gone to Westminster. Most of the new gang were pro-Europeans and there was little dissent from the party line.

Glenys Kinnock was Labour's new star and beneficiary of most of the press attention as well as attracting three out of four votes in her constituency. Not since Castle had there been an MEP that the public could name. Labour's vote was the highest since the 1966 general election and offered a hopeful marker to victory to come. Lowest turnouts were in the North West. In the hitherto marginal seats held by the EPLP the majorities were massively increased, although turnouts were generally down from 1989 apart from in London. In Labour heartland seats, however, majorities tended to be down. Wales traditionally always had high turn-outs.

The Maastricht Treaty permitted European citizens to vote and stand for election where they lived, and in Britain two "Europeans" married to British people stood for election, neither of whom was successful. The Conservatives fielded French Christine Adamson, and Labour's Gisela Gscheider lost a marginal seat, which some attributed to her German nationality. In 1997 she stood under her married name of Gisela Stuart to win a seat in the House of Commons. A wealthy British Eurosceptic, James Goldsmith, was elected in France.

In Sussex South and Crawley, Joyce Edmond Smith, who had won a close-fought battle for the selection against another woman, narrowly lost. Duncan Enright, son of former MEP Derek, lost to incumbent Tory James Elles in Buckinghamshire and Oxfordshire East. Lord Plumb's Labour opponent this time was Tessa Kingham, who became one of the many Labour women MPs elected in 1997 as did Melanie Johnson who came second in Cambridgeshire and Bedfordshire North. Another Labour woman, party official Gil Rolles, lost in London South and Surrey East. A former Labour MP, Antony Gardner (Ruschcliffe 1966-70) stood unsuccessfully. Labour's narrowest victories over Conservatives were Kent East (Mark Watts) and Herefordshire and Shropshire (David Hallam). Oona King, who worked for Ford, tried hard to be selected in London, standing against both Newens and Balfe, and also for the seat for which Evans was selected. It was probably good for her career to miss out, as she, too, was elected to the House of Commons in 1997.

There was one piece of bad news, and that was Labour's first loss of a seat since 1979 with the SNP beating Henry McCubbin in Scotland North East. It put a damper on the celebrations. Although an individualist on policy, he had been well liked in the group.

Routed Conservatives

It was a rout for the Conservatives. They came third behind the Liberal Democrats and Labour even won seats in the shires and leafy suburbs. In the eighteen seats where the Conservatives hung on the majorities in fourteen were not large, with recounts in at least ten. Their highest profile candidate, pro-European Edwina Currie MP was unsuccessful. Their campaign slogan "A Strong Britain in a Strong Europe" fell flat due to their highly-publicised policy divisions, particularly on the single currency. Cabinet Minister Kenneth Clarke spoke out against a referendum whilst Norman Lamont spoke in favour. Their vote was the lowest share in a national election since the establishment of universal suffrage, a source of great satisfaction to Labour and forcing Major into a reshuffle. They had disowned the Christian-democrat manifesto that supported a single currency, Social Chapter, common foreign and security policy, European Constitution and a goal of unification, but still rejoined that group.

The Conservatives had six new Members or retreads and were down to only two women. The Earl of Stockton, grandson of Harold MacMillan, was beaten by Labour's Ian White in Bristol (but elected in 1999). Sir James Scott-Hopkins, a respected supporter of the Parliament moving to Brussels, retired. In five seats their losses could be attributed to anti-Maastricht candidates. The closest run seats held by Conservatives were two against Liberal Democrats: Devon and East Plymouth, and Dorset and East Devon. Against Labour the tightest seats held were: Sussex South and Crawley, Thames Valley, Worcestershire and South Warwickshire. Two Conservatives who would gain seats in 1999 were beaten by sitting Labour MEPs: Philip Bradbourn by Hughes, and Robert Goodwill by Bowe. Mel Read in her new seat defeated Conservative Martin Brandon-Bravo, who had been an MP from 1983-92 and then Deputy Leader of Nottinghamshire County Council.

Other parties

Liberal Democrats won two seats from Conservatives: Robin Teverson defeated Christopher Beazley and Graham Watson won from Margaret

Daly. They were unhappy because they felt they should have won a third seat in Devon and East Plymouth where their candidate lost by only 700 votes because a "Literal Democrat" polled over 10,000 votes. They took this to court but did not win. The Liberal group in the European Parliament were to the right of the UK Liberal Democrats and had voted at least 150 times in the previous two years with the Conservatives. Andrew Duff, who won in 1999 for the Lib-Dems, in this election came third in Cambridgeshire.

The SNP were glad to add North East Scotland, won from Labour's McCubbin, to their traditional stronghold of Highlands and Islands. Scottish Militant under Tommy Sheridan came third in Glasgow behind Labour and the SNP. The Greens were unhappy as their protest vote of 1989 had largely returned to the Lib-Dems. Welsh nationalists failed to win a seat. The Northern Ireland story was the same as usual – one seat each for the three main parties, returning the "heavyweights" Hume for the SDLP and Revd. Paisley once again for the DUP, still with their dual mandates, plus Jim Nicholson for the UUP.

UKIP, a party born in 1993 from the anti-Maastricht campaign, made an appearance under Dr Alan Sked and beat the Greens in a number of seats. It attracted some excited coverage from the *Daily Mail* and ran twenty-four candidates plus the five by-elections, entitling them to one election broadcast. It was the only party in the UK campaigning for withdrawal from the EEC and its candidates for the European Parliament said they would not take up their seats if elected. It won no seats, but had put down a marker for the future.

Tony Blair leads from the centre

Nominations for the Labour Party leadership contest opened the day after the election. Pollack's valued chief of staff Kim Dewdney took leave to work on the Blair campaign with John Carr, and Ford led it in the EPLP. The election was held under OMOV rules put in place by Smith only the year before, giving MEPs a vote in the electoral college. Tony Blair, John Prescott, Margaret Beckett and Denzil Davies put in for the election held on 21 July. Blair, Shadow Home Secretary after a fairly meteoric rise in the Commons, made much of his strong pro-European credentials and won handsomely with more than half the votes in each section. Prescott defeated Beckett for Deputy Leader.

Larry Whitty was soon moved on from General Secretary of the party to become Labour European election co-ordinator from 1994-97 and a peer in 1996. Blair put Tom Sawyer, seen as a "moderniser", in his place. Sawyer had been deputy General Secretary of NUPE up to its merger with UNISON but did not get the top job, so was looking to move on, but says he would have preferred to have been a trades union adviser in the Cabinet Office if he had had a choice. He was Europe-friendly, and liked by the MEPs, paying several visits to Brussels and Strasbourg during his term of office which ran up to 1998. He now says he never felt the party had as close a relationship as it should have had with the MEPs and that their "outstanding" contribution to winning the 1997 general election was completely underestimated.

Lots of new boys and still not many girls

Labour MEPs had rarely thought when they first embarked on public life that they would find themselves in the European Parliament. Many were still standing with half an eye on Westminster for which a sprinkling had tried before, and roughly half were Councillors. They were university educated and most could speak at least a bit of another language. There was a group of young Members in this intake, many of whom struck up long-term friend-ships. Only six of the original 1979 intake remained: Adam, Balfe, Collins, Lomas, Megahy and Seal, still neatly divided 50-50 on Europe. From the pre-vious parliament in addition to this six there remained Barton, Bowe, Coates, Crampton, Crawley, David, Donnelly, Elliott, Falconer, Ford, Green, Harrison, Hindley, Hughes, Martin, McGowan, Newens, Newman, Oddy, Pollack, Read, Simpson, A.Smith, Titley, Tomlinson, Tongue, West, White, Wilson and Wynn. Of that lot only Falconer, Smith, West and Wilson could be described as anti-EEC, though Hindley and Newens remained sceptical of the institutions whilst being pro-European.

The new players were:

Angela Billingham, an Oxfordshire County Councillor, French speaker and former professional tennis player, in Northamptonshire and Blaby. The seat was not predicted to swing to Labour and all its seven Westminster seats were held by male Conservatives. She won from Anthony Simpson, a former Quaestor.

Tony Cunningham, leader of his local Council with a VSO background, won Cumbria and Lancashire North, knocking out Lord Inglewood who returned in 1999 under the regional list system.

Robert Evans, a French speaking schoolteacher, won London North West from Lord Bethell, who also reappeared in 1999.

David Hallam, another Methodist lay preacher, on his third attempt nar-rowly won Herefordshire and Shropshire, beating the Conservative Leader Sir Christopher Prout, who was made a life Peer.

Veronica Hardstaff, a language teacher (German and French) and former Sheffield Councillor, won Lincolnshire and Humberside South from Conservative Bill Newton Dunn who came back in 1999.

Mark Hendrick, a computer science engineer and lecturer and Salford Councillor sponsored by the Co-op, won Lancashire Central after having been inspired by Castle in the 1984 campaign. He was Labour's first min-ority ethnic MEP and one of the youngest, a German and French speaker and beat Conservative Michael Welsh.

Richard Howitt, a Harlow Councillor and disability rights worker won Essex South. Conservative MEP Anne McIntosh had migrated to the safer Essex North and Suffolk South seat and became MP for the Vale of York in 1997.

Hugh Kerr, a left-wing Harlow Councillor, unexpectedly won Essex West and Hertfordshire East from Patricia Rawlings, who went to the House of Lords. The seat had seven Conservative MPs and 10,000 votes went to an anti-EU candidate. The one-time member of the Trotskyist International

Socialist group says that a senior Labour official once said to him: "Hugh, if we thought you would have won we would never have let you stand".

Glenys Kinnock, a teacher, development expert and wife of the former Labour Leader, won South Wales East with an enormous majority of 120,247 – more than most people's total votes.

Arlene McCarthy, an academic and German speaker who had worked in local government and universities in the UK and Germany, won the Peak District.

Eryl McNally, a language teacher and Councillor won Bedfordshire and Milton Keynes against high-profile Conservative MP Edwina Currie.

Bill Miller, a local authority worker and Strathclyde Councillor, responsible for that region's work in Europe, took over from Buchan in Glasgow.

Eluned Morgan, the youngest in the Parliament at 27, a journalist and speaker of French, Spanish, Welsh and German, won Mid and West Wales.

Dr Simon Murphy, an academic who had worked for John Bird, replaced him in Midlands West, winning a very tight selection battle by eleven votes against Adrian Bailey from the Co-op, who is now an MP. Murphy, with a PhD on Northern Ireland, could speak French.

Clive Needle, who had fought South Norfolk in the 1992 general election, could speak French and was a party agent, won in Norfolk from Conservative landowner Paul Howell.

Peter Skinner, a further education lecturer in European studies, won Kent West from Tory Ben Patterson who went back to work in the Parliament.

Shaun Spiers, Co-operative sponsored and Secretary of the South East Co-operative Party political committee, an Oxford graduate with an MA in War Studies and another of the younger crew but Eurosceptic, won London South East from Peter Price, another Tory who had argued strongly for Brussels.

Michael Tappin, a university lecturer in American politics and County Councillor, French speaking, won Staffordshire West and Congleton, a boundary change seat.

David Thomas, a Suffolk County Councillor and former policeman won Suffolk and Norfolk South West from Conservative Amadee Turner.

Peter Truscott, a Russia expert and former Labour Party official, speaking French, Spanish and Russian, won Hertfordshire. He had contested Torbay in 1992.

Sue Waddington, Leader of a Labour Group and community education expert, won Leicester in a re-drawn boundary. She had fought Leicester NW in the 1987 general election.

Mark Watts, a planner and Labour Group Leader in Maidstone, narrowly won Kent East with the tiny majority of 625.

Phillip Whitehead, a former frontbench MP, consumer expert, former *Times* columnist and award-winning TV producer, won Staffordshire East and Derby.

Three by-elections were triggered during this term. Ken Stewart in Merseyside died on 2 September 1996 and Richard Corbett, a pro-European Socialist Group official, was elected at the subsequent by-election on 12 December of that year. Norman West in Yorkshire retired in 1998 and Linda McAvan was elected on 7 May. The other was North East Scotland, not Labour held and not won back.

Politically the newcomers were a very mixed group. The majority were pro-

European, only Shaun Spiers being Eurosceptic although he was no Campaign Group supporter. A division into "old" and "new" Labour can only be subjective but those who generally supported a "modernizing" agenda were Billingham, Evans, Hardstaff, Hendrick, Howitt, Kinnock, McCarthy, Morgan, Murphy, Skinner, Truscott, Watts and Whitehead. Those with a more traditional bent were Cunningham, Hallam, McNally, Miller, Needle, Spiers, Thomas and Waddington. None of these joined the Campaign Group. In the main the latter bunch were as loyal and certainly as constructive as the former and occasional policy differences with the party at home were not confined to one or the other group of individuals. Neither set acted as a block. Tappin described himself as a pro-European centrist – conservative on economic policy and radical on social policy (supporting workers' rights) who had voted for Blair. Most were not keen on joining sub-groups, though many would sign up to advertisements in *Tribune*. The one who stuck out was Kerr, with a Scottish Socialist tradition but a vigorous opponent of Militant. He was a member of Newens' General Committee in Harlow where he is remembered as "always obstreperous". His own view is that he was always "critical and vocal in defence of socialist values". A supporter of John Smith but never on the right, he was dismayed by the policies pursued by Blair.

Elsewhere in Europe

Turnout was down everywhere except Belgium, Greece and Luxembourg where voting was compulsory. Socialists were the largest group on 198, the EPP close behind on 157, damaged by the loss of so many British Conservatives. Women numbered 169, making up 27% of the Parliament but only 17 (or 20%) of these came from the UK. Finland, when it joined the following year, sent 50% women.

Socialists lost ground in Italy, France, Spain, Greece and Denmark but the Group was the largest because of Labour's fine showing. The centre-right gained in Germany, Spain and Italy and in the latter the far right Alleanza Nazionale won eleven seats. The Greens were split, some joining a few nationalists in the United Left/Nordic Green Group, but gained two in Ireland and one in Luxembourg. They were down in France. Ripa di Meana, formerly Socialist, then Commissioner for Environment, was back in Parliament in this group. In Denmark anti-European parties did well.

Votes largely went against governments, except for Germany and Italy. Berlusconi's Forza Italia (with whom the Socialists decided not to co-operate), were successful. Fringe and extreme parties picked up seats, the anti-immigration Vlaams Blok gaining in Belgium, the far right holding on in France but falling back in Germany. Everywhere campaigns were on national lines. In France there was an anti-Maastricht swing (the national referendum on the Treaty having only narrowly squeaked home the year before) and The Other Europe party, led by Sir James Goldsmith, who described himself as an anti-free trade campaigner did well. Orla Guerin, the BBC's Middle East TV correspondent, fought Irish Labour MEP Bernie Malone in Dublin and lost, though Labour did badly in Ireland generally.

The rise in small parties on the right made the left the more cohesive side of Parliament. The grand coalition of Socialist and Christian Democrat groups (which continued to include the semi-detached Conservatives) to a large extent was to continue but rather more shakily, held together by the need to obtain qualified majority votes for legislation under the powers of the Maastricht Treaty that was now in force.

Minority ethnic Members were down from the previous Parliament, and reduced to one each from French dependent territories Guadeloupe and Guyana, and Mohammed Ali with the GUE plus Labour's Mark Hendrick who is half-Somali.

In the Group of the PES Elisabeth Guigou was a former advisor to Delors and Mitterrand and former Minister of European Affairs. Jack Lang was former French Minister of Culture, and there was still Michel Rocard, former Prime Minister and Catherine Trautmann, Mayor of Strasbourg. Bernard Kouchner was on the Socialist delegation – a former Minister of Health and Humanitarian Action, much later to join the Sarkozy government.

The Liberal wife of Danish social democratic Prime Minister Poul Nyrup Rasmussen, Lone Dybkjaer, became a Vice-President of the influential Environment, Public Health and Consumer Affairs Committee. Former heads of state or government elected were: Poul Schluter of Denmark, Wilfried Martens and Leo Tindemans of Belgium and Michel Rocard. Otto Habsburg was still there and Nana Mouskouri, the Greek folk-singer, was elected for the New Democracy Party.

AGM in two parts

Sixty-two excited Members attended the AGM on 14 June in London, with lots of visitors. Cunningham, the Shadow Foreign Secretary, welcomed the Group as Labour's voice in the European Parliament and suggested it would be diplomatic for them not to throw their weight around. Coates, Bowe and others made a couple of attempts, finally successful, to have election of officers postponed until July. There was still some resentment about the organized coup that had taken place in 1989. This meeting simply decided on some standing order changes largely tightening up on discipline, received the annual reports from officers and agreed nem con to the nomination of Pauline Green as Leader of the Group of the Party of European Socialists.

Some standing order changes would be used later:

> "Withdrawal of the Whip, [i.e. expulsion from the EPLP] may be decided by the EPLP at a meeting at which prior notice has been given by the Liaison Group and that such withdrawal shall be reported to the NEC. Any Member against whom disciplinary action is proposed shall be given at least three day's notice and shall have the right to be heard at the EPLP before the motion is put to the vote... whilst EPLP recognizes the right of members to abstain from voting on matters of deeply held personal conviction, this does not entitle Members to vote contrary to a decision of an EPLP meeting or Socialist Group meeting in the absence of an EPLP decision to the contrary".

The reconvened AGM on 6 July in Brussels again had all present and visitors. Tappin and Kinnock proposed a working party to review standing orders, the operation of the Labour Group and efficient use of its time. It was to report in three months and to include at least two of the new Members. An emergency resolution from Crawley on gender balance was carried. This was still a tricky matter, because of the tiny number of women, so its wording was: "This AGM agrees that the EPLP moves towards 40% of its positions being held by women amongst the EPLP officers, and also in key posts in the EP. In the interim at least two of the EPLP officers shall be women".

With Green in place in the Socialist Group, there was an open contest for a new Leader between David, Ford and Wynn. On the first ballot the votes were: David 21, Ford 18, Wynn 23. On the second ballot Tribunite David was elected by 33 to Wynn's 29, which was seen as a victory of the left and centre against the right. From the outset of his leadership David worked to minimize the huge political and often personal differences within the EPLP but antagonism was to grow later over the direction of the Labour government.

For Deputy Leader, those nominated were Crawley, Titley and Simpson but after the prior decision on female quotas Crawley was elected on an affirmative ballot 48 – 8 with four blank, one abstention and four spoilt papers. The gender rule tipped in again for Chair, where Hendrick and Hardstaff had been nominated and Hendrick was the loser. There was an affirmative ballot for Hardstaff, 55 – 3 with 3 abstentions and one spoilt paper. Tappin was elected Secretary with 54 – 5 and two blank. He was to hold this post until 1999, equalling the record of Allan Rogers in the first parliament. Newman was elected Treasurer with 51 – 8, one abstention and one blank and for Whip Alex Smith was elected with 54 – 4, one abstention and one blank. Hallam was elected auditor. This meant that there were two Campaign Group Members amongst the officers, and two new Members.

Mel Read would have liked to have continued as Quaestor, having done some excellent work on the creche, supporting gay and lesbian staff members, and for some poorly treated assistants, but it was not to be. She was opposed by Balfe, who won the election by two votes to be put forward as the EPLP nominee to the Socialist Group.

John Carvel in *The Guardian* wrote up the story on 15 July, as being about Labour MEPs wanting more perks, a line also taken in other British newspapers:

> "Labour MEPs are supporting plans for a big increase in their perks and allowances in spite of criticism during the Euro elections last month that they were already making huge profits from officially approved travel expenses. They have voted to support Richard Balfe... In a personal manifesto... Mr Balfe promised his colleagues that he would work to get them increased allowances for travel, technology and secretaries... including being allowed to take their partners on overseas parliamentary delegations [which had only recently been abolished]. His proposals were causing embarrassment in the Labour leadership in Brussels yesterday. Wayne David, the new leader..., said the Balfe manifesto was not party policy. 'We have been leading the campaign to have the rules tightened up' he said. Balfe's document said 'I do not believe that we should apologise for or indulge in lengthy explanations of our resources as MEPs. If they are used correctly they enable us to assist the Labour movement and to do the job for which we were elected... MPs receive extremely generous car allowances, whereas MEPs have to finance travel within Great Britain out of the general allowance'."

For committee chairs, after some debate Collins was put forward for

Environment; Donnelly wanted EMAC, but lost. Despite their differences, Falconer supported Collins. Billingham and Needle became Socialist Group Whips.

The MEPs threw themselves into their work with vigour and lots of meetings. Not only were there EPLP meetings, but there were also regular meetings of regional groups, trades union groups, Tribune Group (Spiers now organizing those, which included dinners), Campaign Group, Socialist Group, intergroups (many and varied), Liaison group meetings, delegations, committees and pre-meetings of the Socialists. The Transport Committee group even decided to hold Labour pre-meetings before the Socialist pre-meetings. And of course there were the plenaries, often lasting until midnight, plus various dinner groups. Some people even managed a social life on top of this and all the travel. A continental Member once asked whether the Brits did anything besides politics.

Greening the Socialist Group

In autumn 1993 Smith consulted in the Socialist Party and with Priestley then decided it was time for Labour to run for Leader of the Socialist Group. There was choice as to whether to put in for President of Parliament, but it was felt that political leadership would be more advantageous for the party than the ceremonial post. The SPD also wanted one or the other. Labour's sixty-two versus the SPD's forty meant the former could choose. Labour took Group leadership and the SPD the Parliament Presidency. Party Leaders met on the fringes of the Corfu Council on 23-24 June and confirmed the deal. Beckett was there for Labour as acting Leader and made a substantial speech (drafted by Priestley) arguing the case for Green in terms of Labour's now-strong pro-Europeanism. At the first meeting of the Group on 6 July Green became Leader with only two votes against and two abstentions. Ken Stewart was the doyen d'age who chaired the opening proceedings.

Instead of the habitual smooth, conciliatory style of negotiations, Green shocked Priestley by going headlong into confrontational poker-style negotiations with the EPP about positions in the Parliament. It was, however, successful. Green set up a system of monthly dinners with the "left" group leaders in Strasbourg, to discuss key strategic and policy issues. From November 1995 she also attempted to set up similar dinners quarterly with the Socialist Commissioners, but says it did not work. Green saw that this had been successful for the right, and felt that it put the Socialists at a disadvantage, because their opponents were more organized. There were, however, meetings of as many of the socialist family as possible during plenary weeks.

Green encountered some constraints, in that Jean-Pierre Cot may have liked a second term as Leader, and had some concerns about the Socialist Group leadership going to such a large delegation. Priestley soon moved to a new position as Head of the Office of President Hansch, and the new Group General Secretary was Juan Cornet Prat, who was felt not to be a scintillating choice. Capable Jesper Schunck from Denmark might have been a strong contender and was liked by the British, but he suffered from coming from a small country and as such remained a deputy. Green took with her into the Group her own personal adviser and agent, Ray Collins, from whom she took advice on all matters. She says that he was treated by staff as something of a pariah as he was not a proper official but paid from her own allowance. Some did not know this. British David Blackman, long a senior deputy-general secretary, had since retired back to academia and Jean-Marc LaForest was Deputy General Secretary responsible for finances. There was an unofficial national quota for Group administrators, based on electoral success, but Labour wisely never took up its full allowance, realizing that what went up could come down. EPLP Leader David became a Group Vice-President with Crawley, Martin and Balfe all on the Bureau.

Green worked closely with President Hansch in bringing in reforms in the way Parliament did its business, supporting moves to more hearings and topical debates with the Commission President in which back-bench Members could in theory catch the eye of the Chair rather than the stultifying group rotation. This was not entirely successful, as the officials at the elbow of whoever was in the Chair still tended to point out key figures to be called to speak. Priestley points to the success of the hearings, however and he pays tribute to this "unique... form of public scrutiny of office-holders."

As Leader of the Socialist Group Green saw Blair every month and then would report to the EPLP. She also attended the NEC as Socialist Leader and would give reports of her meetings with other party leaders in Europe. This tended to be more interesting than the rather more technical reports from the EPLP Leader. She became so careful not to show favouritism to the British Members that they were almost shut out from access to her, although she would hold regular meetings with the multi-national Group "co-ordinators" (spokespersons), calling them her "Cabinet".

Parliament gears up

It was the turn of German Socialist Klaus Hansch to win the Presidency of this Parliament of 567 Members from twelve countries (to become 624 after enlargement in 1995, a quarter of whom by then would be women). More than half were new. Martin was again a Vice-President. Balfe was duly elected Quaestor with the support of the Socialist Group. Priestley moved from his position as General Secretary of the Socialist Group to take up a post as Head of Cabinet for the President.

Labour won Chair of the Committee on Environment, Public Health and Consumer Protection for Collins again, Chair of the Committee on Social Affairs and Employment for Hughes and Chair of Petitions for Newman. David put him forward and says there was some fuss because of his former Militant sympathies but felt that it worked. His strategy was an attempt to reflect the political balance of the EPLP. The former two were the most powerful legislative committees in this parliament, giving the EPLP unprecedented influence. For six months the group enjoyed a period of relative harmony.

Because of its size, Labour could have won more posts, but Priestley and Green worked on David to concede some of their entitlement to enable smaller delegations within the Group to have some of the spoils. Vice-Chairs were obtained in a number of committees: Security and Disarmament for Truscott, Energy and Research for Adam again, REX for Hindley, ACP for Glenys Kinnock under the chairmanship of Lord Plumb. Crawley did not make it as Chair of the Women's Rights Committee, that post being taken by Nel van Dijk, a Green from the Netherlands. Red-headed socialist feminist Christa

Randzio-Plath became Chair of the Monetary Committee rather than Donnelly.

For the various standing inter-parliamentary delegations, elections were held over until autumn. When they did take place, Labour took some plum posts. Chairs went to Donnelly for USA, Kerr for Australia and New Zealand, Simpson for Switzerland and Iceland. Vice-Chairs were awarded thus: South Africa for White, Poland for Thomas, Czech for Titley, Mongolia for Crampton, Transcaucasia for Needle, Central America and Mexico for Newens, SAARC for Pollack.

Let the business begin

Parliament acted fast in the first piece of business on 19 July when Mel Read piloted rejection of the directive on ONP (open network provision) voice telephony and the rights of users of services. This was a roll call vote, using the new Maastricht powers for the first time, and came after the failure of Parliament and Council to agree during the conciliation process. Voting for the motion to reject was overwhelming with 379 – 45 with 13 abstentions. In a later study of legislative rejections (Earnshaw and Judge, 1995), Una O'Dwyer, then Commission official responsible for relations with the Parliament said of the staff in the responsible Directorate-General: "all they wanted was for their legislation to go through. They were heartbroken... They can't understand it." Read said:

> "during the many hours of the conciliation procedure it was daunting to see how little leeway the Council was prepared to give. There was no real acknowledgement that after Maastricht the balance of power really has changed."

The sticking point was a disagreement between Council and Parliament on a regulatory committee for the most important bits of implementation. This rejection served notice on the Council and Commission that now Parliament had to be taken seriously. Labour voted with the Socialists, but their Danish colleagues abstained. A revised proposal was put forward in May 1995 but at second reading in September 1997 Read complained again that Council did not even consider some of Parliament's amendments and several were carried again, sending it into the conciliation procedure from which it did not emerge until the spring of 1999 after issues such as strengthening consumer rights had been resolved.

Next day Glenys Kinnock, founder (with Joan Ruddock and Joan Lestor) and president of the development charity "One World Action", raised the problem of Burma. That country and Africa became her main focuses of activity. Being elected as a star could not have been easy. Her fame at the outset was as the high-profile wife of the former Labour Party Leader and she was followed around by TV cameras and journalists, giving her no breathing space to settle in. The press attention annoyed a few of her less tolerant comrades. In time it was clear to all that she was not only extremely hard-working, but knowledgeable and passionate about development matters and she earned her high profile in that area. Oona King was part of her Brussels office team 1994-96 then went back to the UK to be elected to Parliament in the 1997 landslide.

A decision to set up a year-long Temporary Committee on Employment, pushed for by the Socialists, was also taken on 20 July, with a remit "to examine all aspects of employment policy in order to develop a coherent strategy for combating unemployment and creating sustainable employment." Coates became rapporteur and McCarthy and Seal also served on it, with Hendrick a substitute. Coates had been involved in a prolonged campaign about unemployment and published several books on the subject. In 1992 he had written to Delors, proposing a European Recovery Programme, after preparing a discussion paper for the EPLP, with Delors responding in supportive terms. Coates circulated the Delors response around European churches and convened meetings in the Parliament in which both Catholic and Protestant European church organizations participated. In December he spoke of the thirteenth state of social exclusion of unemployed citizens. The committee's report was carried in July 1995 by a large majority, its pivotal demands including a European borrowing instrument to allow investment in job creation. Coates and Stuart Holland published a book, *Full Employment for Europe* (1995), following this up, arguing that much job creation would have to come from a reduction in working time, an approach supported by Rocard.

The Commission's term was to conclude at the end of the year and from now on would be co-terminus with that of the Parliament. Tortuous negotiations over the choice of Commission President had taken place in Council, where Britain was not happy with the original proposal of Jean-Luc Dehaene (Belgium) or Ruud Lubbers (Netherlands), because they were seen to be too federalist. Major vetoed Dehaene in June. Jacques Santer emerged as the nominee, although Sir Leon Brittan had some support from the UK at first. Major eventually backed Santer who was no less federalist than the others, but was seen as more malleable, although in his first speech to the EP Santer called for an end to Britain's social opt-out. Neil Kinnock was nominated as the UK's second European Commissioner, to serve alongside Brittan who was serving a second term. For the first time the Parliament had consultation rights on this Commission, albeit *en bloc*.

Parliament's first vote on the Commission President-elect was on 21 July. Green was against ratifying Santer, saying it was not so much the person but the manner of his nomination that was the problem for the Socialists – the secrecy of Council meetings and lack of involvement of Parliament in the process. She spoke about countries "willing to connive at the most squalid, shabby, ill-judged practices to put in place what is essentially the most important position in Europe..." Most Socialists including the EPLP, and the Greens and Liberals opposed him, but twenty Spanish Socialists voted in favour, supporting their government in Council. Danish Social Democrats also were not party to rejection. Irish Labour MEP Bernie Malone and some of the French Socialists voted for him, not being prepared to vote against a candidate where Socialist leaders Felipe Gonzales, Francois Mitterrand, Andreas Papandreou, Poul Rasmussen, Wim Kok, Willy Claes, Jacques Poos and Dick Spring had made their decision. British Conservatives were in favour. The affirmation vote for Santer was 260 – 238 with 23 abstentions. The next day Winnie Ewing pointed out that 36% of the Socialists did not support the line but at least the EPLP were not amongst them. Titley for the EPLP said the problem was a European Union of secrecy and closed doors (in the Council). Deputy Leader Prescott came out on 20

September to an EPLP meeting where the future Commission was high amongst the agenda items, but the Members were put under no pressure.

Green paid tribute to John Hume over the IRA's cessation of violence in Northern Ireland, and Hume himself spoke of the thirteen walls in Belfast, saying that Strasbourg was the capital of hope and that this was the Parliament of hope. The peace fund for Ireland would come into play. The next day the Group decided to nominate Hume for the Nobel Peace Prize.

Given the large number of Labour Members, one or more spoke every day the plenary was in session. By the end of the year the only one who had not spoken in plenary was Mike Tappin. He was busy being secretary of the EPLP but by the next autumn was rapporteur on for the Budgets Committee on the satellite agencies, a large task entailing visiting all of the agencies strewn around different European cities. By October Harrison was a rapporteur on SMEs, a subject on which, with tourism, he was engaged throughout this five year term, with Billingham in full support.

In November the Petitions Committee considered candidates for the first European Ombudsman (a Maastricht Treaty provision). Hopefuls included an array of former MEPs, including Henry McCubbin. It failed to decide and after a couple of attempts at voting put more than one name to plenary (not Henry). The Socialist Group in December was not happy with the procedure, there being a growing view that the post should not go to a former MEP and Green complained there appeared to be indecent haste to appoint before the applicant countries came in. She succeeded in having it delayed, saying: "we want an ombudsman who has dignity and respect and not one who is the result of a political carve up". In the end it went to Jacob Soderman, appointed in July 1995, taking up post at the end of September that year.

Blackpool conference

The huge new MEP contingent was all over party conference that autumn. The *Guide* carried a large report on the elections, with photos of Kinnock and Tongue, another with ten of the thirteen women, something with Whitehead and an article on "Eryl Goes to Strasbourg" (she had a high profile having fought Edwina Currie). The EPLP was now holding a substantial fringe meeting every year and this one featured Joyce Quin MP, Shadow Europe Minister and Cunningham, Green, Hardstaff and David with guest speaker Hansch. On the fringe EPLP speakers were everywhere.

Conference endorsed an NEC paper *Economic Renewal in the EU* with Resolution 45, this supporting the European Commission's White Paper on EMU and another paper, *Jobs and Social Justice*, which endorsed the European Green Paper on social policy.

The conference banner was "New Labour, New Britain" and a new era had begun. Tony Blair, in his first speech as Leader of the party, surprised conference (although Kinnock had overseen a draft text changing the clause some time before) and "stunned and outraged the left" (*The Times* 5 October 1994) by proposing to modernize and rewrite the hallowed Clause IV, part 4 of the party Constitution:

> "To secure for the workers by hand or by brain the full fruits of their industry and the most equitable distribution thereof that may be possible upon

the basis of common ownership of the means of production, distribution and exchange, and the best obtainable means of popular administration and control of each industry or service."

Blair announced a rather speedy consultation period with a special conference to be held in the spring, saying a new draft text would be circulated in December for consultation. It was described variously as a "theatrical coup", "Tory Party Mark II", and "a breath of fresh air" by the broadsheets. Quite a few in the party were startled by the idea of replacing this sacred text, in place since the previous century, feeling change was unnecessary, although many supported additions. The MSF and GMB unions supported the move, but the T&GWU and UNISON, hamstrung by mandates dating from before conference, helped swing a narrow defeat (50.9% – 49.1%) on the proposal after an impassioned debate and several recounts of the vote, leaving the leadership slightly embarrassed but insisting that the review would go ahead nonetheless.

Various affiliated societies began consultations on including up-to-date ideas such as environment, equality and co-operation and Jack Straw produced a pamphlet with his suggested new wording. There was an inevitable backlash from the Campaign Group, insisting that this was the core of the party and that it was a right-wing attack on socialism from within.

The Clause IV debacle – keeping the red flag flying

Coates produced a document shortly after conference in support of keeping the old Clause IV. The winter 1994-95 issue of his *European Labour Forum* made a feature under the heading "Witnesses for Clause IV". Newens turned Coates' text into a one page statement which was circulated around the EPLP in November to seek supporting signatures. The plan was to publish it in *Tribune* as part of the debate. Peter Skinner recalls, however, that Falconer went round on a plane saying the advertisement was also going in *The Guardian*. Thirty-one MEPs signed the statement according to a printed version produced by Falconer where the names in order of appearance are: Newens, Crampton, McNally, Coates, Falconer, Needle, Seal, Elliott, Alex Smith, Thomas, Megahy, White, Hughes, Hindley, Barton, Kerr, West, Balfe, Donnelly, Oddy, Hallam, Stewart, Newman, Wilson, Waddington, McGowan, Lomas, Spiers, Bowe, Morris and Evans. Number 32 was reached with McMahon. This was many more than the Campaign Group and a document such as this for internal use in an open debate in theory should not have been problematic. It called for the retention of Clause IV in its present form, not mentioning anything about additions or amendments. It was the timing, prominent placement and spin from the accompanying press release that was the main problem. Ford says he had told Labour's General Secretary this was happening but news did not reach Downing Street.

Matters came to a head in January 1995. On the 9th Labour launched a spring offensive with a meeting in Central Hall Westminster setting out new Labour values. David, Leader of the EPLP, was on TV that night in a prerecorded interview, saying Labour must hold fast to its traditional values, suggesting that he supported building on the original text and thought the majority of the NEC would like to keep it, wanting Blair to reassure MEPs that the Labour Party will keep its commitments. Perhaps unwisely David allowed himself to be drawn on broader issues. It has been suggested that Blair was particularly annoyed by his criticism of sending his son to a grant-maintained school.

After the European election victory, business people were taking a closer interest in Labour, beginning to see it as a future government with which they needed to make links. The EPLP, with the help of a Labour consultancy, Hobsbawm Macaulay Communications, organized a £500 per head gala dinner with top names in the business community at which Tony Blair would make his first Europe keynote speech. Kingfisher, Whitbread and other companies felt that since Labour had won three-quarters of the seats at the election it was in their interests to keep their options open and listen to what Labour had to say. It was Blair's first visit to Brussels as Leader and was meant to showcase Labour as a progressive party that business could trust. Prescott, Cook and Whitty were all in town for the event. Hallam says there was a Tribune meeting that day and a note came round saying MEPs had to pay £200 (a discount rate) for the dinner about which there were some grumbles.

On Tuesday 10 January, the day of Blair's visit to Brussels, *The Guardian* carried an advertisement on its front page (trailed the night before in the media) purporting to be signed by just over half the EPLP (32 MEPs), supporting the retention of Clause IV. The advertisement read:

> "LABOUR MEPs DEFEND CLAUSE IV. Common Ownership has been a key part of Labour's programme to give ordinary people a decent future. With Britain and much of the world in crisis, this is no time to jettison this powerful weapon for social and economic justice. We are opposed to privatisation and believe that common ownership should remain part of Labour's core beliefs and values which offer: OPPORTUNITY EQUALITY FAIRNESS JUSTICE DEMOCRACY. Common Ownership ensures the economic power resides with the community rather than in the hands of a few private individuals or multinationals. That is why 32 Labour MEPs, more than half the European Parliamentary Labour Party, have called for Clause IV part 4 to remain in Labour's constitution perhaps added to but not replaced. We are concerned that the debate has been shortened, and ask Labour Party organizations and affiliates who require a speaker, or more information to write to: [Falconer's address and telephone number]".

The front page main banner headline was "MEPs Fight Blair Reform, Defiant advertisement backs Labour's Clause 4 and common ownership". The article, by Michael White and Stephen Bates, and clearly co-ordinated by those placing the advertisement, said: "Tony Blair's call for a united Labour movement to lead a crusade for 'national renewal' suffered a damaging blow last night when 32 MEPs challenged his authority with a renewed attack on Clause 4 modernisation." Most of the front page was taken up with negative reporting for Labour. There was a list of the alleged signatories, under the heading: "The 32 challenging the leader". An accompanying press release had gone out more widely.

The party's spin doctors were livid, not to mention the Shadow Cabinet. Major in the House of Commons gleefully spoke of Labour policy running into difficulties and had the furious front bench squirming. Big guns such as

Gordon Brown were hauled before the cameras to criticize the "pre-empting of debate by the MEPs" and pointing out with a certain amount of satisfaction that "the values set out in the advertisement are not currently in Clause IV".

Within a few hours Donnelly, McMahon and Bowe had dissociated themselves from the advertisement. They wrote to Alex Falconer, copying the letter to the Leader and Deputy Leader of the EPLP and it, too, was released to the media. Their letter in part said:

> "It is astonishing that the advertisement should have been placed without formal consultation with all of the signatories of the original statement which differs in content and tone from your press release... The timing of the advertisement has been designed in our view, not to further the debate but to create embarrassment for the Leader of the Party on his first visit to Brussels as Leader... In view of this we entirely dissociate ourselves from the content of the press release and the timing of both the press release and the advertisement."

McMahon says he signed the original document but did not know it was going in *The Guardian* and if he had known he would not have done so, though he thought the proposal for change was an unnecessary debate. Bowe says he was ambushed to sign by Falconer and it was presented as being in *Tribune* and he was furious and then reneged when it was in *The Guardian* which he found out about from Radio Cleveland.

Falconer for the Campaign Group maintained that all had known about the advertisement, but insisted that it was for purpose of debate not for embarrassment. This was disputed by Donnelly who maintained he had not agreed to anything other than an advertisement in *Tribune* and that what had happened was calculated to do mischief to Blair. ITV News said Blair had been upstaged and angered by the advertisement and would tell the EPLP how important the reform was.

Astonishingly, in the face of this fracas, the business dinner went well. Large firms were reassured about Labour's policies on Europe, on environment and on monetary policy. Blair sitting next to Wayne David was very frosty, doubting he knew nothing of the advertisement in advance. The latter is adamant that he knew nothing of the advertisement until it appeared but felt he was always after that having to repair the damage.

There were disputes about paying for the advertisement. Evans signed the document but had no idea it would be in *The Guardian*, did not formally withdraw his signature but wrote to Blair explaining his position. Hughes was furious with Falconer about it. Rather than what he thought was a private debate in *Tribune* it was a public row with Blair and he did not approve. He thought the clause could be amended to include co-operatives and feels that the leadership of the party did bear grudges. Seal signed but did not realize it would be an advertisement, although he stuck up for it on TV. He later thought the advertisement was designed to maximize publicity and debate but not intended to embarrass but that Blair never forgave the EPLP. The same went for Waddington. Elliott thought there was safety in numbers, believed in gradual change and that abolishing the clause was too drastic, supporting amending it with texts on sexism, racism and environment. He did not know it was going in *The Guardian* and was not happy. Spiers did not recant though he thought it was only going in *Tribune*. He thinks the placement and timing was a disgrace and also refused to pay, though he did not like Straw's pamphlet on Clause IV and the full flow of market forces. White thought the clause did not need changing as it was like a biblical text, saying "GCs would ask do you support Clause IV?" However he, too, thought it was for *Tribune*.

Then there was the other side of the story. Coates says the timing of the advert was malicious but he didn't personally know in advance of the timing as Falconer was in charge. He was concerned that Blair wanted to do away with the mixed economy in favour of pure capitalism, to which he was opposed. Newens agrees the advertisement was deliberately planned and that having thirty-two sign was seen as a tremendous boost to the campaign to save the clause. He sees the abolition as the start of the downward slope of right-wing policies in the party. Hindley, who signed, thinks the timing was accidental but also that it was a clever propaganda stroke. He saw the change as something that had to be stopped. Hallam (who was ill with pneumonia but still there) says he helped write the advertisement on Alex Falconer's laptop. He supported the idea of a golden share to bring public utilities back into public ownership and says the *Daily Mail* offered to pay him to set the record straight but he did not take it up. Alex Smith knew it was going in the paper, saying they wanted to beat the Labour spin machine.

Big Alex (as Falconer is known) says he negotiated with the paper for the precise date. He thought the clause was "symbolism" and changing it was sacrificing the Labour movement. Barton signed the advert and saw it as a challenge to a proposal and not an insult, feeling strongly there should be room for discussion but said Mandelson had said that anyone who challenged it was evil. He thinks the row was a symptom and not the cause of the problems with the relationship with the party at home and feels he saw the hijacking of the party stage by stage. McNally signed but did not expect it to be embarrassing. She disapproved of the reform of Clause IV as being a gesture by Blair to demonstrate his leadership, feeling that it was dismantling a symbol of what she was in the Labour Party for. Crampton knew it was going in *The Guardian* and did not feel it was a problem as there were many in the Labour movement against the change and he was cross at the prospect of losing Clause IV. McGowan supported retention of the clause, whilst believing that "common ownership" covered much more than nationalization, such as co-operatives and mutuals, and had written a piece about that. Newman says he knew it was happening and thought they all knew, saying that Blair did not raise changing Clause IV during his leadership campaign and he felt that was wrong. He thought Campbell's game plan was that Blair had to get the "grow up" thing out because the press had been told he would say it. Needle signed and on TV said Clause IV was a clear and distinctive touchstone for the party. He was opposed to abolition though he thought the clause could do with some improvement and says he was involved in the meetings and paid his share of the advertisement. He thought the timing was wrong and said Mo Mowlam tried to persuade him to withdraw his signature.

Of those who did not sign the plea to retain Clause IV, not all were in favour of change. Read did not sign but thought it was a mistake on Blair's part to meddle with it. Simpson was not thrilled about abolition. On the other hand, Watts did not see the problem on Clause IV, saying it wanted rewriting. Pollack thought a bit of modernizing in favour of a social market economy with inclusion of environment and equality would reflect today's reality, but did not see it as the end of socialism. Miller signed neither the advertisement nor the letter the next day. He was fairly ambivalent on Clause IV and thought something better might come from the change. Tappin supported abandoning the clause.

Wintour and Carvell in *The Guardian* on the 11th under the heading "Clause 4 front not learning says Blair", wrote: "Tony Blair picked up the gauntlet thrown down yesterday by 32 Labour MEPs ... telling them they 'were living in history and not learning from it'." *The Independent* said: "'Infantile' MEPs get a scolding from Blair" on its front page and elsewhere: "Anti-reform MEPs split on front page broadside".

Both Glenys Kinnock and Newens appeared on Breakfast TV, with Glenys, aware that Blair was extremely angry, supporting his courage and leadership. In contrast Newens was unrepentant. He proudly recalls that he was also on Radio 4 and said it was the wrong time to give a signal on this issue. He said that some of the EPLP were enraged, that David made what some saw as a cringing apology and that Margaret Hodge wrote to him saying he had insulted the Leader. He felt David was cold-shouldered by Blair after the event. Morris took umbrage at a Walworth Road staffer's description of MEPs as "nonentities".

Blair entered the EPLP meeting on the 11th with Alistair Campbell in tow looking like thunder. Billingham described him as ashen. Coates wrote that "his winning smile looked a little strained, even nervous." Hayter was present, tight-lipped with rage. At the start of the meeting David as Leader made a statement strongly criticizing those Members who had placed the advertisement, saying it was one thing to contribute to a debate and express a point of view; it was another to deliberately seek to embarrass the Leader of the party on his first visit to Brussels. That was greeted by a stony silence. Blair spoke next and, to many people's surprise, he did not angrily criticise the EPLP. Instead, his tone was one of disappointment. He then took questions.

Hardstaff in the Chair rather unwisely, but in the absence of indications from more "moderate" Members, took a question from Hallam (Billingham described this as asinine as he was a loose cannon) about renationalizing the water industry to which Blair responded that Hallam, whom he had known for a long time, should grow up. This was the cue for Campbell to leave the room and brief the press that Blair had read the riot act to the MEPs. It was hurtful to the many who were loyal and keen to hear more about Blair's thoughts on Europe and annoyed Hardstaff who believed in a sense of collective responsibility and discipline. Newens was then called and made a similar point, harking back to the 1945 manifesto, to the crisp response that 1945 was not today. (A reference to likening the position of the Clause IV supporters to those in North Korea and Labour not being a preservation society had appeared in the *Daily Telegraph* that day and on ITV the night before.) Tomlinson recalled with relish that "Blair demolished Newens and Hallam". MEPs were met with a media scrum on leaving the room. The loyalists were all glum. Martin thinks it suited Blair's purpose to be angry but that it was perhaps a bit synthetic, saying "Campbell wanted the story that he gave us a kicking". He thought it marked the cards of those who had caused the bad publicity. But it also made the whole Group feel as if they were being treated as pariahs. Aside from all this there was a further EPLP meeting early in the afternoon, with Robin Cook, Shadow Foreign Affairs spokesperson, speaking to a subdued Group.

Much pressure was exerted on some of those who were named as supporting the advertisement. Campbell told Ford it was his job to get thirty-three signatories opposing the advert and he went round gathering them at the dinner with the aid of Christine Crawley. On 12 January a letter appeared in *The Guardian* signed by thirty-six of the MEPs, saying they welcomed the debate, under the heading "Euro MPs support Blair on Clause Four". The text of this letter was:

> "The Labour Party is engaged in a lively, democratic debate on constitutional issues, including the future of Clause 4. We welcome that debate because we need to renew ourselves continually as a labour movement, while always being confident in our core values. This is a healthy and progressive discussion, in which no socialist should have anything to fear and from which the whole of Britain has a great deal to gain.
>
> As members of the European Parliament we welcome Tony Blair's initiative in inviting the Labour Party to debate how best to serve the interests of the British people into the next century. Our ambition is to serve British men and women with every jot of our creative energy and understanding and not to be museum curators of constitutions set in stone."

The signatories were: David (as Leader of EPLP), Crawley (Deputy Leader), Hardstaff (Chairwoman), Green (Leader of Socialist Group), Martin (Vice-President of EP), G. Kinnock, Ford, Collins, Adam, McMahon, Howitt, Thomas, Oddy, Cunningham, McCarthy, Skinner, Billingham, Hendrick, Tongue, Tappin, Watts, Tomlinson, Harrison, Titley, Hughes, Wilson, Donnelly, Pollack, Read, Simpson, Wynn, Whitehead, Truscott, Murphy, Bowe and Morgan. Seven of these were alleged to have been signatories of the advertisement.

Morgan was in Mexico and signed in absentia via her assistant. She says she would have signed anyway but was cross about the way it was done. Oddy also wrote separately to the press supporting a debate and saying she did not find Blair's arguments persuasive.

Simpson was told by Campbell that Prescott wanted him to sign. He flew back to the UK on the same plane as a still-angry Blair who allegedly said he would never meet the EPLP again. There may have been something in that, since only once was EPLP invited to No 10 after Labour won the election. Even regional groups of MPs were invited there more often.

In his *History of the Labour Party*, Andrew Thorpe (1997) says of Clause IV: "32 Labour MEPs published a statement against change. But no-one cared about MEPs... Barbara Castle... criticized, but no-one was going to take such a veteran figure very seriously against the party leaders." The event had a long-term effect. Meacher, Short and Hain soon wrote an article in *The Guardian* effectively aligning with the Blair line.

Long years later the wounds were still there. Billingham said "We were all tarred with that brush and we never won back the respect. The lesson was we don't count." Truscott felt the confrontation with Blair made the introduction of PR for the 1999 elections inevitable and opined: "the dinosaurs in the EPLP had to be sorted out." Evans later said: "some of those elected in 1994 were a bit of a surprise". Whitty didn't think it was quite as apocalyptic as some but acknowledged that it did affect Tony's view of MEPs though he would still take the views of some such as Martin and Ford later on the Amsterdam Treaty for instance.

At the conference on April 29-30 the new clause was approved, with CLPs giving 90% support for abolition of the old Clause IV. OMOV was used for the vote and the unions supported it by 54.6%. New Labour was definitely the name of the game. The new clause stated that Labour was "a democratic socialist Party".

A core of the EPLP remained publicly opposed to the change to Clause IV even after the conference. *The Independent* on 2 May listed them, with the ballot figures in favour of the change from their constituencies which in every case was between 73% and 89%, as Coates, Falconer, Hindley, Kerr, Lomas, Morris, Newens, Oddy, Alex Smith, Stewart and West.

Newman quietly left the Campaign Group during this year, later saying that he felt it was increasingly following the agenda of the anti-EEC House of Commons Group and he differed from it in tactics. He was by this time half-way through an Open University degree course and spent little time socializing. Being unannounced, it was not a move of which the ruling group in the EPLP were aware.

Magic moments

President Mitterrand made the opening speech for the French Presidency on 17 January 1995. He was frail and dying and it was the last time he would address this Parliament. Members from Austria, Finland and Sweden were present for the first time in the hemicycle with many new women Members. Most MEPs interviewed said it was one of the great moments they remember.

Mitterrand had great charisma and in a long speech he touched on peace and the responsibility of us all to keep it and denounced nationalism. He paid tribute to Delors, who was leaving the Commission after two terms, spoke of a social Europe, supported public services, tackling unemployment and preparing for further enlargement, but also of strengthening the Community and a range of policy matters. After three-quarters of an hour on his feet, he referred to his personal history in two world wars:

> "...my generation has almost completed its work; it is carrying out its last public acts, and this will be one of my last. It is therefore vital for us to pass on our experience... It is vital to pass on not this hatred but, on the contrary, the opportunity for reconciliation which we have, thanks... to those who, after 1944-45, themselves blood-stained and with their personal lives destroyed, had the courage to envisage a more radiant future which would be based on peace and reconciliation... War is not only our past, it could also be our future! And it is us, it is YOU... the Members of the European Parliament, who will henceforth be the guardians of our peace, our security and our future!"

The standing ovation was a poignant moment and there were many damp eyes. Pollack was in the hemicycle near colleagues Pepe Pons Grau from Spain who had opposed the fascist dictatorship and Willy Piecyk from

Lubeck in Germany, whose father had been in the Luftwaffe. There was a feeling of being part of something important. Mitterrand died a year later.

That night the Socialist Group held a farewell cocktail party for Mitterrand, and the following evening a farewell dinner for Delors whose last speech to the Parliament had been a passionate plea for Europe to unite. Coates was a great admirer of Delors and tells that he went up to the top table to bid him farewell, whereupon Pauline Green made a wisecrack that he was a subversive man. Delors said "this man is a militant and that is the most honourable profession of all." It was a busy week, with Tom Sawyer, Labour's new General Secretary, also visiting the EPLP to get acquainted in his new role.

Parliamentary committees interviewed Commissioner-designates early in January and Neil Kinnock, who had been awarded the Transport portfolio, put in a good performance at his test, coincidentally on the same day as the Clause IV events. He understood more than some nominees the importance of winning the support of parliamentary committees and benefited from the advice of Labour MEPs and the experience of Jan Royall, who moved her family to Brussels to take up a post in his Cabinet.

There were few moments of controversy in what was a relatively tame scrutiny process. At the end of the scrutiny procedure Green, after an almost hour-long speech from President-designate Santer on 18 January, pronounced her group pleased with the improved gender balance and spoke about democracy and accountability, racial hatred, equalities and the need for a revised code of conduct. The Socialists had settled their objections but demanded removal of the equalities brief from Irish Social Affairs Commissioner-designate, Padraig Flynn, who was a strong opponent of abortion. After pressure he agreed to step down as Chair of the Equal Opportunities Working Party. Approval *en bloc* of the nominations for the new European Commission went through on the 19th by roll call vote (416 – 103 – 59 abstentions) with most Socialists and Labour in favour. Some Germans in the Socialist Group and Cot were against, as were a tiny very mixed minority of the EPLP: Falconer, Miller and Tongue, with abstentions from Collins, Martin, Morris, White and Whitehead. The Environment Commissioner-designate, Ritt Bjerregaard, had annoyed some by telling the Danish press this was not a proper parliament and that gratuitous insult affected some votes. Five of the eighteen Conservatives, including Provan, their Chief Whip, voted against. One of the provisions of ratification in a Commission code of conduct was to transmit information and documentation simultaneously to both the Parliament and the Council. It also agreed that it would normally withdraw a legislative proposal if it were rejected by Parliament.

Barton still biking

Outstanding from the previous parliament was the directive on high powered motorbikes, the Commission still trying to ban bikes of over 100 bhp, now subject to the conciliation process. Barton, who had taken over the report from Conservative Peter Beazley who had not been returned, ensured that he attended the hearings for all the new Commissioners, bearing in mind that there were now more powers for the Parliament post-

Maastricht, and asking them whether they would support the will of Parliament if it was clear. German Liberal Commissioner-designate Bange-mann in particular committed himself to a Yes.

Barton and other British Members (this being a cross-party effort) demanded the Commission's assertions on safety be backed up by research. Agreement in principle was reached in December 1994 and on 18 January, just after the new Commission was formally approved, Barton asked for a month's delay on deliberations. It took longer. The joint Parliament and Council text emerging from the negotiations was finally approved in May. The Brits had their way and the Commission promised a thorough study. Barton pointed out that the only option before the Maastricht procedure had come in to play was to reject the whole proposal, but the conciliation com-mittee had brought results, and he invited the Commissioner for a celebra-tory ride around Strasbourg. He says the victory was due to canny political manoeuvring and was important for British industry. It was a lengthy case of Parliament being in the driving seat with a vigilant Member at the wheel.

This was not the end of motorbike sagas or of unrealistic ideas from the Commission. Many of these had at their root support for national industries. A compromise package on noisy exhaust systems was reached in June 1996. The biking fraternity assisted Barton by lobbying vigorously and bit by bit realistic agreements were reached.

Turkey customs union rumbles on

Turkey was still controversial. In a proposal for a customs union in February 1995, Green raised Cyprus, human rights and the Kurds, saying we had an unbalanced package and suggesting the matter be put off. The resolution spoke of a deterioration in human rights too serious to allow the formation of the proposed customs union at present, and wanted a system of interim reporting. Labour and the Socialists voted for this but Balfe abstained. A lengthy resolution on EC-Turkey relations with Socialist rapporteur Ray-monde Dury had been carried back in December 1992 following a Com-mission report, suggesting that Turkey did not fulfil the conditions necessary for membership but supporting the renewal of the association agreement.

Agreement to unblock the EU-Turkey Joint Parliamentary Committee membership came in November, 353 – 47 and 20 abstentions. This commit-tee had been frozen in September 1994 and the decision reconfirmed that December. Some of the EPLP voted against the unblocking, an unlikely mix-ture of Falconer, Lomas, Pollack, Read and Smith. However in December Parliament agreed to customs union by 344 – 149 (many Germans) and 36 abstentions. Together with this went a proposal for a regulation on special financial cooperation. Socialists wanted this fund put in the budgetary reserve, but all they managed was a working group between Commission and Parliament to approve every project. The Group set up a Turkey Watch to monitor the human rights situation staffed by the British Patrick Costello. Green said most of the group would vote for it and was concerned that Kurdish politician Leyla Zana, awarded the Sakharov prize in 1995, re-mained in prison. The resolution said Parliament "will remain vigilant". Most of the Socialist Group voted in favour, Morris was against and several abstained: Bowe, Falconer, Lomas, Smith, Stewart, Waddington and West.

The EPLP had a full exchange of views with Robin Cook on the subject, voicing their concerns about human rights and Cyprus. The home leadership wanted it approved. David recalls Campbell on the phone insisting they vote for the Association Agreement with Turkey, saying that Tony Blair and the CBI were demanding it.

Green in September spoke of oppression, intimidation and blatant denial of human rights in Cyprus since customs union was passed with Turkey, saying "my group will make efforts to freeze all financial commitments to Turkey". There were several other debates and more resolutions in 1996, 1998 and 1999. Turkish membership of the EU continues to have strong opponents both in Parliament and Council and problems with this relationship carried over into the next parliament.

Nuclear Pacific

By the end of the French Presidency in June 1995 the Socialists in France had been defeated by the right and the new government resumed nuclear weapons testing in the South Pacific, incensing the European left. President Chirac, a former MEP, was in Strasbourg in July and a good head of steam was generated by protestors. Indigenous people from the South Pacific were in the Parliament along with Australian and New Zealand MPs. One Socialist commented that: "We met him like a hungry shark patrol".

Throughout Chirac's speech on 11 July there was uproar and heckling from the left; the Greens were waving posters but the session was not adjourned. Priestley says Chirac told President Hansch he would walk out if he had to interrupt his speech and somehow sufficient order was maintained. As soon as he finished Green weighed in on behalf of the Socialists:

> "At a time when the international community is in the process of renegotiating the nuclear non-proliferation treaty, President Chirac personally took the totally incomprehensible decision to resume testing of nuclear weapons in the Pacific... we in Western Europe watched with disbelief as armed French commandos stormed, holed and boarded *Rainbow Warrior II* this weekend and did so with blatant disregard for the tragic ten year anniversary of the last time French troops attacked the *Rainbow Warrior* with such final and deadly results. You, President Chirac, need to tell us today what strategic purpose is served by the proposed nuclear tests, what political message are you giving? Why are you doing it? My group – 221 members from every state in the EU – pleads with you to think again."

Chirac's reply after all the group leaders had spoken finally included a few words on the test, saying that it would complete France's programme and allow it to sign the nuclear test ban treaty in the normal way. Then he invited the group leaders to lunch.

The tests in the Pacific continued to cause concern and in September Santer told Parliament the Commission had no power in this and that calls for boycotts were not in the spirit of Europe. Green made another strong speech to substantial applause throughout. Does "he really believe the resumption of nuclear testing to be in the spirit of Europe... my group believe that the President of France is doing more damage to European integration than anyone else in Europe today... It is going to take a long time before the world forgets the arrogance and colonialism behind this decision". There was a demonstration outside. Elisabeth Guigou for the French Socialists said they were totally opposed to the renewal of nuclear testing but not in favour of giving up France's nuclear deterrent. Collins, not normally anti-nuclear, spoke of the "overwhelming sense of outrage in this Parliament" and McNally on the threat to world peace and environment. Tory Tom Spencer attacked the Socialists for focusing on France and disregading China. A joint text from the Socialists, Greens and the left was carried and Hansch called the tests "ecologically and politically dangerous".

Labour and others continued to complain about the nuclear tests in October with Collins pointing out that part of Mururoa had sunk into the sea as a result of tests over twenty years. Collins reported on the Environment Committee's hearing on the French tests, where experts (one of whom was the famous French adventurer Jacques Cousteau) had told them the tests were not safe environmentally. In another resolution that month Socialists found part of their resolution voted down by the right who condemned China but not the French.

Biotech conscience time

A controversial proposal on patenting of biotechnological inventions was the subject of a huge amount of lobbying from all parts of the spectrum, some labelling it the "Frankenstein directive". One distasteful aspect highlighted in the press was the Harvard/Dupont "oncomouse" – a mouse with an ear grafted on to its back, roundly condemned in a resolution as far back as February 1993, when Parliament opposed the granting of the patent and called for the patent office to revoke it.

Labour was divided, being heavily lobbied by both sides of the argument and receiving mixed messages from home. The Greens were against and German Socialist rapporteur Rothley had a hard time with opposition in the Group from his fellow SPD member Evelyn Gebhardt. Originally rejected in 1994, after much amending and discussion it had emerged from the conciliation process but Members were still unhappy. The Socialists narrowly decided to vote against it on grounds that the building blocks of life should not be patentable and after a number of passionate speeches from Labour Members about animal welfare. The vote on 1 March 1995 was 188 – 240 and 23 abstentions. Labour apart from Adam voted against and the matter was sent back to the drawing board for the Council to find more compromises. It set up a biotechnology working group.

The Energy and Research Committee was dealing with growth, competitiveness and biotechnology in March 1996 and Green rapporteur Hiltrud Breyer had resigned, refusing to put her name to what had been agreed in committee. Adam took it over, saying that the regulatory regime in Europe was driving away investment to the US and Japan and supporting gene cell therapy.

A White Paper on biotechnology was debated in July 1997 with Bowe as rapporteur, dealing with GMOs and advocating the precautionary principle. There were over a hundred amendments and huge numbers of split roll call votes.

On the Rothley report the same month, Martin said it now balanced the need to protect inventions and be fair to patients' groups. White was still concerned about "designer children". Collins said we were making some progress and there were sensationalist claims. Most of the Socialists and Labour voted for the final amended text but a few voted against.

The patenting directive came back for second reading in May 1998 to face a huge banner from the Greens saying "no to biopiracy", their members wearing pirate uniforms. Oddy gave it broad support, saying it was a delicate balance between granting a patent and respect for animal welfare and dignity of the human. White repeated his demands for an ethical committee. An attempt to reject the common position was defeated by 78 – 432 – 24, then a bunch of amendments were all rejected one by one, with the EPLP voting every which way. Two-thirds voted for at least some attempts to make the text more acceptable. The common position was eventually approved after a suspension of the sitting, heavy lobbying outside the chamber and packed galleries from pharmaceutical firms. Hallam said it was a black day for Europe, that "we have given the go-ahead for large multinational companies to plunder and play fast and loose with the world's genetic resources". Martin said he was not convinced the common position had done enough to meet the concerns. Spiers said he could not support it because there was a serious danger of the poorest people in the world becoming further exploited.

There was more from Rothley on legal protection of inventions in February 1999, supported by Oddy. She said this proposal would allow researchers a year to publish before the need to file a patent.

EPLP matters

The IPPR published a paper by Donnelly, David and Ward in January 1995, on a single currency, arguing there should be a referendum on the issue as this would give "those broadly in favour of monetary union the chance to debate the issue free from the accusations of elitism, conspiracy and betrayal that are so often thrown around by those fundamentally opposed to Britain's membership of the EU".

A number of working lunch meetings with the UK shadow front bench were held in July 1995. In London on the 4th Blair told them the general election campaign would have Europe policy as a central theme and that Labour should be the party of constructive engagement with Europe. He stressed the importance of the ever-improving liaison between the EPLP and PLP in ensuring that European issues were fought with the party being sure of its ground. Hoon wrote an "engagement plan" for Blair on how to improve the relationship between the EPLP and Labour, particularly with a view to Labour in government. By the next decade there were "Hoon days" taking place in London with meetings with Ministers.

At the AGM on 12 July peace of sorts reigned with little major change. David was re-elected Leader, Crawley remained Deputy, Hardstaff continued as Chair and Tappin as Secretary, Oddy was Treasurer and Clive Needle became Whip. Alex Smith, rooted in the Campaign Group, had seen his role as Whip in terms of letting the Socialist Group know how many of the Labour Group they could count on for votes and he worked hard within that fairly limited perspective. He stood down and supported Needle.

The two regular monthly EPLP meetings were these days conducted much more tightly, with speaking restricted to three minutes per person. The Members' staff group was still meeting twice a year, this time in Birmingham in May and York in November, although there were gaps in attendance, notably by those who were MEPs' family. Computers were improving and e-mails began to be used which enormously helped communication between offices and particularly from Brussels to the UK.

Party conference in 1995 had before it "The future of the European Union", a document that was partly a result of the work of the IGC working group but written largely by Robin Cook, committing the party to reversing the social policy opt-out. It also took a more relaxed line on EMU than in the past.

MEPs collaborated on a book on Europe hoping to influence the debate in the run-up to a general election. Ford in his introduction to what was entitled *Changing States* (Ford *et al*, 1996) said: "A strong commitment to Europe does not involve abandoning British culture; nor does it involve renouncing national sovereignty." Donnelly wrote on the benefits of a single currency, Hendrick about employment and prosperity and the Delors approach, McNally on R&D and added value, McCarthy on Europe of the regions, building economic and social cohesion and recent reforms of the structural funds. Crawley wrote on women in Europe and her five years chairing the Women's Rights Committee from 1989-94, equalities and child care, Ford on racism, residents and refugees, Glenys Kinnock on combating poverty in the global village, Tongue on European media, cultural and audio-visual policy. Watts wrote on transport – safety, TENS, accessibility and need to shift from road to rail, Thomas on CAP and rural development policy, including animal transport. Pollack wrote on Europe and the environment, global warming, energy, cars and healthy cities, green accounting and people power. Whitehead turned his pen to protecting the citizen as consumer, Martin, on power to the people, democratic deficit, merging the pillars, enlargement and institutional reform. Titley wrote on developing the Brussels-Westminster axis, on effective inter-parliamentary co-operation, and links. Proceeds from the book went to One World.

Also in 1996 came another pamphlet from the Tribune Group of MEPs, "The Challenge for Labour in Europe". Articles in this were by David, Needle, Oddy, Howitt, McCarthy, Bowe, McNally, Thomas, Titley, Truscott and Spiers, covering a variety of areas. The EPLP produced a pamphlet, "Working in Europe" in the spring prior to the IGCs, setting out its positive approach to Europe. In spring, too, it put out an attractive "Europe Special" broadsheet entitled "Going Forward in Europe", featuring mostly Social Chapter and employment rights issues. In the summer it began to publish *Labour EuroNews* for circulation around the Labour movement. Normally eight pages, paid for out of Information money, these featured the numerous activities of this large group of Members. The first one majored on environment.

IGC rebellions

The Maastricht Treaty had specified there should be a further IGC in 1996 to examine extension of co-decision and whether to integrate the "pillars" of the common foreign and defence policy and justice and home affairs. A "Reflection Group", was set up after the Corfu European Council in June

1994, to prepare the way, composed of Foreign Ministers and two MEPs. The Socialist Group held a seminar on it in February 1995. Elisabeth Guigou, former French European Affairs Minister was the Socialist Group nominee, assisted in her work by Corbett, by then a Deputy General Secretary. The group met from June to December and then the MEPs continued working with the Council's IGC negotiating group. Corbett points out that the politicians were aware Labour would probably win the general election and that its views were substantially different from those of the Conservatives; they would ask him, on many points, "what would Labour do?" Many of these points were left open until after the general election in 1997. Labour at the same time had a working group of Blair, Brown, Cook, Prescott, Quin, Green, David, Crawley and Martin, also assisted by Corbett. The PES, too, had its own working party which later broadened its work to include enlargement.

Prescott replaced Cunningham as a Vice-President of the PES in March 1995. Labour conference that autumn endorsed an NEC statement "The Future of the European Union", drafted by the working group, outlining its position on the IGC. Many papers and pamphlets were being produced to contribute to the debate on EMU and on democratic reform of the European Community, not least from the new Centre for European Reform, which published "Reshaping Europe" in 1996.

Martin, a co-rapporteur on the IGC, expressed some reservations on the Reflection Group report in May that year, saying decision-making was too complex and there was a need to enshrine the rights of public services more fully. (This was only a month after Hendrick and Read were supporting liberalization of telecoms and cable TV being mooted in a Green Paper.) David for the EPLP expressed some caution, saying that Labour did not support abolition of the pillars. Both Labour and Conservative MEPs were split and John Palmer in *The Guardian* on 17 May wrote: "More than a dozen Labour MEPs backed by the Socialist Group and headed by Pauline Green intend to defy demands from party leadership in London to abstain on the restrictions to the national veto." Labour's official thrust was concerned with more democracy and transparency and not federalism. After a three-hour voting session on amendments in plenary Crampton and Balfe expressed themselves in broad agreement with the report, McCarthy, Tongue and Pollack abstained amongst others and made explanations of vote but were not happy. Tomlinson, Collins, Coates, Kerr and White voted in favour.

Palmer followed up the following day saying that more than a quarter of the sixty-two Labour MEPs had voted to weaken the veto, whilst most of the eighteen Conservatives had abstained. There was intense pressure from London not to support the resolution and McMahon remembers receiving a phone call to the effect that he must abstain. James Elles for the Conservatives said his Members were "split every way".

Did the MEPs go native? There is no doubt there was some heady enthusiasm for building Europe and making it more democratic. Members were firmly rooted in their constituencies and aware of opinion on the ground but sometimes missing was an appreciation of the extent of the daily battle front-benchers and governments faced with the Eurosceptic media. Lord Truscott (a one-term MEP) has voiced the view that MEPs should be limited to two terms to guard against going native, but many of this group were first-timers.

This pressure not to support what many felt was a reasonable extension of majority voting led to a mini-rebellion. A group, normally loyal (Tongue, Ford, Billingham, Kinnock, McCarthy, McMahon, Read, Pollack and Truscott) signed a private letter sent by Phillip Whitehead to Blair on 16 May 1995, copied to David but oddly not to Martin, saying that their loyalty to the party leadership was being threatened by the increasingly negative stance in the run up to the 1996 review of the Treaty.

The letter to Blair, which was not circulated to the EPLP, said:

> "...We are writing to you after the debate on the Martin/Bourlanges Report in the European Parliament. The EPLP decision was to abstain in the final vote, after what seems to us an inadequate process of consultation and discussion with the Party...
>
> All of us believe that most of the Martin/Bourlanges Report merits our support, along the lines of that campaign for a deeper and wider Europe which we undertook in 1994. To abstain on the final report and to vote against all of the recommendations of the PES Bureau makes us at best supine at worst accessories to a flawed report. What we fear now is that Labour seems to be simply responding to the essentially negative Tory view of the IGC rather than engage in a proper debate. We cannot compete in xenophobia with a desperate and discredited government. Nor should we. We cannot go through the whole IGC year keeping in step with their strategy of relentless negativism. It is a failure to argue our case and stand our ground that will damage our credibility, disowning the Martin/Bourlanges report is an unpropitious start. We do not want to become a sheepish and defensive faction in the Socialist Group, nervously arguing against reform because we dare not seem more positive than the Tories... We don't want to be an autonomous element in policy making on Europe, but we *are* an element in it and like every other element in the party we do not want to be seen as a rubber stamp for Walworth Road."

The letter was leaked by someone to Palmer of *The Guardian* who wrote it up on 20 May under the heading "Buck up on Europe, 'negative' Blair told": "it became clear yesterday that many who abstained did so only after considerable arm-twisting", quoting Pollack as saying:

> "Many of those who abstained felt very sick about what we had to do... we believe in a more effective and democratic EU and this involves limits on the national veto. This should be Labour's policy too."

Ford said:

> "I am worried that the Labour leadership is moving backwards on Europe. Even though we have a massive lead in the polls, some of the leadership such as Robin Cook and John Prescott seem scared to death of a pro-union Jack campaign by the Tories over the 1996 conference".

With hindsight it may seem that feelings had heightened rather more than necessary.

Blair brusquely replied to Whitehead, slapping down their point of view and making no concessions. Dated 25 May 1995, his letter said:

> "I do not accept the assertion that the party is 'simply responding to the

essentially negative Tory view' or that the position the party were asking the EPLP to accept was anti-European. Nor do I accept the assertion that the EPLP had not been engaged in the discussion leading up to the agreement on the position.

Representatives of the EPLP participate in the IGC working group, which I chair. The deliberations of this group have been reported back to the EPLP on several occasions, and the EPLP have adopted, by a large majority, the position as reported by Wayne David.

As to being anti-European, the reverse is the case. We have spelt out our positive stance in clear terms, including some extension of QMV, and an enhanced role for the European Parliament. We do not, however, support the merger of the two inter-governmental pillars into the treaty, nor the creation of a defence capability for the institutions of the Union, nor the abandonment of the unanimity principle implied in the Bourlanges/Martin report...

It will be of great importance that we try to stay together on European issues in the run up to the general election. The division in the Tory party on Europe is an important advantage to us as a party..."

The letter concluded with a hand-written PS:

"I have fought all my time in the Party for a pro-European perspective. I will continue to maintain it. But we must guard against Tory misrepresentation and lies and ensure we take people with us."

There were two days of debate in March 1996 and a two-and-a-half hour voting session on the final document. Labour MEPs were again advised by London to abstain in the final vote because of reservations on the foreign and home policy sections. A number of the EPLP voted in favour: Balfe, Billingham, Coates, Crampton, Green, Hughes, Morgan, Tomlinson, Tongue, White and Whitehead. Quite a few EPLP Members were absent for the final vote.

The Irish Presidency in the second half of 1996 put forward a draft of what was to become the Amsterdam Treaty. After Labour came to power in the UK in May 1997 there was a period of hectic diplomatic activity in the run-up to the Amsterdam Summit to finalise a text. The Labour government reversed the Conservative positions on extending QMV and co-decision, revising the co-decision powers to strengthen Parliament, joining the Social Chapter, the proposed employment chapter and integrating part of the third pillar into the first, all of which the Conservatives had opposed. It also dropped a Conservative proposal to give Council the right to overrule judgements of the Court of Justice.

Getting on with the job

Labour MEPs were everywhere, getting involved in the work undertaken by their committees, or taking up matters originating from their constituencies. During the course of the following year or so they were active on Rwanda, ship safety, opposing fascists, social policy, opposing big trucks, protection for time-share property buyers, fire safety in hotels, food additives, safety of Eastern European nuclear plants, accession, agriculture and fisheries, energy strategies and funding for renewables, economic policy, budget, development, pollution control, foreign policy, toxic waste, women, health and safety (Skinner and Hughes), raising concerns about proposals for a Severn barrage, animal welfare, warning labels on alcohol for pregnant women (Miller) and setting up a Ceramic Intergroup (Tappin). There were a few jibes about the poor attendance of Sir James Goldsmith, whose group was not thriving but now he had turned to the home front and founded an anti-EU Referendum Party in November 1995. They continued to table hundreds of probing questions. In this Parliament there was almost never an "urgency" (i.e. foreign affairs and human rights) debate in which Newens did not take part. Many were still taking language lessons, some doing German with Ukrainian feminist Lena Seel. Harrison produced a booklet "Supporting Small Businesses".

Throughout their term most Labour MEPs helped students wherever they could as part of their contribution to the future. There were requests for work experience from sixth formers, interviews from university students, stagiaireships for anything from a month to six months and of course much visiting of educational establishments at home. Many students who benefited in this way later turned up working in European institutions, NGOs, journalism, lobbying companies or other influential organizations.

Watts found that not only did the Labour Transport Committee Members hold meetings before Socialist pre-meetings, they also wanted to approve any press release of a Member prior to it going out. As they only met once a month he did not find this a practical demand and found himself in trouble with some of the old guard on occasion.

A huge petition against tobacco advertising was presented to Parliament, supported by President Hansch. The second reading of the directive on restricting advertising was held in May 1998 where the common position was approved unamended against the votes of most Germans. The battle against tobacco subsidies (still part of so-called "compulsory expenditure") continued as part of the budget debate and the Europe Against Cancer programme, Pollack saying "it is morally ridiculous for us to be trying to persuade people... to give up smoking, while at the same time... voting for so-called compulsory expenditure on vast monies for tobacco subsidies". This was contentious to the end. In March 1999 Whitehead spoke against subsidies for leaf tobacco followed by Hardstaff complaining that the EU spent over one billion growing a product which killed and maimed its consumers. Public health had come within the remit of the EU since a Council of Ministers resolution on 2 June 1994. Needle had joined Read on the Health Intergroup working on smoking as a health hazard. Kerr was its Vice-Chair and led the campaign to ban smoking in the Parliament.

Eddy Newman produced a political report on human rights in the EU in May 1995 saying the EU should accede to the European Convention on Human Rights. It said that long-standing residents should have voting rights, that there were twenty million unemployed and fifty-three million in poverty, that Britain should sign the Social Chapter, that disabled people should have the same rights as those able-bodied and that people should have rights to housing and to work. The right hated it and shot it down with an unholy alliance of the EPP abstaining and Liberals and Forza Italia voting against, which a furious Green said was a mockery. Newman made a more balanced response, but said they should be ashamed of themselves. On this the Socialists were all with Newman.

Simpson yet again made a spirited intervention on postal services. He and Newman defended a universal public postal service again in May 1996. When the proposal came back for a second reading in September 1997, they thought it had substantially improved, but there was more to come. In Spring 1999 he accused Bangemann of continuing to pursue liberalization plans that had been rejected by Parliament, threatening legal action and saying the Commission had overstepped the mark. Postal services were still being argued about in 2008 in Europe and in 2009 in Britain where the Labour government's change of mind on part-privatization caused the unions and many in the party dismay.

Tomlinson concentrated more on Budget Control where he delighted in highlighting particularly idiotic decisions and exposing fraud; and Wynn became general budget rapporteur where a rather more emollient line was called for. They struggled valiantly with cost overruns, not least for more buildings both in Brussels and Strasbourg. There were protests from Labour when the UK, Germany and France blocked thirty million ECU for the Thermie programme in April 1995, endangering the future of regional energy saving centres across Europe. The committee held a hearing on the cost of enlargement in May 1996. EPLP Members took control of the budget opinions in five important committees: Titley in Foreign Affairs, Adam in Energy and Research, McMahon in Social Affairs and Employment, Crampton in Regional Affairs, Bowe in Environment and Kinnock in Development. Part of Wynn's work was demanding a public register of declarations of interest by Members in October, supported by Ford saying those with a direct financial interest should declare it before a vote. Ford, meanwhile, was attempting to set up a system of registration for lobbyists. Labour supported changes in the expenses system. As a result of a Hansch reform assistants were paid more or less directly from December 1995 (with some loopholes) and in 1996 Members were required to supply boarding passes or other forms of proof of travel. It was a start but nowhere near enough.

Collins, White and Pollack rattled the cage when the Commission prevaricated on producing a long-awaited directive on zoos, originally championed by Tory Sir James Scott-Hopkins who had since died. The Commission saw it as a subsidiarity issue, but the Brits wanted something on the statute book because research had shown many countries had inadequate welfare standards. A directive had been demanded by Parliament in 1993. In March 1995 Pollack said she had then accused the Commission of having "a strange illness starting with cold feet and working up to jelly knees, called the subsidiarity bug", and called on the Commission for action now, and not the wishy-washy recommendation that they had produced. It didn't work.

A trading agreement with post-apartheid South Africa was being slowly and painfully negotiated and the Commission appeared to be being controlled by protectionist elements from the southern Member States. Glenys Kinnock, along with White, Spiers, McGowan and others spent many months pursuing more equitable terms and pushing for the allocated amounts of development aid to be spent in that country instead of being subject to delays.

In October 1995 football and single market rules became again a matter of public concern. In the case of Jean Marc Bosman, the European Court of

Justice ruled that UEFA's system of cross-border transfer could not be maintained under Single Market rules. UK clubs then had a rule of no more than three foreign players. Bosman had early on sought the assistance of Billingham in her constituency, saying he was being held against his will by his club. She found that the Conservative Sports Minister did not want to get involved. The perceived problem with the Court judgement was a danger that clubs would get into the state they are now, with top clubs having very few indigenous players. In January 1996 Murphy was demanding a statement and trying to ensure that the judgement only referred to end of contact transfers between Member States, and not within them. After a long struggle a directive was agreed that in general, Billingham says "only hurts those trying to take unfair advantage", although they would have liked to have had something built in that might modify the free-market effects. A Sports Intergroup was set up in which this team played an active role. Wynn and Simpson also had a Rugby League Intergroup on the go so there was plenty of discussion about sport.

Hindley for the REX Committee produced an opinion on Asia and GATT in June which was the first use of the Gomes procedure – where the lead committee was committed to include the report of opinion-giving committees without substantial changes. (For more on this procedure see Corbett *et al*, 2007.)

Not wishing to be stuck on bikes, Barton was also working on a directive on lifts, pushing with Howitt for better provision on access for people with disabilities. In June he reported that following a hearing with lift manufacturers and representatives of disabled groups, co-decision procedures had produced an agreement. Other members of the trades union intergroup were also involved, including Miller. In May 1997 he was also working on pressure equipment, with some cross-party agreement attempting to modify a Commission proposal that could have been problematic for British domestic boilers.

On fur and leghold traps the Commission pushed the deadline for a ban back a year, just three weeks before it was to come into force. In December 1995 Collins said that "people have been conspiring to ensure that the will of this Parliament, expressed in 1991, is not implemented." Again in June 1996, the Commission wanted to wait until an international committee in Geneva had developed a humane trap. Pollack lambasted the decision saying there was no such thing as a humane trap and no case for this pathetic new proposal: "anyone with a grain of backbone would have been able to face up to the Canadian threat to go to GATT". In February 1997 the Commission and Dutch Presidency sought to exclude Russia and Canada from the ban, fearing a trade war, causing Collins to declare: "The Commission cannot allow principle to be subsumed in a desire to placate trading partners", adding that it had stirred up a hornet's nest. Again Pollack enjoyed a rant:

> "the Commission has manoeuvred itself into an utterly indefensible position... defied Parliament and also Council ... truly breathtaking. In the interest of unfettered free trade the Commission seriously expects the EU to lie down and effectively chew off its own leg just as 600,000 fur-bearing animals caught in these barbaric legholds do every year in Canada so that fashionable women in Europe can wear fur coats and the fur trade and Canadian government can continue to make millions of dollars".

Together with the Eurogroup for Animal Welfare she organized an exhibition on the iniquities of the leghold trap themed "furry animals are not a soft option" and brought out Barbara Castle to add some spice to the event, who also addressed the EPLP. The Commission put forward draft agreements in December 1997 between the EU and Canada and the EU and Russia. Parliament did not have much power to change them, but Pollack leapt into the fray once more saying it was a non-agreement, fundamentally flawed, permitting the use of trapping underwater leading to slow death by drowning of the animal, that it was unworkable and would perpetuate the use of the leghold trap. She said: "I would liken it to the Cheshire Cat because all you can see is its smile... has enough loopholes for a pack of wolves to run through." In 1997, according to Wall, it was stonewalled by officials who shifted it off the Environment Council agenda and put it onto that of the General Council, composed of Foreign Ministers. In other words political diplomacy won out over principles.

Newens, Truscott and McGowan shared a rare moment of agreement in January 1996 on EU-Cuba relations, speaking against sanctions and saying that actions must avoid destabilization of the regime. It was the time of the Helms-Burton Act in the USA and Newens was rapporteur. On the common foreign and security policy (CFSP) Newens was rapporteur in July that year, Titley speaking against him.

Simpson and Pollack were involved in conciliation on Trans European Networks (TENS) with Commissioner Kinnock in the summer of 1996. After a string of late nights and with help from an Italian Socialist Minister, agreement was finally reached to include more rail and better environmental assessment in the plans. Whilst they were seeking to curb road development, Billingham now praises the regenerative properties of the A14 in Britain that was one of the TENS spinoffs. Also on transport, Seal was rapporteur on a directive on ground handling at airports in July that year. He was unhappy with the proposals and unsuccessfully attempted, with Socialist support, to have the common position rejected.

Tony Cunningham called for a ban on manufacturing, distribution and stockpiling of land mines and parts, and for resources for mine clearing in June 1997. He kept up this campaign for most of his term in Parliament as part of his work on the Development Committee. He argued for cutting sporting links with Nigeria on the occasion of that country's execution of environmentalists. Later he was responsible for the Development Committee budget and won a small increase for saving tropical rainforests. On the Development Committee Glenys Kinnock and McGowan did not always agree.

Constituency interests played a large part in MEPs' work and sometimes bemused their continental colleagues, who operated on list systems with less local accountability. Billingham took up the cudgels on behalf of the Nottinghamshire boot and shoe industry where twenty thousand jobs were lost in a decade, pressing the Trade Commissioner, Sir Leon Brittan, for fairer import quotas. The industry shifted into the quality or niche markets with the aid of some Objective 2 funding, later epitomised in the film *Kinky Boots*. She also relentlessly pursued the problem of protectionist discrimination against ski instructors in the French Alps, where qualifying tests for non-French instructors were of the level of Olympic downhill slaloms. Over a period of years, working with Commissioner Mario Monti, eventually there was improvement.

There were many other events where Members found opportunities to pursue their interests. Kerr, Vice-President of the Tibet Intergroup, led a delegation to meet the Dalai Lama in Dharamsala. Tessa Jowell, then Shadow Women's Minister, visited in January 1996, giving Sue Waddington an opportunity to showcase her work on child poverty, domestic violence, equal pay and parental leave. She wanted children's rights included in the IGC. Ford lobbied the Commission for regeneration funds after the Manchester city centre was bombed by the IRA. McMahon battled for years for equal pay for foreign lecturers at Italian universities. It started as a constituent's problem (one David Petrie) and became a struggle against injustice. Miller became involved with a campaign to ban silicone breast implants as dangerous. It began with case work, turned into a petition and carried on into the next Parliament.

In South West London the proposal to build a fifth terminal at London Heathrow Airport had a planning appeal that took several years to complete its work. Local authorities supported HACAN, a campaign against the plans and Pollack took on an economist, Gavin Rees, for six months in 1995 to make a full investigation and come up with a reasoned critical opinion for submission to the inquiry at which she also gave evidence in person. Apart from the environmental concerns on pollution, her constituents suffered from aircraft noise. She was restrained from running a full-scale campaign in opposition once she learned that the Leader was in favour.

Hardstaff, Hallam, Thomas, Wilson and Needle threw themselves into agriculture policy because their marginal constituencies were largely rural. They were often the Friday stalwarts as their reports, often on quite technical matters, tended to come up regularly at the end of the week. Hallam always made much of the Members (particularly French) who voted against abolishing Fridays but who then absented themselves, leaving it difficult to find quorums for voting at the end of the week. Hardstaff, with Grimsby in her patch, also worked on fisheries, as did Crampton from Hull. Thomas was the EPLP's spokesperson on Agriculture and Rural Development. When the Temporary Committee of Inquiry on BSE was set up in July 1996, he was a member.

On EMAC Donnelly, Hendrick, Billingham, Murphy and Harrison involved themselves in the details of plans for the forthcoming single currency. Since in the summer of 1996 in Bonn Tony Blair had said he wanted Britain to participate fully in shaping and progress towards EMU, it was at that stage believed that if a Labour government were to be elected it would agree that the UK would join the single currency. They raised problems affecting SMEs, supported tourism and democratizing the system of reporting by the planned European Central Bank.

Hugh Kerr was President of the Friends of Music Intergroup, working with Nana Mouskouri in the Culture Committee and on the copyright directive. He was also active on the Women's Rights and Equalities Committee. He did a substantial piece of work over three years as rapporteur, consulting widely, on a revision of the 1977 acquired rights directive which he says was described by Rodney Bickerstaffe of NUPE as "the most important directive in social Europe". With privatization of public services, ensuring that workers could take their "acquired rights" of pay, holidays and benefits with them to a new employer was important to the trades union movement. At the first reading of this in December 1996 Kerr paid tribute to the work of Hughes, Waddington, Oddy and the committee staff. It became a priority of the Labour Presidency to get this through and it was agreed and published by July 1998; in June, however, Kerr accused the British Presidency of watering it down in the Council, not least due to the Minister removing pension provision. He says it was the opinion of the Parliament's legal department that the Council revision was so major that Parliament should take Council to the ECJ but nothing came of it.

While Chair of the Australia and New Zealand delegation Kerr had been criticized in the Australian Parliament for supporting Aboriginal rights on one of the visits, saying that he received "widespread support in Australia" for doing so and that "according to the ABC [Australian Broadcasting Corporation] he was the most effective chair of the delegation in its history". Rocking the boat in that way was not Parliament's idea of how an inter-parliamentary delegation should behave.

Collins continued terrorizing any Commission officials who were less than forthcoming and was assisted by the immensely committed Clare Wells, with Birgitte Nouaille-Degorce and later Henrik Hansen and British Rosemary Opacik on the secretariat. The Brits worked well with their Socialist Co-ordinator, Dagmar Roth-Behrendt and Austrian Wolfgang Hiller from the Socialist Group, but sometimes found other colleagues a bit hard to take. The Swedes tended to be smug about their own high environmental standards and intolerant of difficulties faced by others. At the other end of the spectrum, some of the Spanish could be obstructive. The Greens were utopian. In dealing with industry, Members found business organizations were always pessimistic about meeting higher standards and inflated the costs of meeting strict directives. Bowe found the landfill directive inadequate, having been watered down too much by Council and its legal base changed. He led Parliament's rejection on 22 May 1996. In the same week he was also rapporteur on two other heavy subjects – dealing with chemicals PCB/PCT and on pollution prevention and control, the latter having spent six years in Council. Pollack won the Green Ribbon Award for best environmental MEP of the year in May and again in January 1999. She continued with energy saving and air pollution reports, temporarily aided by a bright young stagiaire, Julia Stuart-David, who later went on to work in the Foreign Office. The European Commission had set up an Auto-Oil working group (consulting with industry and health experts but not at that stage, environmentalists) that was preparing the way for a raft of air pollution directives.

A vote in Parliament in July deleted the second October 1997 week in the Strasbourg programme, by just one vote, with Labour's support. There was much ribbing of Goldsmith (as a Member for France), who had not been present. This was later contested by France and taken to the ECJ which eventually ruled against the decision. A second October session had to be reinstated in October 1998.

Richard Howitt, then Foreign Affairs Link person, got into hot water after a visit to Colombia. He had uncovered evidence of serious human rights abuses by BP, was righteously enraged and put down an urgency resolution in Parliament. The Colombian Embassy, when it got wind of the text, complained to the British government, and he says BP tried to suppress the resolution. Concern was expressed by the Leader's Office at No 10 and this was conveyed to Howitt by the Leader of the EPLP. Nevertheless, Howit persisted. Whilst not wishing to be seen as anti-corporate, he stood firm, supported by a fellow Socialist MEP Dutch human rights campaigner Martje Van Putten, and in the debate in October 1996 he spoke out on military human rights violations and the implication of BP and says that as a result BP changed their practices.

Ken Stewart, Liverpool stalwart of the Transport Committee, who argued endlessly for Objective One status for his city, died on 2 September 1996. He was seventy-one and had struggled with diabetes for years. His colleagues paid tribute to his work on safety at sea. His friends say that in contrast to the dour image he presented to many and although decidedly "un PC", he was kindly, funny, a generous tipper and dedicated to his constituency. A by-election was held on 12 December 1996, with turnout at 11.3%. Richard Corbett from the Socialist Group secretariat romped home as Labour's candidate with 53.8% of the vote and was now able to pursue for himself his passion for constitutional matters. His maiden speech on 29 January 1997 was on the future development of the EU. (Corbett lost his seat at the 2009 elections to a BNP candidate.)

David Hallam ran a prayer group on Wednesday mornings during Strasbourg weeks at which Wynn was an active participant. Prayer breakfasts had been taking place since the beginning in 1979 with cross-party attendance. Unnoticed by the atheists amongst the Group, there were some interesting things going on. Reverend Ian Paisley refused to join these prayer meetings, so Hallam made a point of meeting him later in the day. Hallam, who is a Methodist local preacher is evangelical about his religion and says that Paisley would give him useful tips for sermons, and feels it was a useful discussion forum. He was open about his meetings with Paisley, then seen as a risky friendship, and made sure McCarthy, the Northern Ireland link person was aware of them. The issues covered in the discussions with Paisley, however, remained confidential between the two of them.

Throughout his term Hallam complained that there was no TV coverage on Fridays, which tended to be when he made most of his speeches on agriculture. Press people from the Socialist Group always put a damper on the idea, because they would show the chamber at least three-quarters empty.

Tom Megahy pursued his efforts for European recognition of disabilities when he was rapporteur in December 1996 agitating for an EU-wide parking card for disabled people. Howitt supported his demands for reciprocal recognition of disabled badges which was agreed in 1998. By this time many in the EPLP were campaigning for disability discrimination legislation.

Hughes gets procedure

Towards the end of the previous parliament it was becoming evident that with the growing powers, co-operation between committees with a shared responsibility must be improved. Earlier Hughes had been rapporteur on a Social Action Programme and in working on that, aided by his excellent Socialist Group staffer Ana Colombo and dedicated committee people Nick Lane, Silvio Gonzata and Alex Kleinig, they realized that a hard-worked Opinion voted through one committee could be ignored by the main one. To combat this they set a precedent by having a working group of people from the committee and co-rapporteurs from other committees, with the Commission cabinet, thrash out areas of disagreement in advance. The aim was to maximise the job creating potential of the ESF fund. It was the first use of the "Hughes procedure" before it was officially so-named. A similar exercise also was used prior to the reform of the structural funds in 1993.

Several formalized "procedures" were developed to improve matters, this one at the impetus of Hughes in the Conference of Committee Presidents. It suggested that a timetable must be jointly agreed by both committees and there must be an attempt to agree on texts. (Much more on the Hughes, Gomes and Enhanced Hughes Procedures can be found in *The European Parliament* (Corbett, 2007).)

Anti-racism continues

As a result of Ford's relentless pressure over many years and his report from the previous parliament, the Council of Ministers (the impetus coming from Francois Mitterrand and Helmut Kohl) set up a consultative committee during the German Presidency in the latter half of 1994. Ford was the full parliamentary representative on it. His proposed text on the formal Declaration was carried the next year and included a proposal to designate 1997 as European Year Against Racism.

The annual debate on racism in October 1995 saw Ford pointing out that to date only two of the 77 recommendations from the 1989 Committee of Inquiry had been implemented, and putting the case for an anti-racism article in the forthcoming Treaty. In July 1996 the Council adopted a resolution on objectives for that year. At the beginning of 1997 Commissioner Padraig Flynn invited the Presidents of Parliament, Council and Commission to sign a Declaration of Intent saying that racism, xenophobia and anti-semitism still existed and contravened fundamental human rights. In a further parliamentary debate in February 1997, Ford complained that the British government was still vetoing the Observatory on Racism and Xenophobia. He and Tappin debated budgets for this in April. Finally agreement for setting up this Monitoring Centre came as part of the anti-discrimination wording in the Amsterdam Treaty.

One of the manifestations of racist Europe was that legal non-white residents of Britain were often stopped at borders when part of groups of visitors to the European institutions. Sometimes visits had to be cancelled because some of the group, often schoolchildren, could not get visas. At other times the groups were harassed at border crossings. EPLP Members raised these instances repeatedly in Parliament and wrote to governments but there was little improvement.

The Year Against Racism was very successful with hot competition for project funding and a football tournament against racism. Ford had led all the way, never succumbing to complacency, pointing out the persistence of racist attacks and far-right politics. He continued as President of the European Parliament's branch of the Inter-parliamentary Council against Anti-Semitism until he lost his seat at the 2009 elections.

Broadcasting and audio-visual

Whitehead and Tongue defended public service broadcasting, consumer choice and competitive audiovisual policy. They spoke out against an oligopoly of media owners with the capacity to overwhelm the market, undermine competition and diminish freedom of choice and diversity. The TV Without Frontiers directive had been adopted in 1989 to increase the circulation of European TV and film programming, saying all channels should carry 51% of home grown programming outside of news, current affairs and sport. However, the British Conservative government with encouragement from the Americans inserted a clause modifying this provision to "wherever practicable", with devastating effect on terrestrial TV, particularly children's programmes. In 1995 a new version was put forward proposing to delete these words. Tongue and others on the left argued that new channels should invest at least 5% of turnover in indigenous production. A colossal Hollywood lobby, fearful of selling fewer "B movies" and series in Europe won enough support to see this defeated. UK cable and satellite channels are still not asked by government to contribute to home-grown programming, leaving ITV to compete with Disney, Nickelodeon and Warners children's TV channels which have deep pockets and vast catalogues. Tongue's Italian friend Luciana Castellina was Chair of the Culture Committee, with Doriano Dragoni on the staff and Tongue was Socialist co-ordinator (spokesperson). There was another angle too, in that the Swedes wanted to outlaw children's advertising, which was never going to win a majority at the time.

Tongue worked with Gregory Paulger and Jean Michel Baer at the Commission and formed a consortium of representatives from the UK audio visual industry (mostly the unions) meeting regularly from 1994-99. Her media advisor was a renowned independent film director, Midge Mackenzie. In order to counter lobbying from America and UK scepticism, she held a high-profile press conference in February 1996 around the time of the first reading, stuffed with actors and producers and supported by actor Bob Hoskyns. Michael Grade of Channel 4, launching *The Madness of King George* in Brussels, supported Tongue's position.

In May that year Tongue argued for an amendment to the TVWF directive giving the right of all Member States to have a list of sporting and other major events that must be broadcast free to air. She argued that media moguls (such as Leo Kirch, Silvio Berlusconi and Rupert Murdoch) should not be able to deny citizens free access to the World Cup and other major events by buying the rights and airing them solely on Pay TV. Murphy spoke on SOS – Save our Sport. On this matter all political groups were united and given Parliament's co-decision powers, meetings with Ministers succeeded in inserting this provision into the final directive.

When it came to the second reading of the TVWF directive on 22 September 1996, former French Culture Minister Jack Lang supported her in Parliament but there were only 292 votes in favour, 22 fewer than the required majority to remove the legal loophole of "wherever practicable". The results are seen today in little or no broadcast or investment by cable and satellite channels in home grown drama, film or children's programmes.

The Commission's Competition Directorate was pushed continually by commercial broadcasters to rule against public service broadcasting (PSB) on the grounds of creating a level playing field for commercial competitors. Tongue produced an "own initiative" report on the future of public service broadcasting in the digital age, adopted in September 1996. It won the support of the Irish Presidency and their Culture Minister and poet, Michael D.

Higgins. The Irish handed the baton to the Dutch Presidency, whose Hague PSB conference was addressed by Tongue arguing for a separate article or protocol in the new Amsterdam Treaty defending PSB as central to democracy. As soon as the Labour government was elected Tongue turned her attention to getting support for this amendment and tackled the new Europe Minister, Doug Henderson, in an airport lounge on his first visit to Brussels. She sought to give him courage to resist heavy commercial lobbying against the idea and persuaded him that Labour must support it. She is proud that a text in defence of public service broadcasting was signed into the 1997 Amsterdam Treaty as a Protocol.

Tongue held a fringe meeting at Labour conference in Brighton that year with UK Culture Minister Chris Smith, Italian Deputy Prime Minister Walter Veltroni and Jack Lang. On some parts of audio-visual policy the messages coming from the Department of Trade and Industry and the Department of Culture, Media and Sport were not always in tune and this was also reflected in the EPLP with occasional clashes between Tongue, Read, Donnelly and Billingham. During the UK Presidency Tongue produced many briefings for Ministers hoping to inspire them to be pro-active on a number of fronts where little had happened under previous Conservative governments. It has been suggested that her vociferous opposition to Murdoch and determination that BSkyB should invest in British film production and broadcast was a factor in her unfavourable position on the list of candidates for the 1999 election.

Whitehead was rapporteur in October 1997 on an Audiovisual Green Paper, saying we needed a proper legal framework on freedom of speech. His main angle was consumer protection and he complained that there were two separate responsible directorates in the Commission. He pursued the case for rationalization, which led to the setting up of the Consumer Directorate, then known as DG XXIV.

Car safety and auto oil

After John Smith died, his assistant David Ward came to work for Donnelly for a time, concentrating on the car industry. The Commission produced a strategy on the industry and Donnelly began to work on car safety, calling for a high level panel of car manufacturers' chief executives. Labour called for bull bars to be banned and for proper fitting of child seats. A number of highly technical proposals were put forward and first debated in July 1995 on crash standards dealing with front and side impact safety. The pair of them worked hard on Commissioner Bangemann to accept higher crash standards than the car industry wanted after the visit of a Formula One driver, Gerhard Berger, to Parliament for a hearing. Donnelly in debate in September 1996 said the crash safety proposals could prevent nine thousand deaths and serious injuries a year in the UK alone. The resultant crash legislation probably saved thousands of lives and credit goes to the proactive work of Labour Members. Murphy and others repeatedly called for seat belts on coaches after a series of crashes, some involving children. Billingham raised the problem that airbags could crush babies in special seats that faced the in wrong direction, pushing for warning labels.

After a time Ward set up his own company one of whose clients was the

International Automobile Association. Donnelly and Ward created an Auto Users Group. There was a bit of an internal culture divide on this, since the Environment Committee members were pushing for reduced car use and were uneasy with the enthusiastic car lobby.

In an attempt to improve both the environment and public health the Commission launched the first Auto Oil programme in 1996. Industry and the Commission had been involved in lengthy working groups on the subject and the oil companies and car manufacturers tended to play each other off. Following a common position in October 1997 Parliament reinstated more demands in February 1988 in the face of aggressive lobbying from the oil industry umbrella organization EUROPIA concerned about costs. Trialogues were a product of the Amsterdam Treaty changes but Collins was critical of the make-up of the committee, saying if you put fifteen people on each side then the only thing you can realistically do is play rugby. At one point, with several different Commission directorates putting forward different views, Collins had told them to leave and come back when they could agree amongst themselves. After four conciliation meetings during the British Presidency and three trialogues, Parliament emerged the winner.

Before the first programme was approved the Commission presented its work schedule for Auto Oil II in January 1997. This time environment NGOs were also included in the consultation. (A full discussion of the Auto Oil programme can be found in Wurtzel, 2002.)

BSE ban

The beef crisis in British agriculture had been around for years. Parliament raised a resolution in February 1995 critical of British beef where Thomas asserted that there had been no BSE in cattle in UK born after 1 January 1992 and that there was not a scrap of evidence to support the motion. The vote was postponed. Scientists in Britain could not rule out a link between BSE and the human variant CJD and in March 1996 the government announced a slaughter of all cows aged over thirty months. Parliament's resolution considered a "total ban on the production and use of meat meal or by-products of slaughter in animal feed to be essential", and called for monitoring of the action plan to eradicate BSE to apply not only to the UK but to all Member States.

The government had inadequately informed the Commission of the situation and at this point the export ban was put into place by Commissioner Franz Fischler. Collins pointed out that it was a European matter of public health, requiring more research to restore consumer confidence and the EU should re-examine intensive agriculture production methods. Ford supported the notion of compensation for victims. The Commission statement with a constrained debate took place in April. David asked why it was taking so long for Britain to submit proposals which would allow the ban to be lifted and Collins pressed for a Committee of Inquiry, asking whether there had been discussions with Health Ministers on the transmissibility of BSE to humans. Morgan called for labelling for animal feed and Morris highlighted with concern that the protein bonemeal was also used in horticulture.

By May the British government was proposing to disrupt the entire work of the EU because of the export ban. Its policy of non-cooperation hung over the Florence Summit. Green said that if the British government disrupted the Council it would be an act of folly and stupidity. It did so.

At an extraordinary Council on 3-4 June 1996 the UK Agriculture Minister produced a comprehensive plan as a result of which Fischler for the Commission lifted the ban on derivatives, welcomed by Plumb. David observed that it was absurd that the government was damaging everyone's interest by indiscriminate blocking measures. Collins attacked Plumb for omitting to tell us how the mess was caused in the first place. Thomas wanted an aid package extended to more than farmers (such as those in the processing industries hit by the export ban). Hallam complained of an hysterical attack on British beef on German TV. At the Florence Council at the end of June over a hundred pieces of legislation were vetoed by the British including the multi-million Thermie and SAVE programmes and funding for Trans European Networks. On 18 July Parliament agreed to set up a Temporary Committee of Inquiry into BSE.

Collins organized an Environment Committee hearing jointly with the Agriculture Committee on 24-25 June, being keen to highlight the health risks but also to make the authorities aware that it might not simply be a British problem. It was held in the largest committee room of Parliament which was packed to the rafters.

The government ended its cull of cattle in September but Collins and Green continued to say that BSE was a major European concern and that there was a threat to humans. A report from the Agriculture Committee outlined steps needed for a system of identifying the origin and quality of BSE-free beef. In September there was a censure motion in the House of Commons where the Conservatives scraped home, said David, "by the skin of their teeth".

The Committee of Inquiry reported on 19 February 1997 and was critical of the UK government. Green blamed the crisis on the British government and complained of the refusal of Agriculture Minister Douglas Hogg to come to the committee. Labour made much of this refusal. Hogg insisted it would be an abnegation of his authority to the European Parliament and in the House of Commons Major was said to have referred to it as "a load of tosh". This added heat to the anti-British atmosphere. In contrast, Lord Plumb said it was "political folly". Following the debate on the report the Conservatives voted against it and a Belgian Member of the Agriculture Committee, Jose Happart, and seventy-one other Members tabled a motion of censure against the Santer Commission. This was rejected by plenary (188 – 326) including the majority of Socialists. Green said that although there was a litany of shambolic decision-making throughout she would not support a censure motion.

As a result of the report a follow-up committee was set up on 23 April to monitor the action taken on its recommendations. Whitehead was particularly effective on this committee, which reported on 18 November. One of the first pro-European acts of the new Labour government was for the Agriculture Minister, Jack Cunningham, to come to Brussels and address the committee where he was warmly greeted for his positive and informed attitude. He attended six times in six months. Socialist Roth-Behrendt was Chair, and another German, Reimer Boge, was rapporteur. At home Prescott led a "task force" with which Thomas worked closely, attending meetings attempting to influence Commissioner Fischler and others. Whitehead in a final debate in November 1997, following a visit of the Committee to the UK, said the Commission had made advances which would make a vote of censure by Parliament inappropriate and that the UK was not setting an example in health and safety standards.

Strenuous efforts were made by some Labour Members to have the export ban lifted, but it was not until November 1998 that this happened, with the government claiming credit for bringing the outbreak under control. By this time, Whitehead said, thirty-eight people had died of CJD. The report of this second Committee of Inquiry came to plenary in April 1999 where Whitehead underlined the need to follow the precautionary principle. Then there was another outbreak in February 2001 with the horror of burning pyres of slaughtered livestock.

One prominent SPD Member, Gerhard Schmid, ventured an aside that Pauline Green could never catch CJD because first one had to have a nervous system.

The internals

With a group as large as sixty-two it was inevitable there would be disagreements; in fact the group, bedevilled by factionalism, was split almost neatly in half with thirty-two at times close to loathing the other thirty. It was no longer about being pro or anti EEC, but often about personalities. There was a bit of class tension too. One assistant referred to "the blatant sexism and general uselessness of those old, Northern gits who opposed Europe while taking its money". Ian White, believing in the idea of a European socialist party, took the principled position that the EPLP should not have separate meetings or a separate whip from the Socialist Group and ceased to attend EPLP meetings. He later said he felt that may have gone against him in the Stoke Rochford interviews, for selection of candidates in 1999, since he was unprepared for some of the questions such as the Five Pledges.

Following its European conference in Birmingham in February the EPLP held another high-profile Europe event in Brussels on 5 March 1996, again aimed at business with a range of workshops fronted by MEPs, all designed to widen support for election of a Labour government via the work of its representatives in Europe.

The annual meeting in 1996 again registered no large appetite for change. David remained Leader, Crawley as Deputy, Tappin as Secretary. Barton won the post of Chair from Hardstaff, Oddy remained Treasurer and Murphy took the post of Whip as Needle wanted to focus more on health policy which was growing in importance. Overall political balance remained much the same.

Labour's habit of producing separate whips had proliferated as a general election approached and European policy-making became extremely sensitive on the home front. It did not endear the EPLP to their colleagues in the Socialist Group who were annoyed at Labour Members being handed a whip on entry to voting sessions, when the official Socialist whip was on their desks. The group was, however, generally careful to announce any differences of voting intention during Socialist Group meetings and the EPLP Whip or a staffer would be in touch with the Socialist Whip.

At the party conference in 1996 efforts were made to exert more discipline within the party in the run-up to an election. Following heckling of Blair at fringe meetings by Kerr, David as Leader became fed up with the latter's tactics and gave *Guardian* journalist Stephen Bates a full-scale negative briefing. It was written up on 18 December with a front page photo of Kerr under the heading: "The MEP: I only offered Tony some advice. The Party: You're out, comrade." The piece stated:

> "...Kerr, unreconstructed Old Labour MEP... is being threatened with deselection after regular public criticism of the party leadership. If he loses his nomination for the marginal seat at the European elections in two years' time, he will be the first elected member to be deselected under Labour's new disciplinary code. Wayne David... said Mr Kerr had brought the party into disrepute by heckling at meetings and badgering Mr Blair as he attended a reception organised by the privatised gas companies..."

David said: "From now on people who do step out of line will be dealt with." It was a portent of things to come.

The women in this intake added to the feminist influence which was sometimes too much for the more traditional men in some of whose souls lurked a hard core of misogyny. Some had useful contact with Joni Lovenduski, a UK academic, who acted as a consultant on gender politics for the Commission during 1996-97. This was a confident and able intake of women though small. They were mostly mature professionals and all university educated. Five out of the seven had teaching backgrounds. Half had far more Conservative than Labour MPs in their constituencies and put much effort into helping win marginal parliamentary seats.

Angela Billingham had been an Oxfordshire County Councillor, a former professional tennis player and was a force to be reckoned with on economic matters. She shared a flat with McCarthy. Veronica Hardstaff had a Sheffield Council background and with her languages built up strong links with members of other delegations. She was one of twenty MEPs to attend an all-European conference in Vienna on enlargement because she spoke all the working languages. She concentrated on outreach work at home, particularly in Lincolnshire where there was little Labour representation. Glenys Kinnock devoted herself to development and human rights work and her Welsh constituency. She particularly battled on democratic freedoms, women, childcare, humanitarian aid, AIDS, family planning and reproductive health, conflict prevention and at that time Rwanda. Arlene McCarthy was ambitious, another fine linguist, knowledgeable about Europe and European funding, articulate and feisty which led to many clashes with some of the less dynamic and more bullying men. Eryl McNally, also with local authority experience, was interested in science and tackled energy and research, campaigned in marginal areas and made many friends outside the EPLP, particularly French. She was one of the few who could put up well-argued opposition to some of the pro-nuclear proponents and she battled for a greater role for renewables and energy saving before it was as common as it is today. Eluned Morgan, young and enthusiastic and also a linguist, pursued youth and culture policy, made friends, stayed with a local family in Strasbourg and in those early years spent a good deal of time in her geographically large Welsh constituency. Sue Waddington, having been a Leader of a Labour group in Leicester, concentrated on women's issues and education policy to great effect, working enormously hard on subjects that were not always top of the recognition pile in the Labour Party including the DAPHNE fund against violence to women. She worked on the Parental Leave Directive of 1996 which was the first to give legal validity to a Social Partner Framework Agreement (a procedure that had emerged after the Maastricht Treaty).

Dianne Hayter expressed surprise that there was never a formal women's group of Labour MEPs as there was after 1997 in Westminster but such a grouping was never discussed. The prevailing feeling was that there were more than enough meetings in life without creating more for the hard-pressed women, and there was a fairly good strand of sisterhood amongst the women in the Socialist Group.

Hayter moved on to another job at the end of this year and her successor was Peter Coleman, formerly Director of Organisation at Labour Party headquarters, the position also being contested by David Gardner. The final run-off was between Coleman and Maggie Coulthard who ran the Brussels office but there was no animosity between the two. Both Sawyer and Tappin had confidence in Coleman and the latter wonders if his lack of support for Gardner went against him later. Coleman proved effective in his post, emanating an easy-going ambience combined with shrewd tactical abilities, and was certainly as loyal as his predecessor without being as confrontational. Some were a little concerned at having a "party hack" in the post rather than someone with European expertise, but the latter was being effectively supplied by Coulthard in Brussels and it proved not to be a problem.

Commissioner Kinnock always had an open door for the Labour Members and in Parliament had numerous transport-related issues to deal with. His stints in the Parliament sometimes drove him to frustration. He had to take his turn at Question Time and put up with the late hours, last-minute changes of agendas, and debates over-running, often without any apology to the Commissioners who were expected to turn up when required in Strasbourg.

Half-time changes

Following the terms of the traditional deal between the two big groups, Spanish Christian Democrat Jose Maria Gil-Robles Gil-Delgado, an opponent of the former Franco dictatorship, was elected President of Parliament in January 1997 with the usual grumbles from the left and small groups. His vote was 338 versus 177 for Catherine Lalumiere. David Martin retained his Vice-Presidency and Balfe continued as Quaestor.

Green continued as Chair of the Socialist Group and David, Crawley, Martin and Balfe were members of the Bureau. Elliott became Chair of the Animal Welfare Intergroup. Chairs of committees were again Collins for Environment, Public Health and Consumer Protection and Hughes for Social Affairs and Employment and for Tomlinson a Temporary Committee on Community Transit System. Vice-Chairs went to: Truscott for the Security Subcommittee, Adam for Energy and Research, Howitt for Regional Affairs, Corbett for Institutional Affairs, Tomlinson for Budget, Evans for Rules, Newman for Petitions and Kinnock for ACP. Julian Priestley in 1997 became Secretary-General of the Parliament.

Delegation posts this time were: Donnelly Chair of USA, Pollack Chair of SAARC, Simpson Chair of Switzerland; Green managed to keep Kerr out of the Australia Chair. Vice-Chairs were: Elliott for Poland, Whitehead for Czech, Watts for Bulgaria, Titley for Slovenia, Skinner for Latvia, Ford for Japan, Needle for the "little Stans" (Kazakhstan, Kyrgyzstan, Uzbekistan, Tajikistan, Turkmenistan and Mongolia), Read for SAARC.

Tomlinson really got his teeth into his work as Chair of the Temporary Committee on Transit Fraud. There were huge scams going on concerning suspended VAT. In illustration, he says, a lorry load of tobacco from a bonded warehouse in Antwerp could be worth a million euro in suspended VAT, not due to be paid until it reached its final destination in the EU. However much dodgy paperwork was in use and it could, for instance, be declared at a port, say Algeciras, as being exported to North Africa where no VAT would be required to be paid, but the tobacco could circulate in Spain, thus avoiding VAT. The rapporteur on this committee was Edward Kellett-Bowman of the Conservatives and Parliament put another senior Brit, Michael Shackleton, in place to service it. They held hearings where companies such as Philip Morris, who Tomlinson felt might be potentially complicit in cigarette smuggling, gave evidence. The companies were given a hard time and found it necessary in due course to change some of their practices after it reported in March 1997. The Commission was also pressed to create the UCLAF anti-fraud unit in November 1996.

Unemployment conventions

A "European Appeal for full employment" was published in the summer 1996 European Labour Forum, signed by dozens of left MEPs from various groups, MPs, NGOs, writers, academics and artists, churches and local government leaders. Its main thrust was to argue that over-rigid adherence to the Maastricht criteria on monetary union could aggravate unemployment unless it was offset by joint and combined action at the European level, including reductions in working time. Rocard was a frequent contributor to the journal on this subject.

Following the earlier resolution on unemployment from the Committee of Inquiry, Coates' next project was to call for a "people's assize" and two Conventions of the European Unemployed were held, as a logical follow on to his earlier work with widespread demonstrations against unemployment. One convention was held in February 1997 and with the aid of the left movement and European trades unions, a further convention was held in Brussels on 22- 23 May that year. Coates says that in the beginning the Socialist Group supported these but he accuses Priestley of withdrawing interpretation facilities for the second convention, necessitating a direct approach to Jacques Santer, President of the European Commission, who "saved the day by furnishing a team of highly competent interpreters from his own secretariat".

Working for victory, the workers and Europe

A controversial directive on artists' resale rights was proposed by the Commission and was opposed by the UK, fearing potential loss of the fine art market to Switzerland. The UK on a cross-party basis seemed to be out of synch with the prevailing mood across the water. There were two opposing camps. UK auction houses such as Sotheby's lobbied government to say that the fine art market in London would be ruined if the Commission's proposal that an artist would be entitled to a percentage of the re-sale price of their painting, according to a sliding scale of value, was approved. Tongue pointed out that the big artists would indeed gain, but further down the chain much poorer artists would also benefit. Over ten EU countries had such a system in operation. She argued for the proposal, convinced that the rich auction houses were scaremongering. In the debate in April 1997, however, Oddy, speaking for the EPLP said the delegation was not convinced that the proposal would help artists and voiced concerns that the art market could move to New York and Switzerland. At the vote on the Commission proposal twenty of the EPLP supported it and a further thirty-one abstained. Eventually the resale rights directive was carried in Council by QMV but not without a fight from Britain.

Environment Committee members continued to be involved in numerous policy issues: Tongue on fire safety, Bowe on GMOs and on export of dangerous waste and the Basle Convention, Whitehead on food labelling, irradiation, novel foods and consumer guarantees. Collins was pushing for strict standards on lead levels in drinking water working closely with fellow Scotsman Grant Lawrence in the Commission, at that time responsible for water. In February 1999 White was rapporteur on the water policy framework directive piloting it through first reading, which involved over two hundred amendments and a long and complicated vote.

Robin Cook always had a strong commitment to the environment and was a long-standing member of SERA, Labour's environment organization. In January 1997 when he was foreign affairs spokesperson, he launched an ad hoc, voluntary and unpaid advisory group on environment, the Green Globe Task Force. Most of the hand-picked members were eminent environmentalists but Pollack was invited so as to input the European angle. The group was headed by Hugh Raven (later to become a Sustainable Development Commissioner). Members, who included Peter Madden from Green Alliance, David Baldock from IEEP, James Cameron from FIELD, Duncan Brack and Michael Grubb from the Royal Institute of International Affairs, Felix Dodds and Derek Osborn from UNED-UK, Richard Sandbrook of IIED, and occasionally others, would put together briefing notes on climate change, reform of the UN and the like and offer inputs to major environmental speeches being made by Blair and other government Ministers. After the election its status had to be regularized and a conduit to Cook via his adviser David Clark and John Ashton, Head of the Science and Energy Department at the Foreign Office, ran until 1999. Pollack at this time was sharing with Tongue an immensely talented researcher, Rebecca Willis, who later went on to become Director of the Green Alliance.

Fishing proved very controversial in April and May. Crampton was rapporteur on some international fishing agreements which had meant trips to Namibia with Morris and Greenland with White. He took a stance supportive of third world countries, saying that exporting the EU fleet's excess capacity was not a valid option for the future and took a strong line against drift nets. He was supported by Commissioner Emma Bonino, but it was the subject of some rows in the Socialist Group. Spanish, Portuguese and some other Members did not support the line Labour was taking and Crampton acknowledged it did create some problems for the Spanish. In the end it was sorted out and the report was well-received both in the press at home and with governments in Namibia, South Africa and others.

Parliament moved out of its old rue Belliard building in Brussels in the summer of that year, with Tomlinson complaining about the costs. (It is now renovated and home to the Committee of the Regions and ECOSOC.) By December 1998 the budget included even more money for buildings and by then Parliament owned many of the new buildings in the Brussels EU quarter as well as the IPE IV building in Strasbourg.

Arlene McCarthy worked on the structural funds, having become an expert whilst serving as a European officer of a local authority prior to being elected. The funds were being revised (this and reforms to the CAP to deal with impending enlargement being known as Agenda 2000). With her fluent German, McCarthy had ready access to Socialist Commissioner Monika Wulf-Mathies, in whose Cabinet Gerhard Stahl, formerly of the Socialist Group, was now working. They had pushed through a one hundred million "peace" dividend fund for Northern Ireland. There were always numerous claims from the UK for various areas to be included in eligibility, but McCarthy was also concerned to ensure an urban regeneration component was included and sought to stop the funds subsidizing privatization of utilities in the UK, being pursued with vigour by the Conservative government. The government continued to be lax about taking up all opportunities under the ESF and both she and other EPLP Members raised this repeatedly.

McCarthy was also enthusiastic about Article 10 of the structural funds enabling network exchanges for good practice without huge bureaucracy.This fund was used for a London project, in advance of the restoration of London government, initiated by Pollack with the aid of a friendly expert, Graham Meadows in the Commission, and Jim Murphy, former member of Clinton Davis' Cabinet, now back in the UK at the Henley Research Centre. London MEPs lobbied the Commissioner in March 1998 for some Objective 2 funding to address pockets of deprivation. David argued for Objective 2 funding for Wales to continue to 1999, on sustainable jobs and less on road construction. After much work this was successful.

Seizing an opportunity to hit the government on the use of structural funds in the UK, McCarthy as rapporteur sent out two thousand letters and questionnaires and held hearings in nine regions of the UK. The Regional Committee held a hearing in March 1997 to which the government again refused to send a representative. Her report, which was voted in April just before the general election, said the EU funds were filling gaps in falling government investment in the regions. She highlighted a litany of disasters and delays in the ESF, saying these were mostly due to government incompetence, provoking Giles Chichester (Conservative) to deplore the "manipulation of the Parliamentary timetable". He was unhappy that the rapporteur was British and accused her of being negative and kicking her country. On her part she insisted the report was a result of the research undertaken and was not partisan. Crampton, Crawley, David, Skinner and Donnelly spoke in favour, outlining problems from their own areas.

Ford, Needle and Thomas took themselves off to North Korea in October

1997. On their return they said the country must open up. Ford was to become somewhat of an expert on this country in years to come.

Most MEPs were involved in delegation visits to parliaments all over the world on a regular basis, normally with a meeting in the foreign country one year and a return visit the next. It was always difficult trying to fit them into the timetable, because they required at least five days to a week away. Most used these as opportunities to visit EU funded projects, listen to human rights groups and the like in addition to the formal meetings. A complex delegation was SAARC, comprised of seven countries, all demanding visits and all jealous of India, the biggest. Experience had shown that it was impossible to visit more than two countries at a time. The very first parliamentary visit to Bhutan took place in November 1997, led by Pollack, assisted by Walter Masur and Raymond Herdies of the staff, Rosetti having been moved to a different area. At that time the National Assembly was appointed by the King and his advisers. The delegation also went to Nepal, testing the abilities of the interpreters because of the very heavy accents of the rather elderly politicians and visiting an innovative project. Marvellous photos of the group with the King of Bhutan were unusable however, because one of the French National Front Members was on the delegation and always inserted himself next to the Chairperson when the cameras came out.

Yes, we have no bananas

A long-standing trade battle with the USA over the EU's import rules for bananas surfaced in 1992. Labour wanted to ease access to EU markets for bananas from small farmers in the Caribbean islands but other countries, particularly Germany, had traditionally imported from the giant American-owned Latin-American plantation chains such as Del Monte, Dole and Chiquita who used non-unionised labour. There were huge rows and matters came to a head when the USA threatened to take the matter to the WTO.

Wynn and Glenys Kinnock after a visit to the Windward Isles went to see the Trade Commissioner, Sir Leon Brittan. The problem was that favouring the small producers was against WTO rules, and Labour's sense of moral justice was outraged. Many of the Labour MEPs tabled questions and urgencies, spoke in debates and generally battled for a fair allocation of the import quota for the Caribbean, assisted by Socialist colleague Manuel Medina Ortego raising the case for bananas from Madeira. In May 1997 Wynn and Glenys Kinnock called for an appeal against the WTO decision. It didn't help that United Fruit was a donor to the Clinton election campaign, although his administration denied to Foreign Secretary Cook that this had anything to do with the US position.

Thomas was a rapporteur on a proposal for assistance for ACP bananas in 1998 which passed its second reading with some amendments in January 1999. The issue rumbled on.

A new dawn breaks

Labour swept to power in the UK general election of 1 May 1997 with a majority of 179 seats. Conservative Leader John Major stepped down after this landslide, and William Hague was elected to lead the depleted party.

Tony Blair was walking on water and as the slogan went, things could only get better. It was a wonderful time in Labour politics. Our team had invested huge amounts of time and resources into the victory, helping prospective MPs in marginal seats in particular, and they basked in the glory. After eighteen years of Conservative rule there were high expectations of a new start and warmer relations with the EU. The new government was committed to support democratization of the EU. Colleagues from all parties spontaneously hugged Labour Members in the corridors. The head of the UK Representation, Sir Stephen Wall, wrote reminding them that "we are here for you", which generated some mirth but was well-meant. Wall (2008) says that his office was sending briefings to all UK MEPs from 1995 and that some Labour Members told him they liked to get the government briefings because they immediately knew which way to vote – the opposite of what was being recommended. Clearly this was to change, and many MEPs said they had constructive dealings with UKRep. Wall addressed the EPLP meeting on 9 July. From this time the EPLP were sometimes told at short notice to change a vote after things had been negotiated in committee and Group. He wrote (Wall, 2008) that after the election there was a "step change" policy implemented in all government departments requiring them to make an effort to find areas of substantive co-operation with other Member States and that this work was overseen by the Europe Minister.

Labour's Link Members had worked with Shadow spokespersons in the years running up to the victory and now the system, with access to government Ministers, was formalized. Brian Simpson was appointed European PPS to the Deputy Prime Minister Prescott and Titley to the Foreign Secretary Robin Cook. Because of Balfe's NATO connection he was liaison to the Duchy of Lancaster, dealing directly with David Clark, Cook's political adviser. Ford was Justice and Home Affairs Link to Jack Straw. Other committee Link Members likewise had regular access to Ministers. To cement the image of a new start, Labour moved its party headquarters from Walworth Road to the more modern Millbank Tower on the Embankment at Westminster, closer to Parliament.

At the start of the campaign in April Blair made a speech in Manchester on Europe saying: "I want Britain to be one of the leading countries in Europe... the hardest question remains EMU... we will keep options open..." He was hedging his bets, careful to continue criticizing the CAP.

On Blair's election Priestley (John Fitzmaurice lecture, 2007) was later to say:

"The Party leadership that Blair inherited in July 1994, following Smith's untimely death was a model European social democratic party in the mainstream. And Blair, personally and culturally more European than any British party leader... seemed just the right person to complete the country's and the party's reconciliation with the European idea. His spectacular success in completing the modernisation and broadening its appeal served as a model for other Socialists parties in Europe and in September 1998 Schroeder, campaigning on the slogan of the 'Neue Mitte' brought the SPD into office. For the first time a genuine co-operation between progressive parties, in the driving seat, seemed likely to take Europe in a progressive direction."

This put Socialists in government in eleven out of the fifteen EU states.

Green remembers being at the first meeting between Prime Ministers where there was a real sense we could change the agenda in Europe.

By the autumn plans were launched for regional government in Scotland and Wales, and a Green Paper on London government had been published. Individual EPLP Members campaigned for the success of these proposals.

New Labour and old Socialists

At the PES congress in Malmo in the first week of June, although his victory was enormously welcomed, there were mixed reactions to Blair's speech. He spoke about the third way and the centre and social democracy rather than the left and democratic socialism, exhorting the comrades to "modernize or die" and saying "we do not believe that the Social Chapter means that Europe should seek to harmonise and regulate wherever it can". And he said that socialists should "stop talking about European theology and start doing things for which real people can see real benefit – jobs, environment, internal security". He came and went to fanfare but without much communication with his fellow European socialists. Lionel Jospin, whose views were more statist and who had won his election in France a few weeks after Labour, went about the congress chatting and glad-handing the comrades. Blair's high-handed lecture left some a little flat. Foreign Secretary Cook, popular and now a Vice-President of the PES, was there to mop up.

The AGM of 1997 took three bites to complete taking about seven hours, beginning on 11 June. The officers had asked Peter Coleman to update EPLP standing orders and code of conduct, based roughly on those of the PLP. There were thirty-seven changes to be made and Coleman proposed that the new party rule book was simply voted section by section. This did not meet with approval, West threatening Coleman with legal action if it were not done meticulously. At the first AGM a section saying "do nothing which brings the party into disrepute" was rejected and this part had to be revised and brought back the following year where it was put into the Code of Conduct. Ford believes this was the tipping point with Straw and his special adviser Ed Owens for bringing forward PR. Coates and others argued that the national party could discipline them for almost anything. The meeting resumed on the 12th to continue voting on the rules and deal with electing officers. Donnelly challenged David for Leader but the incumbent held on, as did the remainder of the officers: Crawley as Deputy, Barton as Chair, Murphy as Whip, Tappin as Secretary and Oddy as Treasurer. It concluded its business on 26 June.

The party was keen to ensure a smooth ride for this first Labour government for eighteen years and not permit the mistakes of the past with attacks from within. Headquarters had drawn up a document "Partnership in Power", suggesting two-year rolling policy programmes, based on work of the National Policy Forum, and this was carried at conference that year. The workings of party conference itself and elections to the NEC were restructured. The New Labour brand was not entirely to everyone's satisfaction, however, and Livingstone defeated Mandelson for the NEC. The EPLP Leader was made a full member of the NEC. It was the end of MEPs having a clear run at the fringe meetings: the huge number of new Labour MPs were flavour of the month and MEPs were taking second place again.

In November the EPLP plus spouses were invited to a reception at Downing Street with the Prime Minister and some of the Cabinet. It was a first for most because of the long Tory years and the event was savoured. Most of the Campaign Group did not make the trip.

Amsterdam Treaty

Six weeks after his electoral victory Tony Blair rode a bicycle to the Amsterdam Summit on 16 June and signed the Social Chapter. The Protocol was now incorporated as a Social Chapter in the Treaty and there were several other provisions (see Corbett, 1998 for more detail). The formal signing of the Amsterdam Treaty was in October and it eventually came into force on 1 May 1999. It was not so much a new European Treaty as a collection of amendments. The government did, however, refuse to sign up to the new border-free area agreed by other Member States. Within days of the end of the opt-out on the Social Chapter Blair again sounded a note of caution: "I don't think there is any appetite for great rafts of additional legislation under the Social chapter." He called for labour market reforms to improve employability.

Tobacco and Formula One

David Ward (former advisor to John Smith and then Donnelly's assistant) had put Donnelly in touch with Formula One and this led to some controversy. On the Environment Committee, Members were still battling to ban tobacco advertising. In October 1997 Bernie Ecclestone, boss of Formula One, gave £1 million to the Labour Party shortly after a visit to Downing Street. Not long after that the government negotiated a temporary exemption of the sport from the ban on tobacco advertising, allegedly following pressure from Blair. By this time there were strong divisions in the Labour team and many alleged Donnelly had been involved. Rawnsley (2000) wrote that Ward was lobbying for the racing car industry. The donation from Ecclestone blew up badly in the press and Rawnsley reports that David Hill (then Director of Communications for the Labour Party) said it was his worst week in more than ten years. The party gave the money to charity. Donnelly rejects any suggestion of involvement on his part and also suggests that Ecclestone did not need tobacco advertising because his Formula One team made their money from TV and that other brands were more needful of the advertising. He says that Moseley and Ecclestone were also horrified at the bad publicity.

Proportionally strife-ridden

Kinnock, Smith and Cook all favoured proportional representation and the party's Plant Commission report had been shelved during 1994-95. Titley had served on this as a representative of the EPLP and says that he and Margaret Beckett agued for the first past the post system (FPTP) but the Plant Commission decided by 5 – 4 in favour of PR for the European elections. Electoral reform for the new devolved institutions and European Parliament was then agreed by the Labour-Liberal Democratic Joint

Consultative Committee on Constitutional Reform in March 1997, jointly chaired by Cook and Robert Maclennan (President of the Liberal Democrats), including a regional list system for the European elections. Westlake (2000) records that in his press conference Cook said it was Labour's intention to introduce PR in time for the next European elections. Blair had been holding talks with Liberal Democrat Leader Paddy Ashdown in the run-up to the general election and there had even been some talk of bringing him into the Cabinet, leading to some wry comments that it was easier for Ashdown to get in to see Blair than it was for the Leader of the EPLP. Inside the Labour Party there was growing pressure from the Labour Campaign for Electoral Reform, and outside from a cross-party coalition, Charter 88 to which some Labour MEPs belonged.

After the election landslide, fervour within government for change for the House of Commons abated, but commitment was there to do something about the European Parliament, where the FPTP system had led to such wild swings in the political balance of British MEPs. The election manifesto had been committed to PR for the proposed Scottish Parliament and National Assembly for Wales. In July plans were announced to change the voting system for the European Parliament. Then a Commission under Lord (Roy) Jenkins was set up to investigate electoral reform for the House of Commons, reporting in October 1988 recommending replacing FPTP with the additional member system.

There was some doubt as to whether a bill would be brought in time for the 1999 elections, but Blair and Ashdown agreed on this, it is said on a return flight from Hong Kong in July 1997. It was complicated by the fact that the year before, the Boundary Commission had been to work on adjusting Euro-constituencies to conform to the 1997 Westminster boundaries. It had published its review paper in October 1996 and held consensus meetings in November but suspended this work after the announcement that PR would be brought in. Westlake (2000) points out they had to restart in haste in December 1998 when it was thought the bill would not get through in time.

The EPLP had been consulted and set up its own working party, sending a questionnaire to Members. Although there were quite a few vociferous supporters of a proportional representation system, there were arguments about systems. There was concern about party control of a fixed list, but fears about public battles in the media in an open list system. Supporters of FPTP including Titley and David were in the majority and some, including Tappin and Donnelly, argued with the party that there was no need to change until 2004. McNally produced a comparison of selection systems in the various European parties to assist debate in November 1997. Green supported change. The European Treaties had long demanded some form of closer alignment of electoral systems and numerous attempts had been made to put this into law, none gaining the approval of Council until 2002.

Hayter pointed out to Tappin that the EPLP would be reduced drastically in size under PR. McCarthy felt that the change of system had been in the general election manifesto and with the aspiration for Labour as a one-nation party it was a logical way to deliver a greater degree of fairness in regional representation. In one of the many EPLP meetings held on the subject one of the Northern men said it would mean mediocre women on lists, whereupon Read shot back that it would make a change from the mediocre men that had dominated for years. The Group's view was put forward by the Leader to Whitty and Sally Morgan. Ford argued that the maximum size of regions should be four to six seat, which would stop a Green and UKIP breakthrough at the election, but Blair and Straw were determined on change as were some of the EPLP officers, supported by Green. David says that Straw, no supporter of Europe, was convinced that the introduction of PR for the European election would discredit PR as an electoral system for the House of Commons. Hayter considers it was near-revenge for the treatment he had earlier received from the EPLP and certainly there was a view that a list system would give more control to the party centrally over errant MEPs. Blair was keen on keeping the LibDems on board for a possible future coalition with Labour, so the EPLP's view was over-ridden.

Rules are made to be broken

The NEC, encouraged by David, sent a Code of Conduct to the EPLP on 7 October after party conference, which prevented Members from discussing the new electoral process. This "gagging order" caused problems. Falconer, Smith, Coates, Hindley and Kerr were against signing the declaration and wrote to the Prime Minister asking for the same rights enjoyed by dissident Labour MPs in the run up to the referendum on Welsh devolution. Murphy as Whip asked them to give an assurance by 23 October that they would abide by the Code of Conduct and this deadline passed without compliance. Four were provisionally suspended on the 22nd. There was substantial coverage of this on the BBC (who interviewed Coates, Falconer, Kerr and Hindley – the latter says his comments upset Blair) and in *The Scotsman* on 23 October, where Morris was also named as saying he did not support the Code.

The European Parliamentary Elections Bill was duly published on 29 October 1997, suggesting a closed regional list system. It was controversial on a variety of counts; disliked by those who opposed PR, those who opposed closed lists, those who pointed out the contradiction of Northern Ireland remaining under STV, those who supported a constituency base, those who feared dictatorship of the party machine and those who opposed the choice of the d'Hondt counting system. There were endless arguments in Parliament, in the press, in the political parties and amongst MEPs. It took four attempts to push it through Parliament, where the Lords kept up a barrage of objections, including a successful attempt from Lord Bethell to bring in Gibraltar (see Westlake, 2000 for a full account) and it did not receive Royal Assent, having been passed under the Parliament Act, until 14 January 1999.

Kerr accused Blair of "Stalinist tendencies" for planning to abolish all current Euro-constituencies and stifling criticism by Labour MEPs. He said the gagging showed that New Labour was increasingly authoritarian and centralized. Coates insisted that under EP rules the Labour Members could not be given such a mandate. Falconer, Coates, Kerr and Hindley who (not alone) opposed the closed regional list system said so publicly, becoming known as "the Strasbourg Four".

Hindley and Falconer had already decided not to stand at the next election and thought the restrictions did not apply to them. The EPLP took a different view and sought to suspend all the dissidents for breaching the Code.

David put down a resolution to suspend Hindley and Falconer for six months and Coates and Kerr for a year, thus making them ineligible to stand for re-selection. As Whip, Murphy spoke to Sally Morgan's office saying he wanted to suspend them and says Downing Street felt it was the EPLP's call.

Coleman spoke to Hindley before the EPLP meeting and it was agreed he would apologise. Hindley had an eye to the future, possibly back in local government, and did not want to be outside the party. Barton was Chair for an unhappy meeting and produced a "Memorandum of Understanding" to try to accommodate those who objected to the electoral system; there was a small retreat and the suspensions were lifted. *The Times* on 12 November 1997 wrote:

> "Labour's Euro-MPs last night defied the party leadership by refusing to agree to the suspension of four rebel MEPs. The four… had been told that they faced suspension after refusing to accept a code of practice that effectively banned any statements to the media about changes to the party's selection plans for the next European elections. They claimed it was a device to get rid of Labour's 'old guard' MEPs. The code of conduct remained in place last night but the… group… voted overwhelmingly in Brussels for a 'memorandum of understanding' to clarify their rights on speaking out. The four insisted that they had been vindicated in their fight for free speech. … Wayne David said 'There were misinterpretations about the code of practice and I hope tonight we have cleared them up'."

Falconer later said that "Coates and Kerr wanted to get expelled", an interpretation corroborated by Hindley who said that the two voted against withdrawing the suspension. Certainly they continued their vocal opposition to the system. Kerr says he briefed the press after the EPLP meeting that "they would continue to speak out against the undemocratic selection process".

Breaking the constituency link was anathema to many in the EPLP, not all on the hard left. Coates and Kerr published a highly critical article attacking Blair in *The Observer* on 28 December. The front page coverage spoke of six MEPs but the other four unnamed, said to be from London, the North West, Scotland and Wales were said to be "taking private soundings before committing themselves." It was a step too far for the party.

According to Kerr's account in *Labour Left Briefing* in February 1998, he and Coates were expelled from the EPLP on 30 December, from the Socialist Group on the 31st (following an attempt to remain as Independent Labour Members) and by fax from the Labour Party on 1 January 1998. The formal expulsion was on 8 January. However, in advance of that and before the old year ended, they had carefully informed the President of Parliament that they were removing their funds from the Socialist Group and transferring them temporarily to the Greens. Officials saw this as tantamount to resignation from the party. Kerr was suspended by the NEC and later expelled along with Coates; he became the first Scottish Socialist Party MEP, locating himself in the Green Group. The two of them set up an Independent Labour network in the grassroots at home.

Coates now vigorously denies wanting to get expelled. He says:

> "I made it clear I would accept no gag [in opposition to the plan to abolish European constituencies] and was instantly expelled. The expulsion was

found to have been illegal, so I was then reinstated. At no point was I consulted about the exclusion or the reinclusion. I therefore wrote to Tom
Sawyer asking him to explain the position, and give undertakings about
my future status. He never responded, so, with Hugh Kerr, I asked the
Green Group if they would be kind enough to hold our Parliamentary
allowances for information money until our status had been regularized.
This did not constitute an application for membership, but it was misrep-
resented as such. When my expulsion was confirmed, I joined the United
Left Group (GUE) whilst following the whip of the European Socialist
Group."

Coates complains that he was denied a hearing but says he enjoyed his
time in the GUE because it was a friendly group. "They could not mandate
any one to do anything because they couldn't agree on anything but they
had good discussions." They also made him Vice-Chair of the US delegation. Some of the Members were rather sad to see Coates go and thought
Labour should be a broad enough church to accommodate him although
most acknowledged he had an oppositionist streak and had brought it on
himself. He is a respected figure in the left community at large mostly
because of his many publications and this episode was regretted. His apparent move to an opposition group was, however, seen as unavoidable
grounds for expulsion.

Hindley from then on kept his head down and concentrated on network-
ing to sustain his post-election career.

Neil Kinnock says he told Blair and Straw that they had picked the wrong
system and there should have been a constituency interest kept. The Plant
recommendations during his time had advocated the alternative preference
system. Kinnock and many others thought the regional list system was so
bad that it would not be used again, but it has not been changed. It is almost
impossible to find anyone in the Labour Party who is in favour now of
breaking that constituency link and the system has very few friends in any
other party with the possible exception of UKIP.

Saving the planet at Kyoto

The UN conference on climate change was held from 5-10 December 1997 in
Kyoto, Japan, with Prescott playing a pivotal role, working with the
Japanese and Americans and brokering an agreement. He says they saw him
as a European rather than as British.

Pollack was one of three Members from Parliament, accompanied by
Rosemary Opacik, a Japanese speaker from the Committee staff, who went
to Kyoto. GLOBE organized a seminar including Al Gore that attempted to
bring on board the G77 developing nations. They aired the "Contraction and
Convergence" strategy developed by Aubrey Meyer of the Global
Commons Institute. The Green Globe Task Force had met with Robin Cook
at the Foreign and Commonwealth Office on 6 November to hone Kyoto
messages and also discuss the British Presidency. At Kyoto there was unfortunately little communication between the European camps of the Council,
Commission and Parliament and at home the media (even *Tribune*) was not
interested in taking stories from MEPs. Simpson as Prescott's European PPS

says that his intelligence about the attitudes of other delegations in the run up to the conference was particularly useful. There was little liaison with the Members on the relevant committees, Environment and Energy.

Beforehand, in October, McNally complained that the lack of an EU legal base on energy meant we would send our delegates to Kyoto with little in their bags. Collins in the debate the following February hoped that Parliament's delegation would be closer to the heart of the EU delegation at the follow-up in Buenos Aires and indeed liaison did improve from that time on.

West bows out

Norman West suffered a heart attack in early 1998 and took a retirement package on grounds of ill-health. His departure triggered a by-election in South Yorkshire, held on 7 May. Linda McAvan was elected for Labour with 52.2% of the vote on a turnout of 23.4%. Two names that were to be seen after 1999 fought for other parties: Robert Goodwill for the Tories and Peter Davies for UKIP. The Liberal-Democrats at this election beat the Conservatives who had always previously been second.

In contrast to West, McAvan from Sheffield was pro-European. She had worked for the Socialist Confed in Brussels between 1985 and 1988, then for the Coalfields Communities Campaign (CCC) based in Yorkshire and as European officer for Barnsley Council. There was a traditional difference of opinion between the NUM and the CCC. The latter was looking for aid to rebuild the ravaged mining communities but the miners were still doggedly battling against closures and felt that this compromised their position. Her selection was a culture change for the area.

The first Labour Presidency

Britain once again held the Presidency of the EU in the first half of 1998 and Labour MEPs had been heavily engaged in preparing ministerial briefing notes, helping with the agenda and policy priorities for the new Labour government. Doug Henderson had rather surprisingly been appointed Europe Minister instead of Joyce Quin and Green was critical of his lack of vision.

Cook began in the EP on 14 January saying "Britain is now a committed player in Europe", that we wanted EMU to be a success and to get enlargement negotiations off to a flying start, launch Europol as soon as possible and put environmental considerations centre stage. He launched an EU code of conduct on arm exports, warmly welcomed by Titley. *The Observer* carried the headline "goodbye xenophobia". There were some reservations about the naff tie and scarf the government had produced to mark the occasion, designed by schoolchildren and featuring symbols supposed to delineate each country, such as a pizza for Italy. Few Members sported this particular trophy.

MEPs welcomed ministerial visits of which there were plenty. For the first time British Ministers were happy to attend committee meetings and respond to questions. It was hardly possible to get into a lift in the Parliament without meeting yet another Labour Minister and entourage. The advisors and civil servants were more snooty in their attitude to MEPs than the Ministers themselves, many of whom had longstanding relations with the Labour MEPs.

Quite a number of Labour Members were Socialist Group co-ordinators, and Hendrick in this role for EMAC was not alone in finding himself torn between voting with the Group or abstaining with the EPLP on matters of concern to the government at home. He had a substantial row with the EPLP Whip Miller on one occasion.

Iraq and the looming concern about Saddam Hussein's alleged weapons of mass destruction were being discussed as early as February with Green telling Henderson, the Europe Minister, that many in her group believed passionately that the UN and only the UN should decide what happened. Kerr was now making it his mission to attack the Labour government at every opportunity and *The Guardian* and *The Observer* offered him opportunities to air his views as did his Green Group compatriots. During this debate about Blair supporting President Clinton over Iraq, he suggested that Green was privately critical. This prompted Titley to respond angrily: "In my nine years in the Parliament I have never before heard a speech of such distorted, self-indulgent drivel", Titley also making some disparaging remarks about "care in the community". It did not stop Kerr, who came back asking Henderson whether Britain was prepared to use nuclear weapons in Iraq and the following day on the aspersions cast on his mental health. When the Iraq resolution came to a vote Kerr said he would be circulating the names of those Members who voted for the resolution. After some attacks he withdrew and apologized.

Europe-building during the Presidency

With water, air and waste listed as priorities, Pollack had seized a piece of draft legislation, the first "daughter directive" on air pollution, and taken on new staff to assist. Prescott announced to Parliament in February that this was a priority for the Presidency. A highly-committed expert, Lynne Edwards, was the Commission official, whose first comment to Aaron McLoughlin and Christian Farrar-Hockley (Pollack's assistants) was "I have a black belt in Karate – mess up this file and I will do you".

The Commission had run working parties for two years before producing the draft, based on WHO health advice. Pollack was astonished to find oil companies pouring scorn on this in private meetings with her. A TV production company "Partners in Production" (Charles Stewart and Malcolm Hurst) shadowed the making of this piece of legislation with an intensive "fly-on-the-wall" filming process running right through until its approval. It was shown on Channel 4 as a three-part programme, "Brussels Behind Closed Doors" in April 1999. Filming was permitted in some of the Council working parties and Pollack had close contact with both Commission and British civil servants both from UKRep and the Department of Environment, finding Chris Leigh helpful. Her assistants would rush to their assiduously courted contacts in the Italian permanent representation to obtain minutes of Council working parties before the Commission. Research on particulates was being undertaken by the Health Effects Institute in the USA and the team began to work with Bob O'Keefe and Dan Greenbaum who ran a seminar in Massachusetts in March 1998 on the health effects of air pollution.

The Commission and Parliament had also set up the CAFE programme to monitor emissions control. Local authorities would be the ones to have to implement this directive but it proved difficult to raise any interest from them in the emerging legislation. There was not one response to a letter sent to them all. It was to be the first time legally binding emission levels were set for CO_2, NOx, SO_2 and lead. Parliament approved the report in May 1998 just in time for the Presidency to deal with it.

The level of EPLP activity continued to be high. Hughes carefully dealt with a common position on risks from chemical agents. Skinner was happy that the Presidency had unblocked it but there were some concerns it did not go far enough. Harrison concerned himself with the development of the euro and tourism and Watts with road safety and also continuing to pilot through legislation on registration of ship's passengers. At second reading the following March he was pushing the case for black boxes on ferries in case of disasters. Waddington and Morris were supporting vocational training and apprenticeships. Murphy was rapporteur on bus and coach design including safety and access for the disabled, supported by Billingham and Donnelly, against the right. Donnelly and Harrison continued their work on the European Central Bank and transparency. Titley kept up his work on future accessions and concerns about the Kosovo crisis and Serb brutality. An accession process for sic countries was launched in April, another of the Presidency's priorities.

Bowe and White carried on trying to get an acceptable text for the landfill directive and supporting abolition of co-disposal, something that would mean a change in the UK system. Bowe began to give cautious support to GMOs but demanded careful labelling, saying that we had to build public confidence and trust in the technology and ensure ethical public health and safety were respected. Whitehead was still engaged with food safety, wanting the directive on irradiation to go to conciliation where it was successfully concluded in February 1999. Collins was still pushing for studies on endocrine disrupters and for the most stringent possible water quality parameters, particularly on lead and copper, against extraordinarily high levels of lobbying and Conservative opposition.

Lomas and a few others supported return of the Elgin Marbles, opposed by Culture Minister Chris Smith. Lomas, whose daughter was married to a Greek, tabled a "written declaration" which by the following January had gained sufficient signatures to become official policy, despite efforts from the government to dissuade Members (such as Tongue) from signing. The text in part said that Parliament "takes the view that the return of the Elgin marbles to Greece would be a key move in promoting Europe's common culture". The Labour Members who signed this were: Coates, Crampton, Elliott, Falconer, Hallam, Hardstaff, Hindley, Hughes, Kerr, Kinnock, Lomas, McGowan, McMahon, McNally, Megahy, Morgan, Morris, Newman, Oddy, Pollack, Seal, Simpson, Waddington, White, Whitehead and Wilson. The signing system for this sort of declaration was tedious and sometimes cut-off deadlines occurred before MEPs managed to find their way to the room where signatures could be appended.

Oddy was rapporteur on investment services, saying in May that conciliation had failed because Parliament believed the chosen system of comitology was anti-democratic. There was some disagreement amongst the team on proposals to end duty free. Those with an eye on their constituencies were worried about it because duty free was popular, and Watts pointed out that it kept fares low on cross-channel ferries. Corbett, on the other hand, felt it was an anomaly in a single market Europe. Ford recognized the logic of eventual abolition but stalled, wanting a study, supported by Miller. Hendrick insisted the entire rationale behind duty free was flawed.

Kinnock, Spiers and Smith expressed concerns over the proposed agreement on trade with South Africa. The following February they were supporting a draft agreement after four years of negotiations, saying the Commission had been at its protectionist worst and were determined to show solidarity. The government had invited President Mandela to the Cardiff Council.

McCarthy raised problems about late approvals and blockages to cohesion funds and Howitt blamed underspends for some funds on poor management in Brussels. There were five reports on the regulations for Agenda 2000 going through the system and Members were being heavily lobbied. One of the most effective of these was Claudia Hamill of the National Trust who always supplied well-written briefings and specific forms of words for amendments. Hardstaff had things to say about tobacco subsidies and rural development in CAP reform. McNally argued for more gender balance and sustainable development in the 5th Framework Research Programme.

No euro please, we're British

Even though the new Labour government was hesitant about EMU, many Labour MEPs thought it was definitely on its way for the UK and accordingly became highly involved in the technicalities of the new currency. Green had pressed Blair to introduce it immediately after the election but says he feared the euro would unite the Tories and Labour dissidents against the Labour government; she feels he lost the opportunity. When Gordon Brown announced his "five tests" that had to be met prior to Britain joining the single currency it effectively ensured that Britain would not be part of the first wave of eleven countries to adopt the new currency in January 2000. The slogan at home became "prepare and decide". Single currency, enlargement and democratic deficit problems led to some concern about the possibility of a "two-speed Europe" developing

Donnelly had been a first co-rapporteur on EMU and in January 1998 together with Hendrick took part in the debate, stressing the growth part of the Stability and Growth Pact. Parliament held a special session on Saturday 2 May to debate the single currency, led, ironically, by Gordon Brown. The night before, Council unanimously agreed on the eleven countries that would adopt the euro. Green saw it as a momentous day and numerous others saw it as a way of tackling unemployment. With no restraint shown for their Presidency Labour speakers Donnelly and David were in favour but Hindley and Megahy were against. Newens said he was in favour in principle but that "provisions to safeguard the most vulnerable sections of the people have been gravely neglected in the present proposals" and abstained, as did Spiers, regretting that the whole project was "driven by faith, not by reason". Morris also abstained. The EPLP produced a pamphlet entitled "A Single Currency for Europe" shortly after Donnelly was elected Leader, with his introduction saying: "I believe Britain cannot afford to stay out of a successful European single currency. I would urge anyone who cares about jobs and Britain's future prosperity to call for a 'yes' vote in a referendum to join..."

There was a little difficulty for Labour in that Chancellor Brown was unable to attend meetings of ECOFIN Ministers. Some MEPs were unhappy when Brown set a pattern of not attending Socialist Ministers' dinners before Council meetings.

Changing places in the EPLP

Change was in the air. David announced at the AGM in June 1998 that he would retire as Leader and not stand in 1999 in order to concentrate as a candidate on the Welsh Assembly elections due in May that year. (He was unsuccessful in this attempt because Labour's internal battles in Wales led to a poor result, but was eventually elected to the House of Commons in 2001.) Donnelly was elected Leader in a contest with Needle (39 – 20). Donnelly says he had a difficult relationship with Green who did not want him to be Leader, preferring Needle. Simpson had also considered standing but dropped out the day before the contest.

Next, Crawley stood down as Deputy Leader (she was made a life peer on 24 July) to be replaced by McNally. Tappin remained Secretary and Oddy as Treasurer, but Murphy was ousted as Whip by Miller, he thinks possibly for his support for Donnelly as Leader. Tomlinson, who had married Paulette Fuller, also became a life peer on 21 July.

With the group down to sixty and McAvan having replaced West, reformers were in the majority, and the revised standing orders and code of conduct, including the rule about not bringing the party into disrepute, were carried.

Alan Barnard, head of the elections unit, came out on 1 July to talk about how the elections might play with a regional system, carrying a bunch of "key messages" that had been tested to play well with the electorate. MEPs had some input into a Europe policy paper published in August 1998 for endorsement at conference as a background for the next election manifesto.

The European selections fired up the left in the autumn along with an assortment of other discontents, and left-wingers won four of the seven constituency places on the NEC at conference. Michael Cashman, Blair loyalist later to be an MEP, was however succesfully elected.

Painful selections and extinction of the dinosaurs

It was not clear until the end of January in election year, 1999, under which system the European elections would be fought in the UK, but the year before was fraught with tension and tears.

With half of the EPLP out of favour with headquarters, the new electoral system proved an effective mechanism for getting rid of the troublesome. Ever since the landslide in 1994 it had been known that senior staff were disparaging of some of the intake. Some were gleefully in favour of the list system as a potential cleansing mechanism. The expectation was that approximately forty-five would be the most that could be elected, and the announced retirements were not going to be sufficient. The party was also very keen to ensure a higher proportion of women and some minority ethnic members. There would be blood on the walls. In the election that followed party predictions were shattered when it won one fewer seat in each region than expected, leaving some of the more favoured MEPs unelected.

Labour's NEC anticipated the change. A reselection ballot procedure was put in place in the spring of 1998 under OMOV, the procedures for which were outlined in the NEC document: "Elections for the European Parliament 1999, nomination and selection of candidates: procedural guidelines". Candidates seeking reselection had to express their interest by 10 May. Instead of the existing "trigger ballot", there would be two parts, with first a YES/NO section for affirming whether or not individuals agreed the sitting Member should go through to a national pool of candidates for a party list.

New candidates were invited to obtain nominations from branches and parties then attend hustings at ECLPs in July. Sitting MEPs did not have to attend these hustings but were permitted to attend and be invited to speak if members desired. This was confusing to party members, who did not understand why their sitting Members were not putting forward CVs for this open selection process. The procedure following the hustings would be a three part trigger ballot (where there was a sitting Member). Part One was the trigger vote along the lines of "Do you wish xxx, your current MEP, to be re-selected as a candidate for the 1999 European elections?" Part Two invited members to choose between all the duly nominated women candidates to go forward to the national pool of additional nominees, and Part Three did the same for all nominated male candidates. Results sheets had to be sent to regional party offices by 3 August. Some Members had already decided they would retire at the next election, perhaps partly prompted by the expected new list system: Newens, Lomas, Collins (who had never been a backbencher in all his twenty years), Hindley, Megahy, Falconer, Crampton and David, plus Crawley and Tomlinson who had been appointed to the peerage. All the remaining Members passed their trigger ballot in their constituencies with scores in excess of 80%, most of them over 90%.

All the successful candidates (MEPs, and the top women and men from the ballot process – quite a large pool) then had to submit themselves to interview by a team of interrogators. The candidates were to be scored and the panel and NEC would then allocate them to numbered places on regional candidate lists. Interviews were held for Scotland in Edinburgh and for England and Wales at a trades union college at Stoke Rochford in Lincolnshire in the middle of September, clashing with a Friday of the Strasbourg plenary. A by-election style aggressive interview was hardly a good test for an MEP. Their job required good negotiating and diplomatic skills and it was rare for them to face a great deal of media attention.

A further, more complicated and lengthy application form had to be filled out at this stage consisting of a person specification and a job description and requiring candidates to make a first and second choice of the region they would like to be in. There were to be no hostages to fortune. As part of the form applicants had to sign up to the following statement:

> "I agree to abide by the rules and procedural guidelines laid down by the party for these selections and accept that the decisions of the selection boards as approved by party conference shall be final. I undertake to be

bound by the rules and constitution of the party at all times and to sign the
Memorandum for prospective European parliamentary candidates agreed
by the National Executive Committee and the standing orders and declarations of interest required by the EPLP when asked to do so."

The interviewees had four minutes to make a presentation on "Why I
would be a good MEP/Candidate", scored by appearance, communication,
vision and values. A reduced number were then selected for a further interview by a panel of at least eleven "in press conference mode" for ten minutes. At the same time a Memorandum of Agreement had been drawn up,
tortuously agreed by the EPLP and Labour Party governing agreements for
the operation of new regional teams. This was a demand that MEPs agree to
locate their office with that of the regional Labour Party or at least to pay
that body a proportion of their office allowance. Coates had earlier insisted
that as under Parliament's rules "MEPs shall not be bound by any instructions and shall not receive a binding mandate", all this was illegal. He complained to Parliament's President who referred it for investigation by the
Rules Committee where it met a dead end.

Margaret McDonagh took over from Tom Sawyer as General Secretary of
the party at around the same time in September 1998, adding to a bunch of
tough women running the party, with Green in Europe and Anji Hunter and
Sally Morgan in Blair's office. She was described in *The Guardian* as "charm-
ing, dedicated and ruthless". David Gardner was in charge of candidate
selection and it was he who devised the system. MEPs felt distinctly
unloved by these two and by the aggressive and unfriendly process.

Shock and awe

The Stoke Rochford event has been described by many as brutal and insen-
sitive. A sour taste remained even a decade later. The panel comprised five
NEC members (Richard Rosser, Ian McCartney, John Allen, Margaret Wall
and Maggie Jones), three representatives from the relevant regional board,
one from the national TU Liaison Committee and the outgoing General
Secretary, Tom Sawyer. The ranking decisions made by the panel were supposed to be final, but in the event proved much more acrimonious and there
remains a feeling that the lists were fixed according to different criteria than
the official ones. There is a lasting impression that party hacks had
favourites not only amongst the existing MEPs but amongst other candidates and were determined to construct lists to suit that agenda, with no
appreciation of or even interest in the parliamentary record and standing of
the MEPs. Members were not given their "scores" and were warned that
anyone complaining about the procedures would be open to disqualifica-
tion, which kept many mouths shut. An atmosphere of fear and acrimony
prevailed. Panorama made a TV programme about it, screened in February
1999. Those MEPs who wished to stand were guaranteed a place on the list.
There were over a hundred other candidates and many were whittled out
after the first interview.

Even loyal Members felt that many on the panel enjoyed watching them
squirm and deliberately asked questions unrelated to Europe, such as their
views on nurses' pay. Some panellists had been overheard joking offen-

sively about Members in the bar. It was not only the "usual culprits" who were penalised, but many strange decisions were made despite the intricate points system which Gardner had introduced in the hope of safeguarding the party against challenges. Most were sure that Number 10 had a hand in the ranking and it was clear that absolutely not a squeak of dissent from the new Labour line was to be tolerated. The list that was put to party conference in the autumn was not the same as that on which the election was finally run and was the subject of dissent on the NEC. Even the *Financial Times* reported that the leadership had been accused of ensuring no left-wing Labour MEPs were returned.

In the North West region the ten seats were all held by men. Newman and Hindley had decided to go. Newman was a strong opponent of PR who won over 80% in the trigger process; he resigned rather than submit to the interview but would have stayed for another term under the old system as he loved the work. He felt headquarters were out to get him for his old associations with Militant, even though he had worked conscientiously and had good relations with the Regional Executive. McCarthy, whose constituency was largely in East Midlands but who had spent time living and working in Manchester, was moved into top place on the list. Donnelly had suggested to Titley that he would be in this place but the latter says he was happy to be in a winning slot. McCarthy and he had never hit it off, being entirely different personalities. Titley says he was hoping that Ruth Turner (who later worked in Blair's Downing Street office) would get into a high place and she was also favourite with some of the officials such as Coleman. Attempts were made to transfer Hendrick to the West Midlands or Yorkshire but he did not want to be moved. It was still far too top heavy with people the party would have liked to have kept.

Harrison was then shifted across the border to Wales, causing uproar there because this meant putting both Wilson and Morris at risk. Wayne David says that in normal circumstances this would probably have been accepted by party members in Wales, as he had a good reputation and was known across the border. But following the Welsh Secretary's "moment of madness" on Clapham Common, Tony Blair had insisted that Alun Michael MP should be the Leader of the Party there rather than the popular but possibly more independent Rhodri Morgan. As a consequence the Welsh party was in a state of near-civil war and in no mood to accept what many saw as the imposition of an outsider. Harrison was unwell and in hospital that autumn and after a great deal of tension withdrew, a strategy happily accepted by the NEC. (He was given a peerage shortly after the election.) Morris, aged 69, pulled out. The *South Wales Evening Post* of 30 September said this was after he was placed fifth out of five and that Labour Party members were angry at the selection panel. On 23 September the same paper had reported that Morris was in real danger of losing his seat following his own party's decision to import a candidate from England (Harrison).

Corbett was moved across from the North West to Yorkshire and the Humber, where Crampton had retired, which shunted Barton, Seal, Hardstaff and McGowan down the list. Hardstaff was very disappointed, having worked hard and loyally during her five year term, and in particular contributed much effort in marginal parliamentary seats. McGowan, placed last, pulled out. Ford, originally from the West Country, was shifted out of the North West across to the South West region. There was then a danger, with the aim of interleafing a woman, that White could be placed number three, but Ford says he insisted on him being second. Ford closed down his Manchester office and set up in the South West, making his assistant of twelve years redundant, who then made allegations about his office expenses. This triggered a parliamentary audit which dragged on before eventually clearing him, but the unwelcome publicity during the election campaign was thought (including by White) to have contributed to White's defeat. After Stoke Rochford, Coleman says a number of Members closed offices and there were arguments with some about selling property and ownership.

There was more manoeuvring on the West Midlands list, where two Londoners were parachuted in above Tappin, Hallam and Oddy, one of whom was Indian Neena Gill, the other a well-known gay actor Michael Cashman, disparagingly described by Tappin as a "London Labour luvvy". Oddy, with 90.9% of her party vote, felt insulted and went into dispute with the party, refusing to accept the position she had been given (seventh out of eight) and putting in an industrial tribunal complaint so that she could see her scoring record. All this took some time and she circulated a personal letter to all Labour members in her constituency saying she was resigning, was then suspended by the party and expelled. She then decided to stand as an independent.

The East Midlands continued to have more "acceptable" candidates than had a hope of election even after McCarthy had been moved out and there was talk of inserting Asian Valerie Vaz in a winnable place. There were some negotiations and regional representatives supported placing the candidates in order of merit as they assessed the situation. The agreed list had four women out of six with men in second and sixth places, the first four being sitting MEPs. In Scotland the introduction of several new women higher than Smith and McMahon prompted Smith to retire. In the North East a new woman was inserted above Gordon Adam but he took that in good spirit. He said that he would be 65, it was necessary to have a woman in a winnable place, and at the time they did think they would win four places.

London was another bloodbath. The three female MEPs in that region all thought they were sure to be in winnable positions because of their high profile, loyalty and achievements, but they had reckoned without the skill of Balfe, a friend of McDonagh, and the determination of the party to insert a minority ethnic candidate, Claude Moraes. Balfe was fourth, Pollack was pushed out to the South East region and Tongue was placed fifth, considered a highly risky position. The list ended up as one woman followed by three men then the next woman rather than the promised gender alternation. Polly Toynbee claimed in her *Guardian* column that Tongue had been demoted due to her opposition to Rupert Murdoch. Elliott was put at the bottom of the list (complaining of ageism) but stayed, he says out of loyalty to the party. In the South East, the two men from Kent, including one whose seat had been so marginal he had not expected to be returned, were put at the top rather than gender zipping.

There was said to be no appeal, but some behind-the-scenes attempts were made to change the list put to the NEC, without success. It was suggested that any change would wreck the "package". Diane Abbott, Ken Livingstone and Dennis Skinner on the NEC voted against the list of candidates, but it went through.

Obviously the elaborate points system was not the key factor in drawing up the lists. The party was determined to insert a woman into the first or second place on every list (it did not succeed in doing that; in four regions the highest-placed woman was number three and of these only one was an MEP) and include minority ethnic candidates in wining places in more than one region (it did do that). There was a ruthless determination to eliminate any voices dissenting from New Labour philosophy. No candidate in a winnable place was a member of the Campaign Group.

Was there also a strong streak of ageism? An objective look at the less winnable placements might suggest this was the case regardless of the ability or political stance of the MEPs. In Scotland, McMahon was sixty. In the North East, Adam was sixty-four. In Yorkshire, Seal was sixty-one and Hardstaff fifty-seven. It was not the case in the North West, where Wynn in a winnable place was fifty-two but Hendrick and Cunningham, lower placed but all equally "on message" were much younger. In Wales, Wilson was sixty-one. In East Midlands, Waddington was fifty-four and Billingham was fifty-nine, although both Read and Whitehead were also in this age range, at fifty-nine and sixty-one respectively. In West Midlands, Tappin was fifty-two. It was not the case in Eastern region, where all the others were younger than McNally who was Number one. In London Elliott was sixty-six. In the South East, Pollack, with a 96.6% approval rating from her constituency was fifty-two. None of these were Campaign Group.

Green, top of the list for London, acknowledged that some people would be disappointed with their ranking, but said the party would fight for every seat. Coates (who had not been a candidate) wrote to *The Guardian* on 26 September saying "the selection process was a travesty of democracy" and that "the next set of MEPs will only be accountable to those that appointed them". Life had to go on, and the party held an induction meeting for European candidates in Brussels on 5 November. Those who had attended party conference that year in Blackpool were in a very subdued mood.

Constituency Labour parties were told that they had to pay £2,000 to central election funds and this alienated the grass roots even more. Quite a few refused to pay, mostly citing poverty. Had they been organized, however, this should not have been an onerous burden, as it was well-known that European elections came along every five years and it ought to have not been beyond the ability of parties to set up regular fundraising.

In April candidates had to sign up to a "service level agreement" promising to "share" resources with regional offices. The way these were worded could probably never have been enforced in law, and Members had a number of differences of opinion about how best to comply with the demands from the party on finance. Teeth were gritted and forms were signed, but nothing was resolved until after the election.

The show goes on

John Hume and David Trimble won the Nobel Peace Prize in October 1988. Hume called the EU the "best example... in the history of the world of conflict resolution." He was thereafter in even more demand to speak to British visitor groups. Hume was delighted to be able to welcome members of the first Northern Ireland Assembly in November.

SNP Member McCartney died and the resultant by-election in NE Scotland was held on 26 November 1998. Labour's candidate was Kathleen Walkershaw who had been running the GMB office in Brussels. Former MEP McCubbin had by this time left the party. Labour had an unhappy campaign and came disastrously third after the Conservatives. Ian Hudghton of SNP won with Struan Stevenson (Conservative) second; a convincing win for SNP this time with 47% of the vote and a turnout of 20.5%. Labour was also to do less well than hoped in Scotland in the Scottish Parliament elections the following May.

Most MEPs, though battered by the traumatic period they had been through, continued with their work. There is only space to record a fraction here. The LEONARDO programme was back with rapporteur Waddington. Kerr was unable to resist referring to her less-than-favourable place on the election list. She stoically carried on and it went through in March at the height of criticism about poor management of the fund; she supported the common position with improved evaluation and monitoring systems. Newman, rapporteur on the Ombudsman's report, suggested a code of conduct for the Union's institutions. Harrison had a report on late payments, being particularly concerned about SMEs. Read was still working on telecoms equipment and attempting to reach a working agreement on another directive. Adam was rapporteur on solid fuels and supported a programme.

Kerr, happily residing on the Green benches and pursuing his attacks on Labour, made more speeches in this last year on a wide range of subjects than in his entire time in Parliament, on one day managing to get to his feet six times on different reports. The Greens had made him their spokesperson both on the Culture Committee and Women's Rights and Equality.

Spending its Information money, the EPLP produced a glossy 24-page brochure entitled "A Democratic Europe", tackling meatier issues than many publications in the past. It had sections on co-decision and the democratic deficit, subsidiarity and the nation state and comitology amongst others, written by Donnelly, Collins, Corbett, Martin, Tongue, Howitt, David, Spiers and Wynn.

The "Pro-Europe Conservative Party"

In this parliament approximately two-thirds of the Conservatives were still pro-EU but the tide had been turning since the Thatcher era. The more active pro-Europeans began to find their position uncomfortable. John Moorhouse joined the ELDR (Liberal Group) in October and there were some defections to Labour in the House of Commons after the Labour victory. The news of Moorhouse's defection was greeted by Balfe saying "he is too left-wing to have a place in the modern Labour Party." Hallam cheekily invited pro-European Cassidy to join the Labour Party. He declined.

In the Conservative selections in mid 1998 pro-Europeans Brendan Donnelly and John Stevens were put lower down the list than they had hoped due to their federalist views. The final selections for the Conservatives were mass membership meetings, often packed with Eurosceptics. Donnelly resigned from the Conservative Party in January 1999 and then he and Stevens formed a Pro-Europe Conservative Party, hoping in vain for support from some big beasts such as Ken Clarke. They stood candidates in all regions, thus gaining an election broadcast and put out a manifesto. None of their candidates was elected. Paul Howell stood in the East of England, Andrew Pearce in the North West, John Stevens in the South East and Brendan Donnelly in West Midlands. The party subsequently fought another couple of elections until some of its members drifted away to the Liberal Democrats. Donnelly has now formed "YES2EUROPE" and is Director of the Federal Trust.

Expenses rows

Back in 1996 a TV programme depicted some Members, including British, signing in and then going off to the airport. The ensuing bad publicity spread around Europe's media like wildfire. Tepid parliamentary reforms such as cutting back on trips outside the normal working places continued. From the end of 1997 Members had to be present for a majority of roll call votes (RCV) in a plenary week in order to obtain their daily expenses. For a time the signing-in sheets were placed outside the hemicycle but were soon moved back inside away from the cameras. There was debate as to whether presence in the chamber was sufficient on RCV voting days rather than actual voting and Falconer took up this loophole and made a fuss, announcing his presence at every voting time for months to the eventual exasperation of plenary chairpersons and some of his own colleagues.

After much unfavourable publicity about Members' expenses in Sweden and elsewhere tortuous attempts were made during this year to draw up a Statute for Members. At least part of the problem was seen as being the low salaries for some (MEPs being paid very different amounts according to those in their respective national parliaments), leading to the expenses system being used as a top up. Rothley from the Socialist Group was rapporteur. He was not a great enthusiast for stringent reform and lengthy acrimonious discussions were held both in group and committee, particularly with some of the British who were very anxious to clean up the system. He advocated a common salary and a common European tax system, the latter not being supported by Labour.

Votes on the reform proposals were first held during the Brussels plenary of 3 December. Both the main points were contentious. Green saw it as particularly important to try to quell the bad publicity in the British press. She said she wanted the reform package adopted, but that "we cannot deal with reforming expenses until the problem of inequalities of income have been solved". She also insisted that having reimbursement for travel costs based on "actuals" was fundamental. Voting on the report took many hours and with some Conservatives and many Germans across the board voting against it finally went through albeit including an opt-out clause for sitting MEPs. Votes were 327 – 120 and 43 abstentions. It was generally considered to be a bad text.

After being mauled in Council and subjected to intense negotiations inside Parliament, the statute came back for a plenary vote on 5 May 1999, just before the elections. The Socialists were divided with Green's position outvoted. Voting was 36 against the text with 140 in favour and 31 abstentions. Labour at that stage would have voted for any text that looked like a reform and Priestley writes: "On the eve of a new legislature, it was a mortal blow to Green's authority" but it went back to the drawing board to be fought again in another parliament. Senior staffers say that Green's opposition to the Germans on the Members' Statute contributed to her losing the Presidency of the group the next time around and it may indeed have been a factor. (A more comprehensive account of the expenses reform can be found in Priestley 2008.)

Fraud and resignation of the Santer Commission

An early inkling of the row to come over fraud surfaced in the autumn of 1997 when the European Court of Auditors report outlined serious mismanagement in implementation of the 1996 budget. These annual reports have always highlighted mismanagement, and often problems with maladministration of funds, particularly those for agriculture, in Member States, but this one was much tougher than usual. Parliament postponed granting discharge from March 1998 until more explanations had been received. Tomlinson had succeeded in having an anti-fraud office set up in the Commission in October 1998 and originally thought the fraud problem could be handled. But this time there had been more than the usual amount of whistle-blowing inside the Commission and in the press from a financial official, Paul van Buitenen, and accusations about misspending in various funds such as those for the Mediterranean (MEDA), Central and Eastern Europe (PHARE), and Russia (TACIS), but also by Socialist Commissioner Edith Cresson, with some accusations concerning Socialist Commissioner Manuel Marin and Radical Emma Bonino. A report on fraud was sent to Parliament and the Court of Auditors in July, and van Buitenen sent a dossier of his accusations to the Green Group. The rapporteur for the discharge, Conservative James Elles, had once been a Commission official and smelled socialist blood.

At the Brussels plenary in December Morgan, becoming active on Budget Control, complained about the need for regular investigations of alleged fraud and corruption and that Finnish Socialist Commissioner Erki Liikanen had been tireless in his efforts to clean up the act. President Santer reported that the anti-fraud office should be in operation within six to seven months but his lengthy speech was attacked by Members. Two weeks later in Strasbourg the problems facing discharge of the 1996 budget loomed larger. First, a request to refer the Elles report (which had been highly controversial during its passage through the Budget Control Committee) back to committee was rejected. Socialists in the main (though not some of the Nordic and Dutch) were happy with that as Green felt that referral back was tantamount to refusal to discharge. This was disputed by Elles and the onslaught continued. On 17 December in Strasbourg the Greens and GUE group accused the Commission of blackmail. After numerous votes on amendments to the report Green led the Socialists in a highly risky manoeuvre, tantamount to dancing with wolves, announcing that her group would table a motion of censure on the Commission if Parliament did not support discharge. Her idea was that the group would not vote for its own censure motion.

This tactic came after accusations against Cresson and Marin (both Socialist Commissioners) and her line was that defeat of such a bold resolution was the only way to win confidence for the Commission and stop the bad publicity. There was an acrimonious exchange between the Socialist and Christian Democrat leaders before the final vote on whether to grant discharge during which Green threatened to table her motion of censure. The paragraph concerned was voted against, by 225 – 270 and 23 abstentions. Priestley (2008), who has a lengthy account of this whole event, said this was not the same as refusing to grant discharge.

Green acknowledged later that this was a tortuous procedure but said the French did not want a critical resolution, Cresson was refusing to resign and the right was saying the Commission was corrupt. Parliament has no power to sack an individual Commissioner and she felt they had to create clarity. The debate on the censure motion was held over until January. Donnelly in the mean time was trying to win agreement for some sort of independent review of the allegations against the Commission.

By 11 January there were two motions of censure, one from the Socialists and another, more strongly worded, from an alliance of the right, Liberals and Green groups. Green pointed out that "We do not have the institutional right to cherry pick… why is there no mention of the CAP when fraud there is well documented and ongoing… or PHARE and TACIS…" Speakers were the various group leaders. Everything by now was being played to the pre-electoral gallery.

On the 13th the Budget Committee said it would report to Parliament by the end of March on the discharge. Santer made a statement and Parliament suspended the session for fifteen minutes. Green then said:

> "If we are to demand the heads of certain individuals on the basis of public campaigns before proper investigation is completed, or sometimes even started, then perhaps we should have resigned *en masse* when the media was it its most vitriolic in claiming that MEPs were abusing their allowances."

For the vote on the 14th, she withdrew her group's resolution and the other one was defeated by 232 – 293 with 27 abstentions. Ford's explanation of vote said it was less a vote of confidence than a final warning. In the voting pattern, Members from countries that benefited from the most funding took the most lenient position. A joint resolution from the Socialists and the left was then carried, calling for improved financial management of the Commission and for a committee of independent experts to examine the way in which the Commission detects and deals with fraud, mismanagement and nepotism, including a fundamental review of Commission practices in awarding all financial contracts. This committee was to report by 15 March. It was a hard-hitting resolution, going on for nine paragraphs about the Commission's belated recognition of the crisis facing it concerning management of the Community budget and its lack of transparency and accountability. Staff in the Commission were unhappy about all the accusations of fraud and the services went on strike on two occasions, in February and again in April.

Labour supported Green's approach, but many had misgivings about lengthily drawing out the debates on fraud, conscious that at home voters did not distinguish between the Commission and Parliament and saw only bad news at the beginning of election year. Some thought the strategy was completely mad. Neil Kinnock said that he had wanted an independent committee of inquiry, and felt that no-one would listen to an explanation of innocence if the Commission didn't resign.

The resultant so-called Committee of Wise Men was too much to the right for the Socialists and a Swedish social democratic woman was added. From then things fell apart. Upon investigation the feeling was that no-one in the Commission would co-operate and take responsibility for the errors. After spending more than a month thoroughly investigating a range of problems, not least the operation of the LEONARDO programme that had been Cresson's responsibility, the report that came out was so critical there was no way the Socialist Group could support the Commission. The most damning sentence was: "It is becoming difficult to find anyone who has even the slightest sense of responsibility." After considering the report the Socialist Group decided it had to support a censure vote. Green told Santer of the Group position after a meeting at 8pm on 15 March and at 10pm the Commission resigned *en bloc*. Reporting on 18 March, *European Voice* wrote: "It was Jacques Santer's stubbornness and the French government's refusal to sacrifice Edith Cresson that left their colleagues with no option but to resign *en masse* this week."

Santer made his formal statement to Parliament on 22 March in Brussels. Green made a lengthy speech demanding that Council put forward an experienced, competent candidate for President of the Commission committed to in-depth reform. Wilfried Martens, the leader of the Christian Democrats, did likewise but enjoyed criticizing Cresson. A joint motion for resolution on resignation of the Commission was voted and Green attempted an oral amendment. Donnelly demanded root and branch reform at the Commission.

What followed was a strange period, because most Member State governments had not nominated any replacements, so the lame duck Commission had to stay on. Blair had re-nominated Kinnock.

Heads of government met at the Berlin Summit to find a successor to Santer. When Romano Prodi was put forward Green advised Blair that he was a federalist, but Blair thought he could be controlled and he became the nominee.

Lame ducks everywhere

During the early part of 1999 Labour MEPs, whether in a happy position on the list or not, pursued their various dossiers. Titley was rapporteur on defence industries in January, supporting Airbus; Bowe was rapporteur on GMOs, expressing some ethical concerns; and White, as rapporteur on water quality, piloted his report through second reading with two hundred amendments.

The March session featured a debate on women. Waddington spoke on the DAPHNE programme on violence against women, congratulating popular Swedish Socialist Commissioner Anita Gradin. Kerr pounced again, saying "by effectively de-selecting three of our women candidates, Sue Waddington, spokesman on women's rights, Oddy and Hardstaff, the Labour Party has made a poor contribution to women's rights." Also in March, Adam was rapporteur on trans-EU energy networks and Truscott was rapporteur on relations with Central Asian countries. More than a third of the EPLP, chiefly those in less-than-safe places on the list, intervened.

McCarthy's work on regulations for the structural funds was coming to a high point. She was still arguing the need to retain the URBAN fund, supported by David seeking Objective One status for South Wales. In March, McCarthy was deploring right-wing votes undermining Agenda 2000. It was debated again in April where she welcomed the Northern Ireland Peace Fund approval but said URBAN was still to be resolved. At the very last moment in May she felt the key principles had been met and in the UK Objective One status was won for Merseyside and West Wales and the Valleys. The latter was to be of some consolation to David when he lost his election to the Welsh Assembly in May. Lord Tomlinson, rapporteur on the budget part of Agenda 2000, said it was better to have something slightly inadequate than nothing.

In April Read was rapporteur on electronic exchange of data between administrations, Harrison on changes to the VAT system, McMahon on working time and Simpson similarly was involved on behalf of transport workers currently excluded from the directive. Oddy gave an official opinion from the Legal Committee on informing and consulting employees saying the provision filled a gap in employment legislation but that "there are some misgivings from my own country".

Commission President-elect Prodi made his statement to Parliament on 13 April. He had spoken to the Socialist Group the previous week and Green welcomed his speech, saying they were keen to see the caretaker Commission leave as soon as possible. The atmosphere was far from subdued, as election fever was in the air. Herve Fabre-Aubespy of the French right accused Green of playing toy town politics all year, to which Green retorted:

> "To those who are shouting at me I actually thrive on it. I note that the level of personal abuse towards me from the right has risen as the right's political fortunes have fallen all across the EU. It was the EPP which split from top to bottom in March on the motion of censure, with the majority voting for the Socialist position."

She attacked their leader, Martens, then the Liberal leader Pat Cox, saying that his statement "was in line with the cheap opportunism for which his political family is famous". At the end of the week Green was having another row with the right, declaring that a resolution they had tabled demanding the Commission resign now was inadmissible. Kerr attacked her on the grounds that the Commission had resigned two months ago but were still drawing salaries.

Last calls again – bowing out gracefully

Goodbyes were being said as early as April. Newman led off with dignity as rapporteur on the 1998 petitions. He said that he was the only MEP with full and continuous active membership of this committee since its formation in January 1987 and thanked those he had worked with and his constituency. He was warmly thanked for the vast amount of work he did by Socialist colleague Renzo Imbeni who happened to be chairing. Titley warmly thanked von Habsburg for his advice over time – the old aristocrat was retiring.

Ken Collins, who was retiring, applauded the decision not to split the big Environment Committee (a battle won yet again). McMahon, too, gave his "swan song" as he called it, as rapporteur on senior citizens in the 21st century on which the Commission was bringing forward a Communication.

Hughes said there was a still problem for atypical workers on fixed term contracts but supported an agreement and also expressed some concerns at second reading on protection of workers from risks of explosive atmospheres. As it was his last speech as Chair of his committee he thanked everyone for their work.

Oddy was slogging away to the last as rapporteur on the legal aspects of electronic trading. She then made a personal statement saying that the General Secretary of the Labour Party had suspended her by fax and that she was astonished and did not know what she had done wrong.

Green thanked the President at the end of a tumultous period. The last words on Friday 7 May were Ford speaking on the minutes, McMahon on Labour's election victory in Scotland and Hallam, ending as he had started on a point of order. A further twenty-two EPLP Members spoke in the April and May plenaries.

Behind the Scenes

EPLP staffers in Brussels were earlier Stephen Brown, Fran Bennett and Cathy Burton. By 1995 Julian Scola and Maggie Coulthard were the key workers. In London it was Dianne Hayter until the end of 1996 then, following the stop-gap Larry Whitty, Peter Coleman and Carol Rawlings, and finally Nick Smith, Andrew Forrester and Emma Whelan.

There were many Brits in the Socialist Group staff but some moved on. Colin Kotz left to train to be an interpreter. Dick Gupwell took an early retirement package in 1996 after the Nordic countries joined, and became honorary secretary-general of the European Institute for South Asian Studies until late 2009 when he retired. Geoff Harris had moved to the Parliament staff. Marion Dewar, daughter of the MP Donald Dewar, joined the Group in 1995, working on the economic committee for a time. Patrick Costello joined in September 1996 to work on foreign affairs, the Asia working group and Turkey, later moving on to a Commissioner's cabinet. Kerry Postlewhite and Katrina Morris were also there, Kerry for some of the time working on the Environment Committee and since moved to Africa. Katrina was on Budgets with Tessa Ryan. Nick Crook had moved by 1997 to the PES as a seconded member of Group Staff. He worked on Budget Control with Tomlinson for some of the time. He now works with the trade union UNISON in the UK and represents the TUC on ECOSOC.

Chris Piening was a British parliamentary official involved in the European Transatlantic dialogue. He was a great comrade: intelligent, witty, sociable, diplomatic and knowledgeable on most matters concerning foreign affairs. Having begun his parliamentary career as a translator in 1973, he worked in various departments including the Cabinet of a President. He took a year out as a visiting fellow at the University of Washington in Seattle in 1995-96, from which came his book *Global Europe: The European Union in World Affairs* (1997). He was a good friend of Priestley and Ford, whose wife Daniela would host dinner parties attended by Pollack and others where

Chris would hold forth on international politics. He became head of the UK office of the Parliament in 1999 and sadly died in 2001 after a long battle with amyloidosis. He is hugely missed and his reputation was so high that his death was reported in the US Congress; the University of Washington set up a memorial foundation, and the European Parliament now offers a Chris Piening Fellowship.

An achievement for the Members' staff group was that they negotiated that when staff were made redundant they should receive an appropriate financial package. When the electoral system was changed and it was clear that many would lose their jobs, there were some training days arranged in the EP offices in London on cv writing and other forms of support.

Gareth Harding, one of the talented assistants, in the autumn of 1995 produced *Under Milk Wood* in Brussels, succeeding in getting the Welsh MEPs to take part plus John Gray, the UK Ambassador who was Welsh and Hywel Ceri Jones, one of the UK's top-ranking Commission officials. It attracted a front page piece in the *Western Mail*.

The EPLP annual reviews continued during the Christmas session each year, fundraising for charities and cementing relations with some other comrades.

Falling off the roundabout

In the European election of June 1999 turnout was much worse than before at 24% in the UK. Labour lost badly with a 10.4% swing against it, losing one more seat in each region than it had thought would be the case. It attracted only 28% of the vote and elected twenty-nine MEPs against the Conservatives 36% and thirty-six MEPs. The era of socialist rule was over. The only upside for Labour was that the new system saw the percentage of women at long last go up to 34.5% and there were two minority ethnic Members.

Of the sitting Members who contested on the Labour list the following twenty lost their seats: Adam, Barton, Billingham, Cunningham, Elliott, Hallam, Hardstaff, Hendrick, McMahon, Needle, Pollack, Seal, Spiers, Tappin, Thomas, Tongue, Truscott, Waddington, White and Wilson. These were mostly loyal high-achievers and most were devastated by their loss, not to mention the dozens of talented staff members they then had to make redundant. Barry Seal was having triple heart bypass surgery on election day.

Three others who had been Labour at the beginning of the parliamentary term also lost. Hugh Kerr stood as number one on the Scottish Socialist Party list and Ken Coates as number one for Alternative Labour in East Midlands, where Nick Clegg was elected for the Liberal Democrats. Christine Oddy stood as "MEP Independent Labour" and gained sufficient votes not to lose her deposit, possibly taking enough votes off Labour to ensure the defeat of Mike Tappin. (A full description of the election can be found in Westlake (2000).)

Former Commission President Santer came back as a Luxembourg MEP. The Socialist Group did badly and was no longer the largest group, winning 180 to the EPP's 233. Green lost her position as its Leader to Enrique Baron and with that went her NEC seat. Within six months both Green and Donnelly announced their retirement from the European Parliament. Donnelly's retirement allowed Gordon Adam back but the position in

London in replacing Green was more complicated. Due to personal circum-stances, neither Tongue nor Spiers (the next two in line) were able to take up the place. Spiers said when the vacancy came up he didn't trust the party enough to come back and thought he would be better off sticking to the executive job he had found. Pollack was marooned on the South East list, and Mary Honeyball came in from seventh place on the list.

Billingham and Truscott were later given peerages, joining Crawley, Harrison and Tomlinson. Simpson returned to the European Parliament in 2006 on the retirement of Terry Wynn and Hendrick became an MP at a by-election in 2000. David and Cunningham were elected to the House of Commons at the 2001 election. The latter had a hard time until then, being unemployed with a young baby. The rest were left to their own devices.

After the resignation drama of the spring of 1999, the Commission that was appointed that summer was more left-wing in composition than the previous one, reflecting the increasingly left balance of power on the Council of Ministers at the time.

Afterword

The European project has often been called a political experiment. In the twenty years covered by this book the world's only trans-national directly-elected Parliament has come a long way both in the power it can wield and in democratic legitimacy. Labour came a long way with it. In 1979 there were nine Member States. By 1999 there were fifteen and the numbers jumped with the accession of ten more in 2004 and two in 2007, mostly from Central and Eastern Europe. Despite their efforts, Members of the Parliament remain largely invisible to the citizens who elect them, and turnout at elections is reducing rather than increasing. This is cause for concern.

Because the European Parliament runs on a committee-based system, MEPs build up real expertise and have been able to evolve with the increasing powers of the Parliament, ensuring appropriate amendments find their way into legislation. In this they have power well in excess of that of a back-bench MP in the House of Commons. Most Members spoke of loving the work and finding it enormously rewarding despite the rigours of endless travel. Many said it was the best job they ever had and hugely enjoyed the privilege of working with people from other cultures and being able to be part of policy-making that made a difference. There has not been enough space, even in a book of three hundred pages, to do full justice to all the efforts and achievements of every Labour MEP.

Many of the Members enjoyed the travel with the Socialist Group, their delegations and their committees, not only to other countries in the EU, but to the rest of the world, meeting interesting people, seeing projects relevant to their work and advancing the cause of social democracy. Occasionally it was a bit like local Councillors on holiday, but the prevailing view, despite the long hours and pressures of work, was that it was a privilege to be a Member of the European Parliament, and able to be part of building a peaceful and prosperous Europe.

Labour's policy on Europe changed dramatically over these two decades, from demanding outright withdrawal in 1979 to full participation in Treaty amendment, reform and European governance. Former Leader Neil Kinnock was Vice-President of the Commission in his second term of office beginning in 1999. The Labour delegation from Britain in these two decades went from strength to strength; from 17 to 32 to 45 to 62, losing only two seats (in 1984 and 1994) until the crash of 1999. Members gave unstintingly of their time and resources to help elect a Labour government in 1997 and provided British politicians, both in government and before, with hundreds of detailed policy briefings. They worked closely with trades unions and civil society.

Of the eighty-three Members who served during these twenty years, the House of Commons claimed thirteen, of whom at least half have had a government position. Seven became Peers and at the time of going to press ten had died. One was knighted, one a Dame, one became a Conservative, one a Scottish Socialist, and at least nine more were no longer in the Labour Party. The Labour Group's first administrator became Leader of the House of Lords.

Sir Stephen Wall, Permanent Representative to the EU from 1995 to 2000 wrote: "the quality of British MEPs is generally high as is the professional standard of their work" (Wall, 2000). He said that in areas such as financial services, a critically important British interest, the MEPs have helped advance the British agenda. They certainly did so in many other fields too, particularly environment and consumer protection and workers' rights. The majority had been there for high aims and scored a number of achievements, living up to Jean Monnet's statement: "to be, not of those who want to be something, but those who want to do something."

At Ken Collins' retirement party there were over 400 people, mostly non-British, an indication of the amount of respect he had built for his work on the environment and that he had won friends cross party. Whilst sometimes temperamental, he put environment and public health in the forefront of European policy and cleverly used Parliament's growing powers to set the agenda.

From the landslide intake of 1994, a young Eurosceptic Shaun Spiers later said he had felt slightly rudderless in the Parliament and believed that much of the legislation going through should have been dealt with at Member State level. Nevertheless, as with the rest of the Labour team, he was very active on the home front, particularly in the campaign for the 1997 Labour victory. His position on the EU contrasts with that of Mark Watts, another of the younger intake that year, but a modernizing pro-European who relished the work and was happy to forge friendships in the European arena based on common values and interests and who was distressed by what he calls the North-South cultural divide within the EPLP.

The 1999 intake worked under an entirely different system, that of a regional list. Their adjustment to that system and to Labour as a much smaller force in the Parliament, is for another volume.

WHERE ARE THEY NOW?

ADAM, Dr Gordon MEP Northumbria 1979-99 and North East Region 2000-04. Retired.

BALFE, Richard MEP London South Inner 1979-99, London Region 1999-2004. Excluded from Labour Party December 2001. Joined Conservative Party March 2002, the first defection from Labour to the Conservatives since Reg Prentice in 1977. Retired from European Parliament in June 2004 but continues as Chair of European Parliament Members' Pension Fund. Conservative trades union envoy.

BARTON, Roger MEP Sheffield 1989-99. Contested Yorkshire and Humberside region 1999. Founded a llama trekking company, now retired.

BILLINGHAM, Baroness Angela MEP Northamptonshire and Blaby 1994-99. Contested East Midlands region 1999. Life Peerage May 2000. Chair of "Catalyst Corby" urban regeneration company 2003-08 and succeeded in having a passenger railway station built in the town. Regular appearances on Sky TV.

BIRD, John MEP for Midlands West 1987-94. Died 18 November 1997.

BOWE, David MEP Cleveland and Yorkshire North, then Cleveland and Richmond, then Yorkshire and Humberside Region 1989-2004. Contested Yorkshire and Humberside Region 2004 and 2009. Public affairs consultant.

BOYES, Roland MEP Durham 1979-84. MP for Houghton and Washington 1983-97, Shadow Spokesman on Environment and Defence. Died, suffering from early onset of Alzheimer's disease, in June 2006.

BUCHAN, Janey MEP Glasgow 1979-94. Founder, Centre for Political Song, Glasgow Caledonian University. Retired, living in London.

CABORN, Richard MEP Sheffield 1979-84. MP Sheffield 1983 – Minister for Sport in Labour government of 1997. To stand down from Parliament in 2010.

CASTLE, Barbara MP Blackburn 1945-79, MEP Greater Manchester North then Greater Manchester West 1979-89. Cross of Order of Merit of FDR (Germany) for services to European democracy 1990. Award from South Africa for outstanding contribution against apartheid. Life peerage 1990. Died 3 May 2002.

CLWYD, Ann MEP for Mid and West Wales 1979-84. MP Cynon Valley (by-election) in 1984 – the first woman in a Welsh Valleys constituency. Special envoy to the Prime Minister on Human Rights in Iraq from 2003.

COATES, Ken MEP Nottingham 1989-99. Excluded from Labour Party 1998 and sat with the GUE group in European Parliament in the last year. Contested 1999 European election as Alternative Labour. Chairman of the Bertrand Russell Peace Foundation. Author of numerous books, articles and pamphlets. Not a member of any political party.

COLLINS, Sir Ken MEP Strathclyde 1979-99. Chair of Scottish Environment Protection Agency 1999-2007. Knighted 2003 "for services to environmental protection". Chair of Scottish Alliance for Geosciences, Environment and Society since 2008.

CORBETT, Richard MEP Merseyside West 1996-99 and Yorkshire and Humberside Region 1999-2009.

CRAMPTON, Peter MEP Humberside 1989-99. Retired in 1999. No longer in Labour Party.

CRAWLEY, Baroness Christine MEP Birmingham East 1984-99. Life peerage 1998. Chair of Women's National Commission 1999-2002. Government Whip House of Lords 2002-2008.

CRYER, Robert (Bob) MEP Sheffield 1984-89. MP for Keighley 1974-83 and MP for Bradford South 1987-94; died 13 April 1994.

CUNNINGHAM, Tony MEP Cumbria and Lancashire North 1994-99. Contested North West Region 1999. MP Workington 2001 – Government Whip since 2005 and from 2008 Pairing Whip.

DAVID, Wayne MEP South Wales 1989-99. Contested Rhondda for Welsh Assembly election in May 1999. MP for Caerphilly 2001-. Parliamentary Under-Secretary of State for Wales 2008-.

DONNELLY, Alan MEP Tyne and Wear 1989-99, then North East Region 1999-2000. Awarded Knight Commander of the Order of Merit by Germany for work on German unification. Founder and Chief Executive Sovereign Strategy.

ELLIOTT, Michael MEP London West 1984-99. Contested London Region in 1999. Returned to Ealing Council 2002 – Mayor of Ealing 2005-06.

ENRIGHT, Derek MEP Leeds 1979-84, contested Kent East in 1984. EC Ambassador to Guinea Bissau 1985-87. First foreigner to be awarded the Order of Merit in Guinea Bissau. MP (byelection) Hemsworth 1991-95. Died 31 October 1995.

EVANS, Robert MEP London North West then London Region 1994-2009.

FALCONER, Alexander MEP Mid Scotland and Fife 1984-99. Retired.

FORD, Glyn MEP 1984-99 Greater Manchester East and South West Region and Gibraltar 1999-2009.

GALLAGHER, Michael MEP Nottinghamshire 1979-84. Contested Lancashire Central for SDP in 1984, later set up Moderate Labour Party in Nottingham. Rejoined Labour in the 1990s and stood for Mansfield Council in 2007. Long-standing consultant for Bellway Homes. Became Director of Simple Solutions 4U. Retired.

GREEN, Dame Pauline MEP London North and then London Region 1989-2000. Chief Executive of Cooperatives UK 2000-2009. Awarded DBE 2003.

GRIFFITHS, Winston (Win) MEP South Wales 1979-89. MP Bridgend 1987-2005. Chair, Bro Morgannwg NHS Trust – June 2005-March 2008. Chair, Abertawe Bro Morgannwg University NHS Trust (merger of Bro Morgannwg and Swansea) – April 2008-October 2009. Chair, Abertawe Bro Morgannwg University Local Health Board – October 2009 – Chair of Wales Council for Voluntary Action (WCVA) since January 2006.

HALLAM, David MEP Hertfordshire and Shropshire 1994-99. Contested West Midlands Region 1999. Labour candidate for Hereford and Worcester in 2001. Freelance media and interim management consultant Horizon Glen Ltd.

HARDSTAFF, Veronica MEP Lincolnshire and Humberside South 1994-99. Contested Yorkshire and Humberside Region 1999. After supply teaching and community activities, re-elected to Sheffield City Council 2002-07 with responsibility for children's social services then served as first Cabinet member for Children's Services including Education. Involved in community activity and campaigning for the Labour Party.

HARRISON, Lyndon MEP Cheshire West 1989-99. Life Peer July 1999.

HENDRICK, Mark MEP Lancashire Central 1994-99. Contested North West Region 1999. MP Preston (by-election on death of Audrey Wise) 2000-

HINDLEY, Michael MEP Lancashire East 1984-99. Founded Michael Hindley and Associates undertaking research work for European Commission and Council of Europe. Lancashire County Councillor 2001-05.

HOON, Geoffrey MEP Derbyshire 1984-94. MP Ashfield 1992-. Various Ministerial posts in Labour government: Europe, Defence, Chief Whip, Transport.

HOWITT, Richard MEP Essex South and East of England Region 1994-

HUCKFIELD, Leslie MEP Merseyside East 1984-89. MP for Nuneaton 1967-83. European consultant. Works in planning and regeneration.

HUGHES, Stephen MEP Durham, then North East Region 1984-.

KERR, Hugh MEP Essex West and Hertfordshire East 1994-99. Contested Scotland region for SSP in 1999. Excluded from Labour Party 1998. Founding member of Scottish Socialist Party, now Solidarity. Freelance journalist.

KEY, Brian MEP Yorkshire South 1979-84. Returned to local government, now retired. Active in local Labour Party, school governor and board member of Barnsley College.

KINNOCK, Glenys MEP South Wales East then Welsh Region 1994-2009. Life Peerage and Minister for Europe June 2009-.

LOMAS, Alfred (Alf) MEP London North East 1979-99. Retired and enjoying painting and playing chess. No longer in Labour Party.

McAVAN, Linda MEP Yorkshire South then Yorkshire and Humberside Region 1998-.

McCARTHY, Arlene MEP Peak District then North West Region 1994-.

McCUBBIN, Henry MEP Scotland North East 1989-94. Was a candidate for European Ombudsman in 1994. Editorial member *Scottish Left Review*. No longer in Labour Party.

McGOWAN, Michael MEP Leeds 1984-99. Leeds City Councillor 2001-04. Moved resolution for Leeds to become a Fair Trade City. Chairman of Leeds Co-operative Party and on NEC of the national Co-operative Party, Director of Leeds City Credit Union, Director of Positive Action for Refugees and Asylum Seekers, board member of the Centre for African Studies at Leeds University and co-ordinator of Olof Palme Annual Peace Lectures.

McMAHON, Hugh MEP Strathclyde West 1984-99. Contested Scottish Region 1999. University lecturer and consultant in Scottish, British and European politics.

McNALLY, Eryl MEP Bedfordshire and Milton Keynes then East of England Region 1994-2004. Gained an Open University Science Degree, lives much of the time in France, active in local French Socialist Party. Awarded the Chevalier of Legion d'Honneur by France in December 2003 for promoting Anglo-French understanding on industrial and research sector and for being a "European" MEP.

MARTIN, David MEP Lothians 1984-99 and for Scotland 1999-.

MEGAHY, Thomas (Tom) MBE MEP South West Yorkshire 1979-99. Died in 2008 after a long illness.

MILLER, Bill MEP Glasgow 1994-04. Contested Scotland Region 1999. Head of Western Scotland European Office in Brussels.

MORGAN, Eluned MEP Mid and West Wales then Welsh Region 1994-2009.

MORRIS Reverend David (Dai) MEP Mid and West Wales 1984-99. Died 2007.

MURPHY, Dr Simon MEP Midlands West then West Midlands Region 1994-2004. Director of City Region of Birmingham, Coventry and Black Country and Chair of Sandwell Local Improvement Finance Trust Company.

NEEDLE, Clive MEP Norfolk 1994-99. Contested East of England Region 1999 and 2004. Independent policy adviser including with WHO and EuroHealthNet. No longer in Labour Party.

NEWENS, Arthur Stanley (Stan) MEP London Central 1984-99. MP Epping 1964-70, Harlow 1974-83. Chair of Harlow Civic Society and officer-holder in other local, historical and Essex organizations. President of Liberation (formerly the Movement for Colonial Freedom), Chair of Labour Heritage. Author of books, pamphlets and articles.

NEWMAN Edward MEP Greater Manchester Central 1984-99. Returned to Manchester City Council 2002-.

ODDY, Christine MEP Midlands Central then Coventry and North Warwickshire 1989-99. Excluded from Labour Party 1999. Contested 1999 election as Labour Independent. Active on patient advisory committees.

PITT, Terence MEP Midlands West 1984-86. Died 3 October 1986.

POLLACK, Anita MEP London South West 1989-99. Contested Southern Region 1999 and London 2004. Head of European Policy English Heritage 2000-06. Freelance European consultant.

QUIN, Baroness Joyce MEP South Tyne and Wear 1979-89. MP for Gateshead East, then Gateshead East and Washington West from 1987-2005, Minister for Home Office 1997-98, Europe 1998-99, Agriculture 1999-2001. Life peerage 2006. Chair of Franco-British Council since 2007.

READ, Imelda (Mel) MEP Leicester, then East Midlands Region 1989-2004. Chair of Health First Europe.

ROGERS, Allan MEP South East Wales 1979-84. MP for Rhondda 1983-2001. Retired.

SEAL, Dr Barry MEP Bradford 1979-99. Ran a horse breeding enterprise and was Chair of North Kirklees Primary Care Trust in 2002. Since 2006 Chair of Bradford District Care Trust.

SIMPSON, Brian MEP Cheshire East 1989-99. MEP North West region 2006-.

SKINNER, Peter MEP Kent West and South East Region 1994-.

SMITH, Alex MEP Scotland South 1989-99. Retired. Resigned from Labour Party in 2000 after being blocked from consideration as candidate in Ayr by-election.

SMITH, Llewellyn MEP South Wales East 1984-94. MP Blaenau Gwent 1992-2000. Retired. No longer in Labour Party.

SPIERS, Shaun MEP London South East 1994-99. Contested London Region 1999. Chief Executive of Campaign to Protect Rural England.

STEVENSON, George MEP Staffordshire East 1984-89. MP Stoke on Trent South 1992-2005. Retired and running a Labour Party branch in southern Spain.

STEWART, Kenneth, MEP Merseyside West 1984-1996. Died 2 September 1996.

TAPPIN, Michael MEP Staffordshire West and Congleton 1994-99. Contested West Midlands Region 1999. Chair, Stoke South Primary Care Trust 2001-06. Stoke-on-Trent City Councillor 2004-08, Leader of Labour Group 2007. Lecturer in American Politics Keele University. Unpaid Member of Governance Transition Board 2008-.

THOMAS, David MEP Suffolk 1994-99, contested East of England Region 1999. After a period of illness returned to Suffolk County Council 2001-. Also Waveney District Council 2002-07, Leader of Labour Group for 2007. Eastern Region political officer for CWU.

TITLEY, Gary MEP Greater Manchester West, then North West Region 1989-2009. Awarded the Grand Commander of the Order of the White Rose for his work on Finnish accession to the EU.

TOMLINSON, John MEP Birmingham West 1984-99. MP for Meriden 1974-79, Life peerage 1998. Member of UK delegation to Council of Europe.

TONGUE, Carole, MEP London East 1984-99. Contested London Region 1999. Consultant and lecturer.

TRUSCOTT, Lord (Dr) Peter MEP Hertfordshire 1994-99, contested East of England Region 1999. Life peer June 2004. Energy Minister 2006-7. Suspended from the House of Lords 20 May 2009 for six months; the Labour whip was withdrawn and he left the party the same month.

WADDINGTON Susan MEP Leicester 1994-99, contested East Midlands 1999. Returned to Leicester Council for one term. European Programme Director, NIACE.

WATTS, Mark MEP Kent East then South East Region 1994-2004. Contested South East Region 2004. Associate Director, The Waterfront Partnership until mid-2009, then Director, Luther Pendragon, Brussels.

WEST, Norman MEP Yorkshire South 1984-98. Retired for health reasons.

WHITE, Ian MEP Bristol 1989-99. Contested South West region 1999 and 2004. Returned to family legal practice.

WHITEHEAD, Phillip MEP Staffordshire East and Derby, then East Midlands Region 1994-2005. MP Derby North 1970-83. Died 31 December 2005.

WILSON, Anthony (Joe) MEP Wales North 1989-99. Contested Wales Region 1999. Retired. Active in local Labour politics.

WYNN, Terence MEP Merseyside and East Wigan then North West Region 1989-2006. Methodist Lay Preacher.

REFERENCES

Debates and Minutes of the European Parliament plenary sessions between 1979 and 1999 as published in the Official Journals were consulted and have been quoted liberally. Interviews, sometimes face-to-face, sometimes by telephone, were conducted with eighty-two of the eighty-three Labour MEPs and former MEPs. Many were kind enough to respond to repeated questions, e-mails, phone calls, letters and a questionnaire, as were the many other European stakeholders. They are all listed below and their time is greatly appreciated.

Books, pamphlets and articles referred to:

Bainbridge, T and Teasdale, A: *The Penguin Companion to European Union*, Penguin Books, 1995

Barber, Lionel: *Britain and the new European agenda*, Centre for European Reform, 1998

Batory, Agnes: *European Elections in Britain*, Federal Trust for Education and Research, 2000

Blair, Cherie: *Speaking for Myself*, Little, Brown, 2008

Bond M, Smith J and Wallace W, (eds): *Eminent Europeans*, The Greycoat Press, 1996

Broad, Roger: *Labour's European Dilemmas*, Palgrave, 2001

Brussels Labour Group: *British Withdrawal from the EC?*, Brussels, 1982

Butler, D and Marquand, D: *European Elections and British Politics*, Longman, 1981

Butler, D and Westlake, M: *British Politics and European Elections 1994*, St Martin's Press 1995

Butler, D and Westlake, M: *British Politics and European Elections 1999*, Macmillan 2000

Butler, D and Westlake, M: *British Politics and European Elections 2004*, Palgrave MacMillan 2004.

Butler N, Dodd P, Flanders S, Garton Ash T, Grant C, Hughes K: *Reshaping Europe*, Centre for European Reform, 1996

Castle, Barbara: *Fighting All the Way*, Macmillan, 1993

Castle, Barbara: "Let them throw us out" *New Socialist* 17 September 1982

Clwyd, Ann: "Why I have changed my mind on the Common market", *New Socialist* 19 February 1982

Coates K and Holland S: *Full Employment for Europe*, Spokesman books, 1995

Corbett, Richard: *The Treaty of Maastricht*, Longman, 1993

Corbett, R: *The European Parliament's Role in Closer EU Integration*, Macmillan, 1998

Corbett R, Jacobs F and Shackleton M: *The European Parliament* 7th edition, John Harper Publishing, 2007

Crick, Michael: *Militant*, Faber and Faber, 1984

David, W *et al*: *The Challenge for Labour in Europe*, Tribune Group of MEPs, 1996

Earnshaw D and Judge D: *Prelude to Codecision: A Qualitative Assessment of the*

Cooperation Procedure in the 1989-94 European Parliament, European Parliament Directorate General for Research Project IV/93/54, February 1995 (unpublished)

European Labour Forum Numbers 1, 2, 4, 5, 8, 10, 11, 14, 15, 16, 17, 19, 20, Spokesman, 1990-99

Ford *et al*: "Kamikaze Politics or the Collective Madness that Grips Labour in Europe" *Tribune*, 12 December 1986

Ford *et al*: *Changing States*, Mandarin, 1996

Ford, Glyn: *The Evolution of a European*, Spokesman books, 1993

Ford, Glyn: *Making European Progress*, Watase Publications, 2002

Gould, Philip: *Unfinished Revolution*, Little, Brown and Company, 1998

Grant, Charles: *Can Britain Lead in Europe?*, Centre for European Reform, 1998

Harris, Geoffrey: *A Wider Europe*, Fabian Society, 1976

Hayter, Dianne: *Fightback*, Manchester University Press, 2005

Hix, Simon and Lesse, U: *Shaping a Vision: A History of the Party of European Socialists 1957-2002*, Party of European Socialists, 2002

Hix, Simon: *What's Wrong with the European Union and How to Fix it*, Polity, 2008

Hix, Noury and Roland: *Democratic Politics in the European Parliament*, Cambridge University Press, 2007

Holland, Stuart: *The European Imperative: Economic and Social Cohesion in the 1990s*, Spokesman, 1993

Hoskyns, Catherine: *Integrating Gender: Women, Law and Politics in the European Union*, Verso, 1996

Hoskyns, C and Newman M (eds): *Democratising the European Union: Issues for the twenty-first century*, Manchester University Press, 2000

Judge, D and Earnshaw, D: *The European Parliament*, Palgrave Macmillan 2003

Keegan, V and Kettle, M (eds): *The New Europe*, Guardian Books/Fourth Estate, 1993

Kendall, Liz: *Wherever Next? The Future of Europe*, Fabian Society, 1996

Kereva, G, Savill, R and Percival, D: *The Defence of Coal*, British Labour Group, 1986

Kinnock, Neil: *Making Our Way*, Blackwell, 1986

Kerr, Hugh: article in *Labour Left Briefing*, February 1998

Labour Movement for Europe: *The Economic Consequences of Withdrawal*, 1982

Lewis, Enright, *et al* (eds): *The Man Who Sang Yellow Submarine in Latin*, Pontefract Press 1996

Lloyd, John: "Interview: Robin Cook", *New Statesman* 14 August 1998

Martin, David: "Whither the Left in Europe", *Radical Scotland,* 1986

Martin, David: *Bringing Common Sense to the Common Market: A Left Agenda for Europe*, Fabian Society, 1988

NEC EEC Liaison Committee paper RD2271 "1984 European Elections"

Palmer, John: *Europe Without America?*, Oxford University Press, 1987

Palmer, John: *1992 and beyond*, European Commission, 1989

Piening, Christopher: *Global Europe: The European Union in World Affairs*, Lynne Rienner, 1997

Pillinger, Jane: *Feminising the Market: Women's Pay and Employment in the European Community*, Macmillan, 1992

Plumb, Henry: *The Plumb Line*, Greycoat Press, 2001

Plumb, Tongue and Wijsenbeek: *Shaping Europe: Reflections of Three MEPs,* Federal Trust, 2000.

Priestley, Julian: 3rd John Fitzmaurice Lecture, Brussels, 17 October 2007

Priestley, Julian: "Labour's Long Winding Road" *e!Sharp*, Brussels, January-February 2008

Priestley, Julian: *Six Battles That Shaped Europe's Parliament*, John Harper Publishing, 2008
Radice, Giles: *Offshore: Britain and the European Idea*, I.B. Taurus, 1992.
Rawnsley, Andrew: *Servants of the People – the Inside Story of New Labour*, Hamish Hamilton/Penguin 2000
Read, Mel and Simpson, Alan: *Against a Rising Tide*, Spokesman, 1991.
Scully, Roger: *Becoming Europeans?*, Oxford University Press, 2005
Thatcher, Margaret: *Margaret Thatcher: The Downing Street Years*, Harper Collins, 1993
Thorpe, Andrew: *History of the Labour Party*, Palgrave Macmillan, 1997
Times Guide to 1979 European Election, Times Books 1979
Times Guide to 1984 European Election, Times Books 1984
Times Guide to 1989 European Election, Times Books 1989
Times Guide to 1994 European Election, Times Books 1994
Tribune Group of MEPs: *Going Forward in Europe*, Cardiff, 1994
Tribune Group of MEPs: *The Challenge for Labour in Europe*, London, 1996
Wall, Stephen: *A Stranger in Europe*, Oxford University Press, 2008
Westlake, Martin: *Britain's Emerging European Elite?*, Dartmouth Publishing, 1994
Wurtzel, R K W: *Environmental policy-making in Britain, Germany and the European Union*, Manchester University Press, 2002
Wynn, T and Kitt, R: *A Guide to the Community budget*, Local Government Information Bureau, 1994
Wynn, Terry: *Where are the Prophets?*, Troubador Publishing, 2006

LABOUR MEPs or former MEPs interviewed

ADAM, Gordon	GREEN, Dame Pauline
BALFE, Richard	HALLAM, David
BARTON, Roger	HARRISON, Lord Lyndon
BILLINGHAM, Baroness	HENDRICK, Mark
BOWE, David	HINDLEY, Michael
BUCHAN, Janey	HONEYBALL, Mary
CABORN, Richard	HOON, Geoff
CASHMAN, Michael	HOWITT Richard
CLWYD, Ann	HUCKFIELD, Lesley
COATES, Ken	HUGHES, Stephen
COLLINS, Sir Ken	KERR, Hugh
CORBETT, Richard	KEY, Brian
CRAMPTON, Peter	KINNOCK, Glenys
CRAWLEY, Baroness Christine	LOMAS, Alf
CUNNINGHAM, Tony	MARTIN, David
DONNELLY, Alan	McAVAN, Linda
ELLIOTT, Michael	McCARTHY, Arlene
EVANS, Robert	McCUBBIN, Henry
FALCONER, Alex	McGOWAN, Michael
FORD, Glyn	McMAHON, Hugh
FALCONER, Alex	McNALLY, Eryl
FORD, Glyn	MILLER, Bill
GALLAGHER, Michael	MORGAN, Elunid
GILL, Neena	MURPHY, Simon

NEEDLE, Clive
NEWMAN, Eddy
NEWENS, Stan
ODDY, Christine
O'TOOLE, Barbara (Mo)
QUIN, Baroness Joyce
READ, Mel
ROGERS, Allan
SEAL, Barry
SIMPSON, Brian
SKINNER, Peter
SMITH, Alex
SPIERS, Shaun
STEVENSON, George
STIHLER, Catherine
TAPPIN, Mike
TITLEY, Gary
TOMLINSON Lord
TONGUE, Carole
TRUSCOTT, Lord
WADDINGTON, Sue
WATTS, Mark
WEST, Norman
WHITE, Ian
WILSON, Joe
WYNN, Terry

*OTHER STAKEHOLDERS
interviewed*

ANDERSON, Janet, MP
ASHTON, Terry
BEAZLEY, Christopher
BUNDRED, Steve
CARR, John
CASIDY, Bryan
CLARKE, Rt Hon Charles, MP
CLARKE, Frazer
COLEMAN, Peter
COOK, Greg

COSTELLO, Patrick
COULTHARD, Maggie
CROOK, Nick
DONNELLY, Brendan
EARNSHAW, David
ENRIGHT, Jane
GAPES, Mike, MP
GOULD, Baroness Joyce
GUPWELL, Dick
HACK, Reinhold
HARRIS, Geoff
HAWORTH, Lord (Alan)
HAYTER, Dianne
HEALY, Pat
KINNOCK, Lord (Neil)
KURLEMANN, Jan
LOWE, David
MICHEL, Manfred
MURPHY, Jim
OXENBOULD, Joanne
PALMER, John
PRESCOTT, Rt Hon John, MP
PLUMB, Lord (Henry)
PRIESTLEY, Sir Julian
PYKE, Belinda
REED, Derek
ROBINSON, Tony
ROTH-BEHRENDT, Dagmar
ROYALL, Baroness (Jan)
SAWYER, Lord (Tom)
SIGLER, Nick
SIMPSON, Anthony
SMITH, Lord (Chris)
STAHL, Gerhard
STOWELL, Jane
THORNTON, Baroness (Glenys)
TRIESMAN, Lord (David)
Van HEMELDONCK, Marijke
WHITTY, Lord (Larry)
WOOD, Michael

INDEX